DISCOUNTING LIFE

Extrajudicial, extraterritorial killings of War on Terror adversaries by the US state have become the new normal. Alongside targeted individuals, unnamed and uncounted others are maimed and killed. Despite the absence of law's conventional sites, processes, and actors, the US state celebrates these killings as the realization of "justice." Meanwhile, images, narrative, and affect do the work of law, authorizing and legitimizing the discounting of some lives so that others – implicitly, American nationals – may live. How then, as we live through this unending, globalized war, are we to make sense of law in relation to the valuing of life? Adopting an interdisciplinary approach to law to excavate the workings of necropolitical law, and interrogating the US state's justifications for the project of counterterror, this book's temporal arc, the long War on Terror, illuminates the profound continuities and many guises for racialized, imperial violence informing the contemporary discounting of life.

JOTHIE RAJAH is Research Professor at the American Bar Foundation. She is committed to excavating rule-of-law violations and analyzes law in context. Rajah is also the author of *Authoritarian Rule of Law: Legislation, Discourse, and Legitimacy in Singapore* (Cambridge University Press, 2012), which shows how Singapore's narrative of national vulnerability combines with authoritarian politics to undermine rule-of-law ideals.

CAMBRIDGE STUDIES IN LAW AND SOCIETY

Founded in 1997, Cambridge Studies in Law and Society is a hub for leading scholarship in socio-legal studies. Located at the intersection of law, the humanities, and the social sciences, it publishes empirically innovative and theoretically sophisticated work on law's manifestations in everyday life: from discourses to practices, and from institutions to cultures. The series editors have longstanding expertise in the interdisciplinary study of law, and welcome contributions that place legal phenomena in national, comparative, or international perspective. Series authors come from a range of disciplines, including anthropology, history, law, literature, political science, and sociology.

Series Editors

Mark Fathi Massoud, *University of California, Santa Cruz*

Jens Meierhenrich, *London School of Economics and Political Science*

Rachel E. Stern, *University of California, Berkeley*

Past Editors

Chris Arup, Martin Chanock, Sally Engle Merry,
Pat O'Malley, Susan Silbey

A list of books in the series can be found at the back of this book.

DISCOUNTING LIFE
Necropolitical Law, Culture, and the Long War on Terror

Jothie Rajah
American Bar Foundation

CAMBRIDGE
UNIVERSITY PRESS

Shaftesbury Road, Cambridge CB2 8EA, United Kingdom

One Liberty Plaza, 20th Floor, New York, NY 10006, USA

477 Williamstown Road, Port Melbourne, VIC 3207, Australia

314–321, 3rd Floor, Plot 3, Splendor Forum, Jasola District Centre, New Delhi – 110025, India

103 Penang Road, #05–06/07, Visioncrest Commercial, Singapore 238467

Cambridge University Press is part of Cambridge University Press & Assessment, a department of the University of Cambridge.

We share the University's mission to contribute to society through the pursuit of education, learning and research at the highest international levels of excellence.

www.cambridge.org
Information on this title: www.cambridge.org/9781316513682

DOI: 10.1017/9781009075848

First published 2023

A catalogue record for this publication is available from the British Library.

Library of Congress Cataloging-in-Publication Data
Names: Rajah, Jothie, 1963– author.
Title: Discounting life : necropolitical law, culture, and the long war on terror / Jothie Rajah, American Bar Foundation.
Description: Cambridge, United Kingdom ; New York, NY : Cambridge University Press, 2022. | Series: Cambridge studies in law and society | Includes bibliographical references and index.
Identifiers: LCCN 2022030679 (print) | LCCN 2022030680 (ebook) | ISBN 9781316513682 (hardback) | ISBN 9781009074650 (paperback) | ISBN 9781009075848 (epub)
Subjects: LCSH: United States–Foreign relations–Law and legislation. | United States–Foreign relations–21st century. | Law–Social aspects–United States. | BISAC: LAW / General
Classification: LCC KF4651 .R35 2022 (print) | LCC KF4651 (ebook) | DDC 342.73/0412–dc23/eng/20220831
LC record available at https://lccn.loc.gov/2022030679
LC ebook record available at https://lccn.loc.gov/2022030680

ISBN 978-1-316-51368-2 Hardback
ISBN 978-1-009-07465-0 Paperback

For my mother,
Gnanambigai Sivasamboo Saunthararajah,
with love and gratitude

CONTENTS

TABLES

ACKNOWLEDGMENTS

At a time when scholarship and critical thinking appear to be under siege, I feel very lucky to be at the American Bar Foundation (ABF), where sociolegal research is protected and nurtured. I am very grateful for the many forms of support for this project extended by the American Bar Foundation and its Fellows, as well as the American Bar Endowment. Warm thanks to the ABF directors, Ajay Mehrotra and Robert Nelson, whose leadership has created the crucible for this book, and to former and current members of the ABF Board leadership, including Doreen Dodson, David Houghton, Thomas Sullivan, Jimmy Goodman, Sandra Chan, and the Hon. Eileen Kato, whose enthusiasm and encouragement have meant so much.

The Internationales Forschungszentrum Kulturwissenschaften (IFK) in Vienna's Senior Fellowship has also provided support for this research, as well as a welcoming and collegial fellowship community, despite pandemic ruptures. Many thanks to all at the IFK, especially Thomas Macho, Johanna Richter, Julia Boog, and Petra Radeczki.

Friends and colleagues who generously read multiple (painful) drafts of early versions of this book, and helped improve it in so many ways, include Beth Mertz, Nick Cheesman, Winni Sullivan, Eve Darian-Smith, Eve Lester, Susan Shapiro, Gary Lee, Jinee Lokaneeta, Jon Goldberg-Hiller, Keally McBride, Ben Golder, Yoriko Otomo, and Bill V. Mullen. I am indebted to all, but in particular to Bill Mullen, whose close reading and careful engagement with every page has nourished the writing process in too many ways to count. Rick Abel, John Comaroff, Frank Munger, Pip Nicholson, Chris Tomlins, and Peer Zumbansen have extended much-needed support at different times, and in many ways, and I am forever grateful. Salvatore Poier gave generously of his time and expertise to help me understand the nuances of Agamben's body of work in relation to law, and I thank him. At the inception of this project, Bonnie Honig asked probing, encouraging questions and introduced me to fabulous books. Her insights have been invaluable.

Also in support of this project, those who have kindly made time, offering insights, encouragement, and critique, include Fred Aman, Kirsten Anker, Mark Antaki, Andrea Ballesteros, Olivia Barr, Bob Bennet, Leigh Bienen, Pablo Boczkowski, Sandra Brunnegger, Ruth Buchanan, Matt Canfield, Yasmine Chahed, Kevin Davis, Meghan Dawe, Lauren Edelman, Paul Frymer, Ilana Gershon, Carol Greenhouse, Priya Gupta, Jack Heinz, Michael Hor, Iza Hussin, Sheila Jasanoff, Hye-Yun Kang, Martin Krygier, Camilo Leslie, Shaun McVeigh, Sally Merry, Sherally Munshi, Mark Osiel, Genevieve Painter, Justin Richland, Kim Scheppele, Bettina Scholdan, Nan Seuffert, Dale Spicer, Mark Suchman, Barry Sullivan, and Umut Turem. Throughout the pandemic, James P. Driscoll, Circulation Services Manager at the Pritzker Legal Research Center, Northwestern Law School, has been a sympathetic and responsive facilitator of access to books. At the ABF, Marcilena Shaeffer, Sophie Kofman, Jeff Swim, Ann Pikus, and Matt Parr have supplied multiple administrative and technological life rafts in times of need. At Cambridge University Press, Rachel Stern and Mark Massoud have been wonderfully supportive series editors, and Matt Gallaway and his team have efficiently shepherded this book through the many steps leading to its delivery. Christy Parzyszek has provided invaluable research assistance.

Friends and family have been incredibly vital to sustaining book-writing in the face of life's twists and turns. My heartfelt thanks to Bill Mullen, Susan Shapiro, Beth Mertz, Carol Heimer, Winni Sullivan, Carole Silver, Meredith Rountree, Mikaela Luttrell-Rowland, Teoh Seok Hoon, Vaani Rajah, and Mahendran Navaratnarajah. My children, Ravindran and Shrimoyee, continue to deepen love's meanings and experiences beyond anything I might have imagined.

CHAPTER ONE

NECROPOLITICAL LAW

1.1 INTRODUCTION: DISCOUNTED LIVES

Osama bin Laden was killed by US Special Forces in his home in Pakistan on May 1, 2011 (Obama 2011) and later buried at sea in accordance with Muslim rites – or so goes the official US account (Wilson et al. 2011). Renowned journalist Seymour Hersh has written that his body was hacked into bits and flung out of a helicopter over the Hindu Kush mountains (2016: 47). According to YouTube clips, bin Laden is still living.[1] And news of very uncertain provenance reports Edward Snowden saying that he is doing it in luxury on CIA money in the Bahamas.[2] This proliferation of competing accounts distracts us from three crucial elements in the bin Laden narrative. First, at least four others were killed in the raid on bin Laden's home (CNN 2013). These killings were discounted as incidental to the killing of bin Laden, their legality barely questioned by media and artfully elided in the official announcement of the death of bin Laden by the US state (Obama 2011).[3] "A small team of Americans carried out the operation

---

[1] At www.youtube.com/watch?v=oGPatAC_TTc; www.youtube.com/watch?v=bHhalz3iy7g.
[2] At https://worldnewsdailyreport.com/bin-laden-is-alive-and-well-in-the-bahamas-says-edward-snowden/; www.snopes.com/fact-check/snowden-bin-laden-alive/.
[3] The category "civilian," in the course of the long War on Terror, has become especially contested, leaving unclear the role played by the others who were killed. We have no reliable information, for example, as to whether these others were armed. Some reports do note the killing of these four others in the raid, but the legality of these killings is generally not questioned; for example, CNN (2013) and Marks (2018).

1

with extraordinary courage and capability," said President Obama. "No Americans were harmed. They took care to avoid civilian casualties." Second, the extraterritorial, extrajudicial killing of bin Laden took place outside of law's conventional sites, processes, and actors, such as courts, trials, and judges. Third, and perhaps most crucial, starting with bin Laden, each such extraterritorial, extrajudicial killing in the War on Terror has been celebrated publicly in the United States as the realization of justice and the delivery of security.[4] All but unacknowledged are the unnamed and uncounted others who have died and been maimed alongside the targeted individuals. Despite law's seeming absences, the invocations of justice and security legitimize the discounting of these lives so that others – implicitly, American nationals – may live. How, then, proceeding through this unending War on Terror, are we to make sense of law in relation to the valuing of life?

This book argues that texts, images, and events emanating from the United States discount life by eclipsing the values and institutions of rule of law while fostering the secretive, belligerent values and institutions of the long War on Terror.[5] By discounting life, I mean in the first instance "life" in the straightforward sense of the distinction between life and death. But this book also shows how lives are discounted by the US state along a continuum, from the brute violence of intentional killing to the less obvious violence of lives actually or potentially stripped of dignity, sociality, and rights.[6] In opposition to

---

[4] See, for example, President Biden's authorization of killings of alleged ISIS-K terrorists that resulted in the killing, by drone strike, of ten civilians in Afghanistan, including seven children (Aikins and Rahim 2021), and the Trump administration's February 2020 announcement on the killing in Yemen of Qassim al-Rimi, the leader of Al Qaeda in the Arabian Peninsula (Helsel 2020). While the details remain murky, it seems probable that a US drone attack in late January is what killed al-Rimi, along with uncounted others who were in the building that was bombed; see Helsel (2020) and Al Jazeera (2020). In January 2020, Trump announced the killing of Iran's Quds Force leader, Qassem Suleimani (Trump 2020). Ten others were killed in the drone strike that killed Suleimani (Entous and Osnos 2020). In October 2019, Trump announced the killing of ISIS leader Abu Bakr al-Baghdadi (Trump 2019). In the al-Baghdadi raid, at least nine others, including two women and a child, were also killed by US forces (Syrian Observatory for Human Rights 2019).

[5] Rule of law is discussed below at Section III.B. As elaborated in Section IV, this book makes its argument by reading for law across legislative, policy, and popular cultural texts.

[6] These two senses of life are explicated by Agamben in *Homo Sacer* (1998 [1995]) as prefiguring and conditioning bare life. In holding open the possibility of a socially

positivist notions of law's apartness as a sphere of specialized knowledge and activity, I make my argument by delving into texts, images, and events because, like all cultural artifacts and dynamics, these hail us into our ways of being and knowing.[7] Animated by Robert Cover's seminal argument on culture as the medium for "the creation of legal meaning" (1983: 11), by Lawrence Rosen's important elaboration of law *as* culture,[8] "creating the categories of our experience . . . knit[ting] together disparate ideas and actions . . . to fabricate a world of meaning" (Rosen 2006: 4), and by Renisa Mawani's theorizing of law as archive, to highlight the key roles played by law's record, power, and dominant narratives in simultaneously justifying and obscuring law's violence (Mawani 2012), this book traces the discounting of life legitimized and globalized via cultural texts emanating from the United States after 9/11.[9] Through this tracing, I show how law values (and discounts) life. The texts, images, and events that pervade our everyday existences[10] reveal the way relations and ideologies of sovereignty,

and politically empowered human life, even in the context of states of exception, I draw, first, on Bonnie Honig's excavation of the possibilities for democratic politics in emergency contexts; possibilities, she notes, that work against the closures and indistinguishability between these two forms of life in Agamben's bare life (2009: xv); and, second, on Jinee Lokaneeta's demonstration, against Agamben's totalizing conception of bare life, of the compelling presence of resistance in states of exception (2017: 81).

[7] Some influential scholarship on how everyday life and ordinary culture hail us into being in relation to all things social (power, law, language, affect, media, and shared infrastructures and environments) includes Kahn (1999); Sarat and Kearns (1998); Hall (1980); Althusser (1970); Williams (1959).

[8] James Boyd White is widely credited with introducing this heuristic of "law as. . ." in his original readings of law as literature (White 1973), literature as law (White 1984), and more, writing, "I could imagine a course not in law and history, or sociology or economics or anthropology, but law as each of those things" (White 1990: 19). Also influential is Sally Falk Moore's compelling study *Law as Process* (1978). More recently, in addition to Rosen's *Law as Culture* (2006) and Renisa Mawani's theorizing of law as archive (2012), the ongoing, multipart "Law As. . ." project led by Christopher Tomlins has revitalized the heuristic to grapple with law's inextricable enmeshments with multiple facets of the social.

[9] At the risk of stating the obvious, expressions and sites of culture include but far exceed texts, images, and events such as those I analyze. I keep my focus on texts, images, and events because of my methodological reliance on interpretive socio-legality and close textual reading as found in *Critical Discourse Studies* (discussed at Sections 1.3.2 and 1.4.2).

[10] Section 1.3 details and discusses law's compound and contested meanings, attributes, and relations.

nationalism, and imperialism – all inextricably enmeshed with law – condition us to discount some lives so as to value and secure others.[11]

In relation to law, life is discounted via a double move, in which liberal legality's insistence on rule of law, nation-state sovereignty, and the valuing of all human life as equal is notionally upheld even as an exceptionalist narrative of the War on Terror scripts justification for departures from these same principles. The exceptionalism narrative is a version of the state of exception (Schmitt 2005 [1922]; Agamben 2005 [2003]), the state in which, as Hansen and Stepputat write, by suspending "rules and conventions ... a conceptual and ethical zero point [is created] from where the law, the norms, and the political order can be constituted" (2005: 301). In de-centering and disrupting dominant notions of law, this book contributes to scholarship on sovereignty that contests received understandings of the concept as being coterminous with nation-state sovereignty. I highlight Hansen and Stepputat's definition of the state of exception in part because their foregrounding of sovereign power in relation to violence resonates with critical approaches to law, in which violence is understood as foundational to law and inextricably enmeshed with it (Derrida 1992; Benjamin 1996 [1921]). And, as Renisa Mawani points out in her important essay on law in relation to contestations over "power" and "truth," law, understood as "an expansive and expanding locus of

---

[11] In reading cultural texts of imperialism for the co-constitution of the valuing of some lives in tandem with the discounting of others, I draw on a tradition which, from Edward Said's groundbreaking studies, *Orientalism* (1978) and *Culture and Imperialism* (1993) onward, understands cultural texts forged in the crucible of Euro-Atlantic imperialism as producing knowledge, shaping subjectivity, and disseminating ideologies that reinscribe the racialized relations of domination and subordination inherent to imperialism and neo-imperialism. Also pertinent to this book's concern with legitimations of US imperialism, a critical body of scholarship illuminates the simultaneous figuring of the United States as "nation" in relation to its "foreign" other. For example, Melani McAlister focuses on "the cultural politics of encounter" (2005: xvii) through a reading of representations across genres (news media, films, popular novels) to show how the "uncoordinated conjunctures" of cultural products "have the knitted-together power of a discourse" (2005: 307) to shape US responses to 9/11 (2005: 268). And Amy Kaplan's influential analytic insight, again through a reading of US cultural texts across genres (including Supreme Court judgments, domestic manuals, films, and novels), has been that "international struggles for domination abroad profoundly shape representations of American national identity at home" [such that the] idea of the nation as home ... is inextricable from the political, economic, and cultural moments of empire" (Kaplan 2002: 1).

juridico-political command," cannot be disaggregated from "struggles over sovereignty, authority, violence, and nonviolence" (2012: 337). Mawani's examination of the entwining of sovereignty, law, and violence provides a foil to the more positivist notion of law in Schmitt's now-canonical formulation of the sovereign as "he who decides on the exception" (2005 [1922]: 5), with the decision empowering the sovereign to step outside and beyond the law of "ordinary legal prescription" (Schmitt 2005: 6).

Departing from Schmitt, and in line instead with critical, sociolegal, and cultural understandings of law as a compound and relational social fabric, with violence and sovereign power inevitably part of the weave, this book approaches law as plural, everyday, and embodied. Understood in this way, law is discernible in sovereign power's plural, everyday, and embodied expressions. It may "be spectacular and public, secret and menacing, and also can appear as scientific/technical rationalities of management and punishment of bodies" (Hansen and Stepputat 2005: 3). Put differently, because law is articulated in part through the intersections of power and violence, in states of exception it cannot disappear or be discarded. Law is, rather, reconstituted and reconfigured by the exception. In part, contingent and socially constructed and in part the product of deeper histories, ideals, and politics, law is always present, no matter the state, condition, or fragmentation of sovereign power.

In *Discounting Life*, I depart from doctrinal law's dominant frameworks for thinking about sovereignty, law, and exception by foregrounding Achille Mbembe's crucial contribution to thinking on the state of exception. In his book *Necropolitics*, Mbembe illuminates the large-scale discounting of life that is inherent to the state of exception by understanding sovereignty, not according to the legal fictions of nation-state sovereignty or "supranational institutions and networks" (2019: 197) but instead in terms of the visceral and totalizing "power and capacity [of the sovereign] to dictate who is able to live and who must die" (Mbembe 2019: 66).[12] Alert to formal, legal, and

---

[12] *Necropolitics*, the book, includes an almost identical version of the 2003 essay, "Necropolitics," as well as a detailed "reflection on today's planetary-scale renewal of the relation of enmity and its multiple reconfigurations" (2019: 1–2). Mbembe draws, in part, on Foucault's analysis of biopower and the sovereign right to kill (Foucault 2003: 240) as a major launching point for his argument on necropolitics. Both in *Necropolitics* (2019) and in other work, Mbembe has emphasized that

philosophical notions of sovereignty, Mbembe refuses the tendency in "late modern political criticism" to overlook the fact that "modernity is at the origin of multiple concepts of sovereignty" (2019: 66–67). Repudiating "the romance of sovereignty, ... defined as a twofold process of *self-institution* and *self-limitation*" (2019: 67–68), Mbembe looks instead at "politics as the work of death" and "sovereignty defined as the right to kill" (2019: 70). His focus is on "those figures of sovereignty whose central project is ... *the generalized instrumentalization of human existence and the material destruction of human bodies and populations*" (2019: 67–68).[13] These figures of sovereignty, he writes, "constitute the *nomos* of the political space in which we continue to live" (2019: 68). Tracing how the long durée for racialized,[14]

sovereignty expressed as power over bodies, territories, resources, and populations need not necessarily be the sovereignty of state power. Such sovereignty might be exercised by corporations, private armies, neighboring states, and religious organizations (Mbembe 2000).

I draw on Hansen and Steputtat's succinct definition of the state in exception (quoted above) in part because Hansen and Steputtat hold in common with Mbembe an acute attention to sovereignty articulated through violence over peoples (2005: 2). Hansen and Steputtat review a vast literature on sovereignty (2006) and theorize sovereignty in relation to postcolonies (2005) to offer their definition of the state of exception, which is shaped by an "ethnographically informed look at the meanings and forms of sovereignty in postcolonial zones" with particular attention to "historically-embedded practices and cultural meanings of sovereign power and violence" (2005: 3). Importantly, these ethnographies show how, in practice, sovereign power may be "exercised by a state, in the name of the nation, or by a local despotic power or community court [and] is always a tentative and unstable project whose efficacy and legitimacy depend on repeated performances of violence and a "will to rule" (2005: 3; see also Greenhouse and Davis 2020). Additionally, while their theorizing of postcolonial sovereignty builds on zones conventionally understood as former European colonies, Hansen and Steputtat draw on Hardt and Negri's influential framing of contemporary globalized imperialism as a network of power with "no outside" (2005: 2). In other words, we are all postcolonial today.

[13] In *Necropolitics*, elaborating on terror and killing as "the means of realizing the already known telos of history" (2019: 74), Mbembe traces politics as the work of death, and sovereignty as the right to kill, with regard, first, to slaves in the contexts of the plantation system (74–76); second, to sovereignty as "colonial terror" over colonized "savages" (76–78); and, third, to sovereignty as violent territorialization and fragmentation in apartheid South Africa and in the West Bank and Gaza (79–83).

[14] As an analytic category, racialization signifies an ideological process "that produces race within particular social and political conjunctures" (HoSang and LaBennet 2014: 212).

imperialized violence finds its contemporary expression through the long War on Terror, Mbembe argues that "the state of exception and the relation of enmity have become the normative basis of the right to kill" (2019: 70).[15] Drawing on this scholarship, and grounding analysis in texts, images, and events, *Discounting Life* asks what law, norms, community, and political order have been constituted from the zero point of the War on Terror's state of exception? What bearing does this particular confluence of law, norms, community, and political order have on the manner in which we value life?

Scholarship on the relationship of law to the state of exception in colonies, in postcolonies, and under imperial power (past and present) details the manner in which ostensibly rule-of-law states have deployed the state of exception to centralize state power, reinforce the state's coercive apparatus, and amplify executive prerogative (e.g., Jayasuriya 2001, 1999; Hussain 2003; Hansen and Stepputat 2005; Johns 2005; Hussain 2007; Lokaneeta 2011; Rajah 2012; Khalili 2013; Saito 2021). As these studies show, when "the exception becomes the norm" (Jayasuriya 2001), law, far from being suspended (as posited by Schmitt 2005) or emptied of its connection to life (as posited by Agamben in his bleak genealogy of the state of exception),[16] may be intensified and amplified. This amplification can take the form of hyperbolic and excessive legality "constraining or avoiding experiences of the exceptional" (Johns 2005: 615), or the hyperlegality of proliferating new laws "in an ad hoc or tactical manner" while repurposing

---

[15] Because *Necropolitics* draws on Foucault's thinking on biopower, Mbembe's use of "normative" invites associations with Foucault's arguments on the "prescriptive character of the norm" in effecting disciplinary normalization through the apparatuses of security that shape contemporary society (Foucault 2007 [2004]: 57). That killing on the basis of War on Terror enmity has become simultaneously "normal," valued as desirable, and no longer treated as abnormal or unlawful speaks to these compound meanings imbuing Mbembe's "normative."

[16] For Agamben, the state of exception is "an empty space, in which a human action with no relation to law stands before a norm with no relation to life" (2005: 86). Agamben's understanding of the category "law," here and in *The Sacrament of Language* (2010), seems to be squarely *state* law. It is interesting to note that while in *Homo Sacer* Agamben uses the category "juridico-political," pointing perhaps to law, politics, and the social as enmeshed and co-constituting, in his other work, he also segregates law from politics and the social. In *Emergency Politics* (2009), Honig interrogates Agamben's reading of both "law" and "politics" in *State of Exception*, pointing out Agamben's failure to perceive plural legalities of "popular law and popular justice, both formed and formless ... as elements of a democratic state of exception" (Honig 2009: 89).

older law (Hussain 2007: 741), or the "aggressive hyperlegality" designed to narrow law's protections for vulnerable parties and expand law's accommodation of excess state violence (Lokaneeta 2011: 70).

This scholarship also shows how, in relation to the state of exception in colonies, in postcolonies, and under imperial power, law – a compound category – becomes disaggregated and reconfigured in particular ways. Framed by narratives of "nation" and "security," this disaggregated law is liberal in some arenas of life (typically commerce) and illiberal in others (typically civil and political rights).[17] Similarly, within the United States, when narratives of "nation" and "security" herald exception to (re)constitute law and normalize emergency, civil and political rights are also eroded, while state secrecy, executive power, and the excesses of hyperlegality are amplified (e.g., Margulies 2006; Lokaneeta 2011; Chesney 2014; Dudziak 2015; Abel 2018a and 2018b; Saito 2021;). I extend this scholarship by analyzing texts that demonstrate how the long War on Terror, as a state of exception, evidences a point from which law, norms, community, and the political order are constituted, rather than suspended (Schmitt) or rendered meaningless (Agamben).

If exception *constitutes* law, then much depends on how the concept and category "law" is understood. In this book, I draw on scholarship that perceives law and its attributes – such as ordering society and social relations through norms, rules, and notions of community, alongside assertions of authority and legitimacy – as pervasive in social life. For those on the receiving end of the long War on Terror's pervasive necropolitical law, there is a painfully acquired expertise in how "[c]-ulture, law, politics, and theory ... [e]ach significantly informs the other" (Bayoumi 2015: 17). Section 1.3 addresses the many meanings, dynamics, and sites of law this book grapples with. For now, it is important to highlight that I approach law as both state law and beyond state law, and as inextricably enmeshed with and discernible in politics, society, and culture. From a reading of and *for* law (reading for law as a methodology is detailed in Section 1.4.2), this book argues that the apparent zero point generated by war-on-terror exceptionalism has scripted a law invested in the discounting of some lives so that others may live, that is, necropolitical law.

---

[17] Scholarship understanding law in this disaggregated way (e.g., Jayasuriya 1999, 2001; Rajah 2012) owes much to Ernst Fraenkel's *Dual State* (1941).

1.1.1 Necropolitical Law

In naming necropolitical law, I conjoin Achille Mbembe's highly influential theorizing of necropolitics to interdisciplinary understandings of law as that which orders society by expressing norms, legitimacy, and authority, both through state law and through ostensibly nonlegal texts, images, and events.[18] Necropolitics fosters not life but death, and it does so selectively, on a *relational* basis, in that the designation "enemy" justifies killing (Mbembe 2019: 70). Through the lens of necropolitical law, the extraterritorial, extrajudicial[19] killing that is such a hallmark of the long War on Terror[20] becomes its own rationality. The right to murder enemies constituted by war-on-terror exceptionalism makes sense of the elisions and discounting of human life embedded in the category "collateral damage" and in the practice of targeted killing.[21] The celebratory tone and language deployed by the US state when it triumphs in the extrajudicial killings of its war-on-terror enemies (Obama 2011; Trump 2019, 2020) become platforms for the necropolitical legitimation of these murders. Exalting American virtue, valor, and superiority through accounts of how exceptionally brave American armed forces risk themselves so as to protect the United States and the world from "evil terrorists," these narratives of

---

[18] While Mbembe does not use the category "law" in his essay on necropolitics, he does trace a genealogy of sovereignty that unpacks sovereignty's multiplicities, and he does identify norms, beliefs, and historically enacted evidence of psychologies, which, I would argue, amount to a deconstructive reading of law's reliance on founding myths, beliefs, and conventions, and well as of law's attributes and operations.

[19] The term "extrajudicial" points to a paradox that arises in reading for law through culture and events, as well as through the institutions and discourse of conventional state law. In highlighting the extrajudicial nature of these killing, I am highlighting departures from conventional law that need to be scrutinized and interrogated for the manner in which publicly sanctioned violence has been enacted in the long War on Terror. I am grateful to Ian Hurd for prodding me to articulate the implications of "extrajudicial" in this project.

[20] In his history of targeted killing, Markus Gunneflo traces the intensifications of extrajudicial, extraterritorial killings by drones after the events of 9/11 (2016). Struggling to compile data and able to offer only a partial accounting, the Bureau of Investigative Journalism estimates that in the course of the War on Terror, as of the end August 2021, between 8,858 and 16,901 people have been killed through drone warfare alone in Pakistan, Somalia, Yemen, and Afghanistan. Of these an estimated 910–2,200 are civilians and 283–454 are children.

[21] Collateral damage is unpacked below at Section IV.C. Targeted killing is addressed in Chapters 3, 4, 5, 6 and 7.

legitimation weave together belligerent patriotism, American exceptionalism, and discourses of security to constitute an unbounded territorial sovereignty for America's right to kill, alongside an unbounded
jurisdictional sovereignty to formulate, enact, and enforce necropolitical law. Crucially, it is only by seeing law through an interdisciplinary
lens, and by grappling with the role of narrative, images, and affect in
making and disseminating law, that it becomes possible to perceive
how law's compound meanings have been represented, reconfigured,
and globalized to justify and authorize the long War on Terror's discounting of life through a unidirectional ennobling of violence. This
book excavates and defines this process of discounting life as necropolitical law to make visible an occluded and coded legal transcript of US
state power and state-sanctioned violence. Put differently, necropolitical law is being expressed and enacted all around us, while we, distracted by narratives of exception, fail to recognize these norms,
practices, relations, and legitimations *as law*.

Our failure to perceive necropolitical law is unsurprising, in that
deception is central to necropolitics, which engages "a force of
separation ... that, while pretending to ensure the world's government,
seeks exemption from it" (2019: 1).[22] Through analytic attention to
separation, deception, and exemption, Mbembe excavates "the contemporary ways in which the political, under the guise of war, of
resistance, or of the fight against terror, makes the murder of the enemy
its primary and absolute objective" (66). Understanding the role of
culture in our processes of meaning-making thus becomes crucial to
perceiving the workings and guises of necropolitical law (as argued in
Section 1.4). This is especially the case because, as Melani McAlister
writes, culture works in "sly" ways (2005: 269). Culture, unlike the
presumed rationality and legibility of law in positivist thinking, "packs
associations and arguments into dense ecosystems of meanings; it
requires us to know a thousand things about politics, social life, and
correct feeling in order to 'get it'; and then, in a remarkable sleight of
hand, it makes the reactions it evokes seem spontaneous and obvious"
(269). And the "work of culture" after 9/11, Alex Lubin argues, has
been to facilitate "actively forgetting US complicity in a global world
order that made life across large parts of the globe unlivable ... as the

---

[22] This force of separation works against life by impeding "a relation with others based
on the reciprocal recognition of our common vulnerability and finitude" (Mbembe
2019: 3).

United States framed itself as victim rather than perpetrator" (2021: 30–31). And, as elaborated in Section 1.5, drawing on Bonnie Honig's (2017) theorizing of the relationship between democracy and public things, the enactment of necropolitical law in our present can be discerned through the *displacement* of law's public thingness. It is, thus, by reading *for* the law embedded in and expressed by war-on-terror texts, images, and events, that it becomes possible to shine a light on how necropolitics works, not in a legal void or in legal indeterminacy but through a set of practices, norms, and relations that constitutes the often-disguised corpus that is necropolitical law.

In addition to dislodging the liberal legal principle that all human life should be valued and protected equally, necropolitical law reconfigures the liberal legal understanding of nation-state sovereignty. Rather than the (notional) primacy of state sovereignty within a state's own borders and the (notional) containment of state sovereignty to state territory, such that states rule only within their own borders,[23] necropolitics is animated by sovereignty expressed "in the power and the capacity to dictate who may live and who must die" (Mbembe 2019: 66). This form of sovereignty – directed at bodies – is not constrained by borders or by liberal legality, as illustrated by the killings of bin Laden and (often uncounted) others. Under liberal legality, the categories sovereignty, jurisdiction, territory, control, and law are tethered together as foundational pillars underpinning the same socio-political terrain. However, war-on-terror tactics disaggregate sovereignty, territory, jurisdiction, law, and control such that power over populations and territory may be exercised without concomitant obligations to extend law's protections to these populations.

1.1.2 Death Worlds: Global and National

The brute violence of extraterritorial, extrajudicial killing is an obvious expression of how necropolitical law unfolds beyond the borders of the

---

[23] For example, Cornell University's legal dictionary, Wex, offers a conventional definition of sovereignty that straightforwardly presumes the containment within nation-state borders of sovereign power: "Sovereignty is a political concept that refers to dominant power or supreme authority. In a monarchy, supreme power resides in the 'sovereign,' or king. In modern democracies, sovereign power rests with the people and is exercised through representative bodies such as Congress or Parliament. The Sovereign is the one who exercises power without limitation. Sovereignty is essentially the power to make laws, even as Blackstone defined it. The term also carries implications of autonomy; to have sovereign power is to be beyond the power of others to interfere"; at www.law.cornell.edu/wex/sovereignty.

United States, discounting life in the straightforward sense of delivering death. In addition to the spectacular killings of high-profile war-on-terror enemies, the post-9/11 wars initiated by the United States have killed, maimed, and displaced *millions* of people. Brown University's Costs of War project has provided estimates as follows: 801,000 killed through direct war violence, with several times that many killed indirectly "due to ripple effects like malnutrition, damaged infrastructure, and environmental degradation"; 387,000 civilians killed; 38 million war refugees, with displaced peoples in Afghanistan, Pakistan, Iraq, Syria, Libya, Yemen, Somalia, and the Philippines.[24]

Consistent with the co-constitutions of nation and empire, as argued by Amy Kaplan (2002), within the domestic terrain of the United States, a necropolitical discounting of life is also violent, explicitly racialized, and historically embedded. Foundationally, the United States is a state "based on the ideology of white supremacy, the widespread practice of African slavery, and a policy of genocide and land theft" (Dunbar-Ortiz 2014: 2). Indeed, necropolitics has been expressed, in part, through the complexities of a historical matrix characterized by the "law of inequality" governing the constitution of the United States as "both a state and a *pro-slavery democracy*" (Mbembe 2019: 17). The continuation of the practice of lynching from slavery into the early twentieth century (Berg 2011)[25] illustrates the persistence of necropolitics through an "arresting, grotesque, and exhibitionist form of racist cruelty" (Mbembe 2019: 18). The "ritualized torture" of lynching constitutes "a form of terrorism within a liberal democratic state [through which] a racially privileged part of the population systemically terrorizes its racialized stigmatized fellow citizens" (Asad 2007: 98–99).

Further affirming Kaplan's important analytic insight on the many "interconnections between internal and external colonization in the imperial constitution of American national cultures" (Kaplan 1993: 18), reverberations between nation/empire and past/present are evident in the "profound historical resonance" to be registered between images of lynching in the United States that circulated in the early twentieth century and photographs of brutalized and tortured detainees at Abu Ghraib that became public early in the twenty-first-century War on Terror (Pugliese 2007: 247). As Melani McAlister writes, the

---

[24] At https://watson.brown.edu/costsofwar/.
[25] While Blacks were the primary victims of lynching, victims also included Mexicans, Native Americans, and Chinese and Italian immigrants (Berg 2011: 117–43).

"photographs from Abu Ghraib were images of a new kind of racial politics, one that brought the symbolics of domestic racism – itself a product of the history of colonialism and imperialism – into the service of new, overtly imperial American power" (2005: 302).

In tracing continuities between empire and nation in US "violence work," Micol Seigel highlights how, historically, "US soldiers and cops have never been distinct" (2018: 20), with shared and overlapping tasks, personnel, equipment, and tactics long predating the contemporary and spectacular militarization of the police. She highlights, how, throughout the United States' eighteenth- and nineteenth-century imperialist and expansionist wars, police and soldiers worked together, with enduring effects for the co-constitutions of nation/empire in terms of state-sanctioned racialized violence:

> Police and military are often in the same places, pursuing the same goals, applying the same lethal means. Following the suppression of rebels in the Philippines after 1898, for example, US police "came home to turn the same lens on America, seeing its ethnic communities not as fellow citizens but as internal colonies requiring coercive controls." Domestically, the brunt of this mission miscegenation falls on African Americans, disproportionately sighted in police crosshairs. Conflating them fully with targets abroad, police in Black areas "view each person on the streets as a potential criminal or enemy."
> (Seigel 2018: 20; quoting Skolnick and Fyfe 1993: 77)

Thus, agents of the state's violence such as the police perceive racialized minorities less as fellow citizens than as inherently subordinate subcommunities akin to the colonized Other, needing management through coercion. Indeed, so persistent and entrenched was the terrorizing of the racialized Other that in 1951 the Civil Rights Congress, a coalition of radical Black and White activists, looked for justice beyond US borders, appealing to the United Nations to intervene in the genocidal and "continuous history of lynching and extralegal violence, police murder, and diminished life expectancy of Black people in the United States" (Mullen and Vials 2020). And extending the necropolitical penal infrastructures of the United States into the long War on Terror has also been achieved, Michelle Brown notes, through exporting "supermax levels of confinement" to Guantanamo, then to Iraq at Abu Ghraib (2010: 129).

In our present, when "environmental justice activists, Black Lives Matter protesters, and Indigenous water protectors have faced the forces of War on Terror-inspired counterinsurgency warfare," then "it is increasingly the case that the War on Terror is staged globally *and* within the US" (Lubin 2021: 5). Alert to the disproportionate targeting of racialized communities by state violence, scholars and activists deplore "the war on black life and ... the extent to which black lives [have been] deemed disposable, killable, and structurally less worthy within the context of the United States" (Méndez 2016: 96), with state violence and policing practices creating the "*death world*" in which "blackness is a metonym for crime and disorder" (Kwate and Threadcraft 2017: 535). In May 2020, the killing of a handcuffed African American man, George Floyd, suffocated to death by the White police officer using his knee to pin him to the ground, sparked protests against police brutality that spread from Minneapolis across the United States and outward into the world. The police killing of Floyd was but one instance of a systemic targeting and killing of unarmed African Americans in recent years; killings so egregious that the tragic roll call of victims killed by White police officers and, in some cases, by armed vigilantes, have become familiar names worldwide. Trayvon Martin is one such name, the unarmed teenager who was carrying home a bottle of Arizona Iced Tea and some Skittles when he was shot dead by neighborhood vigilante George Zimmerman in Florida in 2012. The killer's acquittal precipitated the Black Lives Matter movement (Ransby 2018; Lane et al. 2020: 792). Another unarmed teenager, Michael Brown, was killed by a White police officer in Ferguson, Missouri, in 2014. Also in 2014, an unarmed African American man with a history of mental illness, Dontre Hamilton, was shot and killed by a White police officer in Milwaukee. Unarmed and Black, suspected of illegally selling cigarettes, Eric Garner was killed by a White police officer's chokehold in New York (2014). Twelve years old and playing with a toy gun in a Cleveland park, Tamir Rice was shot and killed by a White police officer, who was quick to presume Rice to be criminal and dangerous (2014). And, as Laurence Ralph points out, when a seventeen-year-old suspected of having punctured the tires of a police car is shot sixteen times by a White police officer, and turns out to have been holding a knife, not a gun, then we can be sure that the US mythology of the dangerous, predatory Black criminal is at work, as it has been innumerable times before and since the police killing of Laquan McDonald in 2014 (Ralph 2019). In Georgia, Ahmaud Arbery was unarmed and jogging when he was shot and killed by White neighborhood vigilantes for no apparent reason other than jogging while

Black. In Kentucky, Breonna Taylor was shot and killed when White police officers forcibly entered her home, raiding the wrong address to search for drugs.[26]

The list of victims runs far longer (O'Kane 2020). Black Lives Matter is a movement demanding in its very name that African American lives not be discounted any more. And while the movement may have been precipitated by the 2012 killing of Trayvon Martin, the necropolitical violence of discounting certain racialized lives bears a long history in the United States. The resilience of necropolitical law in the domestic sphere of the United States is also evident in the disproportionate incarceration of Black and Brown communities, in the frequently lethal violence directed at these populations, and in continuing evidence of torture experienced by African Americans at the hands of police and the legal system (e.g., Alexander 2010; Ralph 2020). Conjoining Mbembe's analysis of the necropolitics entrenched in the United States to Judith Shklar's insight that, in the modern dual state, "some of its population is simply declared to be subhuman, and a public danger, and as such excluded from the legal order entirely" (1987: 1), necropolitical law is to be recognized as a deeply embedded feature of US domestic politics.

1.1.3 Discounting Life: A Necropolitical Continuum

In addition to brute violence, within the domestic terrain of the United States the necropolitical discounting of life has unfolded through a particular historical conjuncture of militarism and globalization. In 1973 "an unholy alliance of military hawks and economists from the University of Chicago" launched the practice of "forcing the leaders of developing countries to address their growing foreign debt by privatizing their economies in ways that benefited US-based multinational corporations and severely harmed local and national economies" (Lubin 2021: 13). By the end of the Cold War, alongside disinvestment in public goods and public infrastructure, the "politics of enforced austerity . . . made new low-wage labor and production markets globally available to US corporations" even as "vast swaths of the US industrial economy was also being gutted and American workers faced

---

[26] On Michael Brown, see Pulliam-Moore and Myers (2014); on Dontre Hamilton, Eric Garner, and Tamir Rice, see Sanburn (2015); on Breonna Taylor, see BBC News (2020a); and on Ahmaud Arbery, see BBC News (2020b).

joblessness, declining wages, and fierce limits on their ability to organize" (Lubin 2021: 13).

A further reverberation between empire/nation is evident along the continuum of discounting life involving, in part, an altered relationship between state and citizen. Joseph Masco names the current US state "the counterterror state," highlighting a particular mode of governance (Masco 2014: 1). The counterterror state has harnessed the "very real violence of September 2001 ... to a conceptual project that mobilizes affects (fear, terror, anger) via imaginary processes (worry, precarity, threat) to constitute an unlimited space and time horizon for military state action" (2014: 1). The counterterror state orients governance away from "national boundaries and citizenship," toward an "expansive universe of terroristic potentials" (Masco 2014: 1). In doing so, as Masco notes, the counterterror state sets aside a range of "everyday forms of suffering and vulnerability that Americans experience," such as "poverty, bankrupt municipal governments, spectacular white-collar crime, energy scarcity," and "cities lost to storm surges." In setting aside "these everyday insecurities endured by citizens," the counterterror state subordinates the terror citizens *actually* experience to the imagined terrors of fearful future possibilities (2014: 2). In other words, through governance, necropolitics within the domestic sphere of the US expresses an attenuated version of necropolitical law's discounting of life.[27] To borrow Rob Nixon's compelling metaphor of slow violence (2011), the counterterror state's sustained governance oriented *away* from citizenship (Masco 2014; Lubin 2021), does not so much set out to kill, as to diminish and devalue life qualitatively, socially, and politically.

This book provides a critical taxonomy of the overlapping processes, histories, tactics, and ideologies of necropolitical law. This taxonomy maps and describes how the dynamics of separation, deception, and exemption that are key to necropolitics (Mbembe 2019: 1) inform and shape necropolitical law. These include dynamics of deception through (1) language that obfuscates, masks, and deceives; (2) military technology that is represented as precise but is more accurately understood as annihilatory; (3) the strategic management of media to construct narratives of legitimacy that underpin necropolitical law's workings; and (4) the conjoining of liberal legal features (regulations, procedures, laws) to illiberal practices. Necropolitical dynamics of separation are

---

[27] These critiques of how public funds are distributed are also foundational arguments of the social movements #defund the police. See, for example, Levin (2020).

evident in (1) a narrative of existential crisis that fosters fear, to cultivate citizen acquiescence for de-democratizing practices, and anger, to cultivate citizen consent for vengeance and war; (2) the marginalization of counternarratives critiquing the War on Terror; (3) and representations of patriotism and national security that overtly or covertly amplify racism and Islamophobia. Necropolitical dynamics of exemption are evident in (1) revitalizations of American exceptionalism; (2) valorizations of violent imperialism; (3) a normalizing of preemptive and vengeful US state violence on a global scale; (4) the disaggregation of sovereignty, law, jurisdiction, and control; and (5) representations of rule-of-law values, processes, actors, and institutions as inadequate to meeting the exigencies of the long War on Terror.

1.2 THE LONG WAR ON TERROR

In choosing to write of "the long War on Terror" – a category that both acknowledges and disrupts the US state's "War on Terror" – I foreground the centrality of narrative to law's meaning-making[28] and the key role played by language in simultaneously justifying and obscuring the discounting of life embedded in necropolitical law. Specifically, injecting the durational marker into the term challenges the US account of the War on Terror as an emergency response precipitated and necessitated by the events of 9/11.[29] By inserting "long," the provocation is to grapple with the histories and power

---

[28] In addition to Robert Cover's influential argument about the meaning-making that occurs through the co-constitution of law and narrative (1983), scholarship that has shaped thinking on law and narrative includes White (1973), Scheppele (1989), Fitzpatrick (1992), the edited collections Brooks and Gewirtz (1996), and Bellow and Minow (1996).

[29] The language and logics of 9/11 as precipitating event, alongside the War on Terror as a "necessity," can be seen in a range of war-on-terror texts. For example, the opening clauses of the Preamble to the *Authorization for the Use of Military Force*, passed on September 18, 2001, read, "Whereas, on September 11, 2001, acts of treacherous violence were committed against the United States and its citizens; and Whereas, such acts render it both *necessary* and appropriate that the United States exercise its rights to self-defense and to protect United States citizens both at home and abroad ..." (emphasis added). In his September 2006 speech justifying the secrecy of military commissions and detention without trial, President George W. Bush invoked "necessity," as did President Obama in his May 2011 speech announcing the killing of Osama bin Laden: "The American people did not choose this fight. It came to our shores."

relations of necropolitics' long durée informing the long War on Terror.[30] These histories illuminate liberal legality's deep embeddedness in and co-constitution with a counter-humanist racism stemming, in large part, from European colonization and what Mbembe terms the United States' "pro-slavery democracy" (2019: 17). In his analysis, the colonizer's ideology that constructs colonies as inhabited by "savages" informs a politics through which racism and lawlessness converge. Of course, it is a key argument of *Discounting Life* that the dynamics Mbembe characterizes as "lawlessness" are better understood as expressions of necropolitical law. By reframing lawlessness as necropolitical law, I draw on the scholarship on law in relation to imperial dynamics and exception (discussed above) to reiterate the point that necropolitical law has long been an unacknowledged partner of liberal legality. Put differently, the ostensible lawlessness of necropolitical law has historically relied on power's capacity to spatially and racially segregate populations. Through this segregation, the seeming prevalence of "normal" liberal legality in the Euro-Atlantic sphere – for those *not* racially stigmatized – has been deceptively split from, while ideologically and temporally coexisting with, necropolitical law in colonies, on plantations, in postcolonies, and (as discussed above) in the contemporary death worlds of both the United States and the world in the global War on Terror.[31]

In addition to acknowledging the long durée of racialized, imperialized violence, I use the term "long War on Terror" to repudiate the US state's narrative claiming that the events of 9/11 inaugurated the War on Terror. With the War on Terror "having a long history undergirding the structure of US settler colonial formation," it becomes crucial to grapple with this war as "both new and old – it is staged within a new

---

[30] While Nikhil Pal Singh does not use the analytic category of necropolitics, his *Race and America's Long War* (2017) traces the "dimly acknowledged, disavowed, or defensively protested" histories of "imperial expansion, colonial dispossession, and racial domination" in US history from its founding to its present (2017: ix).

[31] And to add to the point made above in Section I on the necropolitical law fostered yet disavowed by exception, the temporal coexistence of liberal legality and necropolitical law might also be understood as key to dual state legality, and to excavating the neglected "multiple genealogies" of modern democracies, which include the coexistence of a "*community of fellow creatures* governed, at least in principle by the law of equality" with "a category of nonfellows ... [with] no right to have rights" (Mbembe 2019: 17). The plantation and the penal colony, Mbembe highlights, are entangled within histories of modern democracies (2019: 22).

epoch in American imperial culture, but it is continuous with a long history of American national development" (Lubin 2021: 6). *Discounting Life* is alert to the War on Terror's profound continuities with the founding logics and practices of the United States (e.g., Saito 2010, 2021; Dunbar-Ortiz 2014; Singh 2017), as well as Cold War ideologies, practices, and institutions (Dudziak 2012; Masco 2014; Lubin 2021). These continuities link the War on Terror to the concept of permanent war (Lens 1987; Lutz 2009). Permanent war, from 1945, has worked to "rearrange old institutional patterns, . . . modify attitudes toward law and order, alter traditional beliefs, refashion the economy and above all, sire a new form of government," that is militarized and that, in turn, militarizes "the American state of mind" (Lens 1987: 4). For Catherine Lutz, the War on Terror is the current expression of "the long Permanent War" (2009: 367).[32]

Within this broader category of "national security state," the Cold War state might be distinguished from the counterterror state on three counts: geopolitical, governmental, and temporal. Geopolitically, the Cold War state was constrained by contestation with an opposing superpower such that the former could not exert its power over the entirety of the globe. In contrast, the counterterror state, unchecked in the absence of an opponent with equivalent geopolitical heft, claims the entirety of the planet as its "homeland."[33] In turn, planetary

---

[32] Indebted to Lutz's "long Permanent War," the category "long War on Terror" also honors the centrality to *Necropolitics* (2019) of sustained and systemic dynamics of terror in racialized, imperialized violence, past and present. Lutz usefully summarizes Lens's argument: "Permanent War began in 1947 with passage of the National Security Act and a variety of executive orders. They produced a revolutionary rupture in US state organization, instituting what Lens argued was a second, secret government that was housed in a set of new organizations, including the National Security Agency (NSA), National Security Council (NSC) and the Central Intelligence Agency (CIA). At the head of this second state was a new, more imperial President permitted, or better created by, the National Security Act. From the Act's passage on, military activities fell under heavy mask from public oversight. The US became a 'national security state'" (Lutz 2009: 368).

[33] The *9/11 Commission Report*, in Chapter 12 (entitled "What to Do? A Global Strategy"), asserts, "9/11 has taught us that terrorism against American interests 'over there' should be regarded just as we regard terrorism against America 'over here.' In this same sense, the American homeland is the planet" (362). The paradoxical conjoining of the globalized imperialism articulated by the *9/11 Commission Report* and post-9/11 xenophobia is illuminated by reading "planetary homeland" through the lens of Amy Kaplan's analysis of the sacralizing post-9/11 use of "homeland" in US political and popular discourse. She demonstrates how the

homeland produces a global and imagined (Masco 2014), "shadowy, but omnipresent" (Kaplan 2018: 240), enemy. In terms of governance, through much of the Cold War the "total social formation" of nuclear fear was "balanced by investments in a welfare-state apparatus devoted to improving the conditions of everyday life for citizens in terms of health, education, and the environment" (Masco 2014: 7). In contrast, as noted above, the counterterror state selectively allocates resources in favor of the necropolitical, disregarding "everyday forms of violence that require other nonmilitarized forms of governance" (Masco 2014: 27).

Temporally, in addition to nineteenth-century colonialism and the Cold War, a third, more recent past informs the long War on Terror, and that is the violent conflict between the United States and al Qaeda throughout the 1990s (Jackson 2005; Dower 2010; Tierney 2016). In 1993, explosives were detonated in a parking garage of New York's World Trade Center (Diplomatic Security Service 2019). It took US intelligence six years (Dower 2010: 54) to establish the link between that bombing and al Qaeda. In 1996, Osama bin Laden – that "telectronic phantom of the Information Age" (Lawrence and Karim 2007: 539) – issued his first declaration of war against the United States through the power of "not just any fatwa but an online fatwa," signaling bin Laden's "skillful use of self-representation on global satellite television and other electronic outlets" (Jacquard 2002; Lawrence and Karim 2007: 496). In 1998, after bin Laden issued a second declaration of war, al Qaeda bombed the US embassies in Kenya and Tanzania, and the United States retaliated by launching cruise missiles at an al Qaeda training camp in Afghanistan (Young 2003: 10–11; Dower 2010: 28). In 2000, al Qaeda "suicide bombers in a small boat" attacked the US naval destroyer USS Cole when the ship was berthed in Yemen (Dower 2010: 29). And throughout the year 2001 prior to the 9/11 attacks

term "puts into play a history of multiple meanings, connotations, and associations that work on the one hand to convey a sense of unity, security, and stability, but more profoundly, on the other hand, work to generate forms of radical insecurity by proliferating threats of the foreign lurking within and without foreign borders" (Kaplan 2003: 64). Put differently, in the long War on Terror, "homeland" has become a keyword in the sense theorized by Raymond Williams in terms of the structuring relations of "significant binding words ... and their interpretation" (Williams 1983 [1976]: 15); these are words that are compound, capacious, and inherently ideological, with a taken-for-granted resonance that defies easy definition, thereby perpetuating the obfuscations of ideology.

taking place, US intelligence personnel alerted the government of George W. Bush "as many as forty times of the threat posed by Osama bin Laden but this is not what the administration wanted to hear, and it did not hear it" (Powers 2004). In short, for at least seven years before the 9/11 attacks, the United States and al Qaeda had been in conflict. By inserting these pasts into the narrative – nineteenth-century colonialism, the Cold War, and the pre-9/11 conflict between al Qaeda and the United States – it becomes possible to perceive how much of the justification of the War on Terror has been constructed for the purpose of legitimizing an apparently liberal legal state's necropolitical legality. Contesting the war-on-terror origin story is crucial to unpacking the co-constitutions of law and culture shaping necropolitical law.

Importantly, as a category the "long War on Terror" is also future-making, which is consistent with repeated formulations by key US state actors of the War on Terror's probable unending duration (McAlister 2002; Dudziak 2015) and with the counterterror state's deliberate generation of "imagined terrors of fearful, future possibilities" to legitimize its governance (Masco 2014: 2). This future-making matters because "the future we imagine is a well-spring of law," and because the future is "a cultural construct that depends, in part, on the way we remember the past," it is vital to scrutinize and challenge the memories, narratives, politics, and values through which we shape our futures (Dudziak 2015: 592).

It is noteworthy that a generative slippage inheres in labeling the current counterterror project a "war."[34] Conventionally, wars are conducted between states, their temporalities framed by a distinct opening moment, such as a declaration of war, and a definitive closing, such as surrender. Conventionally, wars have winners and losers, beginnings and endings. To invoke "war time" is also to construct the War on Terror as an episode that has "interrupted regular time," thereby muting and reconfiguring the law and politics of "peacetime" (Dudziak 2012: 3). Mary Dudziak emphasizes the significant effects that "the assumption of temporariness" in the idea of wartime has on law, in that the

---

[34] On September 12, 2001, the day after the 9/11 attacks, Bush made a speech characterizing the attacks as "more than acts of terror. They were "acts of war"; see Bush (2001a). Four days later, in remarks to the press that were broadcast across the United States and reported worldwide, Bush articulated the coinage "war on terrorism"; see Bush (2001b).

"temporariness becomes an argument for exceptional policies such as torture" (2012: 4). And war is also inextricably enmeshed, Caren Kaplan argues, with the concept and lived experience of wartime's *aftermath*. Aftermath renders our sensed experience of post 9/11 as an "always already undeclared war, the endless war that cannot locate a stable origin or believe in a definite conclusion, offering a present perceived through various states of denial, anger, numbness, or engagement" (Kaplan 2018: 16). In short, the category "war" in the label War on Terror imports into the term capacious and confounding meanings, affects, and associations that matter for the War on Terror's narrative and cultural enmeshments with law.

Importantly, despite being depicted as a war, for the War on Terror there was no formal congressional declaration of war (Franke-Ruta 2013). In legal-doctrinal terms, rather than voting on a declaration of war, Congress passed an Authorization for the Use of Force (AUMF),[35] which scripts law in terms that are consistent with two pillars of necropolitics. These are, first (and as noted above), "the state of exception and the relation of enmity ... [as] the normative basis of the right to kill" (Mbembe 2019: 70) and, second, the constitution of "the ultimate expression of sovereignty ... in the power and the capacity to dictate who may live and who must die" (Mbembe 2019: 66). The AUMF declares a state of exception and emergency[36] and identifies US citizens as bearers of "the right to self-defense ... both at home and abroad" in a manner that constructs a necropolitical relation of "enemy" out of an expansive global population of those who are not US citizens.[37] In other words, the United States' necropolitical sovereign power to kill or not kill follows the bodies of individuals or groups, no matter where in the world those bodies might be.

The necropolitical law of the AUMF links this planetary sovereignty to a long War-on-Terror temporality in two senses. First, the AUMF was in force for eighteen years, from September 2001 to

---

[35] Public Law 107-40, 107th Congress, September 18, 2001. At www.congress.gov/107/plaws/publ40/PLAW-107publ40.pdf.

[36] Among the characterizations of exception and emergency in the AUMF is the assertion, in the preamble in reference to the 9/11 attacks, that "such acts continue to pose an unusual and extraordinary threat to the national security and foreign policy of the United States."

[37] The second clause of the preamble to the AUMF reads, "Whereas, such acts render it both necessary and appropriate that the United States exercises its rights to self-defense and to protect United States citizens both at home and abroad ...."

June 2019,[38] and over the course of those years it has been used to authorize the long War on Terror's ever-expanding activities (Kelly 2016). Second, while Bush may deserve derision for using "terror" where "terrorism" or "terrorists" would have been grammatically correct (Jones 2001), by taking seriously the former president's lexical choice, Masco illuminates key points about the logics and temporality of the War on Terror:

> [C]ounterterror is not only a highly flexible mode of security, based on an ever-expanding concept of terror and a highly elastic set of core concerns in the figuration of the WMD [weapons of mass destruction]. It also addressed an unwinnable problem, for when can one say that terror – a basic emotional state – has been finally purged from American experience? Counterterror *colonizes the American future* by identifying an ever-shifting series of peoples, objects, technologies, hypotheticals, and contingencies to secure in the name of planetary defense.
>
> (Masco 2014: 196; emphasis added)

To summarize, in addition to the imperialist appropriations and racialized violence underpinning the founding of the United States, the state's war-on-terror narrative denies at least three strands of the past: the racialized imperialism of nineteenth-century colonialism; continuities between Cold War logics and institutions and those of the War on Terror; and the conflict between the United States and al Qaeda throughout the 1990s. It also displaces the present, in part by disregarding the terror *actually* experienced by US citizens in favor of channeling resources toward fighting future imagined terrors (Masco 2014). In denying these pasts and displacing the present, the state eclipses the viability of an alternative future, rendering the War on Terror endless, permanent, and future-making (McAlister 2002; Der Derian 2009; Lutz 2009; Masco 2014; Dudziak 2015). The blanket exclusion of any understanding of "terrorism as an expression of social conflict reflecting comprehensible grievances (albeit not necessarily justifiable)" (Brysk 2007: 4), alongside the insistent inscription of terrorists as "the universal enemy" (Li 2020), effects de-politicizing closures in public discourse. As Melani McAlister notes, when the terrorism of 9/11 is explained in pathologizing, moral, and abstracted terms, the public space for much-needed

---

[38] The June 20, 2019, repeal of the 2001 AUMF appears to have been prompted by fears that the Trump administration would rely on it to authorize war with Iran; (Edmondson 2019; McArdle 2019).

historically and politically informed analysis is foreclosed, as is any possible path to peace (2005: 278). Cumulatively, these discursive, ideological, and temporal features weave into an encompassing and globalized social fabric. In the process, "terror" and "war" become central enabling terms for necropolitical law's expansions and enactments, discounting life through the unbounded temporality of the long War on Terror.

1.3 LAW'S MANY MEANINGS

1.3.1 An Interpretive Sociolegal Epistemology

In this section, I disaggregate the compound category "law," and argue for the need to uphold the ideals that inform the socio-political concepts rule of law and liberal legality. Writing and reading in the English language, I (principally) understand "law" through Anglo-American and "Western" traditions, in which law occupies a semantic field intersecting with morality, ethics, and power.[39] In keeping with these traditions, and as a humanist, sociolegal scholar, I understand justice as inseparable from law[40] and law as inseparable from the cultural and the

---

[39] Law's compound meanings might be mapped usefully (although partially) in terms of the following lists of law's arenas and institutions, law's actors, law's attributes, and law's forms. A non-exhaustive list of law's arenas and institutions includes bureaucracies, courts, governments, legislatures, prisons, police, the public sphere, and trials. A non-exhaustive list of law's actors includes asylum seekers, bureaucrats, citizens, dissidents, elected representatives, individuals, intelligence and security personnel, judges, lawyers, legislators, police personnel, prisoners, and refugees. A non-exhaustive list of law's attributes, values, dynamics, and effects includes adjudication, authority, contestation, deliberation, due process, duty, equity, ethics, evidence, fairness, governance, obligation, obedience, order, incarceration, justice, jurisdiction, legitimacy, mediation, morality, privacy, proof, protection, secrecy, violence, punishment, prescription, proscription, reparations, restitution, surveillance, scrutiny, separation of powers, security, and transparency. A non-exhaustive list of forms through which law is made manifest includes bodies, built structures, conduct, contracts, national constitutions, corporations, images, judgments, legislation, partnerships, pardons, procedure, regulations, rules, sound, and treaties.

[40] Perhaps the most acute critique of sociolegality's neglect of justice as an analytic category has been articulated by Marianne Constable in her 2005 monograph *Just Silences*. Constable shows how, despite the absence of justice in modern law's texts and despite the inattention to justice in sociolegal scholarship, a sense of justice, which understands "the existence of law is one thing; its justice another" (2005: 9) cannot be erased. I agree with Constable that, despite the elusive, aspirational, potentially unrealizable quality of an ideal justice, justice *is* a social fact. Modifiers

social.[41] Tracing histories and genealogies of law and culture as analytic categories, Rosemary Coombe notes "their mutual interdependence in colonial histories" (1998: 63). Heeding her call to "become more critically cognizant of the historical forces always already at work" in the relationship between law and culture, *Discounting Life* addresses "inequalities of power, legitimizing some identities and delegitimizing others" by focusing on "the everyday practices of signification and their institutional acknowledgement, where material relations between meaning and power are forged" (Coombe 1998: 64). In short, I understand law to be a plural[42] and pervasive strand of life,[43]

like social justice, distributive justice, procedural justice, and wage justice are efforts to translate between the ideal and the real by denoting spheres of social inequity. Aristotle's distinction between natural justice and legal justice informs an enormous body of scholarship that, in one way or another, addresses histories and philosophies of disjuncture between positive law (legislation and judgments) and understandings of justice. The political concepts impelling this book – rule of law and liberal legalism – insist on law's indivisibility from justice. And culture – including popular culture – is an important and pervasive social site through which the call to and for justice is regularly made (Miller 1998).

[41] In approaching law as domain of experience and knowledge that is inextricably enmeshed with "everything" (Rosen 2006: xi), I follow the turn in sociolegal scholarship away from doctrinal law's abstractions, instead understanding law as grounded in and expressed through a "mutually constitutive relationship" with all facets of the social (Darian-Smith 2013: 3). As an approach to law with permeable disciplinary and methodological borders (Mather 2011), sociolegal studies also embraces approaches to law shaped by cultural studies and the humanities, with this interdisciplinarity also drawing on important philosophical and critical thinking about law. Scholarship informing my analysis includes understandings of the co-constitution of law and culture (Rosen 2006); law and narrative (Cover 1983); the experiential and interpretive dimensions of legal meaning (e.g., White 1990; Kahn 1999); images, popular culture, and media materiality as sites and expressions of law (e.g., Sarat and Kearns 1998; Sherwin 2000; Sarat and Simon 2001; Vismann 2008; Mawani 2012; Manderson 2018); everyday life as sites of law (e.g., Ewick and Silbey 1998), and legal consciousness (e.g., Engel and Yngvesson 1984; Merry 1990; Ewick and Silbey 1992).

[42] An invaluable review of the vast scholarship on legal pluralism, tracing its histories, themes, and politics is Greenhouse (2019).

[43] In *Asking the Law Question*, Margaret Davies takes the position that law exists in, and is discernible in, "everything – from literature to science, and everyday experience. The whole world is structured by laws of one sort or another. The law is a form we cannot avoid, whatever its substance. We think and act in relation to laws. There are laws of social behavior, laws of language, laws relating to what counts as knowledge and what doesn't, and laws which say that well, really, law is actually something different from all of these things" (2002: 4). A canonical articulation of an analogous perception of law as pervasive might be read into Derrida's non-

inextricably connected with contestations over power and sovereignty (Mawani 2012), and "with existence at large" (Davies 2017: iii).

In treating law as cultural text, I turn away from narrow doctrinal understandings of law as only state law. Looking at – but also *beyond* – state law is absolutely crucial because "[t]he politics of defining law as limited to state law is composed of a number of factors: the alignment of capitalism with statism; the colonialist downgrading of non-state law; the gendered imagining of law as a man writ large and of legal subjects as mini-sovereigns; the insistence on disciplinary separation; and other matters that serve to isolate law from its social and relational founda-tions" (Davies 2017: 39). Additionally, I look beyond state law and doctrine in part because of the US insistence that the War on Terror exceeds the frameworks of both doctrinal law and conventional war.[44]

Approaching law through an interdisciplinary lens becomes espe-cially crucial in the context of necropolitical law because necropolitical law, like necropolitics, is undeclared, and its workings are often masked. As the discussion of collateral damage (below, in Section 1.4.3) illustrates, the discounting of life fostered by necropolitical law tends to be treated, in dominant discourse, as sporadic and incidental. Through elisions, omissions, and secrecy – facets of the deception Mbembe draws attention to (2019:1) – the systemic discounting of life built into necropolitical law is disavowed and deflected.

Sometimes the masking of necropolitical law takes place through a yoking of liberal legal tropes to necropolitical law. For example, on August 30, 2019, it was reported that the death penalty trial of the five men accused of plotting the 9/11 attacks would commence in January 2021 (Rosenberg 2019). However, in an August 2021 update, the *New York Times* reported that in the interim since the 2019 announcement, "the timetable has been upended by changes in personnel as well as pandemic-related restrictions on travel to the base" (Rosenberg 2021). In

---

exhaustive examples of law in his essay "Force of Law": "the area of laws on the teaching and practice of languages, the legitimization of canons, the military use of scientific research, abortion, euthanasia, problems of organ transplant, extrauterine conception, bio-engineering, medical experimentation, the social treatment of AIDS, the macro- or micro-politics of drugs, the homeless, and so on, without forgetting, of course, the treatment of what we call animal life, animality" (Derrida 1992: 28–29).

[44] Bodies of doctrinal law rejected by the United States include international law, human rights law, the laws of war, and the law applicable to interstate force (Alston 2010: 3).

the public discourse on this long-delayed trial – it has been in pretrial phase since May 2012 (Rosenberg 2021) – gestures, institutions, and dynamics of liberal legality, such as a trial, a judge, the process of selecting a jury, and a public gallery, accompany routine violations of liberal legal principles – indeed, outright criminality on the part of the counterterror state (Alston 2010). The five accused have been tortured, detained without trial in CIA prisons and at Guantanamo for almost twenty years. The trial, if and when it takes place, will have a military jury and a military judge and will follow the rules and procedures of military commissions, a hybrid creature designed to obstruct the rights of accused persons in a range of ways (Abel 2018a: 184–321). The capstone of this discombobulating emulsion of liberal legal discourse and necropolitical law is that the trial will be held at Guantanamo's war court compound: Camp Justice (Rosenberg 2021).

Agreement on language is necessary to legal argument (White 1984: 268) and to basic human communication. The ordinary meanings of "justice" do not encompass the torture,[45] detention without trial, inhumane conditions of incarceration, and extraordinary renditions characteristic of detention at Guantanamo.[46] The ordinary meanings of "trial" do not encompass the contingent audibility and near invisibility of Guantanamo detainees, nor the many ways in which their access to counsel has been obstructed and attenuated.[47] The sinister (mis)naming of Camp Justice is darkly befitting of how Guantanamo, in spatial, temporal, and legal terms, is emblematic of the systemic and

---

[45] In its ordinary meaning "trial" presumes and requires that accused persons have the mental capacity to participate in their own defense. As part of the preliminary steps toward the 2021 trial at Guantanamo, the accused are to receive magnetic resonance imaging scans to determine whether they have suffered brain damage as a result of torture (Rosenberg 2019).

[46] A vast literature has been generated on the legality of, and the conditions of detention at, Guantanamo. Of particular note are Abel (2018), Slahi (2015), Khalili (2014), Hussain (2007), Kaplan (2005), and Johns (2005).

[47] The accused will be behind glass screens that prevent those in the public gallery from hearing them without headphones, and the headphones will only relay what the accused say after a forty-second audio delay to facilitate military censorship; www.nytimes.com/2019/08/30/us/politics/sept-11-trial-guantanamo-bay.html.
Additionally, as Laleh Khalili notes, attorney-client privilege is utterly undone, in that counsel's legal notes and documents are "monitored by the Department of Defense in a warehouse in northern Virginia. Where usually the performative of justice allows the accused to speak for him- or herself, in a military commission, the detainees' voices are smothered" (Khalili 2014: 87).

structural discounting of life in the long War on Terror. And, as this brief discussion of the possible "trial" of Guantanamo detainees shows, with necropolitical law, liberal legal values and processes are undone even as the liberal legal terminology deployed conceals the workings of necropolitical law.

1.3.2 Rule of Law and Liberal Legality

The socio-political concepts "rule of law" and "liberal legalism" might be understood in terms of rendering law's many meanings concrete in accord with specific orientations to power, ethics, and political ideals.[48] At the heart of rule of law, for example, is law's capacity to scrutinize and limit power (e.g., Dicey 1959; Loughlin 2000; Tamanaha 2004).

And as a political concept, unsurprisingly, rule of law is rooted in the history of countering unfettered monarchical power. Conceptually, liberal legalism augments rule of law's wary distrust of power by layering the values of democracy and liberalism upon rule-of-law foundations (Loughlin 2000: 198).

Law's susceptibility to the political and the disjuncture between liberal ideals (such as justice, equality, and rights) and the persistent inequities of material realities has meant that, as socio-political concepts, rule of law and liberal legality may be claimed and invoked while not quite existing in their fully realized expressions (Cheesman 2018: 168). Critical legal scholarship has explicated how rule of law and liberal legality have failed to repair the affiliation between law and power, an affiliation that too often undermines realizations of rights and justice. However, an equally vital body of scholarship shows how law's mythic resonance and the promise of justice held within concepts like rights together yield a vital heuristic against which law's social articulations might be assessed and held accountable (e.g., White 1990; Williams 1991; Baxi 2004; Constable 2005).

The promise of transformation – *alchemy* in Patricia Williams's memorable formulation (1991) – is held within the humanist values of a law oriented to serving rights and justice. Situated, relational, and ethnographic attention to socio-political concepts that may not yet exist in their perfect expressions is key to recognizing these concepts as enlivened – even as they struggle – in the paradoxical coexistence

---

[48] For a recent and useful analysis of rule of law and liberal legality, see Diab (2015).

of orienting ideals and fragmentary realizations (Mertz 2002; Cheesman 2018).

As socio-political concepts, the humanist content, orientation to justice, and attention to due process of rule of law and liberal legality become especially important when law, an already compound category, bristles with the contradictions of a befuddling eruption of war-on-terror terminology, practices, and institutions. Torture memos, a disregard for international law, the violations of human rights associated with Guantanamo Bay and Abu Ghraib, and the rule-of-law transgressions engendered by military commissions are just a few examples of the War on Terror's remaking of law's lexicon and norms. Euphemisms like "enhanced interrogation,"[49] "extraordinary rendition," and "collateral damage" reflect efforts to re-semanticize – and thereby *legitimize* – torture, kidnapping, and the killing of civilians.[50] In short, even though flawed in practice, the orienting values of rule of law and liberal legality – values that insist upon human rights, due process, and the accountability of state power – become a foil against which the practices of our present may be exposed as a vehicle for discounting life through necropolitical law.

1.4 NECROPOLITICAL LAW AND CULTURE IN THE LONG WAR ON TERROR

1.4.1 Media and Counterterror

It is the convergence of necropolitical law's frequent masking of the discounting of life, the co-constitution of law and culture (Rosen 2006), and law's juridico-political command through symbolic and material violence (expressed and evidenced in part through document and documentation; Mawani 2012) that directs my attention to representations of law across a range of texts: legislation, images, and news

---

[49] Elisions between "torture" and "interrogation" in the displays at Washington, DC's International Spy Museum (Small 2019) are a troubling instance of the manner in which "[f]rom a diverse array of representations and cultural expressions, patterns coalesce ... to create a perceptual field ... inviting different meanings from diverse perspectives while effectively ruling out others" (Kaplan 2018: 3).

[50] These re-semanticizations speak, with new intensities, to Robert Cover's influential argument about how "legal interpretation takes place in a field of pain and death" (1986: 1601). The missing element in Cover's argument is the necropolitics of race. As Khalili points out, the "unmentioned axis around which much counterinsurgency revolves is that of 'race' or its euphemisms 'culture' and 'civilization'" (2014: 3).

and entertainment media. While my engagements with language are shaped by critical discourse analysis (detailed in Section 1.4.2), my attention to visual culture draws on Joseph Masco's argument concerning the manner in which visual culture has been central to the formation of "key aspects of US security culture" (2014: 46). He writes:

> [T]he early Cold War state sought explicitly to militarize US citizens through contemplating the end of the nation-state, creating in the process a specific set of ideas and images of collective danger that continue to inform American society in powerful and increasingly complex ways. In the aftermath of the terrorist attacks on New York and Washington in 2001, the affective coordinates of the Cold War arms race provided specific ideological resources to the state, which once again mobilized the image of a United States in nuclear ruins to enable war.
>
> (Masco 2014: 47)

Masco's genealogy of visual culture in relation to national security traces how a specifically American set of "assumptions about mass violence, technology, and democracy" informs the manner in which the War on Terror has been "conducted largely as a campaign of emotional management ... to enable a new kind of American geopolitical project" (2014: 73). Building on his analysis, and on scholarship on the intersections of law and images,[51] my analysis engages with a range of media, in part, to illuminate the co-constitutions of necropolitical law, publicity, and secrecy (Section 1.5).

Relatedly, scholarship shows that the US state has been acutely aware of media's role in shaping public opinion and affect when it comes to engendering popular support for war. When culture yokes affect to militarism, the result is a foreclosing of public debate and critical analysis (Lubin 2021: 27) and mass media is the most efficient and effective vehicle for the generation of widespread consensus (Jackson 2005; Anker 2014). The state's awareness of the role of media is evident from post–World War II depictions of the United States as global superpower through "the use of spectacle into the rise of televisual politics" (Anker 2014: 26), in the planned and synchronized prime-time launching of the 1991 Gulf War (Stahl 2010: 21), and it continues in the "master narratives of airpower and visual culture" that

---

[51] Scholars approaching law from a range of nondoctrinal perspectives have illuminated its pervasive presence in social sites and texts, including popular culture (e.g., Macaulay 1989; Freeman 2004), images (e.g., Sherwin 2000; Manderson 2018), sound (e.g., Parker 2015), and movies (see the essays in Sarat and Kearns 1998).

shape the drone warfare of the long War on Terror (Kaplan 2018: 33). In our present, there has been an "intensification of the relationship between the Pentagon and the entertainment industries" (Stahl 2010: 3), an intensification sometimes amounting to a media-manipulation campaign (McAlister 2005: 292–97), contributing to a vast network "across space and time" with "Matrix-like social effects" (Vavrus 2013: 103). James Der Derian has memorably identified this vast network as "the military-industrial-media-entertainment network" through which asymmetrical and perpetual war has been cast as state "virtue" (2001).

Indeed, even as the long War on Terror renders law's sites and operations secretive and inaccessible, images have been pivotal to the post-9/11 militarization of global culture (Mirzoeff 2006: 4–8; Mirzoeff 2005). In the process, both the domestic space of the United States as nation and the larger sphere of the global have been imbued with the felt unease of "aftermath" (Kaplan 2018). The simultaneously national and global reach and resonance of the texts, images, and events I analyze in this book are attributable to two factors. First, the United States unique standing as "the one and only *global* state" (Falk 2007: 14) has expansive effects of dominance – military, political, economic, as well as cultural – worldwide. And, second, US domination of global mass culture (e.g., Hall 1997; McAlister 2005) becomes especially potent because a "constitutive feature of modern subjectivity" is how media, as Arjun Appadurai notes, renders national borders permeable, shaping our imagination and our sense of self (1996: 3). Put differently, circulations of text, through the internet and otherwise, create consumer-audiences, "connecting people separated by history, geography and language through media in the way that fashion or advertising does" (Devji 2008: ix). These networks and affiliations linking the US state and media, and then traversing across the world, problematize and dismantle distinctions between fact/fiction, news/entertainment, state/nonstate, national/global, and law/not law.

1.4.2 Reading for Law: A Methodology

By tracing how narratives, events, and images emanating from the US script justification, legitimacy, and authorization for discounting life, this book shows how necropolitical law lives and breathes so that Others may die.[52] Alert to "the social power of popular forms of

---

[52] For Mbembe, necropolitics expresses "today's planetary scale renewal of the relation of enmity ... showing how, in the wake of decolonization, war (in the figure of

textuality" and the need to critically interrogate law's "dominant self-representations" (Coombe 1998: 22), the excavating *for* in "reading *for* law" signifies the interpretive process of looking for law and finding (sometimes partial and disaggregated) expressions of it. The *reading* I engage in is reflective, critical reading; alert to contested histories, power interests, and mass-mediated sensationalism. For Edward Said, these are the crucial ingredients of "reading in the real sense of the word."[53] In addition to demonstrating law's pervasive presence, and attending to conditions through which necropolitical law may be masked, muted, or rendered illegible, reading for law draws attention to interpretation as a practice that is "socially determined" and "conditioned by other non-linguistic parts of society" (Fairclough 1989: 24). In other words, reading for law takes into account the affective, temporal, and contextual markers of the long War on Terror.

Methodologically, in addition to performing an interpretive reading *for* law, my analysis draws on critical discourse studies (CDS).[54] CDS is "an inter-disciplinary approach to language in use, which aims to advance our understanding of how discourse figures in social processes, social structures and social change" (Flowerdew and

conquest and occupation, of terror and counterinsurgency) has become the sacrament of our times" (2019: 1–2).

[53] The quote is from Said's May 2003 preface to the twenty-fifth anniversary edition of *Orientalism*. I am grateful to Gary Lee for drawing the text to my attention, in which Said writes, addressing the events of 9/11, "education is threated by nationalist and religious orthodoxies often disseminated by the mass media as they focus ahistorically and sensationally on the distant electronic wars that give viewers the sense of surgical precision but in fact obscure the terrible suffering and destruction produced by modern 'clean' warfare. In the demonization of an unknown enemy, for whom the label 'terrorist' serves the general purpose of keeping people stirred up and angry, media images command too much attention and can be exploited at times of crisis and insecurity of the kind that the post-9/11 period has produced." For Said, the corrective to "the fragmented knowledge available on the internet and in the mass media" is "reading in the real sense of the world," which is reading guided by humanist values and critical thought.

[54] Critical discourse studies, or critical discourse analysis, describes an extensive body of scholarship that attends in particular to the relationship between language and power, for which Norman Fairclough's *Language and Power* (1989) has been seminal. In addition to Fairclough's own considerable body of work, see, for example, the scholarship of Allan Luke on pedagogy, literacy, and race; Carmen Luke on critical media and cultural studies, feminism, and globalization; Teun A. Van Dijk on mass communications, race, and ideology; and Ruth Wodak on critical sociolinguistics. Blommaert and Bulcaen (2000) offer a useful review of CDS. Flowerdew and Richardson's Handbook (2018) is an important resource.

Richardson 2018: 1). CDS's supple alertness to representations of power and social relations, and its attention to the semiotic, sensory, and communicative effects of images, sound, gesture, and dialogue are especially helpful to analysis of text across genres and modalities (Flowerdew and Richardson 2018). CDS is informed by critical theory on language, power, and society, and seeks to render explicit underlying meanings and social relations so as to uncover that which may be hidden or normalized. For example, Richard Jackson's CDS-informed analysis shows how the public language of the War on Terror reflects

> a deliberately and meticulously composed set of words, assumptions, metaphors, grammatical forms, myths and forms of knowledge ... designed to achieve a number of key political goals: to normalise and legitimise the current counter-terrorist approach; to empower the authorities and shield them from criticism; to discipline domestic society by marginalising dissent or protest; and to enforce national unity by reifying a narrow conception of national identity.
>
> (Jackson 2005: 2)

In addition to the public language of the War on Terror, as delineated by Jackson in terms of ideologies and epistemologies of official policies and practices, the discourse of the long War on Terror also saturates our reality of "decades of securitization and counterinsurgency practices" (Lubin 2021: 109) and is refracted in our material landscapes[55] and in the conduct of nonstate actors. Some examples of the long War on Terror's expansive discursive reverberations are versions of the "if you see something, say something" sign visible in cities worldwide; the securitization of airports, air travel, and public entertainment venues; attacks by ordinary citizens on people perceived to be members of the identity category "Middle Eastern, Arab, or Muslim" (Volpp 2002); the new prominence of fields of scholarship like security studies and critical terrorism studies; legislative enactments, such as the Patriot Act and related UN Security Council Resolutions;[56] and the 2008 creation of the US Department of Defense's Minerva Research Initiative, "a DoD sponsored, university-based social science research initiative that

---

[55] On September 11, 2019, the US public broadcaster PBS offered a short list of six ways in which "the world has – and has not – changed since 9/11": (1) life in Afghanistan, (2) oil prices, (3) anti-Muslim violence in the US, (4) changes to air travel and safety, (5) rise in 9/11 related illnesses, and (6) changes in the global economy (Santhanam and Epatko 2019).

[56] These are discussed in Chapter 2.

focuses on areas of strategic importance to the US national security policy."[57] These overlapping state/nonstate, public/private conjunctures in war-on-terror discourse condition and contextualize the cultural texts that I read for necropolitical law.

In CDS, close reading of text is highly valued because each instance of text is understood to yoke the macrocosm of society to the microcosm of a particular text (Candlin 1989: viii). Because every instance of text expresses the conditions of possibility that are the larger structures of the social, the task for the scholar is to uncover the histories, politics, ideologies, and social relations embedded in, and occluded from, a text. Attention to ways in which one text relates to other texts (intertextuality), as well as to historical and synchronic contexts, is also valued as helping to make power more visible (Wodak 1996: 204–10), illuminating the "historical, socio-political, and cultural foundations" of discourse (Flowerdew and Richardson 2018: 2).

An important feature of the *reading for* that I engage in is analyzing text that is publicly available. Publicity is a key feature of law in our mediatized present, an argument that is developed throughout this volume, but an additional goal of focusing on text in the public domain is to demonstrate that reading for law is something that all of us, as globalized, mediatized subjects, can do. Whether that text is conventionally legal in form, as in the Patriot Act, or escapes scrutiny as law because the text's form is not conventionally legal, the project of discerning law's co-constitution with the discounting of life is not predicated on a law degree or the whistle-blower's revelations of dirty secrets. Instead, by reading for necropolitical law in and through text in the public domain, this book equips readers to perceive how narratives of justification and practices of power are fostering the discounting of life by recalibrating the meanings and processes of law. And this methodology – excavating, aware of contested histories and power interests, suspicious of media's alliances with power – becomes especially crucial in the context of our long War on Terror because so much of what is done under the banners of justice, democracy, freedom, and security is shrouded in the amplified secrecy, the distortions of language, and projections of enmity that are hallmarks of the counterterror state (Kaplan 2003; Jackson 2005; Masco 2014).

---

[57] See https://minerva.defense.gov/.

1.4.3 Collateral Damage

In this section, I delve into the category "collateral damage" to illustrate how these strands – reading for law, culture, and the long War on Terror – weave together to construct and disseminate meanings, ideologies, and relations of power central to necropolitical law's discounting of life. First appearing in 1947 to mean "injury inflicted on something other than an intended target,"[58] usage of "collateral damage" has spiked dramatically since the inauguration of the long War on Terror. Google's ngram shows that, between 2000 and 2012, the use of the term in books alone increased by 250 percent.[59] As a pairing of words, collateral damage is an "ambiguous euphemism" designed to minimize "the political impact of civilian casualties" by taking "blood, killing, and devastation out of the picture" while downplaying "suffering and death" (Zambernardi 2017: 331–32). Further, as Christiane Wilke shows, the term works seamlessly with the racialized underpinnings of necropolitical law, in that the civilian/combatant binary

> was developed with a specific spatiotemporal imaginary of war in mind: wars between Western nation states, not wars of colonial conquest or anticolonial insurgency, ... [as] non-European populations under European rule were called "natives," not "civilians." ... Colonial wars were often characterized as police actions, mutinies, or "small wars" because the colonized societies were not recognized as a state and thus lacked the right to go to war. In this logic, where there are no legitimate combatants, there are no legitimate civilians.
>
> (Wilke 2017: 1043)

New technologies of killing, such as drones armed with powerful antitank missiles, mean that the kill and wound radii – the risk of death and dismemberment to civilians – are far greater than they were when "collateral damage" was first coined in 1947 (Chamayou 2015: 140–42). Embedded within the obfuscating category of collateral damage is the US practice of simply disregarding the killing and

---

[58] Merriam-Webster online, at www.merriam-webster.com/dictionary/collateral%20damage.

[59] Google ngram; https://books.google.com/ngrams/graph?content=collateral+damage&year_start=1947&year_end=2019&corpus=15&smoothing=3&share=&direct_url=t1%3B%2Ccollateral%20damage%3B%2Cc0#t1%3B%2Ccollateral%20damage%3B%2Cc0.

maiming of civilians;[60] these are not deaths or injuries that are counted or recorded (Engelhardt 2007; Kennedy 2012).[61] Additionally, as Tom Engelhardt points out, because of US military superiority and the nature of technology deployed in the long War on Terror, the meaning of collateral damage has changed:

> [I]n modern wars, especially those conducted in part from the air (as both Iraq and Afghanistan have been), there's nothing "collateral" about civilian deaths. If anything, the "collateral deaths" are those of the combatants on any side. Civilian deaths are now the central fact, the very essence of war. Not seeing that means not seeing war.
>
> (Engelhardt 2007)

Counts of deaths compiled by activists and civil society lend ballast to Engelhardt's assessment that, in the long War on Terror, it is combatant deaths that are collateral. For example, Brown University's Costs of War project estimates that civilians have been killed at a rate thirty-five times higher than US soldiers in the War on Terror.[62] The language and logics of collateral damage thus involve a semantic sleight of hand: law's foundational protection of civilian life in war is disregarded even as entirely predictable civilian deaths are framed as accidental and incidental. In the category of collateral damage, the removal of protection for civilian life in war sits beneath the calm facade of a dehumanizing characterization of civilian death and wounding as inconsequential and irrelevant even as we are distracted from seeing that "[c]ivilian deaths are now the central fact, the very essence of war" (Engelhardt 2007). It is not obvious in the language of collateral damage that held within the term is a history and politics founded on the assumption that the lives of certain (mostly foreign).[63] Others are human lives that do not count (Wilke 2017).

Necropolitical law and the long War on Terror are supported by a sensory and informational deception: despite our age of hypermediatization

---

[60] The deaths of private military contractors (mercenaries) are not counted either; Taussig-Rubbo (2009: 101).

[61] Emily Gilbert (2015) points to the problematic foreclosure of legal liability when the US military makes cash payments to civilians in a very limited set of collateral damage cases.

[62] At https://watson.brown.edu/costsofwar/papers/summary.

[63] Far greater controversy has attended the targeted killing of US national Anwar al-Awlaki than has attended the targeted killing of non-US nationals. For a discussion, see Banks (2015).

and the contemporary intensification of visual culture (Mirzoeff 2006), collateral damage has been rendered almost invisible. If, as Engelhardt argues, it is combatants that constitute collateral damage in the War on Terror, then the eighteen-year ban on news coverage of deceased US military personnel being returned in coffins is one instance of the media invisibility manufactured for a discounting of life that starkly impacts US citizens and the politics of war.[64] And, relatedly, in the US state's refusal to count, acknowledge, or broadcast images of civilian victims in Afghanistan, Iraq, Pakistan, Syria, Somalia, and Yemen, similar dynamics of erasure and muting are at work.[65] What both expressions of collateral damage share is that public awareness of the discounting of life is minimized. In other words, the "not seeing" (Engelhardt 2007) of civilian deaths is by no means accidental. For publics in the global North, the US state's close management of war-on-terror media coverage converges with the directing of lethal and maiming violence at sites in the global South. These distant, barely visible sites are populated primarily by people with brown skins bearing the religious identity "Muslim," such that the not seeing of war accompanies the not seeing of necropolitical law, producing the discounted racialized subject of the long War on Terror.[66]

1.5 LAW AS PUBLIC THING

1.5.1 Devitalizing Democracy and Law's Archive

Law's interconnectedness with "existence at large" (Davies 2017: iii) prompts attention to the conditions of possibility for the discounting of life. In this section, I set out key ideas relating to "public" and publicity that I draw on to analyze dynamics and modalities through which

---

[64] The ban, put in place in 1991 by the first President Bush during the first Gulf War was conditionally lifted – media coverage would be permitted "only if the families of the dead agree" – in December 2009 by the Obama administration. (Miller 2003; Bumiller 2009). The question that arises is, when, on August 30, 2021, media showed President Biden among those receiving the coffins of US service personnel who had been killed in the August 26, 2021, suicide bombing of Kabul airport, were those families in a position to decline this presidential gesture and the extensive media attention it received?

[65] Scholars and activists look to websites conducted by civil society for a clearer picture of collateral damage. Sites relied on by scholars and analysts include Brown University's Watson Institute Costs of War project (https://watson.brown .edu/costsofwar/papers/summary) and the Bureau of Investigative Journalism (www .thebureauinvestigates.com/projects/drone-war).

[66] I am grateful to Bill Mullen for this point.

standard tropes of liberal legality (such as transparency, accountability, human rights, rule of law, and due process) have been marginalized, ceding ground to necropolitical law. These key ideas are law as archive (Mawani 2012), governance through the de-democratizing disregard for public things (Honig 2017), and the role of publicity and technology in the dynamic for communication between state and citizen marking our present (Dean 2002, 2005). I will describe each of these in turn.

In her important theory and methodology-advancing essay, Renisa Mawani argues for the concept of "law as archive" (2012: 340) to illuminate law as "an expansive and expanding locus of juridico-political command, one that is operative through ... a mutual and reciprocal violence of law as symbolic and material force and law as document and documentation" (2012: 337). Illustrating her argument in part through an analysis of how the US-led 2003 invasion of Iraq precipitated the looting and destruction of Iraq's archives,[67] violations of international law, and the scripting of a new, post-invasion Iraqi Constitution, Mawani highlights law's constitutive relations with violence (and, relatedly, war, force, command, power, authority); sovereignty (relatedly, imperialism, colonialism); documents and documentation (relatedly, practices of governance, knowledge production, and population management through bureaucracy, categorization, quantification, and record-keeping, as well as through the common law's self-referential self-authorization through precedent); history (especially fraught in the imperial encounter and inextricably enmeshed with power); and contestation around "truth." Reading through and across key interdisciplinary scholarship on law and archive, Mawani repairs law's tendency to be disengaged from and unreflexive about its own textuality, sources, and discursive regime of power/knowledge by bringing to bear upon law critical debates in other fields that problematize the archive as uneven and contested, registering the "profoundly asymmetrical" effect of power (2012: 342). For Mawani:

> law's archive recalls and speaks not only to law's past but also to its present and future, sanctioning both the violence of law (invasion, occupation, and the imposition of a new constitution) and the violence

---

[67] Relatedly, on the question of law's archives, Mawani notes how, analogous to Britain's strategic destruction of documents recording its colonial violence, the War on Terror has been marked by US practices of having "willfully destroyed, concealed, and redacted documents under the guise of national security" (2012: 357).

of the archive (preservation/destruction and remembering/forgetting) as violence that is always already necessary. Importantly, this double logic of violence harbors the potential, however limited, to question and possibly attenuate law's claims to legitimacy and authority.

(2012: 341)

Seizing upon the opening created by law's double logic of violence and an expansive interdisciplinary understanding of what counts as legal text, *Discounting Life* attends to the textuality, citational practices, narratives of citizenship and sovereignty of a range of cultural texts in order to excavate necropolitical law's assertions of legitimacy, authority, norms, community, and political order.

In *Public Things: Democracy in Disrepair* (2017), Bonnie Honig describes public things as "things that conjoin people. Shared among users from all kinds of background, classes, and social locations, the public thing calls out to us, interpellating us as a public" (2017: 30). Honig argues that public things are foundational to democracy, in that without them "action in concert is undone and the signs and symbols of democratic life are devitalized" (2017: 4). Her examples of public things include "universities, local, state, and national parks, prisons, schools, roads and other transportation systems, the military, governments, electricity and power sources, including hydropower, gas, and oil pipelines, and nuclear plants, airwaves, radio and television broadcast networks, libraries, airport security, and more" (2017: 4). Importantly, public things, Honig highlights, are not only those objects, spaces, or infrastructures that generate political consensus[68] or bestow an unambiguous public good. Frustrating, obstructive experiences like navigating airport security are also public things because "the infrastructure of security ... bring[s] us together in ways that are not optional" (2017: xii–xiii).

In bringing us together, public things play the crucial role of supplying the shared objects, spaces, experiences, and infrastructures that

---

[68] Honig discusses pipelines as public things in the context of "the Unist'ot'en Camp's ongoing efforts to prevent an oil and gas pipeline from being built on tribal lands" to show that "not all public things are 'good' from every political angle. Nor can they be all bad, surely. At their best, in their public thingness, they may bring people together to act in concert. And even when they are divisive, they provide a basis around which to organize, contest, mobilize, defend, or reimagine various modes of collective being together in a democracy" (2017: 22, 24).

facilitate deliberation, contestation, and constellation, occasioning "the action in concert that is democracy's definitive trait" (Honig 2017: 5). When juxtaposed with necropolitics, which thrives on dividing and dehumanizing selected segments of humanity (Mbembe 2019), the democratizing dynamics facilitated by public things are thrown into sharp relief. Valuing and protecting public things, Honig argues, becomes especially important, given the contemporary dominance of neoliberal logics through which "[a] perfect storm of privatization and austerity politics ... [has] undermined an earlier nineteenth- and twentieth-century commitment to democratic governance as a generator of public goods" (Honig 2015: 624). Drawing on Honig, I show how, in the context of our long War on Terror, despite the very public and globalized events and narratives that generate fear of terrorism, constructing the dangers of terrorist attack as ever present, law has lost its public thingness. Instead of publicly accessible legislative text, vigorously debated by elected representatives, the Patriot Act is obfuscating and almost incomprehensible and was thinly contested when presented to lawmakers for assent (Chapter 2). And, as opposed to the public arena of courtroom trials, accessible "sites of confrontation and encounter, enjoyment and conflict" (Honig 2015: 624), as the discussion above of Guantanamo's Camp Justice has shown, secretive military tribunals generate inaccessible, hidden encounters and redacted records. And when entertainment media shows us what official media does not, such as drone warfare (Chapter 5), and news media celebrates asymmetrical killing (Chapters 3, 4, and 6), cultural text turns away from the values and relations of law as a public thing to instead perpetuate national security's narratives of imminent danger, bolstering a cultural climate of fear that affectively legitimizes secrecy and vengeance (Masco 2014), and reinscribes texts as fragmentary sites of law's symbolic and material violence (Mawani 2012).

1.5.2 Public Things in the Long War on Terror

Honig's analysis of the role played by public things in fostering democracy is especially valuable for understanding law in our context of the long War on Terror because she highlights the other-than-rational when she writes, "all forms of governance and citizenship are enmeshed in desire. They do not just provide rules to coordinate collective action. They also enlist us into imagined pasts and futures, they shape, and then feed or starve, our hopes" (2015: 624).[69] In broad terms, Honig's use of "desire" here may be understood as yoking the rational – rules – together with the other-than-rational – the realm of desire and affect. The desire in which contemporary American governance and citizenship is enmeshed, Masco argues, is counterterror, an affect enlisting us into an imagined future of perpetual existential danger (2014).

For Masco, the counterterror state has remade the social contract (2014: 9), reconfiguring its relationship to citizens by neglecting and devaluing both "the public" and public things. Honig argues that, against this reconfiguration of state/public, and in order to support democratic life, we need to "dedicate ourselves to retaking" state institutions, so that they might "serve their properly public pursuits" (2017: 91). Reading for law, in the manner I have described, offers one path through which, as publics, we might retake law as a state institution serving properly public pursuits. However, in the face of state disregard for publics and public things, the project of reading for law requires an interrogation of contemporary iterations of "the public" in relation to law and media. And, to better grapple with the dynamics of law in relation to contemporary media, I turn to Jodi Dean's analysis.

In her analysis of the co-constitution of publicity and secrecy, Dean traces key Enlightenment conceptions of the public to show how it is, in part, the conviction that public scrutiny restrains state power that has bestowed "the public" and "publicity" with a cluster of legitimizing, authorizing associations, including "ideals of openness, inclusivity, visibility, equality, accessibility, and rationality" (Dean 2002: 2). Additionally, positing the public as a foil to "the state" imagines the public and "the public sphere" as "the unitary site and subject of democratic governance" (Dean 2002: 9) in a manner immediately recognizable as the standard tropes of liberal legality. She writes, "the very premise of liberal democracy is the sovereignty of the people. And, governance by the people has generally been thought in terms of communicative freedoms of speech, assembly and the press, norms of publicity that emphasize transparency and accountability, and the deliberative practices of the public sphere" (Dean 2005: 53).

Dean characterizes our media environment as technoculture, denoting an environment in which the familiar – television, tabloids,

---

[69] Honig writes this to amplify upon Tocqueville's observation that the "art of pursuing in common the objects of common desires [is democracy's] highest perfection" (2015: 624).

newspapers, magazines – is connected to digitalized and networked new technologies (Dean 2002: 1). Dean points out how the affect of legitimacy that attaches to "the public" and "publicity," working alongside technoculture, has altered a key attribute of communication in our time. She vividly illustrates this point by recounting the vigor with which publics in the United States (and elsewhere) expressed opposition to the war in Iraq – both in the form of demonstrations and through media communications (Dean 2005: 51–52). In response, then president George W. Bush said that the people were free to express their opinions (Dean 2005: 52). Public opposition and public opinion were not messages received and responded to by the state. Instead, as if on parallel tracks, the people opposed and the state continued with its war (Dean 2005: 53). Messages, notes Dean, become "contributions to circulating content – not actions to elicit responses" (2005: 58).

Attention to the shifting contours of the meanings, dynamics, and relations of the category "public" is important because the sociopolitical concepts "rule of law" and "liberal legality" both presume states populated by inherently rights-bearing, empowered individuals; that is, people with the capacity to act, speak, and convene as publics so as to be engaged citizens. Law as public – published, accessible, clear, and known – facilitates the engagement of the informed citizenry of liberal legalism's democratic ideal. The legitimizing resonance attaching to "the public" incorporates notions of the sovereignty of "the people" as well as rule of law's conviction that if law is public, then abusive, unrestrained power will be detectable, and abusers of power held accountable (Krygier 2016).

This book shows how, instead of having law as a public thing alongside an ongoing narrative of imminent danger, *publicity* has come to stand in for law's public attributes, where media is the key platform for the coupling of necropolitical law and publicity. Publicity is inextricably enmeshed with commodification and the profit motive of the "military-industrial-media-entertainment network" (Der Derian 2001) and with the "networks of sentiment and spectacle" that are "the golden ring of infotainment society" (Dean 2001: 624). A traumatized, fearful population, dazzled by publicity's spectacles of war and terrorism, is more likely to take on the role of passive spectator than that of the engaged, empowered citizen (Stahl 2010, 2018).

The triangulation of publicity, secrecy, and necropolitical law is powerfully illustrated by the possible trial at Guantanamo's Camp Justice of the five men accused of plotting the 9/11 attacks. And in the analysis offered by the chapters, I show how this triangulation of publicity, secrecy, and necropolitical law animates the workings of the counterterror state in the long War on Terror. Highly publicized events like the enactment of the Patriot Act (Chapter 2) and the killings of bin Laden and ISIS leader Abu Bakr al-Baghdadi (Chapters 3 and 4) obscure the degree to which law has become twinned to illegibility (Chapter 2), and to asymmetrical violence, deception, and secrecy (Chapters 3, 4, 5, 6, and 7). The constituent and meta-legal right to life (Chamayou 2013: 155) is undone by the US state's refusal to protect and account for civilians killed and wounded in the long War on Terror and by its practice of conducting extrajudicial killings based on suspicion rather than proof (Chapters 5, 6, and 7). Law's public texture is also undone by limiting, constraining, or excluding media (Chapters 3, 4, 5, and 6). A politics and a public sphere in which the narrative of imminent danger is conjoined to the deployment of killing technology that is asymmetrical (if not annihilatory), cultivates a citizenry that identifies with violent imperialism, rather than a citizenry that values democracy and liberal legality (Brown 2005).

In short, through the US state's prioritization of the War on Terror (Masco 2014), the intensified fragmentation of law's archive through "profoundly asymmetrical" power (Mawani 2012: 342), a disregard for public things (Honig 2017, 2015), and an altered dynamic for communication between state and citizen (Dean 2002, 2005), our contemporary social fabric is reconfiguring the values, affects, and social relations underpinning rule of law and liberal legality. This disjuncture between the (presumed and ideal) conditions for law and our present is discernible in the texts documenting, denying, and erasing law's violence in the long War on Terror (Mawani 2012). As the chapters show, gestures and symbols of rule of law and liberal legality persist alongside necropolitical law. Collectively, incrementally, exerting the comforting pull of the familiar, these persistent gestures toward rule of law and liberal legality may well distract us from perceiving the configurations of necropolitical law's values, actors, and sites unfolding before our very eyes.

1.6 CHAPTER OUTLINES

To show how texts, images, and events construct, reflect, and disseminate necropolitical law, alongside gestures and tropes of rule of law and liberal legality, I analyze a range of texts across a range of genres. Using

43

conventional legal text as a launching point, Chapter 2 explores the way federal legislation, in the form of the 2001 Patriot Act, in sub-stance scripts necropolitical law. As legislation, its authorship is insti-tutional and inscrutable, the vehicle for an unwieldy and inaccessible legal text. And yet, the Patriot Act takes on the authorizing, legitimiz-ing resonances of the state's voice and the liberal legal order. Debated and passed through Congress and the Senate, the act emerges from the container of domestic legislation to enact this law's global reach, in part through UN Security Council Resolutions. The very opening lines of the Patriot Act legislate necropolitical law's planetary jurisdiction: the Act's purpose is "[t]o deter and punish terrorist acts in the United States *and around the world*" (emphasis mine). Necropolitical law's dynamics of deception are most immediately apparent in the naming of the Patriot Act, a naming that imports spectacle, the closures of meanings for "patriot" in war contexts, as well as the compound meanings of patriot as a peculiarly American keyword. The Patriot Act shows how legal illegibility is part of necropolitical law's deception, operating through law as publicity to undo law as public thing. At the time of writing, the twenty-year anniversary of the Patriot Act's excep-tionalism has passed, and we find ourselves in legal landscapes still conditioned by it. Chapter 2 traces the Patriot Act's role in normalizing and consolidating necropolitical law's planetary jurisdiction for the discounting of life in the unending long War on Terror.

Chapter 3 analyzes President Obama's announcement on the killing of bin Laden to reveal the way discounting life is authorized and legitimized through extrajudicial, extraterritorial killing. Specifically, Obama's celebratory narrative of the killing as a nation-healing, nation-securing achievement codes vengeance as "justice," normalizes US imperialism, implicitly justifies "collateral damage," and remakes the parameters of legitimate state conduct in relation to terrorism. Attending to how Obama's announcement used image, narrative, political myth, and sound to manufacture necropolitical law's author-ity, legitimacy, norms, and community, Chapter 3 argues that we are interpellated by the official announcement, not as liberal legality's empowered citizenry but as docile spectator-subjects. Chapter 3 also shows how the announcement, in avoiding the category "law," enables a lawyer–president–commander-in-chief to invest the category "justice" with a range of meanings that contradict liberal legality, in that they invite us, as subjects, to acquiesce in state secrecy and in necropolitical law's extraterritorial, extrajudicial violence.

Chapter 4 shows how the October 2019 killing of ISIS leader Abu Bakr al-Baghdadi became a platform for President Trump's visual and verbal consolidations of necropolitical law. Announcing the killing at a press conference held at the White House Diplomatic Reception Room, Trump positioned himself in front of a portrait of America's first president, George Washington, visually asserting Trump's lineage in an always already necropolitical state, built, as it is, on the racialized pillars of territorial appropriation, genocide, and slavery. With the many flags of the US armed forces flanking Trump like an honor guard, the visuals of Trump's announcement encode the two bodies of president/commander-in-chief, foregrounding the military as a key actor in the state's implementation of necropolitical law. Chapter 4 shows how Trump used the occasion, first, to deepen the necropolitical separations animating necropolitical law and, second, to stage himself as the White, male, militarized hero central to spectacles of imperialism. Chapter 4 demonstrates how normalizing the necropolitics of imperialism past and present fosters the discounting of life legitimized by necropolitical law.

Chapter 5 analyzes *Eye in the Sky*, a 2016 film on drone warfare, to illuminate popular culture's role in scripting us into being as spectator-consumers while legitimizing the counterterror state's discounting of life through necropolitical law. The gripping plot, stellar performances, and dazzling displays of technology distract us from, first, the de-democratizing and dehumanizing concealments and erasures that accompany drone warfare and, second, the remaking of lawful authority through a dramatization of the (highly contested) principle of international law known as "the responsibility to protect." In the process, the film renders visible a particular set of actors, narratives, and questions, while concealing and erasing others, thereby legitimizing drone warfare and valorizing its actors, institutions, practices, and technologies. As text, *Eye in the Sky* is an instance of the "cultural sensibility . . . in which killing the enemy of the state is an extension of play" (Mbembe 2019: 73). Given the official secrecy accompanying drone warfare and the film's convincing incorporation of "fact" into its "fiction," *Eye in the Sky* amounts to a compelling representation of the necessity of drone warfare as enacted by lawful military actors with the aim of securing civilians worldwide.

Chapter 6 analyzes the April 2017 deployment in Afghanistan of the US military's most powerful nonnuclear weapon, the Massive Air Ordinance Blast (MOAB). The bombing, the secrecy surrounding it, the shock-and-awe media celebrations in the aftermath are all part of the cultivation of global audiences as spectator-consumers fascinated with the annihilatory killing technologies unleased by contemporary US militarized imperialism, which fuel necropolitical law's discounting of life. Necropolitically, the MOAB strike illustrates "innovations in the technology of murder . . . [that] aim at disposing of a large number of victims in a relatively short span of time" (Mbembe 2003: 19). Chapter 7 concludes the book with an analysis of two key speeches delivered by President Biden on the US withdrawal from Afghanistan. Biden's speeches served, yet again, to co-constitute nation/empire, the familial and the political, deploying these co-constitutions to authorize and legitimize American imperial violence. In the process, Biden re-articulated to necropolitical law, relying on political myth to ground his narratives of authority, legitimacy, and community. With myth doing the work of law, imperial violence directed at distant, racialized Others reconstituted America as a community of power identified with asymmetrical violence as the lawful delivery of national security. Chapter 7 highlights how the chaotic US military withdrawal from Afghanistan demonstrates necropolitical law's capacity to discard subject and subordinated populations at will. The combination of spectacle, contradiction, and occlusion in media reports on the MOAB strike (Chapter 6) and the US withdrawal (Chapter 7) point to the urgency of recognizing necropolitical law's consolidations in the continuing unfolding of the long War on Terror.

All in all, this book is impelled by sociolegality's normative project of contributing, through scholarship, "to understanding and refashioning this troubled world" (Merry 1995: 13). The trouble in our world focused on here is the crisis presented to law by the long War on Terror. The methodology I adopt is that of reading for law. Resulting from a study of texts, images, and events traceable to the War on Terror, this book analyzes how institutional and normative shifts in law have been explained, justified, concealed, contested, and consolidated. In the process, it shows how much it matters that we pay attention to the way law, through culture, participates in discounting life. A brute and unambiguous dimension of necropolitical law's discounting of life is enacted when those in the sovereign's crosshairs in the long War on Terror are killed and maimed. But domestically, inside the United States, citizen complicity with necropolitics and citizen acquiescence with the state's channeling of resources to the War on Terror likewise harm quality of life, and they diminish prospects for peace. In engaging in the work of identifying the discounting of life, my hope is that we might re-politicize ourselves as questioning, feeling, interpreting citizen-subjects. Seeing necropolitical law in operation might make it possible to orient governance toward a humanist, relational justice anchored in law as a public thing, a seeing that will move us toward dismantling the discounting of life.

NECROPOLITICAL LAW'S PLANETARY JURISDICTION

The U.S.A. P.A.T.R.I.O.T. Act

2.1 LEGISLATING NECROPOLITICAL LAW

The opening lines of the Patriot Act legislate necropolitical law's planetary jurisdiction.[1] The Act's purpose is "[t]o deter and punish terrorist acts in the United States *and around the world*" (emphasis mine). With the Patriot Act, the US crosses the line separating covert from overt imperialism, twinning liberal legal processes to the substance of necropolitical law. Chapter 2 explores the Patriot Act as a central example of how the discounting of life is authorized and legitimized through the form and processes of conventional law. Necropolitical law, I argued in Chapter 1, is constituted by the practices, texts, norms, authority, and legitimacy for the discounting of life. Necropolitical law does not necessarily declare itself in these terms. *Deception*, Mbembe writes, is central to necropolitics, in that necropolitics engages "a force of separation . . . that, while pretending to ensure the world's government, seeks exemption from it" (Mbembe 2019: 1).[2] Scripting and disseminating necropolitical separation, the Patriot Act has played a key role in the selective fostering of the discounting of life, nationally and globally, through the long War on Terror. Chapter 2 delves into

---

[1] My use of "planetary jurisdiction" as an analytic category is indebted to Markus Gunneflo's careful tracing of the history of targeted killing "in an American home-land which is the planet" (2016: 82).

[2] This force of separation works against life by impeding "a relation with others based on the reciprocal recognition of our common vulnerability and finitude" (Mbembe 2019: 3).

48

the forces of deception and separation in the Act, while also examining it as an exemplary instance of necropolitical law's violence in the sense noted in Chapter 1 as theorized by Renisa Mawani (2012): the violence of law as archive.

Mawani argues for the concept of "law as archive" (2012: 340) to illuminate law as a "locus of juridico-political command" that works through the double violence "of law as symbolic and material force and law as document and documentation" (2012: 337). For Mawani,

> law's archive recalls and speaks not only to law's past but also to its present and future, sanctioning both the violence of law (invasion, occupation, and the imposition of a new constitution) and the violence of the archive (preservation/destruction and remembering/forgetting) as violence that is always already necessary. Importantly, this double logic of violence harbors the potential, however limited, to question and possibly attenuate law's claims to legitimacy and authority.
>
> (2012: 341)

Seizing the opening created by the double logic of violence in law as archive, Chapter 2 attends to the textuality, citational practices, and narratives of citizenship and sovereignty of the Patriot Act, in order to question and attenuate its claims to legitimacy and authority in the following ways. First, the chapter shows how the Act, emerging from the nation-state domain of domestic legislation, works as a cultural text of imperialism, legislating the necropolitical law of "sovereignty defined as the right to kill" on a planetary scale (Mbembe 2019: 70). Necropolitical law's dynamics of deception are most immediately apparent in the naming of the Patriot Act, which imports spectacle and imposes the closures of binaried meanings, as discussed in Section 2.2. Section 2.2 also considers how the peculiarly American reverberations attaching to the lexical item "patriot" engage some of the anarchic convulsions rebounding between empire and nation, affirming yet again Amy Kaplan's highly influential analytic insight on the ongoing and ever-shifting co-constitutions of nation and empire in American cultural texts (Kaplan 2002).

Section 2.3 discusses how, in the post-9/11 moment of empire, the Patriot Act rehearses the imperial nation's anxieties about "turn[ing] aliens into citizens" (Kaplan 2002: 9). By covertly reinscribing presumptions of homogenous racial and religious identities in the space of the United States as nation, the Act authorizes necropolitical separations, exalting these separations as the norms and practices of (formal) law. Through these provisions, the Act also discloses the workings of law as archive, expressing law's symbolic and material violence toward subordinated populations, even as power's instability and contingency are revealed.

Section 2.4 details how the Patriot Act's narrative of emergency further facilitates deceptions fostering necropolitics, first, through fictions of temporality and, second, through the Act's unwieldy and inaccessible text. Taking law's textuality seriously as an attribute of law as archive, Section 2.4 shows how illegibility in law becomes an attribute of necropolitical law's deception. Relatedly, law as publicity becomes the modality for dismantling law as public thing. The analysis of the Act and its global tentacles in Section 2.5 shows how it has functioned in post-9/11 co-constitutions of nation/empire. At the time of writing, November 2021, despite being two decades hence from the emergency exceptionalism of the Patriot Act, we find ourselves in legal landscapes that remain conditioned by it. Chapter 2 traces the Patriot Act's role in normalizing and consolidating necropolitical law's planetary jurisdiction for the discounting of life in the unending long War on Terror.

2.2 NECROPOLITICAL DECEPTION THROUGH SPECTACULAR NAMING

When politics is the work of death, power "continuously refers and appeals to the exception, emergency, and a fictionalized notion of the enemy. It also labors to produce these same exceptions, emergencies, and fictionalized enemies" (Mbembe 2019: 70). Section 2.2 explores the Patriot Act as a product evidencing the labor invested in constructing and appealing to the exceptions and emergencies by which enmity has become necropolitical law's normative basis of the right to kill.

In the Patriot Act, such laboring is discernible in the dynamics of spectacle informing the Act's name. Spectacle, as theorized by Guy Debord, is "a social relation among people, mediated by images" (1977: para 4). In producing a powerful polemic against the manner in which social relations of spectacle discard and obstruct dialogue while inculcating "passive acceptance" (1977: para 12), Debord was sounding a warning against the depoliticizing effects of "a media and consumer society, organized around the production and consumption of images, commodities, and staged events" (Kellner 2003). Spectacle tends to work by "distancing, distracting, and disengaging" (Stahl 2010: 3), transforming citizens into passive consumer-audiences schooled, by the role of audience, into a "larger political helplessness" (Rogin 1990: 103). In other words, the depoliticizing effects and affects of spectacle work against law as public thing. Of course, spectacle
50

contextualizes the Patriot Act, in that the hyper-mediatized and the spectacular mark the horrific events of 9/11, as well as the American state's frequently staged and media-savvy responses to the attacks (e.g., McAlister 2005: 266–307; McBride 2006; Kellner 2007) .

When it comes to law, spectacle is often associated with visible, inherently dramatic, and theatrical sites of (conventional) law, such as the trial (e.g., Sherwin 2000; Friedman 2015). But spectacles of law also subsist in legal language (Richland 2013). As an artifact participating in a web of meaning-making with other facets of culture, histories, and politics, the Patriot Act's production and dissemination of exception, emergency, and enmity through spectacle are most evident in the gap between the Act's two official names and the name by which the Act is most widely known. The Act's first official name is its full legal name: "Uniting and Strengthening America by Providing Appropriate Tools Required to Intercept and Obstruct Terrorism," an unwieldy and immemorable thirty syllables. The Act's second name is its official alternative name: "USA PATRIOT Act."[3] Unsurprisingly, the official full and alternate names have yielded to a third name, the more succinct and politically potent name by which the Act is typically referred to: Patriot Act. The Act's two official names demonstrate the workings of "USA PATRIOT" as a bacronym. The neologism "bacronym" was coined to describe the inversion of an acronym,[4] and in the bacronym-name of this law, the deliberate crafting and clever wordplay associated with branding, marketing, and advertising seem evident. In abstracting recognizable features of consumer culture – branding and advertising – and deploying these features in the "conservative, frozen genre" of legislation (Bhatia et al. 2004: 206), the Patriot Act establishes "indexical resonances" (Briggs and Bauman 1992: 141) between law and consumer culture. These indexical resonances evidence a version of commercial nationalism – a dynamic through which states blend the register and logics of commerce with the mobilization and exploitation of nationalist sentiment (Volcic and Andrejevic 2016: 3).

The commercial nationalism at work in naming a law "Patriot," that is, the marketing logics of branding and advertising, becomes even more obvious when "Patriot Act" is contrasted with the names of

[3] Section 1(a) of the Patriot Act states, "This Act may be cited as the "Uniting and Strengthening America by Providing Appropriate Tools Required to Intercept and Obstruct Terrorism (USA PATRIOT ACT) Act of 2001."
[4] "Bacronym" was coined by Meredith G. Williams and highlighted in the *Washington Post*'s Neologism of the Month Award column (Levey 1983).

legislation initially forwarded as possible legislative responses to 9/11 – the Combating Terrorism Act of 2001,[5] the Public Safety and Cyber Security Enhancement Act,[6] the Intelligence to Prevent Terrorism Act,[7] and the Financial Anti-Terrorism Act.[8] In discarding this raft of possible names – names that straightforwardly describe the content and purpose of proposed enactments – and turning instead to the bacronym USA PATRIOT, the quality of *deception* central to necropolitical law merges seamlessly with the quality of deception generally associated with advertising (Carson 2010).

One straightforward example of the Patriot Act as a platform for deception is how, contrary to President Bush's assertion that the Patriot Act protects "the constitutional rights of all Americans," (Bush 2001c) the Act dismantles fundamental liberties[9] and "turns regular citizens into suspects."[10] In other words, under the rubric of "patriot," and consistent with Sigal Ben-Porath's analysis of how belligerent citizenship reinterprets "key components of democratic citizenship" such that "the measure of civic participation is not so much civic engagement as the readiness to contribute to the war and the survival effort, and possibly to risk one's life for the sake of the country" (2011: 316–17), the Act has altered the content and nature of citizenship in the United States while pretending to strengthen it.

Just as "in advertising the signification of the image is undoubtedly intentional," such that "the viewer receives at one and the same time the perceptual message and the cultural message" (Barthes [1964] 1977: 33, 36), so too with the bacronymed name as image, "Patriot Act," "patriot" becomes a coded, iconic, and symbolic message that

---

[5] This proposed Act was introduced two days after the 9/11 attacks; see https://cdt.org/wp-content/uploads/security/010913senatewiretap2.shtml. Interestingly, before the galvanizing post-9/11 moment, the Combating Terrorism Bill "had languished in the legislature in the past because of its threats to individual rights" (Ball 2004: 37).

[6] This proposed Act was introduced on September 20, 2001; see www.congress.gov/bill/107th-congress/house-bill/2915.

[7] This proposed Act was introduced on September 24, 2001; see. www.congress.gov/bill/107th-congress/senate-bill/1448.

[8] This proposed Act was introduced on October 3, 2001; see www.congress.gov/bill/107th-congress/house-bill/3004.

[9] Richard Abel's thorough detailing of "the uneven impact of 9/11 on fundamental constitutional rights" (2018a: 501–93) might be understood in part as an account of the Patriot Act's erosions of constitutional rights writ large in its social effects.

[10] See www.aclu.org/issues/national-security/privacy-and-surveillance/surveillance-under-patriot-act.

"discourages dissent" (Young 2003: 12). Publics are presented the ideologically freighted cultural message that supporting the War on Terror's key legislative text *constitutes* being "patriotic," even as the use of the word "patriot" opens the door to a complex set of meanings and connotations, some of which I explore below.

2.2.1   Patriot: A Compound and Contested Category

I launch my analysis of the meanings of "patriot" with a general, rather than scholarly, definition to highlight the commonsense, socially embedded meanings of "patriot." The *Oxford English Dictionary* (*OED*) defines patriotism as the "quality of being patriotic; devotion to and vigorous support for one's country." Tellingly, the *OED*'s exemplar of patriotism is "a highly decorated officer of unquestionable integrity and patriotism."[11] This highly decorated officer implicitly reproduces the "old Lie" (Owen 1917), that to die as a citizen-soldier is patriotism's most exalted expression. This belligerent sense of the word is part of a "generic fight/war vocabulary" situating "patriots" among other "parties to war" such as allies, combatants, and enemies (Musolff 2016: 20). Drawing on George Lakoff's influential scholarship on metaphor, Andreas Musolff argues that the "high degree of coherence" for this belligerent resonance attaching to "patriot" as an obedient participant in "nation as family" is unsurprising, given "the millennia-long history" reaching back "at least to Roman Antiquity where the paterfamilias was almost the 'owner' of the whole family" (Musolff 2016: 29).

The "patriot" willing to die for her or his country is also the exalted "patriot" Benedict Anderson probes in the "arresting emblem" of "cenotaphs and tombs of Unknown Soldiers" (2006 [1983]: 9) and the public reverence attaching to them. To love one's country differently, for example, as a critically engaged scholar or dissident (Hage 2006), or to experience shared humanity as the locus of a border-transcending humanist citizenship (e.g., Honig 2003; Azoulay 2008), these non-binaried expressions of patriotism lack the archetypal nationalist resonance conveyed by the *OED*'s top "example sentence." The sacralizing affect of devotion, the visceral quality of vigorous support, is assigned to an account of patriotism that presumes – and implicitly celebrates – the violence of war in a world shaped by exclusionary and intolerant nationalism.

---

[11] See www.lexico.com/en/definition/patriotism.

By situating a law named "Patriot" at the center of the counterterror state's project of legitimacy, the already existing deep roots for civil religion, sacrificial death, and blood sacrifice in the United States (Marvin and Ingle 1996, 1999) have been revitalized for the unending duration of the long War on Terror. In a particularly compelling analysis of civil religion's sacralizing of death by blood sacrifice, Dale Spicer's *Consecrated Steel* tracks how pieces of steel from the World Trade Centers were "preserved, transformed and used to build a net-work of sites" expressing through their materiality an infrastructure of planetary jurisdiction. Exalted and memorialized, this consecrated steel has been carefully distributed to "every state in the US, along with sites at military bases and government buildings from Britain to Afghanistan." Traversing continents and oceans, the approximately twenty-four tons of steel from the World Trade Center were also "repurposed in the bow-stems of three navy warships" (Spicer, in press). On the warships, alongside violence and death, this consecrated steel is the focus of "ceremonial or ritual practices used to create national identity, belonging, and sharing." In short, notions of American belonging that sacralize and memorialize the 9/11 attacks have become enmeshed with the belligerent post-9/11 constructions of "patriot" scripted by the Patriot Act. Through the Act's image-name, the tenor of "patriot," so deeply associated with war's binary of friend/enemy (Schmitt 2007 [1932]), interpellates citizen-consumers into the role of a particular kind of subject: the loyal, unquestioningly obedient subject, prepared to make patriotism's ultimate sacrifice of dying for one's country.

Necropolitics, Mbembe notes, has long taken the form of state power exercised through war, simultaneously exposing citizens and enemies to killing, maiming, and terror (2019: 70–92). In addition to the necro-political exposure to war for citizen-soldiers (and by extension, their civilian families), in a twist away from received understandings of patriotism as a call to the citizen-soldier, the wars in Iraq and Afghanistan are noteworthy for the degree to which noncitizen mer-cenaries – private military contractors – have been deployed (e.g., Scahill 2007; Taussig-Rubbo 2009; Moore 2019; Peltier 2020).[12] Deploring the commercialization marking America's post-9/11 wars, Heidi Peltier's research confronts yet another facet of the discounting

---

[12] See also the discussion of private military contractors in Chapter 7.

of life through necropolitical deception: the US state "camouflages" costs, both in financial terms and in terms of fatalities and injuries. She writes:

> In 2019, the Pentagon spent $370 billion on contracting – more than half the total defense budget of $676 billion and a whopping 164% higher than its spending on contractors in 2001. ... Regarding human costs, in 2019, there were 53,000 U.S. contractors compared to 35,000 U.S. troops in the Middle East. Since the U.S. invasion of Afghanistan in 2001, an estimated 8,000 U.S. contractors have died, in addition to around 7,000 US troops.
>
> (Peltier 2020: 1)

If the sacralizing affect attaching to "patriot" is tied to the so-called ultimate sacrifice of the citizen-soldier dying for her or his country, Peltier's findings and analysis are an important reminder of how law as spectacle works to *conceal* in the naming of the Patriot Act. Against the Patriot Act's invocations of the desirably sacrificial "patriot," the Act's name occludes the degree to which, citizenship is discounted, first, through the counterterror state's spending priorities and, second, to borrow Mateo Taussig-Rubbo's memorable formulation (2009), through the outsourcing of sacrifice by replacing citizen armies with mercenaries and private military contractors.

2.2.2 America's "Patriot"

In addition to generalized understandings of "patriot," grappling with the term as a keyword in American culture becomes crucial to analysis of the Patriot Act's image-name. Briefly, drawing on the argument I set out in Chapter 1, if law is understood as a cultural domain through which "we create our experience, knit together disparate ideas and actions ... [to] fabricate a world of meaning that appears to us as real" (Rosen 2006: 4), attending to the particularly American categories of experience animating "patriot" helps illuminate the world of meaning called into being by the bacronymed image-name of the Act.

In American culture, "patriot" is, and has long been, a keyword. Keywords indicate "powerfully but not explicitly, some central formation of values" and of meaning, linked to understandings of a "particular *way of life*" (Williams 1983 [1976]: 12, 15). Keywords bind together "certain ways of seeing culture and society," pointing to the need to be "conscious of the [key]words as elements of the problems" informing social issues (Williams 1983 [1976]: 15, 16). I argue below that, as a keyword, "patriot" is richly meaningful for an American way of life that narrates crisis, imminent danger, and racial hatred, multiplying enemies to justify the necropolitical right to kill.

As a keyword, "patriot" mobilizes and exploits a particular strand of American nationalist sentiment by reaching across more than two hundred years to invoke valorizing associations with America's original "patriots": those who fought against British colonial rule in the American Revolution of 1776 (e.g., Banvard 1876; Trumbull and Woodward 1896).[13] The annual official holiday in the states of Maine and Massachusetts, Patriots Day, since 1894, has been celebrated to commemorate events key to the Revolution (e.g., *Congregationalist* 1895: 635).[14] From 1897, the Boston Marathon has been held on Patriots Day. And the 2016 film *Patriots Day*, based on the bombings at the 2013 Boston Marathon, deepens associations between America's revolutionary patriots and the patriot invoked by the post-9/11 project of counterterrorism. On December 18, 2001, "a joint resolution of the US Congress designated September 11 as Patriot Day."[15]

In short, in American culture, "patriot" is associated with freedom, independence, and the righteous, armed, revolutionary fight. These meanings and associations occlude the necropolitical dynamics of genocide, territorial appropriation, and slavery that accompanied the project of the founding patriots (Dunbar-Ortiz 2014). Put differently, in its founding associations with America's history of violent settler colonialism, the "patriot" invoked by US culture, justifies war's violence as securing and protecting "freedom," while discounting the lives of racialized Others and eliding the imperial violence of appropriating land and resources.

---

[13] The 2000 Roland Emmerich film *The Patriot* offers one example of the American cultural resonances linking "patriot" as a keyword to the American Revolution as a righteous war for liberty. Donald Pease argues that in featuring a man driven by "revenge and rage" (2002: 37) and in substituting the South as the site of nation-making warring, "*The Patriot* proceeds to designate the South's state founding violence as the occult foundation of the national order" (2002: 40), contributing to legitimations of emergency logics in the 2001 Patriot Act.

[14] From 1897, the Boston Marathon has been held on Patriots' Day; see https://web .archive.org/web/20140424013642/http://216.235.243.43/races/boston-marathon/ boston-marathon-history.aspx.

[15] See www.britannica.com/topic/Patriot-Day.

Threads of continuity run from America's original assertions of patriots fighting through armed violence for freedom and independence into the rallying ideologies of "rebellion, religion, and racism" that mark the contemporary Patriot movement (Abanes 1996).[16] While Richard Abanes, the Southern Poverty Law Center, and others name this social movement "the Patriot movement," Kathleen Belew argues that it is more accurately called "the white power movement" (2018: ix). White power, she explains, is a slogan "commonly used" in a social movement that has "brought together members of the Klan, militias, radical tax resisters, white separatists, neo-Nazis, and proponents of white theologies" (Belew 2018: ix). Tracing the networks, ideologies, actors, arenas, and events of the White power movement from 1975 to 1995, Belew points to the co-constitution of nation and empire that marks it, in its "startling and unexpected origin [in] the aftermath of the Vietnam War" (2018: 3). She writes:

> As narrated by white power proponents, the Vietnam War was a story of constant danger, gore, and horror. It was also a story of soldiers' betrayal by military and political leaders and the trivialization of their sacrifice. This narrative facilitated intergroup alliances and increased paramilitarism within the movement, escalating violence. … [M]ovement leader Louis Beam urged activists to continue fighting the Vietnam War on American soil, … a literal extension of military-style combat into civilian space.
>
> (Belew 2018: 3)

The interconnections of nation and empire were to become a central dynamic of the White power movement, linking together "domestic anticommunism, white power organizing, and intervention abroad" (Belew 2018: 80). Veterans of US overseas wars (Vietnam, Korea, the Persian Gulf) often also became pro-White and anticommunist mercenaries in Rhodesia, South Africa, Nicaragua, and many parts of the Third World (Belew 2018). Devin Burghart explains a further dimension of the co-constitutions of nation and empire; "As a country we have spent so long at war overseas that a small percentage of veterans, but a percentage nonetheless, has warmed to the idea that the way to deal with political conflict is to engage in armed struggle"

---

[16] The Southern Poverty Law Center offers a timeline for the Patriot Movement; see www.splcenter.org/fighting-hate/intelligence-report/2015/patriot-movement-timeline.

(Steinhauer 2020). Put differently, political violence – normalized through the imperialism of the long War on Terror – has damaged democratic political participation both within the United States and globally. The estimated 25 percent of veterans who become militia members (Steinhauer 2020) often join because, according to one former Department of Homeland Security senior terrorist analyst, they fearfully transport to the "homeland" what they have learned to perceive as global and national threats: "communism, Islamic law and Marxism" (Steinhauer 2020).

The White power movement took a revolutionary turn in 1983 when it declared "war on the state. . . . Rather than fighting on behalf of the state,[17] white power activists now fought for a white homeland, attempted to destabilize the federal government, and waged revolutionary race war" (Belew 2018: 104). Predictably, the White power movement's militia groups attracted more members during the Obama presidency (Steinhauer 2020). Again predictably, despite a tradition of hatred toward the federal government, as Heidi Beirich, the cofounder of the Global Project Against Hate and Extremism, points out, "This has completely changed with Trump" (Steinhauer 2020: 13). The headline of Steinhauer's *New York Times* report encapsulates her findings: "Veterans Fortify the Ranks of Militias Aligned With Trump's Views."[18]

Some examples[19] across the twentieth century of the centrality of "patriot" as a keyword for the White power movement include the telling name of the Ku Klux Klan newspaper, *The White Patriot* (Belew 2018: 56); the organized racist and profascist groups of the early years of World War II, such as the Allied Patriotic Society and American Patriots, Inc. (Derounian 1941); the racism and coordinated paramilitary violence of the White Patriot Party through the 1980s (Belew 2018: 136);[20] the paramilitary training camps conducted by the Christian Patriots Defense League in the 1980s (Belew 2018: 52); the

---

[17] Belew notes how the vigilantism of white supremacist violence has served both white supremacy and state power throughout US history (2018: 106–07).

[18] See www.nytimes.com/2020/09/11/us/politics/veterans-trump-protests-militias.html.

[19] This is by no means an exhaustive list. I highlight recent examples involving the lexical item "patriot."

[20] The White Patriot Party, founded in the 1980s by Vietnam war veteran Frazier Glenn Miller, was the renamed Carolina Knights of the Ku Klux Klan. Due to the Southern Poverty Law Center's activism against hate groups, the White Patriot Party disintegrated in its visible, formal shape (Belew 2018: 86, 138).

1986 plans for robberies and violence of the Arizona Patriots (Belew 2018: 171); the 1994 manufacture of a deadly toxin by the Minnesota Patriots;[21] Timothy McVeigh's 1995 bombing of the Oklahoma City federal building (Belew 2018: 209–34);[22] the 2009 anti-Latinx border vigilantism conducted by the Patriots Coalition;[23] the 2008–2009 formation of one of the largest national Tea Party groups, the Tea Party Patriots (Zernike 2010; Peters 2019);[24] the 2017 founding of the "image-obsessed" and "explicitly fascist" White nationalist Patriot Front;[25] the 2018 surfacing of the United Constitutional Patriots, "a border militia ... [that] uses conspiracy theories and President Donald Trump's assertions that immigrants are invading the United States to justify their actions, some of which are illegal, such as detaining migrants at gunpoint";[26] and Patriot Prayer's strategy of deliberately provoking violence from 2018 onwards.[27] Indeed, commonalities between the "patriot" of the White power movement and the politics of Tea Party groups paved the way for the Trump presidency, with its attendant amplifications of racism, hostility to immigration and gun control, and its "politics of outrage and mistrust in government" (Peters 2019; see also Rohlinger and Bunnage 2017; Gervais and Morris 2018; Steinhauer 2020;). In short, as a keyword for this aspect of American culture, "patriot" valorizes armed violence and discounts lives that are nonWhite, non-Christian, and ideologically abhorrent to the White power movement. Put differently, "patriot" is a keyword that both legitimizes and produces necropolitics.

Possibly, the logics of spectacle, branding, and advertising evident in the Patriot Act's image-name were an effort to recruit the White power movement's political support. As noted above, it was not until 1983 that the White power movement turned against the state

---

[21] See www.splcenter.org/fighting-hate/intelligence-report/2015/patriot-movement-timeline.

[22] Against the received account of McVeigh as acting on his own, Belew details how McVeigh "represented the culmination of white power organizing." The bombing, she convincingly shows, was "part of a social movement" (2018: 210–11).

[23] See www.splcenter.org/fighting-hate/intelligence-report/2015/patriot-movement-timeline.

[24] See www.nytimes.com/2019/08/28/us/politics/tea-party-trump.html.

[25] See www.splcenter.org/fighting-hate/extremist-files/group/patriot-front.

[26] See www.splcenter.org/fighting-hate/extremist-files/group/united-constitutional-pat riots.

[27] See www.splcenter.org/hatewatch/2018/10/15/patriot-prayer-again-brings-violence-port land-flash-march-downtown-rounding-out-weekend-far.

(Belew 2018: 104).[28] Up to that point in time, White supremacist violence had mostly "served to constitute, shore up, and enforce systemic power, that is to say, not only overt power wielded by the state but also the many informal structures that upheld law and order. Because white supremacy undergirded state power throughout US history, vigilantes most often served the white power structure" (Belew 2018: 106). In the longer arc of history, then, and in the "uncoordinated conjunctures" and "knitted-together power of a discourse" (McAlister 2005: 307), perhaps naming the Act "Patriot" was an attempt to reach past the White power movement's revolutionary turn of 1983 and revitalize deeper histories and social memories, inviting the White power "patriot" to be on the same side as the state in a war demonizing "terrorists" as a racialized, foreign Other. Possibly, naming a law "Patriot" was an effort to speak to the White power movement through its own keyword, expressing what Ian Haney Lopez (2014) calls dog whistle politics: racially coded language designed to garner populist political support.

Layering upon these foundational, especially American, meanings for "patriot," the naming of the Patriot Act also evokes another set of associations. A mere decade before the events of 9/11, in the first Persian Gulf War (August 1990 to February 1991), a weapon named Patriot played a starring role. Media coverage of the Patriot missile reflected its exalted status in the popular imagination (Huey and Perry 1991: 34; Jeffords 1993). Exceeding "the mere indication of a successful weapon" and entranced by the missile's sleek sophistication and apparent precision, media rhetoric elevated the Patriot missile "into the realm of the mythic" (Jeffords 1993: 537). The first Gulf War's Patriot missile facilitated "tales of righteous and true technology (Patriot missiles) squaring off in the skies against wicked and errant technology (Iraqi SCUD missiles)" (Stahl 2010: 28).

In the first Gulf War, alongside the Patriot missile as mythic weapon, state discourse revitalized the American political myth of overseas warring as an expression of America's exalted role in the world and America's simultaneously national/global delivery of "freedom" through attention to an enmeshed democracy, trade, and the market.

---

[28] In the Southern Poverty Law Center's assessment, it was hostility to the first President Bush's 1990 proclamation of a New World Order that amplified the white power movement's suspicion of and hostility to the state and regulatory governance; see www.splcenter.org/fighting-hate/intelligence-report/2015/patriot-movement-timeline.

Traceable to Woodrow Wilson's 1917 address to a joint session of Congress in which he argued for a declaration of war against Germany, dwelling on how "German submarine warfare against commerce is a warfare against mankind," Wilson yoked trade and access to markets, to "the principles of peace and justice." He insisted:

> The world must be made safe for democracy. Its peace must be planted upon the tested foundations of political liberty. We have no selfish ends to serve. We desire no conquest, no dominion. We seek no indemnities for ourselves, no material compensation for the sacrifices we shall freely make. We are but one of the champions of the rights of mankind. We shall be satisfied when those rights have been made as secure as the faith and the freedom of nations can make them.

(Wilson 1917)

Echoing what came to be known as Wilsonianism (Rosenberg 2014), in August 1990, six days after Saddam Hussein's Iraq invaded Kuwait, the first President Bush announced that the United States was militarily committed to "the security and stability of the Persian Gulf," by ensuring Iraq's withdrawal from Kuwait, and to preserving the sovereign integrity of the United States' "longstanding" friend and security partner, Saudi Arabia (Bush 1990a). If history teaches us anything, Bush said, "[I]t is that we must resist aggression or it will destroy our freedoms" (Bush 1990a). He also made claim to Middle Eastern oil as an American "national interests."[29]

In the first Gulf War, American military-technological superiority delivered a resounding and speedy victory for the US and its allies. Within about five weeks of commencing aerial bombardment, Bush rehearsed the American political myth of delivering "freedom" worldwide when he announced a victorious end to the war, saying, "Kuwait is liberated" (Bush 1991). Crucially, even as spectacle and saturation television coverage characterized the first Gulf War (e.g., Engelhardt 1992; Kellner 1992; Jeffords and Rabinovitz 1994; McAlister 2005), its

---

[29] This claim to Middle Eastern oil as an American national security interest was made in this address and in subsequent speeches on the Persian Gulf War and encapsulated in the necropolitical legal text of Bush's August 20, 1990, National Security Directive 45, which asserts, "U.S. interests in the Persian Gulf are vital to national security. These interests include access to oil. ... The United States will defend its vital interests in the area, through the use of U.S. military force if necessary" (Bush 1990b). See also Chapter 4's discussion of Middle East oil as a US national interest.

imperial and necropolitical dimensions were barely visible.[30] The photo ban that prevented media from showing images of the military's fatalities returning in flag-draped coffins was put in place by the first President Bush in 1991 (Bumiller 2009).[31] The imperial move of turning to war to secure a key resource – oil – was reframed as the American political virtue of standing up for friends and for freedom, confronting a violent Iraq specifically to defend a threatened Saudi Arabia (the world's largest producer of petroleum) and to liberate an invaded Kuwait (Kuwait has about one-tenth of the world's oil).[32] In keeping with this elision of imperialist violence, the Patriot missile was strategically characterized as a *defensive* weapons system (Jeffords 1993: 539), recasting the aggression of war as "a quasi-technological imperial offering" (536).

After the first Gulf War, Tom Clancy's popular novel *The Patriot Games* (1987) was made into the successful 1992 movie of the same name.[33] In the movie, a CIA operative engages in a righteous and victorious fight against terrorists. The CIA operative travels the world, embodying the mobilities of planetary jurisdiction for the United States in its always righteous battle against always evil "terrorists."[34] Consistent with the imperial spectacles of the 1991 Gulf War and a 1992 movie on America's role in fighting terrorism, the 2001 naming of the Patriot Act has facilitated a US-scripted story of a strong and just America, protecting itself and the world, by punishing and deterring terrorism.[35]

---

[30] Iraqi fatalities far exceeded American deaths. America and its allies count fatalities at 343 in the war (McAlister 2005: 348). Estimates of Iraqi military deaths have ranged wildly from 100,000 to 1,500 (McAlister 2005: 236–37). But the human costs of this asymmetrical military encounter were not made visible and much obfuscation accompanied US military statements on the number of Iraqi dead (Heidenrich 1993).

[31] And conditionally lifted by President Obama in December 2009 (Bumiller 2009).

[32] See www.britannica.com/place/Kuwait/Resources-and-power.

[33] See www.boxofficemojo.com/year/1992/.

[34] Harrison Ford plays Jack Ryan, the heroic CIA operative who protects his family, representing the "home" element Amy Kaplan (2002) has identified as crucial to US texts of cultural imperialism, as well as a British cabinet minister (the "abroad" element which, as Kaplan highlights, mutually constitutes "nation" and "empire"), against terrorists affiliated with the Irish Republican Army. As Kaplan has also noted, US texts of cultural imperialism simultaneously constitute home (the family Ford's character protects) and abroad (the British cabinet minister).

[35] In addition to the Patriot Act's overarching statement of purpose, "[t]o deter and punish terrorist acts," specific sections of the Act cite to 9/11 as the compelling

Framed through dramatic and simplistic understandings of good and evil, right and wrong, with sometimes subterranean continuities in race-hatred, the patriot of the American Revolution, the White power/Patriot movement, the Patriot missile, *The Patriot Games*, and the Patriot Act show how the category "patriot" becomes, again and again, a legitimizing trope within US culture. Donning the guises of "freedom," of protecting the weak and the innocent, and fighting evil and injustice, "patriot" mobilizes belligerent, racist, nationalism and becomes a cipher for securing "American interests" while denying the workings of necropolitical imperialism. In the process, dynamics of law as spectacle – dynamics that power has labored to produce – work alongside the Patriot Act's encapsulations of exception, emergency, and enmity to evacuate law as public thing.

2.3   LEGISLATING RACIAL SUBORDINATION

Interrogating the juxtapositions of home/abroad, domestic/foreign in US cultural texts, Amy Kaplan's influential scholarship shows the co-constitutions of nation/empire in US history (2002). Section 2.3 explores how, in the post-9/11 moment of empire, the Patriot Act rehearses the imperial nation's anxieties about "turn[ing] aliens into citizens" (Kaplan 202: 9), while masking this anxiety through necropolitical law's dynamic of deception.

At the time the Patriot Act was signed into law on October 24, 2001, a brute, imperial articulation of the discounting of life was already underway. By then, the United States had been conducting an "intense" bombing campaign over Afghanistan for at least three weeks (History.com Editors 2010). Contextualized by this overt discounting of life, with the passing of the Act, a covert discounting of life in the domestic space of "nation" unfolded through two troubling provisions. Almost like bookends, these two provisions sit toward the opening and the closing of the Act. Section 102, the second substantive provision of the Act (section 101 establishes the counterterrorism fund), is entitled, "Sense of Congress Condemning Discrimination Against Arab and Muslim Americans." The provision reads:

moment of inauguration. For example, section 358, amending bank secrecy provisions, states as a finding of Congress, "given the threat posed to the security of the Nation on and after the terrorist attacks against the United States on September 11, 2001."

(a) Findings. Congress makes the following findings:
  (1) Arab Americans, Muslims Americans, and Americans from South Asia play a vital role in our Nation and are entitled to nothing less than the full rights of every American.
  (2) The acts of violence that have been taken against Arab and Muslims Americans since the September 11, 2001, attacks against the United States, should be and are condemned by all Americans who value freedom.
  (3) The concept of individual responsibility for wrongdoing is sacrosanct in American society, and applies equally to all religious, racial, and ethnic groups.
  (4) When American citizens commit acts of violence against those who are, or are perceived to be, of Arab or Muslim descent, they should be punished to the full extent of the law.
  (5) Muslim Americans have become so fearful of harassment that many Muslim women are changing the way they dress to avoid becoming targets.
  (6) Many Arab Americans and Muslim Americans have acted heroically during the attacks on the United States, including Mohammed Salman Hamdani, a 23-year-old New Yorker of Pakistani descent, who is believed to have gone to the World Trade Center to offer rescue assistance and is now missing.
(b) Sense of Congress. It is the sense of Congress that—
  (1) the civil rights and civil liberties of all Americans including Arab Americans, Muslim Americans, and Americans from South Asia, must be protected, and that every effort must be taken to preserve their safety;
  (2) any acts of violence or discrimination against any Americans be condemned; and
  (3) the Nation is called upon to recognize the patriotism of fellow citizens from all ethnic, racial, and religious backgrounds.

Section 1002, toward the end of the Act (section 1016 is the Act's final provision), is similar to section 102, in appearing to celebrate and protect American Sikhs. And just as section 102(5) acknowledges the sometimes distinctive dress conventions of some Muslim women, section 1002(6) explains (male) Sikh embodiment: "many Sikh-Americans, who are easily recognizable by their turbans and beards, which are required articles of their faith, have suffered both verbal and physical assaults as a result of misguided anger toward Arab Americans and Muslim Americans in the wake of the September 11, 2001, terrorist attack" (s. 1002(6)) Patriot Act).

The first victim of a post-9/11 hate crime was a turbaned American Sikh man, Balbir Singh Sodhi (Basu 2016).[36] He was shot and killed at the gas station he owned and operated in Mesa, Arizona, on September 15, 2001 (Basu 2016). Sodhi's killer described himself as a patriot and an American (Goodstein and Lewin 2001; Thomsen 2001), descriptors disclosing that, in the killer's eyes, by his very embodiment, Sodhi could not qualify as a "patriot" and an American.

Along with similarities, the two provisions are also marked by some very important differences. In particular, Congress finds that "Sikh-Americans form a vibrant, peaceful, and law-abiding part of America's people." In contrast, the Act's characterization of American Muslims is muted. Instead of "vibrant, peaceful, and law-abiding," American Muslims are, arguably, damned by faint praise: "American Muslims ... play a vital role in our Nation"; as if to imply that being vibrant, peaceful, and law-abiding are traits that cannot be assigned to Muslims.

Another significant detail lies in s.102(a)(6)'s exalting of Mohammed Salman Hamdani as a hero and (by implication) as an exemplary patriot. Section 102(a)(6) records that Hamdani was missing. He was later declared to have died in the devastation at the Twin Towers (Schabner 2006). Hamdani was a twenty-three-year-old police cadet at the New York Police Department. He was also an emergency medical technician. These credentials helped him gain access to the site when he rushed to offer help at the scene. Ironically, before he was declared a hero, simple facts about his biography – he was Muslim, he was a police cadet, he had been an exchange student in England – became sufficient to shroud his name under a pall of suspicion, adding to the grief, fear, and official harassment of his family (Gorta 2001). Suspected as a terrorist, redeemed as a hero, the self-sacrificing Hamdani is implicitly offered as a model of patriotism when the provision closes by calling upon "the Nation ... to recognize the patriotism of fellow citizens from all ethnic, racial, and religious backgrounds"

---

[36] The man who killed Sodhi, Francisco Silva Roque, "then proceeded to target a Lebanese family and Afghan, all at gasoline stations. Although only four murders have been confirmed as anti-Muslim hate crimes since 9/11, arson and violent assaults continued around the nation, increasing from 28 to 481 cases in just one year following 9/11" (Poros 2009: 334).

(s. 102 (b)(3)). Reinscribing the dehistoricized, depoliticized binary of good Muslim/bad Muslim (Mamdani 2004), the Patriot Act's implication seems to be that good Muslim citizens can only prove their patriotism by making that ultimate sacrifice of dying for the country.[37] Indeed, post-9/11 Muslim American military personnel speak to the notion of proving their patriotism through sacrifice when they describe their determination to be both Muslim *and* American by serving in the US Armed Forces despite sometimes being mistreated (Sandhoff 2017: 74–77), or subject to suspicion (Sandhoff 2017: 2, 55–57).

While, at a semantic level, sections 102 and 1002 read like a laudable, nation-making statement of American inclusivity, by inscribing certain citizens as always and inherently alien – contemporary embodiments of America's "impossible subjects" and "alien citizens" (Ngai 2014) – sections 102 and 1002 deploy the metapragmatics of Othering.[38] The metapragmatics of segregating for special mention – naming through categories of race and religion, explaining turbans and noting the clothing conventions of Muslim women – spatially and notionally re-inscribe America as White and Christian. Section 102 (4) confirms continuing reverberations for the (unspoken) conviction that only one particular racial identity – White – properly stands in for and represents the US nation: "When American citizens commit acts of violence against those who are, or are perceived to be, of Arab or Muslim descent, they should be punished to the full extent of the law" (section 102(4) Patriot Act).

The violent "American citizens" of section 102(4) is a reference, not to the "race, racism, and fictive ethnicity as mysteries lodged within the 'hyphen' joining the nation and the state, society, and the market" (Singh 2004: 236) but to the whiteness of "the nothing-in-particular American, or the true national subject" (Singh 2004: 20). The violent "American citizens" of section 102(4) need no hyphens or modifiers, thereby implicitly referencing the citizens who are "that mixture of English, Scotch, Irish, French, Dutch, Germans and Swedes" (Singh 2004: 20). Acting through this understanding of who properly belongs

---

[37] At the 2016 Democratic National Convention, the father of Humayan Khan, a Muslim US Army captain who had been killed in Iraq, implicitly reinscribed this binary of what constitutes the "good Muslim" when he described his family as patriotic (Sandhoff 2017: 4).

[38] Warm thanks to Beth Mertz for helping me figure out this particular law-and-language puzzle.

in America, the violent "American citizens" of section 102(4) express their patriotism by killing certain nonWhite citizens who have been discursively identified as enemies in the post-9/11 moment (Volpp 2002). The liberal legal tropes invoked in sections 102 and 1002 – rights, liberties, freedom, safety, individual responsibility for wrong-doing, law's protections, citizenship – all work as forms of deception, occluding the necropolitical discounting of life inherent to the racial subordination and metapragmatic Othering of sections 102 and 1002.

As part of the tension between semantics and metapragmatics, sections 102 and 1002 rely on the dynamic interplay between racial profiling and racial subordination, a dynamic powerfully explored by Leti Volpp in her compelling essay "The Citizen and the Terrorist" (2002). Analyzing the post-9/11 wave of violence directed by private citizens toward those perceived as "Middle Eastern, Arab, or Muslim," Volpp notes the coherence between the "extralegal racial profiling" (Volpp 2002: 1580) of seemingly private acts of violence and official racial profiling instituted by the state. State racial profiling took many forms, including the detentions, dragnet interrogations, and selectively punitive immigration enforcements relating to thousands of Middle Eastern, South Asian, or Muslim noncitizens without any known connection to terrorism (Volpp 2002: 1579–80; see also Bakalian and Bozorgmehr 2009). Official statements and state conduct, Volpp notes, ideologically effected "legitimation of the religious and modern impera-tive to eradicate either from without or within the forces of despotism, terror, primitivism and fundamentalism, each of which are coded as Middle Eastern, Arab, and Muslim." In doing so, state practices, rhet-oric, and subtext instructed the American public "that looking 'Middle Eastern, Arab, or Muslim' equals 'potential terrorist'" (Volpp 2002: 1582). At the same time, the state disavowed its role in the unfolding of post-9/11 racialized hate crime. Volpp writes:

> Simply because the state does not officially sponsor an activity does not mean that the state does not bear a relationship to that activity. In simultaneously advocating policies of colorblindness for citizenry while engaging in racial profiling for noncitizens, and publicly embracing all religions while particularly privileging Christianity, the administration has, in the name of democratic inclusion, disingenuously excluded. Thus, that an epidemic of hate violence has occurred within the context of "private" relations does not mean that such violence is without "public" origins or consequences.
>
> (Volpp 2002: 1583)

Volpp illuminates the pervasive and pernicious effects of racial profiling by contrasting popular and state responses to the events of 9/11 and the 1995 Oklahoma City bombing. In the Oklahoma City bombing, Timothy McVeigh, a Gulf War veteran and White power activist, detonated a truck bomb in front of a federal building. The explosion wounded 500 and killed 168 people. Among the dead were "19 young children in the building's day care center . . . [McVeigh] called the dead children "collateral damage" (Belew 2018: 210). McVeigh and his principal accomplice, Terry Nichols, were "right-wing extremists, part of the anti-government 'Patriot' movement (McVeigh also had white supremacist leanings)" (Pitcavage 2020; see also Belew 2018: 209–39). Volpp writes:

> Racial profiling only occurs when we understand certain groups of people to have indistinguishable members who are fungible as potential terrorists. The Timothy McVeigh analogy helps clarify the strangeness of the present moment. Under the logic of profiling all people who look like terrorists under the "Middle Eastern" stereotype, all whites should have been subjected to stops, detentions, and searches after the Oklahoma City bombing and the identification of McVeigh as the prime suspect. This did not happen because Timothy McVeigh did not produce a discourse about good whites and bad whites, because we think of him as an individual deviant, a bad actor. We do not think of his actions as representative of an entire racial group. This is part and parcel of how racial subordination functions, to understand nonwhites as directed by group-based determinism but whites as individuals. Racial profiling also did not happen because, as a white man, Timothy McVeigh was seen by many as one of "us" – as the New York Times editorialized at that time, there was "sickening evidence that the enemy was not some foreign power, but one within ourselves.
>
> (Volpp 2002: 1584–85)[39]

All in all, Volpp argues, the "redeployment of old Orientalist tropes," alongside racial profiling, helps explain the "ferocity with which

---

[39] Despite the "enemy-within" dynamics of the 1995 Oklahoma City bombing, the Antiterrorism and Effective Death Penalty Act of 1996, legislation passed partly in response to this act of domestic terrorism, also paid a great deal of attention to the threat of the "foreign" (both in terms of foreign states and foreign nationals), probably because of the "foreign" element behind the 1993 World Trade Center bombings and the 1979 taking of American hostages in Iran. In other words, the legislative co-constitutions of "nation" and empire in the Patriot Act has its legislative precedents.

multiple communities [persons who appear "Middle Eastern, Arab, or Muslim"] have been interpellated, both by the state and by individuals, as responsible for the events of September [11]." Through the racialization of this identity category, "members of this group are identified as terrorists and disidentified as citizens" (2002: 1576). The necessary companion to this racialized misidentifying of citizens as terrorists is the nativist, White power ideology identifying only certain bodies as properly American (Lubin 2021: 2). Given the compressed seven weeks between the events of 9/11 and the passing of the Patriot Act, it is illuminating to note that a form of racial subordination has also been enacted in terms of the timing of legislation. Almost thirty-six years passed between the Oklahoma City bombing and a bill introduced to Congress in January 2021 that was focused in part on the violence engineered by White supremacists, the Domestic Terrorism Prevention Act of 2021.[40] In being to some extent prompted by "the violent insurrection at the U.S. Capitol on January 6, [2021],"[41] the timing suggests that it was only when the violence of White supremacists targeted a cherished American institution of democracy that these particular social actors began to be taken seriously by legislators as threats to national security.

2.3.1 Legal Language and Racial Subordination

As narrative action, legal language generates spatiotemporalities (Richland 2013: 218; Valverde 2015). The two Sense of Congress provisions naming Arab Americans, Muslim Americans, Americans from South Asia, and Sikh Americans appear – superficially – to *re-identify* these peoples as citizens, members of the "nation." However, the necropolitical dynamic of deception attenuates this belonging, not just through the contradictions between semantics and metapragmatics or the seeming contradictions of the state's inculcation of hate crime even as it disavowed private violence but also in the way sections 102 and 1002 mimic racial subordination.

Racial subordination in the body of the nation is mirrored by textual subordination in the body of the text, in that the Patriot Act, even as it offers the protestations and affirmations of sections 102 and 1002, has the bulk of its text devoted to the Act's functioning as a key tool in the

---

[40] At www.congress.gov/bill/117th-congress/house-bill/350.
[41] At www.judiciary.senate.gov/press/dem/releases/durbin-reintroduces-legislation-to-combat-rising-domestic-terrorist-threat.

counterterror state's cultural project of nurturing and disseminating Islamophobia, dismantling civil rights, and institutionalizing racial profiling (e.g., Ball 2004: 62; Volpp 2002; Bakalian and Bozorgmehr 2009; Abel 2018a: 501–93). By implicitly appending the condemnatory necropolitical designation "enemy" upon certain Americans, the Patriot Act participates in discounting the lives of multiple, subordinated citizens. The Act also evidences law's double violence (Mawani 2012). As document, it encapsulates the symbolic and material force of the launching of the War on Terror, the widespread incidence of private violence directed at racialized populations, and the necropolitics of discounted lives both within the United States and globally. And, consistent with the expansive reach of the long War on Terror, the double violence of the Act and the space-time of racial subordination in the American nation continue to condition life today. As noted below in Sections 2.4 and 2.5, the Patriot Act persists through multiple national and global facsimiles, extending the necropolitical law and logic of the long War on Terror. And, in relation to the space-time of legal language, reports have surfaced as recently as 2016 of systemic torture directed at Muslim recruits in the US armed services (Hauser 2016; Reitman 2017). Instructors call Muslim recruits "terrorists" and single them out for cruel and inhumane treatment (Philipps 2016). Given the broader post-9/11 context of Islamophobia (e.g., Abel 2018: 501–93) and the overlapping membership between US military personnel and the White power movement (Belew 2018; Steinhauer 2020), this violence directed at Muslim recruits is unsurprising.

2.4 NECROPOLITICAL LAW'S ILLEGIBILITY

On October 26, 2001, a compressed forty-four days after the 9/11 attacks, President George W. Bush signed the Patriot Act into law. To mark the occasion, he made a speech in which he proclaimed:

> Today, we take an essential step in defeating terrorism, while protecting the constitutional rights of all Americans. ... With my signature, this law will give intelligence and law enforcement officials important new tools to fight a present danger. ... The changes, effective today, will help counter a threat like no other our nation has ever faced. We've seen the enemy, and the murder of thousands of innocent, unsuspecting people. They recognize no barrier of morality. They have no conscience. The terrorists cannot be reasoned with. ... These terrorists must be

pursued, they must be defeated, and they must be brought to justice. And that is the purpose of this legislation.

(Bush 2001c)

This excerpt shows key elements of the Bush administration's account of the War on Terror and the Patriot Act's place in fighting that war. Bolstered by repetition across multiple media sites, while plugging into long-established tropes, myths, and genres of American political discourse, the Bush administration account became the dominant account (e.g., Jackson 2005; Anker 2014). As a traumatized population sought explanations and guarantees of safety, Bush presented the Patriot Act as an urgently needed legal response to an emergency: "this law will give intelligence and law enforcement officials important new tools to fight a present danger. . . . [to] help counter a threat like no other our nation has ever faced." This overarching temporality of emergency framed a narrative Bush presented in cause-effect terms. First, the Act's cause: the 9/11 attacks.[42] Second, the Act's designed effect: to pursue, defeat, and bring terrorists to justice. Bush reinforced this cause-effect narrative through notions of emergency's inherently temporary duration; the Act was to be "an essential step in defeating terrorism."

However, against this temporality of emergency informing both the Act and its legitimizing narrative – urgent, provisional, exceptional law designed to respond to a crisis – we find ourselves in 2021 in the temporality of what Mary Dudziak calls "wartime" (2010, 2012). Wartime is characterized by "altered governance . . . when presidential power expands, when individual rights are often compromised" (Dudziak 2010: 1669), such that "[w]artime becomes a justification for a rule of law that bends in favor of the security of the state" (Dudziak 2012: 3–4). And, Dudziak argues, against conventional understandings of war as a time of exception, given the twentieth-century experience of "the longstanding persistence of war, . . . wartime is actually normal time" (2010: 1670). A further strand of the

---

[42] Bush's narrative presents the attacks as "diabolical" and a shock that "came like a bolt out of the blue" (Jackson 2004: 43), a version of events only too coherent with racial hatred and with dehumanizing characterizations of the enemy as "evildoers beyond the scope of human community" (Brysk 2007: 4). By decontextualizing the 9/11 attacks, Bush obscures the fact that the 9/11 attacks were "the latest in a long-running cycle of violence and counter-violence between the American government and al Qaeda" (Jackson 2004: 43), including the 1993 bombing of the World Trade Center (Ball 2004: 10).

somewhat covert normalization of wartime is discernible in the enduring influence, within the national security state, of a 1984 "shift from passive to active defense against terrorism," designed to overcome "the idea of war and peace as distinct phenomena" (Gunneflo 2016: 110, 154).[43]

Bearing in mind these covert temporalities of "wartime" animating the long War on Terror, and despite the Patriot Act's presentation to legislators and publics as law specifically and urgently crafted to meet the exigencies of 9/11, the Patriot Act substantially adopts and reproduces a "very sensitive" and secretive Reagan-era law (Gunneflo 2016: 109–10). The necropolitical legal precedent discernible in the logics of the Patriot Act is the Reagan administration's 1984 National Security Decision Directive 138, through which a "declaration of war against an unspecified terrorist foe, to be fought at an unknown place and time with weapons yet to be chosen" became "the stated policy of the government" (Jenkins 1984).[44] Extending this reproduction of prior legal text, almost three-quarters of the body of the Patriot Act – 67.8 percent, to be precise – consists of amendments to prior legislation (Table 1).[45] By incorporating yet altering prior legislation, these amendments exemplify law's temporalities of precedent – looking to the past for authority – alongside the ruptures of wartime (Dudziak 2010: 1669). There is a necropolitical dynamic of deception in the coexistence of continuities and ruptures, incorporating yet amending prior legislation and a national security decision directive. This deception mimics the common sense understanding of "[a]n altered rule of law" as "tolerable because wartimes come to an end, and with them, a government's emergency powers" (Dudziak 2010: 1669). However, despite being inaugurated as an emergency war effort, the War on Terror has become, as noted in Chapter 1, unending, permanent, and future-making.

---

[43] Gunneflo traces continuities informing the national security state's legitimations of targeted killing, identifying Reagan's 1984 National Security Decision Directive 138 as a key legal text and demonstrating how "Secretary of State George P. Shultz was without doubt the architect of NSDD 138" (2016: 115).

[44] Brian Michael Jenkins, "Combatting Terrorism Becomes a War" (Santa Monica, CA: The Rand Corporation: 1984).

[45] Treating the text as an artifact, I arrived at this figure by measuring the length of the body of text constituted by amendments and calculating amendments as proportions of the main body of the Patriot Act. I excluded the title page and the table of contents in making these calculations.

True to Dudziak's analysis, and contrary to the US state's framing of the Patriot Act's role in the War on Terror as exception and emergency, we find ourselves, two decades after 9/11, living in legal landscapes conditioned and legitimized by the Act's endless discursive instantiation. In keeping with the model for emergency legislation, the Patriot Act features sunset clauses with built-in expiration dates,[46] but they sit within the broader context of the continuing state of formal legal emergency declared by President Bush on September 14, 2001.[47]

State-declared states of emergency are nothing new for the United States (Struyk 2017), which "has been in an uninterrupted state of national emergency since 1979" (Ingraham 2014).[48] The formal, legal emergency declared by Bush in 2001 has been renewed so routinely that it is now in its twentieth year.[49] Like the broader state of emergency, the sunset clauses have, for the most part, been extended.[50]

---

[46] Known as sunset clauses, these built-in expirations originally applied to some but not all sections of the Act. See, for example, section 224, which reads, "SEC. 224. SUNSET. (a) IN GENERAL.—Except as provided in subsection (b), this title and the amendments made by this title (other than sections 203(a), 203(c), 205, 208, 210, 211, 213, 216, 219, 221, and 222, and the amendments made by those sections) shall cease to have effect on December 31, 2005. (b) EXCEPTION.— With respect to any particular foreign intelligence investigation that began before the date on which the provisions referred to in subsection (a) cease to have effect, or with respect to any particular offense or potential offense that began or occurred before the date on which such provisions cease to have effect, such provisions shall continue in effect." In addition to various extensions, the combination of the 2011 PATRIOT Sunsets Extension Act, and the 2015 USA FREEDOM Act, have exposed the temporality of emergency as a fiction.

[47] See Proclamation No. 7463, 66 Fed. Reg. 48199 (September 14, 2001) ("Declaration of National Emergency by Reason of Certain Terrorist Attacks").

[48] The 1979 national emergency was declared by President Carter on November 14, 1979, in Executive Order 12170, "with respect to Iran pursuant to the International Emergency Economic Powers Act (50 U.S.C. 1701–1706) to deal with the unusual and extraordinary threat to the national security, foreign policy, and economy of the United States." It has most recently been extended by President Trump; see www .whitehouse.gov/presidential-actions/notice-regarding-continuation-national-emer gency-respect-iran/.

[49] At www.whitehouse.gov/briefing-room/presidential-actions/2021/09/09/notice-on-the- continuation-of-the-national-emergency-with-respect-to-certain-terrorist-attacks/.

[50] Briefly, to review what exactly in the Patriot Act has become permanent and what is still subject to sunset: Section 201: Permanent as of 2006 Reauthorizations; Section 202: Permanent as of 2006 Reauthorizations; Section 203(b): Permanent as of 2006 Reauthorizations; Section 203(d): Permanent as of 2006 Reauthorizations; Section 206: Sunset of December 15, 2019, due to USA FREEDOM Act; Section 207: Permanent as of 2006 Reauthorizations; Section 212: Permanent as of 2006

And with the May 2015 passing of the U.S.A. F.R.E.E.D.O.M. Act,[51] many of the (ostensibly) temporary provisions of the Patriot Act have become permanent.[52] Like the discounted lives of Guantanamo detainees, trapped in the limbo of indefinite detention, the discounted lives of Americans in terms of civil rights have been (mostly) entrapped in the indefinite extensions of the Patriot Act and its successor, the U.S.A. F.R.E.E.D.O.M. Act. In short, in addition to being law central to the long War on Terror, the Patriot Act has become an enduring feature of our legal present, a present of perpetual wartime. And, at the risk of stating the obvious, war is inherently necropolitical.

2.4.1 The Patriot Act's Illegibility

Another facet of how the spectacle of the Patriot Act's name works to manufacture law as publicity while obstructing law as public thing becomes evident through a consideration of the body of the Act itself. In his highly influential book *The Cultural Study of Law* (2000), Paul Kahn encourages inquiry that offers "a thick description of the legal event." When the legal event is legislation, the thick description, necessarily, dwells on the words that form the text of an Act. As noted above, despite being presented to legislators and publics as law specifically crafted to meet the exigencies of 9/11, almost three-quarters of the body of the

---

Reauthorizations; Section 213: Increased civil rights protection in 2006 Authorization; Section 214: Permanent as of 2006 Reauthorizations; Section 215 (the so-called lone wolf amendment: Sunset of December 15, 2019, due to U.S.A. F.R.E.E.D.O.M. Act. However, "This act extends the authorization for the reformed expiring FISA authorities, along with the "roving wiretap" authorities and "lone wolf" provision to December 1, 2023" USA FREEDOM Reauthorization Act. If these authorities of FISA lapse, US intelligence surveillance programs would mostly revert to their pre-9/11 status, reducing the federal government's powers to investigate terrorism (see www.rpc.senate.gov/legislative-notices/hr-6172_usa-freedom-reauthorization-act; Section 217: Permanent as of 2006 Reauthorizations); Section 218: Permanent as of 2006 Reauthorizations; Section 220: Permanent as of 2006 Reauthorizations; Section 215: Lone-wolf Amendments: Sunset of December 15, 2019, due to USA FREEDOM Act May 2015.

[51] The full name of the USA FREEDOM Act is Uniting and Strengthening America by Fulfilling Rights and Ensuring Effective Discipline Over Monitoring Act of 2015; see www.congress.gov/bill/114th-congress/house-bill/2048/text.

[52] P.L. 114-23. Section 705 of the USA FREEDOM Act extends the sunset on three provisions of the 2006 reauthorizations to December 15, 2019: Section 206's roving wiretaps, Section 215's business records' requests, and the "lone wolf" amendments.

Patriot Act consists of amendments to prior legislation (Table 1).[53] In addition to recording the paradoxical simultaneity of law's continuities and ruptures, the Act is a telling instance of how law, in part through document, is animated by the mutual and reciprocal violence of symbolic and material force expressing law's constitutive relations with sovereignty, authority, and violence (Mawani 2012). Mawani argues,

> [law's] constitutive relations and self-generating qualities are clearly manifest in law's citational and organizational structure of command. Its mutuality and mutability are evidenced in the ways that law conceives of, appropriates, and assimilates some knowledge as pertinent to legality while dismissing others as extraneous and nonexistent. As a self-referential system mandating recall, reference, and repetition, while also drawing selectively from other domains of knowledge, law generates documents and renders them potentially (ir)relevant. In doing so, it continually produces, expands, and destroys that which comprises its archive and in turn, that which constitutes law. ... By referencing statutes ... that came before and by determining which are apposite, law cultivates its meanings and asserts its authority while at the same time concealing and sanctioning its material, originary, and ongoing violence. This reciprocal and reinforcing violence of law as archive ... highlights the preservation and destruction by which law generates the veracity of its own legality.
>
> (Mawani 2012: 340–41)

The two highly problematic Sense of Congress provisions (discussed above in Section 2.3) and the belligerent, racialized meanings attaching to "patriot" (discussed in Section 2.2) are vivid examples of how the Act "conceives of, appropriates, and assimilates some knowledge as pertinent to legality while dismissing others as extraneous and nonexistent" (Mawani 2012: 340). The Act's incorporation and securitization of a vast body of prior legislation (detailed below), and its centrality to the necropolitics of the War on Terror, illustrate law's self-referential, self-authorizing cultivation of meaning and authority "while at the same time concealing and sanctioning its material, originary, and ongoing violence" (Mawani 2012: 341). Paradoxically, an

---

[53] I arrived at this figure by measuring the length of the body of text constituted by amendments and calculating amendments as proportions of the main body of the Patriot Act. I excluded the title page and the table of contents in making these calculations.

especially potent expression of law's violence through the Patriot Act rests in its illegibility.

Like Frankenstein's creature, the hundred-and-thirty-two-page Patriot Act is something of a monster, scavenged and assembled from the corpus of law. This monster consists of substantive amendments to four main limbs of law: crime, immigration, surveillance, and banking.[54] Crudely stitched together, and brought under the bacronym image-name "Patriot," the voluminous, all-encompassing expanse of the Act effects a sweeping securitization of law. In its overarching logic of preemption, securitization, and expansive executive discretion, the Patriot Act is the creature of the counterterror state, deploying emergency to justify the parasitic discounting of life in order to feed the insatiable maw of the long War on Terror.

In the process of amending prior legislation, the Patriot Act cites to the Constitution and fifty-four prior legislative enactments.[55] I list the Acts cited in the Patriot Act in this absurdly long footnote[56] because

54 Almost a quarter of the Patriot Act—23.9 percent—amends title 18 of the United States Code, Crimes and Criminal Procedure (Table 2). Amendments to title 31 of the United State Code, Money and Finance, add up to a hefty 17.5 percent (Table 3). Amendments to the Immigration and Nationality Act and to the Foreign Intelligence Surveillance Act together come close to 10 percent of the Patriot Act (Tables 4 and 5). And amendments to a plethora of other legislation together constitute a further 16.7 percent of the Act.

55 In citing to prior law, the Patriot Act sometimes names acts in a way that includes the year of enactment, and sometimes names acts only by the title letter or number of the United States Code or Public Law.

56 Where the Patriot Act identifies legislation only by a title number, I include, in square brackets the acts' subtitles. The fifty-four legislative enactments cited in the Patriot Act are: Administrative Procedure Act; Antiterrorism and Effective Death Penalty Act of 1996; Arms Export Control Act; Atomic Energy Act of 1954; Bank Holding Company Act of 1956; Bank Secrecy Act; Classified Information Procedures Act; Code of Federal Regulations; Commodity Exchange Act; Communications Act of 1934; Controlled Substances Act Crime Identification Technology Act of 1998 Department of Justice Appropriations Act 2001 Departments of Commerce, Justice, and State, the Judiciary, and Related Agencies Appropriations Act, 2001; DNA Analysis Backing Elimination Act of 2000; Federal Deposit Insurance Act; Federal Reserve Act; Federal Rules of Civil Procedure Federal Rules of Criminal Procedure; Federal Tort Claims Act; Foreign Agents Registration Act of 1938; Foreign Corrupt Practices Act; Foreign Intelligence Surveillance Act of 1978; Foreign Narcotics Kingpin Designation Act; Foreign Relations Authorization Act, Fiscal Years 1988 and 1989; Gramm-Leach-Bliley Act [also known as the Financial Services Modernization Act of 1999]; General Education Provisions Act; Illegal Immigration Reform and Immigrant Responsibility Act of 1996; Immigration and Nationality Act; Immigration and

citation, a "foundational dimension of human language and social life," is especially central to legal discourse (Mawani 2012; Goodman et al. 2014: 449). Citation connects discourses and documents across time (Goodman et al. 2014), and in doing so, "citation never merely repeats an earlier utterance but *reconstitutes* discourse marked as prior (or anticipates future discourse) in relation to emergent concerns" (Goodman et al. 2014; emphasis added). In other words, consistent with law's self-referential, self-authorizing cultivation of meaning, even as the Patriot Act is brought into being as an urgently needed new law, scripted to meet a shocking set of events, the citation to fifty-four other enactments,[57] together with the embedding of substantial amendments to other legislation, expresses expansive connections with past legislation, past discourses, past moments in history, enlisting these times and subjects as participants in a post-9/11 account of law.

The Act's disorienting plurality of citations and omnibus quality thwart the readability and accessibility of the Act. Some of the Patriot Act's effects on comprehension and accessibility might be illustrated by a brief example. Section 201 of the Patriot Act reads as follows:

SEC. 201. AUTHORITY TO INTERCEPT WIRE, ORAL, AND ELECTRONIC COMMUNICATIONS RELATING TO TERRORISM
Section 2516(1) of title 18, United States Code, is amended –

Naturalization Service Data Management Improvement Act of 2000; International Banking Act of 1978; International Emergency Powers Act; International Financial Institutions Act; International Security Assistance and Arms Control Act of 1976; Investment Company Act of 1940; Money Laundering Control Act of 1986; National Crime Prevention and Privacy Compact Act of 1998; National Education Statistics Act of 1994; National Security Act of 1947; Omnibus Crime Control and Safe Streets Act of 1968; Omnibus Diplomatic Security and Antiterrorism Act of 1986; Public Law 91-508 [1970 amendments to the Federal Deposit Insurance Act]; Right to Financial Privacy Act of 1978; Securities Exchange Act of 1934; State Department Basic Authorities Act of 1956; Title 42, Code of Federal Regulations [Public Health]; Title I of Public Law 91-508 [Fair Credit Reporting Act]; Title IV of Public Law 107-42 [Air Transportation Safety and System Stabilization Act]; Title 5, United States Code [Government Organization and Employees]; Title 18, United States Code [Crimes and Criminal Procedure]; Title 28, United States Code [Judiciary and Judicial Procedure]; Title 31, United States Code [Money and Finance]; Title 49, United States Code [Transportation] (115 STAT.381); Trade Sanctions Reform and Export Enhancement Act of 2000; Victims of Crime Act of 1984.

[57] The Patriot Act also cites to text with legal status subordinate to legislation, such as executive orders, the US sentencing guidelines, and the *Code of Federal Regulations*.

(1) by redesignating paragraph (p), as so redesignated by section 434(2) of the Antiterrorism and Effective Death Penalty Act of 1996 (Public Law 104-132; 110 Stat. 1274), as paragraph I; and

(2) by inserting after paragraph (p), as so redesignated by section 201 (3) of the Illegal Immigration Reform and Immigrant Responsibility Act of 1996 (division C of Public Law 104-208; 110 Stat. 3009-565), the following new paragraph;

"(q) any criminal violation of section 229 (relating to chemical weapons); or sections 2332, 2332a, 2332b, 2332d, 2339A, or 2339B of this title (relating to terrorism); or."

The convoluted language of Section 201 tells us that the Patriot Act amends a second piece of legislation, title 18 of the United States Code. The United States Code is "a consolidation and codification by subject matter of the general and permanent laws of the United States," dating from 1948.[58] Title 18, subtitled "Crimes and Criminal Procedure," is the main federal statute governing criminal law and procedure. In amending title 18 of the United States Code, section 201 of the Patriot Act refers to a third enactment, the Antiterrorism and Effective Death Penalty Act of 1996.[59] Section 201(1) of the Patriot Act refers to the Antiterrorism and Effective Death Penalty Act of 1996 in order to note that it was the Antiterrorism and Effective Death Penalty Act of 1996 that had designated paragraph (p) of section 2516(1) of title 18 of the United States Code as paragraph (p) but that the Patriot Act would now be redesignating paragraph (p) as paragraph I. In other words, the amendment that is section 201(1) contains a brief note of legislative history. Section 201 of the Patriot Act then refers to a fourth enactment, the Illegal Immigration Reform and Immigrant Responsibility Act of 1996. Just as the reference to the Antiterrorism and Effective Death Penalty Act of 1996 cites to a prior amendment, so too the reference to the Illegal Immigration Reform and Immigrant Responsibility Act of 1996 notes that paragraph (p) was designated as paragraph (p) by the Illegal Immigration Reform and Immigrant

---

[58] Office of the Law Revision Counsel, http://uscode.house.gov/browse/prelim@ti tle18&edition=prelim.

[59] The Antiterrorism and Death Penalty Act of 1996 was passed as a response to the domestic terrorism of Timothy McVeigh's bombing of federal offices in Oklahoma City in 1995.

Responsibility Act of 1996. Section 201(2) of the Patriot Act then amends section 2516(1) of title 18 of the United States Code by inserting a new paragraph (q).

This new paragraph (q) refers to seven further sections of title 18 of the United States Code. The first of these is section 229, which consists of almost five pages of law relating to chemical weapons. In the course of these five pages, section 229 refers to three other titles of the United States Code[60] and to four other enactments,[61] one Executive Order,[62] and the 1993 Convention on the Prohibition of the Development, Production, Stockpiling and Use of Chemical Weapons and on Their Destruction.

In brief, to read the Patriot Act is to struggle with a disorienting plethora of citations that are primarily meaningful with reference to other pieces of legislation. Like a scavenger determined to uncover *something* of value, a reader must sift, puzzle, scrutinize, and then discard significant tracts of the Patriot Act in a search for meaning. Arguably, the Patriot Act dismantles genre conventions for legislation by being as fragmentary and as other-referencing as it is. Delving into the body of the Patriot Act demonstrates a necropolitical deception: the widely accepted rule-of-law principle, requiring clarity and publication of law[63] – a principle undergirding law as public thing – is superficially observed, in that the Patriot Act has been published and is available online. However, the Act's multiple references render it effectively inaccessible. Through its illegibility, the document works as an almost-closed communication loop, discounting social and political life not just by dismantling civil and political rights but also by diminishing citizens' access to law. As a fragment of law's archive, the Act's documentary and discursive attributes illustrate the violence of law's

---

[60] Title 22, Foreign Relations and Intercourse; title 5, Government Organization and Employees; and title 10, Armed Forces.

[61] In two of the four instances, the acts are named with their year of enactment: the Export Administration Act of 1979 and the Comprehensive Drug Abuse Prevention and Control Act of 1970. The other two are the Immigration and Nationality Act and the Maritime Drug Enforcement Act.

[62] S 229 cites to Executive Order Number 13128 (June 25, 1999).

[63] In Jeremy Waldron's concise restatement of rule-of-law principles, "law should be epistemically accessible: it should be a body of norms promulgated as public knowledge so that people can study it, internalize it, figure out what it requires of them, and use it as a framework for their plans and expectations and for settling their disputes with others" (2016).

archive converging in material, symbolic, and epistemic terms in the long War on Terror. The inaccessibility of the Act's text also redirects attention to the seeming clarity of the Act image-name, which brands the Patriot Act as a law protecting and nurturing citizens, rather than necropolitically discounting life.

2.5   THE NECROPOLITICAL LAW OF PLANETARY JURISDICTION

Up to this point, I have argued that the Patriot Act expresses the discounting of life inherent to necropolitical law by deploying the deceptions and disengagements of spectacle, by legislating racial subordination, by generating law that is illegible, and by being presented as an exceptional and temporary response to an emergency, a representation the passing of time has exposed as a legal fiction. In Section 2.5, I address ways in which the Patriot Act constitutes necropolitical law that discounts life, not merely at the level of nation but also at the level of the planet.

The Patriot Act effects planetary jurisdiction by discarding legal fictions of sovereignty that limit legitimate state power to state territory.[64] Instead of conventional nation-state sovereignty, the Act scripts into being an account of sovereignty consistent with casting necropolitical law's jurisdictional net worldwide. As noted above, the opening lines of the Patriot Act – its statement of purpose – legislate the United States' global necropolitical sovereignty by asserting that the Act purpose is "[t]o deter and punish terrorist acts in the United States and around the world." By the time the Act was signed into law, as noted above, the United States had already demonstrated its determination to execute the Patriot Act's purpose: it had launched an aggressive bombing campaign in Afghanistan.[65] In other words, the Patriot Act, both in terms of text and context, exemplifies necropolitical law's

---

[64] As discussed in Chapter 1, sovereignty, in a formal legal sense, is understood to entwine territory, law, nation, state, people, and the legitimacy to rule. Article 2 (4) of the Charter of the United Nations captures this formal legal understanding of sovereignty: "All Members shall refrain in their international relations from the threat or use of force against the territorial integrity or political independence of any state, or in any other manner inconsistent with the Purposes of the United Nations."

[65] See www.cfr.org/timeline/us-war-afghanistan.

sovereignty: the spatially and geopolitically unconstrained "power and capacity to dictate who is able to live and who must die" (Mbembe 2019: 66).

Even though the Patriot Act, in substance, discards conventional legal sovereignty by transgressing the borders of other, formally sovereign nation-states, the Act retained facades of US (domestic) legal sovereignty. In keeping with ordinary procedures for US federal law-making, the Patriot Act was debated and passed in the House and the Senate. This process permitted the United States to retain the *appearance* of liberal legality while in substance enacting necropolitical, imperial law. This performance of ordinary liberal legal processes in the context of the extraordinary events of 9/11 might be understood as a political spectacle of security. In her analysis of political spectacle, Keally McBride argues that because the 9/11 attacks "were designed to be a spectacular strike at the symbols of American power . . . a reassertion of normalcy and predictability" became necessary aspects of the provision of security (2006: 259). Assertions of normalcy and predictability, McBride highlights, are delivered through spectacle that is "recognizable and routine" (2006: 259). Enacting legislation through recognizable and routine processes, even in the face of exceptional circumstances, surely operates as just such a palliative spectacle of normalcy. Notably, regimes that erode individual rights while seeking to *appear* lawful tend to enact rights-eroding legislation through procedurally correct processes (Rajah 2012).

In addition to supplying the recognizable and routine, when legislation moves through House and the Senate, liberal legality's dynamics of scrutiny, contestation, and transparency are assumed to be at work. In turn, the performance of liberal legality feeds into a narrative of liberal legal legitimation that has become part of the story of the Patriot Act. For example, a 2004 Department of Justice Report characterizes the Act as having been "overwhelmingly passed" by Congress.[66] "Overwhelmingly passed" becomes a shorthand assertion for the values and dynamics of representative democracy. This assertion is contradicted by the muted, truncated debates at both House and the Senate. In both settings, the debates were characterized by representatives

---

[66] At www.justice.gov/archive/olp/pdf/patriot_report_from_the_field0704.pdf.

echoing state justifications for the Act.[67] The narrative of liberal legal legitimation also disregards how the Patriot Act's statement of purpose, in naming and conjoining just two territories – the United States and an undifferentiated rest of the world – functions to undermine liberal legality by legitimizing US imperialism.

Indeed, this coexistence of gestural liberal legality alongside substantive imperialism in the Patriot Act is consistent with law's double move in relation to the discounting of life, as discussed in Chapter 1. To briefly recapitulate, and as evidenced by the Patriot Act, necropolitical law's double move involves the notional upholding of liberal legality through performances indexed to rule of law, nation-state sovereignty, and the valuing of all human life as equal. At the same time, a narrative of War on Terror exceptionalism scripts justification for the state of exception in which, by suspending "rules and conventions ... a conceptual and ethical zero point [is created] from where the law, the norms, and the political order can be constituted" (Hansen and Stepputat 2006: 301). The planetary jurisdiction the US awards itself in the Patriot Act is a startling yet normalizing instance of this double move, enacting domestic law in the sphere of the nation-state according to liberal legality while dissolving conventional sovereignty by reaching into a jurisdictional domain surpassing nation. And, as discussed below, it is UN Security Council Resolution 1373, together with a globalized listing regime, that illustrates some of the planetary jurisdiction effected by the Patriot Act.

2.5.1 Resolution 1373

Alongside comforting but deceptive gestures of liberal legality, and narratives of legitimacy, it is important to note that, as an expression of US imperialism, the Patriot Act has taken on multiple afterlives in multiple jurisdictions. Thirteen days *before* Congress passed the Patriot Act, "while the wreckage of the Twin Towers still smoldered a short

---

[67] In both the House and the Senate, debate was minimal and muted, as was media critique, and the Patriot Act was rapidly passed. Some eighteen months after it was passed, one "former conservative Republican congressman," Bob Barr, described it as "the worst piece of legislation we've ever passed. It was what you call *emotional voting*" (Ball 2004: 71–72).

distance away" (Scheppele 2004: 91), the UN Security Council passed Resolution 1373.[68] Resolution 1373 reads like an executive summary of the Patriot Act.[69] It reproduces the Patriot Act's core logic of emergency – preemption – and requires all member states to prevent, suppress, and criminalize the financing, planning, perpetration, and support for, terrorists and terrorist acts. Resolution 1373 also imports the Patriot Act's logics of crimmigration (Stumpf 2006) by casting suspicion on the claims of refugees and asylum-seekers and by amplifying suspicion of those who seek to travel across borders.

With the Patriot Act, liberal legal processes were performed even as liberal legal content was evacuated. Similarly, with Resolution 1373, in which political spectacles of the recognizable and routine accompanied the gutting of processes of deliberation. The United States drafted the resolution only in consultation with its four fellow permanent members – China, France, the UK, and the Russian Federation. The "10 non-permanent Council members were only given notice the day before the vote. Nevertheless, the resolution passed unanimously at a public meeting lasting only five minutes" (Roele 2013: 58). If deliberation is central to the legitimacy of the UN Security Council (Cronin and Hurd 2008), then the underbelly of Resolution 1373 illustrates how, also at a global level, the appearance of liberal legal process has accompanied the enactment of a law[70] that is in substance necropolitical.

Just as the Patriot Act has discounted life by cultivating a belligerent modality of citizenship (Ben-Porath 2006; 2011) that erodes rights and amplifies secretive, discretionary state action, so, too, Resolution 1373 is at the center of a sinister web through which lives have been discounted, but this time on a global scale. The global rights erosions and annihilations attributable to Resolution 1373 include terrorism watchlists, and no-fly blacklists, and lists resulting in the assets and

---

[68] At www.unodc.org/pdf/crime/terrorism/res_1373_english.pdf.

[69] The concise text of Resolution 1373 expands, like a multiheaded hydra, into the one hundred pages of the Counter-Terrorism Committee's Technical Guide; see www.un.org/sc/ctc/wp-content/uploads/2017/08/CTED-Technical-Guide-2017.pdf.

[70] As Shirley Scott argues, "[T]here was no explicit or implicit time limit to the actions required of states; hence the resolution could be said to establish new binding rules of international law" (Scott 2009: 214).

bank accounts of individuals being frozen (Sullivan 2020). The composition of these security watchlists and blacklists is not necessarily derived from fact or proof. Rather, those listed are often "suspects preemptively targeted, usually on the basis of unseen intelligence material, for potential terrorist association" (de Goede and Sullivan 2015: 82). In other words, many contingencies and suppositions inform these lists – suspicion, preemption, unseen intel, racial profiling – aggregating into potential association with that expansive and undefined category, "terrorists" (Sullivan 2020).

The fear of the racially Other foreigner, a fear so central to the designation of necropolitical enmity (Mbembe 2019) as well as to the enmeshed and co-constituting dynamics of American imperialism and American nation-making (Kaplan 2002; McAlister 2005), might be illustrated through the example of US No Fly List. Compiled, like other security lists, on the basis of suspicion not fact (Bernstein 2013; de Goede and Sullivan 2015; Sullivan 2020); notoriously ridden with error (ABC News 2015; CNN 2015)[71] and administered through Kafkaesque layers of obstructive bureaucracy (ProPublica 2015),[72] the

---

[71] In a December 2015 interview with CNN, Senator Marco Rubio said, "The— former Senator Kennedy—Ted Kennedy once said he was on a no-fly list; . . . there are journalists on the no-fly list. . . . These are everyday Americans that have nothing to do with terrorism. They wind up on the no-fly list. There's no due process or any way to get your name removed from it in a timely fashion" (CNN 2015). De Goede and Sullivan (2015) note that protections and processes available to Americans mistakenly placed on the no-fly list are unavailable to non-Americans. And, in 2017, 99 percent of the 1.6 million people on the no-fly list were foreign nationals; see www.dni.gov/files/NCTC/documents/features_docu ments/TIDEfactsheet10FEB2017.pdf. In a December 2015 interview with ABC's This Week with George Stephanopoulos, then Governor Jeb Bush of Florida, when asked if he believed that people on the no-fly list should be able to buy guns. Bush replied, "I mean, Ted Kennedy and Stephen Hayes (ph) the journalist and Cat Stevens, I mean, this is not a list that you can be certain of" (ABC News 2015).

[72] ProPublica traces the convoluted events, mistakes, and bureaucratic missteps relating to Rahinah Ibrahim's inclusion on the no-fly list. Ibrahim, a Malaysian citizen who was a doctoral student at Stanford when she was first placed on the list, is the only person to date to have successfully challenged her inclusion on a no-fly list. It took her almost ten years through the American courts to do so, and yet, because of the way security lists, in being shared across bureaucracies and countries, take on a life of their own (de Goede and Sullivan 2015), she remains unable to secure a visa for travel to the United States.

dissemination of the US No Fly List to "more than 20 foreign govern-ments" (ProPublica 2015) is part of the globalized security apparatus traceable to Resolution 1373. Compiled by the United States' Terrorist Identities Datamart Environment, the list before 9/11 had named "perhaps a dozen people worldwide" (ProPublica 2015). As of February 2017, the number of people identified as known or sus-pected terrorists added up to 1.6 million. Of those listed, 99 percent were non-US persons.[73] Just as necropolitics relies on "a force of separation" that pretends to ensure government even as it seeks exemption from that same government (Mbembe 2019: 1), security lists are administrative devices, compiled without transparency and circulated globally (de Goede and Sullivan 2015). Security lists govern by engineering the discounting of life through new forms of civil death. Resolution 1373 and the security machinery it has engendered are necropolitical, in that when bank accounts are frozen, visas refused, and travel obstructed, families are fragmented, struggles for survival ensue and individuals' lives are degraded, as people find themselves floundering in the blackholes of adminis-trative nightmares marked by failures of due process, transparency, and accountability (Bernstein 2013; Roele 2013; de Goede and Sullivan 2015; Sullivan 2020). As administrative devices, security lists produce and reproduce necropolitical separations, giving "advantage to the executive by carving out novel logics of inclusion and exclusion" (de Goede and Sullivan 2015: 17).

Resolution 1373 has been characterized as the United States' tool for effecting an imperial scheme of surveillance and correction (Roele 2013). In this, Resolution 1373 might be seen as mimicking the ever-expanding secrecy and bureaucracy of the counterterror state (Masco 2014) on a global scale. Resolution 1373 and the global security apparatus it has facilitated also undo law as public thing through layers of impenetrable official secrecy and inaccessible, labyrinthine bureau-cracies with simultaneously global and national dimensions (Bernstein 2013; Roele 2013; de Goede and Sullivan 2015; Sullivan 2020). In addition to failures of deliberation marking Resolution 1373 as described, this particular resolution represents significant departures

---

[73] See www.dni.gov/files/NCTC/documents/features_documents/TIDEfactsheet10FEB2017 .pdf.

from past practice.[74] These departures include how, consistent with the long War on Terror's unbounded temporality and unlike prior Security Council resolutions, "there was no explicit or implicit time limit to the actions required of states" (Scott 2009: 214). Put differently, as a global facsimile of the Patriot Act, Resolution 1373 reproduces the Patriot Act's claim to planetary jurisdiction and the long War on Terror's anticipation and production of a necropolitical perpetual war.

Kim Scheppele draws attention to how, by transplanting the Patriot Act into Resolution 1373, even as the United States has deprecated and disregarded international law, it has constructed a new body of global security law (2014; see also Scheppele 2010). The "two worrisome gaps" of Resolution 1373, "the lack of any definition of terrorism and the lack of any mandatory concurrent compliance with human rights norms in carrying out the fight against terrorism" (Scheppele 2004: 92) have been amplified, bureaucratized, and rendered continuous by the Security Council's Counter-Terrorism Committee, a committee established under Resolution 1373 to monitor states' implementation of the resolution.[75]

2.6 CONCLUSION

Chapter 2 has shown how the Patriot Act is a central text in the long War on Terror's project of legislating necropolitical law. Incorporating

---

[74] First, prior to Resolution 1373, UN Security Council resolutions tended to address specific situations and specific countries, "whereas 1373 addressed itself to (undefined) international terrorism in general" (Roele 2013: 59). Second, until Resolution 1373, the issue of international terrorism had been addressed by the UN General Assembly, not the Security Council (Rosand 2003: 333). Third, by creating uniform obligations for all member states, Resolution 1373 exceeds "existing international counterterrorism conventions and protocols binding only those that have become parties to them" (Rosand 2003: 334).

[75] From September 2005, the obligations created by Security Council Resolution 1624, also came under the purview of the Counter-Terrorism Committee. Resolution 1624's obligations include to: "(a) Prohibit by law incitement to commit a terrorist act or acts; (b) Prevent such conduct; (c) Deny safe haven to any persons with respect to whom there is credible and relevant information giving serious reasons for considering that they have been guilty of such conduct"; see http://unscr.com/en/resolutions/doc/1624.

necropolitical dynamics of deception and separation to foster enmity and discount civil and political life, and exemplifying the symbolic and material violence of law as archive, the Patriot Act has emanated from the United States to take on a global and tentacular second life through its facsimile, UN Security Council Resolution 1373. The Act also deploys two Sense of Congress provisions to metapragmatically re-inscribe racial subordination in the United States as nation while superficially seeming to protect minority citizens. Strategies of naming, resonant of advertising, branding, and marketing, point to the Patriot Act as commodity. As commodity, the Patriot Act purports to enhance citizenship even as its content erodes civil rights and obscures these erosions through its inaccessible text. The bacronymed image-name of the Act may well be an effort to recruit the political support of adherents of the White power movement, a movement that identifies with "patriot" as a keyword in particularly necropolitical dimensions of American culture. The illegibility of the Act demonstrates one of the ways in which, even as the Act adopts gestural performances of liberal legality, the Act functions to dismantle transparency, accountability, and rights. In short, the Patriot Act illustrates the workings of law as publicity while pretending to function as law as public thing. Read through the lens of necropolitics, the Patriot Act discloses conventional law's role in the long War on Terror's discounting of life.

Departing from Chapter 2's analysis of conventional legal text – legislation – Chapter 3 reads for law in a text not conventionally recognized as legal: Obama's announcement of the killing of Osama bin Laden. Just as the Patriot Act scripts the long War on Terror's authorization of necropolitical law and planetary jurisdiction, Obama's announcement also scripts norms, relations, practices, and authorizations remaking "justice" into vengeance. And just as the Patriot Act crossed the line dividing covert and overt imperialism by asserting the United States' planetary jurisdiction, so too Obama's announcement, the first made by a US president publicly celebrating an extraterritorial, extrajudicial killing, crossed the line dividing the shadowy, secretive world of assassination from practices the US state was now prepared to publicly declare as lawful. Chapter 3 shows how, by legitimizing and authorizing the extraterritorial, extrajudicial killing of an enemy, Obama's announcement made new legitimizing meanings for necropolitical law's discounting of life.

2.7 TABLES

The tables I set out here offer a detailed accounting of the page numbers, sections, and lengths of the Patriot Act in relation to its amendments of prior legislation.

As discussed in Section 2.4 above (Law's Illegibility) almost three-quarters of the body of the Patriot Act – 67.8 percent to be precise – consists of amendments to prior legislation (Table 1). I arrived at this figure by treating the Act as an artifact and measuring the length of the body of text constituted by amendments, then calculating amendments as proportions of the main body of the Patriot Act. I excluded the title page and the table of contents in making these calculations.

Almost a quarter of the Patriot Act – 23.9 percent – amends title 18 of the United States Code, Crimes and Criminal Procedure (Table 2). Amendments to title 31 of the United State Code, Money and Finance, add up to a hefty 17.5 percent (Table 3). Amendments to the Immigration and Nationality Act and to the Foreign Intelligence Surveillance Act together come close to 10 percent of the Patriot Act (Tables 4 and 5). And amendments to a plethora of other legislation together constitute a further 16.7 percent of the Act. These tables detail how, despite the claim that the Patriot Act was new law designed to meet a shocking new set of circumstances, the Act is more accurately described as a portmanteau law that "seriously threatens the liberties of ordinary citizens" (Ball 2004: 3–4).

Tables

TABLE 1.   Amendments Embedded in Patriot Act

Legislation	Length (cm)
Crimes and Criminal Procedure Amendments	568.1
Money and Finance Amendments	416.2
Immigration and Nationality Act Amendments	148.7
Foreign Intelligence Surveillance Act 1978 Amendments	80.3
All Other Amendments	396.7
Total	**1610**
Percentage of Legislative Text	**67.8%**

TABLE 2.   Title 18: Crimes and Criminal Procedure Amendments

Item	Page	Section	Length (cm)	Item	Page	Section	Length (cm)
1	277	104	1.6	27	341	374	19
2	278	201	7.8			375	
3	280	203(1b)	14	28	342	376	9.3
		203(2)				377	
4	281	204	2.7	29	365	505a	10
5	283	209	13.5	30	366	506	2
		210		31	367	506	6
6	284	212	16	32	374	801	6.5
7	285	212	19	33	375	801	19
		213		34	376	801	
8	286	213	7			802	
9	288	216	7			803	
10	289	216	19	35	377	803	19
11	290	216	19			804	
		217				805	
12	291	217	11.5	36	378	805	16.5
13	291	220	2.5			806	
14	292	220	4.2			808	
15	293	223	17.5	37	379	808	19
16	294	223	19			809	
17	295	223	13	38	380	809	19
18	308	315	3.7			810	
19	309	315	9.5	39	381	810	18
20	310	316d	17			811	

Table 2. (cont.)

Item	Page	Section	Length (cm)	Item	Page	Section	Length (cm)
21	311	317	19	40	382	812	9.5
		317				813	
		318				814	
		319a		41	383	814	19
22	312	319a	14.5	42	384	814	15.5
23	315	320	6.8	43	385	815	8
24	315	322	3			817	
25	339	372b	15.7	44	386	817	19
		373		45	392	1004	5.5
26	340	373	19	46	393	1004	2.5
		374		47	396	1011c,d	4.3
				Subtotal			302.5

TABLE 3. Title 31: Money and Finance Amendments

Item	Page	Section	Length (cm)
1	298	311	4.7
2	299	311	19
3	300	311	19
4	301	311	19
5	302	311	19
6	303	311	19
7	304	311	19
		312a	
8	305	312a	16.7
9	306	313a	14.7
10	307	313a	3
11	312	313b	4.2
12	313	313b	19
13	314	313b	3.5
14	315	321	6.5
15	317	325	19
		326	
16	320	351	3
17	321	351	19
18	322	35	19
		352	
19	323	353	19
		354	
20	326	358a,b,c	10
21	327	358d	2.3
22	328	359	7.5
23	329	359	3
24	329	361	4.4
25	330	361	19
26	331	361	19
27	332	361	19
		362	
		363	
28	333	365	5.5
29	334	365	19
30	335	362	13.5
31	337	371c	6.5
32	338	371c	19
		372	
33	339	372	3.2
Subtotal			416.2

TABLE 4.   Immigration and Nationality Act Amendments

Item	Page	Section	Length (cm)
1	343	403	16.5
2	344	403	3
3	345	411	1.7
4	346	411	19
5	347	411	19
6	348	411a,b	9.5
7	349	411c	7
8	350	411c 411d	19
9	351	412a,b	19
10	352	412a,b	12.5
11	353	413	8.8
12	355	417c,d	8
13	394	1006	5.7
Subtotal			148.7

TABLE 5.   Foreign Intelligence Surveillance Act 1978

Item	Page	Section	Length (cm)
1	282	206	15.4
2	283	208	2.5
3	286	214	12
4	287	214, 215	19
5	288	215	12.2
6	291	218	1.7
7	295	225	1.5
8	296	225	2
9	364	504	7.5
10	365	504	4.5
11	392	1003	2
Subtotal			80.3

CHAPTER THREE

NECROPOLITICAL LAW REMAKES JUSTICE

3.1 INTRODUCTION: DEATH-TAKING

Osama bin Laden was killed by US Special Forces in his home in Pakistan on May 1, 2011, and, according to official accounts, subsequently buried at sea.[1] His killing, as signified by the secretive burial and the 1 a.m. raid on his home, is shrouded in the concealments of necropolitical law. Enacted in darkness, and with the material reality of his body annihilated when it was slipped into unmarkable spaces, the killing of bin Laden demonstrates one of the "contemporary ways in which the political, under the guise of war, of resistance, or of the fight against terror, makes the murder of the enemy its primary and absolute objective" (Mbembe 2019: 66). Positioning bin Laden beyond the reach of conventional law's sites and processes – beyond capture, trial, sentencing, and most potently, beyond a burial that acknowledged his (human) ties to kin and community – this was a killing and burial demonstrating the necropolitical sovereign's power to take life, certainly, but also to take death.[2] It is, after all, the very materiality of dead

---

[1] The official account of a burial at sea has been contradicted by renowned investigative journalist, Seymour Hersh (2016: 47).

[2] As Verdery notes, immense political symbolism attaches to death rituals and beliefs, notions of the "proper burial," and national and international contexts relating to particular dead bodies (1999: 3). The dead bodies of the "named and famous" have a heightened significance, and shaping the social visibility of a dead body is part of the larger process of political transformation (1999: 13–20). The 2006 show trial, killing, and burial of Saddam Hussein—also labeled a "terrorist" by the United

bodies and the markable spaces of graves that facilitate the political lives of the "named and famous" beyond death (Verdery 1999: 13–27).

Chapter 3 centers on Obama's announcement on the killing of bin Laden to show how particular meanings have been made for necropolitical law's community, norms, authority, and legitimacy. Archived by the White House as "Remarks by the President on Osama bin Laden,"[3] (hereafter, Remarks), the president's announcement represents the first instance in which the United States made a celebratory public declaration with reference to the extrajudicial killing of a political enemy (Section 3.2). For this reason alone, the Remarks is a paradigmatic, precedent-setting text of necropolitical law. The subsequent extraterritorial, extrajudicial killings of both citizen and noncitizen "terrorists,"[4] alongside the subsequent burials-at-sea of other "terrorist" leaders,[5]

States—offers a telling contrast to the annihilatory logics of Osama bin Laden's killing and burial.

[3] Remarks by the President on Osama bin Laden, Address in the East Room (May 2, 2011); at www.whitehouse.gov/the-press-office/2011/05/02/remarks-president-osama-bin-laden. A copy of the Remarks is appended.

[4] Some five months after the bin Laden killing, this precedent became reauthorized for necropolitical law when US citizen Anwar al-Aulaqi, living in Yemen, became the first US citizen to be targeted and killed by a US drone and jet strike. A notable feature of the al-Aulaqi killing is that Anwar al-Aulaqi's father, Nasser al-Aulaqi, filed a claim with the US District Court "seeking declaratory and injunctive relief" once his son's presence on so-called kill lists became known. The court declined jurisdiction in December 2010 (Gunneflo 2016: 83–87). And in September 2011, Anwar al-Aulaqi was killed by drone strike.

In keeping with the long War on Terror's discounting of life, at least one other US citizen, Samir Khan, who was not "targeted," was killed alongside al-Aulaqi. Two weeks later, al-Aulaqi's sixteen-year-old son, also a US citizen, was killed along with eight others in a US military strike in Yemen. Official US statements did not confirm or deny that the sixteen-year-old was a target of the strike, broadening the precedent and opening the door to the killing of Osama bin Laden's son, seemingly on the basis of biological descent, as discussed in Chapter 4. Importantly, more than a year *before* the al-Aulaqi killing was conducted, the Obama administration prepared lengthy secret legal memos, justifying the extrajudicial killing of a US citizen. In a logical extension of the disidentification of citizens through their reidentification as "terrorists" (Volpp 2002), this memo cast the anticipated killing of al-Aulaqi as legally analogous to the killing of noncitizen enemies. The memo, followed by the killing, illustrate with chilling acuity Mbembe's argument that the War on Terror "makes the murder of the enemy its primary and absolute objective" (Mbembe 2019: 66).

[5] For example, in 2019, when the Trump administration announced the extraterritorial, extrajudicial killing of Abu Bakr al-Baghdadi, it likewise announced that the remains were buried at sea. See Gonzales (2019).

point to this authorizing, legitimizing quality of precedent attaching to the Remarks and related events.[6]

Obama's Remarks is a paradigmatic text of necropolitical law for a second reason: despite Obama's firmly liberal legal critique of the Bush administration's conduct of the War on Terror, a critique through which he explicitly positioned himself as the War on Terror's *lawyer-president-commander-in-chief* (Section 3.2), the Remarks demonstrates a high level of continuity and consistency between the Obama and Bush administrations' war-on-terror discourses and practices.[7] Section 3.2 also traces the twinning that is evident between the ban on assassinations and national security in America's Cold War context to demonstrate necropolitical law's capacity to perform law as public thing in liberal legal terms, while also securing spaces of secrecy and unaccountability for US foreign policy. This doubling dynamic animates the legitimation manufactured in the domestic sphere for the discounting of foreign lives.

Demonstrating necropolitical law's strategic and gestural deployments of liberal legal guises, Obama's Remarks demonstrates how he invokes liberal legal categories to situate and condemn bin Laden, even as he carefully excludes the United States from liberal legal constraints on power (Section 3.3). In addition to strategic deployments of liberal legal discourse, Obama also constructs himself as the embodied realization of a seemingly race-blind meritocracy. Reading the Remarks in conjunction with Obama's famous 2009 address in Cairo, staging himself as evidence of the American dream's multiethnic, multiracial capaciousness, Section 3.4 argues that Obama's race identity minimized the realities of racialized necropolitics in the domestic sphere of the United States, adding new layers to the deceptions wrought by necropolitical law in its global staging of spectacles of American imperialism.

Through his Remarks, at the level of the obvious – his words – Obama constructs legitimacy for necropolitical law by uncoupling "law" and "justice." Broadly speaking, within Anglo-American and "Western" traditions, "law" is understood as a compound category occupying a

---

[6] See Section 3.7 for further ways in which the quality of authoritative precedent attaching to the bin Laden killing has been expressed.

[7] Chapter 5 demonstrates the Trump administration's ideological consolidations and extensions of War-on-Terror discourse established by the Bush administration (January 2001–January 2009), and reinforced by the Obama administration (January 2009–January 2017).

semantic field intersecting with morality, ethics, and power, such that, arguably, "justice" is inseparable from "law."[8] It is therefore significant that, avoiding the category "law," this lawyer–president–commander-in-chief invokes "justice" five times. In each of those five instances, Obama's justice takes on meanings valorizing the discounting of life, justifying extrajudicial killing, and discarding the restraints of rule of law. And, as traced through this chapter, underlying these justifications are the narratives and political myths of American exceptionalism reinscribing the myth of the frontier (Section 3.4) and positioning the United States as the chosen nation (Section 3.5). By simply not mentioning crucial and spectacularly delegitimizing episodes of the War on Terror, Obama's Remarks engages the double violence of law's archive, disavowing US transgressions of law, humanity, and justice so as to re-narrate the United States as always already innocent and therefore *just* in its imperialism and in its remaking of "justice" as vengeance (Section 3.6).

Section 3.6 also analyzes how the two images disseminated by the counterterror state as visuals for the Remarks augment the erasures and historical amnesia effected through Obama's narratives of nation and justice. These images demonstrate that the visual culture accompanying necropolitical law strategically pairs spectacle and secrecy to foster legitimacy, authority, and community for the discounting of life. And Section 3.7 shows how, by re-narrating both nation and justice, Obama minimizes the fractures of racialized public and private violence, such that nation, as loving community, becomes a healing trope. All in all, Chapter 3 shows how the Remarks enacts the double violence of law's archive, constructing authority, legitimacy, and implicitly racialized, exclusionary community for necropolitical law through the triple pillars, first, of revitalizing covert White supremacy; second, normalizing both necropolitical law and the project of counterterrorism; and third, implementing a strategic discarding of law's public thingness.

3.2 BANNING ASSASSINATION, PERFORMING LAW'S PUBLIC THINGNESS

As noted above, the Remarks represents the first instance of a US president making a celebratory public declaration with reference to

---

[8] As elaborated in Chapter 1.

the extrajudicial killing of a political enemy.[9] Obama's celebration of the killing of bin Laden is a telling moment encapsulating how the discounting of life in liberal democracies relies on law's doubled character. As discussed in Chapter 1, liberal legality's insistence on rule of law, nation-state sovereignty, and the valuing of all human life as equal is notionally upheld even as narratives of exceptionalism script justification for departures from these principles. This dual character of a coexisting liberal legality and necropolitical law is potently embodied in Obama's image and identity as the *lawyer*–president–commander-inchief determined to right the wrongs of the Bush administration's conduct of the War on Terror. Within the terms of a liberal legal critique, the Bush administration was notoriously "imperial,"[10] guilty of

[9] Up to 1975 the United States had not officially admitted to conducting extrajudicial killings; see Senate Select Comm. (1975), www.intelligence.senate.gov/pdfs94th/94465.pdf. In the more recent post-9/11 climate, prior to the killing of bin Laden, information on extrajudicial killings appears to have entered the public domain through leaks and comments from officials not authorized to speak. These news reports on killings in Yemen and Somalia are typical of the government's tendency to minimize publicity and links to state authority. See Bloomfield (2008), Schmitt (2002). After 9/11, the United States has argued that extrajudicial killings, euphemistically renamed "targeted killings," are permissible in military operations and self-defense. For a succinct critique, see Alston (2010). In February 2013, a leaked Department of Justice white paper revealed the Obama administration's legal justification for drone attacks on citizens: Department of Justice, "Lawfulness of a Lethal Operation Directed Against a U.S. Citizen Who Is a Senior Operational Leader of Al-Qa'ida or an Associated Force 1"; at https://irp.fas.org/eprint/doj-lethal.pdf. In May 2013 the Obama administration acknowledged that drones had killed four citizens. See, e.g., Friedersdorf (2013).

[10] Prompted, in part, by Nixon's conduct in office, Arthur Schlesinger's influential 1973 history of presidential power characterized the "imperial presidency" as one that awarded itself excessive, unconstitutional power. In the environment of hope for liberal legality's resuscitation under the Obama administration, on January 13, 2009, some eight days before Obama took office as president, the House of Representatives Committee on the Judiciary published its report entitled, *Reining in the Imperial Presidency: Lessons and Recommendations Relating to the Presidency of George W. Bush*. In his foreword to the report, John Conyers Jr. deplores how, "[u]ntil recently, the Nixon Administration seemed to represent the singular embodiment of that idea. But today, as the Bush Administration comes to a close, there can be little doubt concerning the persistence of Mr. Schlesinger's notion. More than three decades later, Mr. Schlesinger himself characterized the Bush Administration as "the Imperial Presidency redux," although he more optimistically predicted that "democracy's singular virtue—its capacity for self-correction—will one day swing into action." Today, in hindsight I can attest to the prescience of Mr. Schlesinger's warnings of unchecked power, even as we vigorously pursue the

dismantling the separation of powers and amplifying discretionary and unaccountable executive power, while fostering systemic abuses of human rights (e.g., Rudalvelige 2005; Savage 2007; Conyers 2009; Schmitt and Bessete 2017; Schmitt et al. 2017). Just eight days before Obama took office, the House of Representatives Committee on the Judiciary published a report cataloging specific transgressions of liberal legality marking Bush's imperial presidency. These include (1) the politicization of the Department of Justice; (2) assaults on individual liberty through detention, enhanced interrogation, ghosting, and black sites; (3) extraordinary rendition; (4) erosions of civil liberties conse-quent upon the Patriot Act, including the warrantless domestic surveil-lance program and the expanded scope and increased use of national security and exigent letters to bypass judicial review; (5) misuse of executive branch authority; (6) retribution against critics; and (7) the institutionalization of government without transparency and account-ability through the workings of executive privilege, secrecy, and the manipulation of intelligence (Committee on the Judiciary 2009).

Campaigning for the presidency, Obama routinely articulated a rule-of-law critique of the Bush administration's practices, asserting, for example, that "nobody is above the law." (Bunch 2008) Just two days after taking office, Obama signed three evidently urgent executive orders addressing key facets of the Bush administration's violations of human rights and liberal legality.[11] One, entitled "Ensuring Lawful Interrogations," was passed "to promote the safe, lawful, and humane treatment of individuals in United States custody and ... to ensure compliance with the treaty obligations of the United States, including the Geneva Conventions."[12] A second was "to effect the appropriate disposition of individuals currently detained by the Department of

much-needed democratic self-correction he anticipated" (Committee on the Judiciary 2009: 10).

[11] Notably, and with reference to issues of law's archive, as legal text, executive orders carry strategic advantages. An executive order is inherently flexible. "Although each order has the effect of law, they are not immutable, and allow the President a variety of ways to circumvent them. The President has the authority to overrule the order, make an exception to it, or ask Congress to legislate its removal. Additionally, the President may designate any of these changes as classified if he considers them 'intelligence activities ... or intelligence sources and methods,' effectively preventing them from ever reaching public view" (Canestaro 2003: 23).

[12] Executive Order 13491 of January 22, 2009, "Ensuring Lawful Interrogations": www .govinfo.gov/content/pkg/FR-2009-01-27/pdf/E9-1885.pdf.

Defense at the Guantanamo Bay Naval Base and promptly to close detention facilities at Guantanamo, consistent with the national security and foreign policy interests of the United States and the interests of justice."[13] And the third was issued "to develop policies for the detention, trial, transfer, release, or other disposition of individuals captured or apprehended in connection with armed conflicts and counterterrorism operations that are consistent with the national security and foreign policy interests of the United States and the interests of justice."[14]

In so rapidly passing these three executive orders, Obama staged a particular account of law as central to his statecraft.[15] As discussed in Chapters 1 and 2, the positive law staged by Bush as his statecraft featured belligerent nationalism in the law-as-commodity naming of the Patriot Act, the confounding illegibility of the Patriot Act as a cover for the dismantling of civil liberties, and the militarized imperialism animating the expansive authority in the authorization for use of military force (AUMF) "to use all necessary and appropriate force."[16] In contrast, explicitly distinguishing himself from the emphasis on force and exception so central to Bush's presidency, Obama's three early executive orders assert his identity as the lawyer–president–commander-in-chief, reminding publics that he had once been a constitutional law professor. Whereas Bush's War-on-Terror discourse was characterized by an explicit or implicit discarding of lawfulness, justice, and humanity in the name of emergency exceptionalism and a threatened national security, in Obama's early, signature staging of his statecraft, lawfulness, justice, and humanity are yoked to – and compatible with – national security and foreign policy. It is thus all the more remarkable that in the Remarks, as noted above, this lawyer–president–commander-in-chief avoids the category "law" while invoking "justice" five times.

But before delving into the specifics of Obama's Remarks, it is important to contextualize the extrajudicial killing of bin Laden in

---

[13] Executive Order 13492 of January 22, 2009 "Review and Disposition of Individuals Detained At the Guantanamo Bay Naval Base and Closure of Detention Facilities," www.govinfo.gov/content/pkg/FR-2009-01-27/pdf/E9-1893.pdf.

[14] Executive Order 13493 of January 22, 2009 "Review of Detention Policy Options," www.govinfo.gov/content/pkg/FR-2009-01-27/pdf/E9-1895.pdf.

[15] In Anderson and Wittes's assessment, in the wake of the lack of transparency, shifts in technology and the conduct of warfare under the Bush administration, the Obama administration came under particular pressure to articulate a legal framework for the War on Terror (Anderson and Wittes 2015).

[16] At www.congress.gov/107/plaws/publ40/PLAW-107publ40.pdf.

terms of a recent phase in the layered temporality of the long War on Terror relating to the legality of killing of foreign enemies. In turn, this recent history illustrates how the deceptions of necropolitical law have long included a statecraft of staging law as a seemingly public thing even as law's public thingness has been twinned to discourses of secrecy and national security.

3.2.1 The Duplicities of Law's Public Thingness

Up to 1975, the United States had not officially admitted to conducting extrajudicial killings.[17] Given the political violence engineered by the CIA throughout much of the postcolonial and third world from (at least) 1945 onward,[18] the plausible deniability retained by the US state speaks to the systemic management of both secrecy and media, a management conditioned by the friend/enemy logics of the Cold War (Herman and Chomsky 1988; Zelizer 2018). This plausible deniability also discloses the double violence of law's archive: asymmetries of power condition the uneven archive through which law's violence is documented and obscured (Mawani 2012). Plausible deniability also speaks to the entrenched co-constitution of liberal legality and necropolitical law. In general, the United States has resolutely staged itself as lawful, transparent, and accountable – the desirable democratic foil to

---

[17] Senate Select Comm. to Study Governmental Operations with Respect to Intelligence Activities, Alleged Assassination Plots Involving Foreign Leaders, S. Rep. No. 94-465 (1975); at www.intelligence.senate.gov/pdfs94th/94465.pdf.

[18] Assassinations are, of course, only the tip of a massive iceberg representing covert and violent foreign policy. Tracing the relationship between foreign intelligence and secrecy, Chalmers Johnson writes, "Actions that generate blowback are normally kept totally secret from the American public and from most of their representatives in Congress. This means that when innocent civilians become victims of a retaliatory strike, they are at first unable to put it in context or to understand the sequence of events that led up to it. In its most rigorous definition, blowback does not mean mere reactions to historical events but rather to clandestine operations carried out by the government that are aimed at overthrowing foreign regimes, or seeking the execution of people the United States wants eliminated by 'friendly' foreign armies, or helping launch state terrorist operations against overseas target populations. The American people may not know what is done in their name, but those on the receiving end surely do—including the people of Iran (1953), Guatemala (1954), Cuba (1959 to the present), Congo (1960), Brazil (1964), Indonesia (1965), Vietnam (1961–1973), Laos (1961–1973), Cambodia (1961–1973), Greece (1967–1974), Chile (1973), Afghanistan (1979 to the present), El Salvador, Guatemala, and Nicaragua (1980s), and Iraq (1991 to the present), to name only the most obvious cases" (Johnson 2004: xi).

an evil communist Other – even as it self-interestedly enacted necro-political law at home and abroad. Not only publics but also political elites have long been kept in the dark as to surveillance and intelligence operations both domestically and around the world (e.g., Hersh 1974; Johnson 2004: xi).

In a striking and parallel prequel to the shock and scandal inside the United States following Edward Snowden's 2013 disclosures of the National Security Agency's extensive surveillance of citizens (Szoldra 2016), it was Seymour Hersh's "groundbreaking" (Nolan 1999) article for the *New York Times*, revealing the CIA's conduct of "a massive, illegal domestic intelligence operation during the Nixon Administration against the antiwar movement and other dissident groups in the United States" (Hersh 1974), that prompted a Senate investigation into the manner in which intelligence agencies were operating.[19] Within a month of Hersh's story, the Senate approved a resolution to investigate federal intelligence operations, appointing what became known as the Church Committee.[20] The CIA operations addressed by the Church Committee include the 1953 coup against Iran's elected prime minister, Mohammad Mossadegh; the 1960 assassination of Congo's Patrice Lumumba; assassination attempts on Fidel Castro and the 1961 attempt to invade Cuba; the 1961 assassination of the Dominican Republic's Rafael Trujillo; the 1963 coup against South Vietnam's President Diem; and the 1970 assassination of Chile's top military officer, General Schneider.[21] Importantly, pointing to law's uneven archive (Mawani 2012), even as the Church Committee acknowledged and addressed certain CIA operations in which foreign leaders were assassinated, it disregarded a host of other CIA activities[22] and the many *uncounted* killed across the Third World in the course of those activities. For example, in Indonesia, the CIA was involved in the 1965–1966 so-called anti-Communist mass killings (Cribb 1990; Roosa 2006; Bevins 2020).

---

[19] According to the law then in force (the Constitution, the National Security Act, the CIA's Charter), CIA operations were to be strictly "foreign." Domestic intelligence was the purview of the FBI. The Senate committee established to investigate federal intelligence operations was known as the Church Committee.

[20] At www.senate.gov/about/powers-procedures/investigations/church-committee.htm.

[21] See www.intelligence.senate.gov/sites/default/files/94465.pdf.

[22] For example, and drawing on Johnson (2004; ix), the following are absent from the Church Committee's deliberations: Guatemala (1954), Brazil (1964), Indonesia (1965), Laos (1961–1973), Cambodia (1961–1973), and Greece (1967–1974).

This political violence – arguably a genocide (Cribb 2001) – killed as many as a hundred thousand to two million people (McGregor 2009). This wide range in the estimates of victims speaks to aspects of the double violence of law's archive. In keeping with the dynamics traced by Mawani (2012), the combination of inadequate records tracking victims of state political violence, the climate of fear created by the killings, and the determined inaction and silence on the part of both Indonesian authorities and its Cold War allies – notably, the United States – has fostered a discounting of life so profound that it is unclear how many hundreds of thousands, or how many millions, have died on account of that particular episode in US imperialism. The excluded, unacknowledged facets of the CIA's activities mark an insidious absence, reminding us that "law and the archive are inextricably linked," and in these linkages informed by history's archive reconceptualized as "a site of epistemic and political struggle" (Mawani 2012: 340).

But to return to the parallels between 1974 and 2013, evident in both instances – Hersh in 1974 and Snowden in 2013 – at the levels of both state and nonstate actors, is a telling reverberation between home and abroad (A. Kaplan 202; McAlister 2005). For intelligence agencies, shadowy foreign puppet masters were surely pulling the strings of domestic dissenters (Hersh 1974; Andrew 1996). And US publics willing to turn a blind eye to its government's violations of liberal legality abroad were galvanized into demanding restraints on state power once confronted with excesses of arbitrary, unaccountable power in governance at home.[23]

Hersh's 1974 investigative reporting precipitated the law of an executive order restraining intelligence agencies and establishing "effective oversight" over these agencies (s.1, EO 11905 of 1976).[24] At the same time, the public scandal prompted official anxiety about the skeletons in the CIA's closet (Andrew 1996: 399–406). When Hersh published his explosive article in December 1974, Gerald Ford had been president for about five months. With the presidency's legitimacy and standing already rocked by the Watergate scandal, Nixon's resignation, and the Vietnam War, within weeks of Hersh's damning

---

[23] For example, the 2013 Snowden revelations precipitated limited revisions to the capacious domestic surveillance powers enabled by the Patriot Act.

[24] Hersh's first story was published on December 22, 1974. Within a month, on January 21, 1975, the Senate approved a resolution to investigate federal intelligence operations; www.senate.gov/about/powers-procedures/investigations/church-committee.htm.

revelations, Ford himself, in a seeming gaffe, added a further damaging revelation:

> At a White House lunch for the publisher and editors of the *New York Times* on January 16 [1975] the president revealed that the intelligence files contained material that it was against the national interest to reveal because it would "blacken the reputation of every President since Truman." "Like what?" asked one of the editors. "Like assassinations!" replied Ford, adding hastily, "That's off the record!" It was by any standards an astonishingly ill-judged remark. ... Eventually CBS's Daniel Schorr got wind of the story and made it national news. "President Ford," Schorr reported, "has warned associates that if current investigations go far they could uncover several assassinations of foreign officials involving the CIA."
>
> (Andrew 1996: 405–06)

Conditioned by Ford's disclosure of assassinations, the executive order designed to address intelligence agencies' abuses of power within the domestic sphere of the United States came to include a prohibition on assassination (s.5(2)(g), EO 11905 of 1976).[25] The heft of EO 11905 reflects this backstory. The bulk of the text sets out policies on the relationship between intelligence and national security, asserts limits on the remit of the various intelligence agencies, and establishes oversight "to assure compliance with law in the management and direction of intelligence agencies and departments of the national government" (s.1, EO 11905 of 1976). The prohibition on assassination is a succinct single subclause.

Ford's executive order banning assassinations was the first such order promulgated by a US president. Through the lens of Honig's concept of public things, the episode precipitated by Hersh's article and leading up to Ford's executive order expresses a version of law as public thing: an object or experience conjoining and interpellating US citizens as a public, facilitating the contestation and action in concert that is vital to democratic life (Honig 2017: 4). A statecraft alert to the value of law's public thingness is also suggested by the redundancy of the ban: assassination was then and continues to be illegal under US and international law (Gunneflo 2016: 113–14).[26] But, layering over the

---

[25] At fas.org/irp/offdocs/eo11905.htm#SECTION 1.

[26] For a nuanced and historically rigorous analysis of the "extensive legal work" that has been conducted to "distinguish between legal 'targeted killing' and extra-legal 'political assassination,'" see Gunneflo (2016).

implicit American exceptionalism of the executive order, the 1974 scandal of intelligence services surveilling domestic dissenters prompted the far more publicity-driven, performative enactment of law's capacity to repair these excesses of intelligence services. Importantly, mirroring the confounding coexistence of law as public thing and law as publicity, alongside the Church Committee's public and televised hearings a series of *closed* sessions were also held.

The committee's report reflects an acute awareness of the democracy-performing public pedagogy thereby achieved, noting that public hearings would "educate" the American public, about the "unlawful or improper conduct" of the intelligence community and that "nationally televised events offered the American public an opportunity to learn about the secret operations conducted for decades by US intelligence agencies."[27] The series of public events, experiences, and cultural objects (including news media) leading up to the executive order performed law's public thingness in a manner that apparently upheld democratic processes and values. Importantly, however, because closed sessions were also held and justified on the grounds of national security, secrecy and security were again co-constituted and enfolded within the legitimizing container of law's public thingness.

Relatedly, this performance of law's public thingness also illustrates a statecraft that deliberately and strategically stages the law of liberal legality as a facade for necropolitical law. Akin to the hyperlegality of tactically proliferating new laws while repurposing older law to entrench and normalize emergency logics and governance (Hussain 2007), less than five years after Ford's executive order, in December 1981, in the shadow of the long-drawn-out Iran hostage crisis[28] and

---

[27] "The committee held a series of public hearings in September and October of 1975 to educate the American public about the 'unlawful or improper conduct' of the intelligence community, highlighting a few carefully selected cases of misconduct. These hearings examined a CIA biological agents program, a White House domestic surveillance program, IRS intelligence activities, and the FBI's program to disrupt the civil rights and anti-Vietnam War movements. These nationally televised events offered the American public an opportunity to learn about the secret operations conducted for decades by intelligence agencies." Senate Select Committee to Study Governmental Operations with Respect to Intelligence Activities, www.senate.gov/about/powers-procedures/investigations/church-committee.htm.

[28] In the intervening years (in January 1987) Carter passed Executive Order 12036, strengthening restrictions on intelligence agencies, strengthening congressional oversight, and extending the prohibition on assassination to include playing an indirect role in assassination; at fas.org/irp/offdocs/eo/eo-12036.htm.

after setting in motion covert support for paramilitary forces in Nicaragua,[29] Reagan passed Executive Order 12333. Reagan's order adopted some of the language of Ford's EO 11905, including the ban on assassination, but with a crucial difference: rather than focusing on the need for intelligence agencies to be subject to oversight as per Ford's EO 11905, Reagan's EO 12333 emphasizes the need for intelligence *effectiveness*[30] and removes some of the restrictions placed on intelligence agencies by Carter's EO 120036. Reagan's order has recently been characterized by former high-ranking officials as the enabling law "at the heart of today's surveillance state" (Farivar 2014).

This statecraft of staging law has accompanied the co-constitutions of liberal legality and necropolitical law. Violating the prohibition on assassination operative in both international and domestic law, the United States continued to plot and direct lethal violence at its foreign political enemies, including "bombing the house of Libyan leader Mu'ammar Gadhafi in 1986 in retaliation for a bombing attack at a Berlin discotheque in April 1986" and the 1998 "firing of cruise missiles at training camps in Afghanistan after the bombings of two US embassies in Africa" (Samuels 2005: 48–49) – strikes that killed up to "thirty people in the camps … but missed Bin Laden by a few hours" (Gunneflo 2016: 158). Also in retaliation for the East African embassy bombings, the United States launched cruise missile strikes at a pharmaceutical plant in Sudan, part of what Richard Clarke described as the launching of "a sustained campaign against Bin Ladin [*sic*]" (Gunneflo 2016: 159).[31] In tracking the roles of social actors enacting the counterterror state's necropolitical law, it is important to note that Clarke, a "counterterrorism tsar," served in the administrations of Reagan, the first Bush, Clinton, and the second Bush (BBC 2004). In 1998, when these

---

[29] At www.brown.edu/Research/Understanding_the_Iran_Contra_Affair/documents.php.

[30] The EO's statement of purpose reads, "Timely and accurate information about the activities, capabilities, plans, and intentions of foreign powers, organizations, and persons, and their agents, is essential to the national security of the United States. All reasonable and lawful means must be used to ensure that the United States will receive the best intelligence available. For that purpose … in order to provide for the *effective* conduct of United States intelligence activities and the protection of constitutional rights, it is hereby ordered as follows" (12333 of 1981; emphasis added).

[31] Faulty intelligence was blamed when they attacked this facility, alleging it was manufacturing chemical weapons. It turned out to be a facility manufacturing medicines; see BBC (2004).

vengeful cruise missile strikes at sites in Sudan and Afghanistan were launched, Clarke was Clinton's National Coordinator for Security and Counterterrorism,[32] and his "Politico-Military plan" included a "multifaceted, detailed" determination to "eliminate" bin Laden (Gunneflo 2016: 160). With Clarke holding this key office, the Clinton administration asserted that it had the "legal right to use deadly force against terrorist leaders such as Islamic extremist Osama bin Laden, despite a 23-year-old presidential ban on assassinations" (Richter 1998).

However, up to at least the first Persian Gulf War, despite the patchy observance of the prohibition on assassination, some effort to assert the United States' formal adherence to this prohibition appears to have been at work:

> In the early fall of 1990, Air Force Chief of Staff General Michael Dugan boasted that if war actually erupted between the United States and Saddam Hussein's Iraq, American planes would probably target Saddam, his family, and his mistress. When Secretary of Defense Richard Cheney learned of Dugan's boasting, he immediately fired him, explaining to reporters that Dugan's comments constituted a potential violation of the US ban on assassinations.
>
> (Johnson III 1992: 401)

That a high-ranking military official comprehended US lethality as seamlessly extending to killing Hussein and his family speaks to the mixed messages delivered by the United States. On the one hand, the formal law banned assassination. Yet, the law enacted through conduct included actual and attempted assassinations, as noted above. These mixed messages disclosed the state's capacity to episodically toggle between liberal legality and necropolitical law. And, as illustrated above by the massive scale of the political killing in Indonesia in which the United States played a role, the discounted lives of the long War on Terror include the many uncounted victims of US imperialism.

---

[32] Also relevant to the military-industrial-media-entertainment network (discussed further in Chapter 6), Clarke began his "public service" career with the Pentagon, and "[a]fter 30 years of public service ... taught at Harvard's Kennedy School of Government for five years, served as an on air consultant for ABC News for ten years, wrote six books, and served as a security risk management consultant. He is currently the CEO of Good Harbor Security Risk Management, Senior Advisor at SRA International, and Chairman of the Board of Governors of the Middle East Institute," www.judiciary .senate.gov/imo/media/doc/1-14-14ClarkeBio.pdf. He is also on the Board of "Khalifa University in Abu Dhabi and several US information technology security companies" (Middle East Institute, www.mei.edu/profile/richard-clarke).

Consistent with its righteous discarding of liberal legal restraints in favor of a no-holds-barred approach to counterterrorism, the Bush administration's early responses to 9/11 included notice, just five days after the attacks, that the prohibition on assassination was being reconsidered. The *Washington Post* reported:

> Secretary of State Colin L. Powell said the administration was reviewing an executive order issued by President Gerald R. Ford in 1976 that bans US personnel from engaging in, or conspiring to engage in, assassinations. Some intelligence and terrorism experts have advocated assassinating Osama bin Laden, the exiled Saudi millionaire who lives in hiding in Afghanistan and has been named the prime suspect in last week's attacks. Powell said on CNN that "we are examining everything: how the CIA does its work, how the FBI and Justice Department does its [sic] work, are there laws that need to be changed and new laws brought into effect to give us more ability to deal with this kind of threat. ... Everything is under review.
>
> (Pincus and Eggen 2001)

Echoing the stance of "intelligence and terrorism experts" eager to assassinate a "prime suspect," media reports that same day quoted Bush both naming bin Laden as the "prime suspect" and pronouncing the death sentence (discussed further in Section 3.3 below). Consistent with the valorization of intelligence services central to the Bush administration's counterterror project, the executive order relating to intelligence services has been amended thrice by Bush.[33] And, in the assessment of one scholar, the September 14, 2001, AUMF, in its sweeping grant of powers to the president, is sufficient to authorize assassination:

> Three days after the terrorist attacks against the United States on September 11, 2001, the US Congress passed joint resolutions authorizing the president to "use all necessary and appropriate force against those nations, organizations, or persons he determines planned, authorized, committed, or aided the terrorist attacks that occurred on September 11, 2001.
>
> (Samuels 2005: 49)

---

[33] In January 2003 Bush amended portions of EO 12333 by issuing EO 13284, a document that reflects the creation of the Department of Homeland Security. On August 27, 2004, Bush issued EO 13355 for the "Strengthened Management of the Intelligence Community." Obama revoked this order the day after he took office as president. Bush issued EO 13470 on July 30, 2008, to amend EO 12333, and to strengthen the role of the Director of National Intelligence, a post created by his administration.

Notably, while it was the overtly necropolitical Bush who spoke eagerly of his desire to assassinate bin Laden (Section 3.4), it was the lawyer–president–commander-in-chief, Obama, who some ten years later delivered this death. How did Obama, who so explicitly positioned himself as a president observant of liberal legality, cast the legality of the bin Laden killing? Section 3.3 shows how one of Obama's strategies was to cast himself as necropolitical sovereign and global lawmaker.

3.3 THE NECROPOLITICAL SOVEREIGN AS GLOBAL LAWMAKER

As we have seen, one striking feature of Obama's Remarks is that he, a lawyer-president, avoids the category "law" while invoking "justice" five times. Importantly, the absence of "law" is accompanied by a cluster of familiar legal categories, including murder, terrorist, and innocence. These familiar legal categories evidence the ordering and interpretive effects of law in everyday life, imbuing acts, events, experiences, and social relations with legal significance.[34] A pattern is discernible in Obama's selective apportioning of legal significance: he avoids legal categories with regard to the US action but relies on legal categories to characterize bin Laden. The opening lines of the Remarks illustrate this move:

> Good evening. Tonight, I can report to the American people and to the world that the United States has conducted an operation that killed Osama bin Laden, the leader of al Qaeda, and a terrorist who's responsible for the murder of thousands of innocent men, women, and children.

Consistent with the discourse established by the Bush administration, as part of Obama's construction of American innocence, bin Laden's

---

[34] Hans Kelsen, in his *Pure Theory of Law* (1967), articulated this argument when he noted that the fact of an action or event does not, in and of itself, carry legal meaning. It is when that action or event is viewed through a legal scheme of interpretation interlaced with values, standards, and rules that the ordering and socially regulating effects of law become evident. Among the examples he offers, "Somebody causes the death of somebody else; legally this means murder" (1967: 4). Law, for Kelsen, is a scheme of interpretation that orders society, legal cognition, and self-interpretation.

guilt is presented stripped of context and cause,[35] such that the political violence he represents is excluded from a "view of terrorism as an expression of social conflict reflecting comprehensible grievances (albeit not necessarily justifiable)" (Brysk 2007: 4). With bin Laden cast as chief perpetrator of an incomprehensible and extreme act of violence, Obama rehearses the temporality, cause-effect narrative, and primarily inscribed identities of the protagonists as cast by the Bush administration a decade earlier, in which good, innocent Americans are pitted against evil terrorists, who are guilty of monstrously inhuman and therefore incomprehensible acts (Jackson 2005: 18). With bin Laden characterized as enemy/terrorist/murderer as well as violator of innocence, he falls under all four categories of state responses to the violence of nonstate actors: conventional war, unconventional war, criminal violence, and, most troublingly, as an "evildoer" "beyond the scope of human community ... forfeit[ing] even the rights of enemies or criminals" (Brysk 2007: 4; see also Falk 2007: 21–23). Consistent with these expansive and designated forfeitures of rights, the annihilatory killing and burial of bin Laden demonstrate necropolitical law's erasures of the "enemy."

As a text of necropolitical law, Obama's Remarks reveals that while legal categories (enemy, terrorist, murderer, and violator of innocence) apply to bin Laden, the nonlegal term "operation" applies to the raid and the killing of bin Laden.[36] The distance and dispassion of "operation" are associated not with law but with the spheres of medicine and the military. In evoking surgical precision and military calculations, Obama sidesteps a range of applicable legal categories (execution, extrajudicial killing, assassination, murder). By avoiding these legal categories, Obama circumvents the binary legal/illegal and deflects attention away from the workings of necropolitics. Key to necropolitics are dynamics of deception and dehumanization (Mbembe 2019). Through necropolitics, communities explicitly or implicitly consenting to asymmetrical violence are cultivated, and "enemies," denied the rights and the meta-legal status of fellow human beings, are targeted and annihilated (Saito 2010; Chamayou 2015 [2013]: 155; Mbembe

---

[35] See Falk, *supra* note 61, at 24–25, for a discussion of the manner in which a refusal to acknowledge grievances, let alone address them, encourages the perception of "the terrorists as evil extremists."

[36] Obama repeats "operation" through the Remarks, characterizing the killing as "the operation," "this operation," "a targeted operation," and twice as "an operation."

2019). In selecting "operation" to characterize the US action, but enemy, terrorist, and murderer to characterize bin Laden, it is as if the ordering and signifying effects of an expansive and necropolitical law apply to bin Laden but not to the United States. Augmenting this appropriative partitioning of law's applicability is the quality of verdict in "murderer" and political ideology in "terrorist,"[37] and of uncontested law-of-war clarity in the use of "enemy."

The contrast between "operation" and enemy/murderer/terrorist is a subtle (and therefore especially powerful) construction of the United States as global, necropolitical lawmaker and enforcer. By engaging in the double move of invoking conventional law as a scheme of interpretation applicable to bin Laden, while implicitly elevating itself above liberal legal constraints on power, the United States asserts the necropolitical sovereign's right to take life and to claim that this taking is lawful.[38] In short, Obama's selective apportioning of legal categories illustrates how necropolitical law invokes the values, relations, and practices of liberal legality to *exempt* the necropolitical sovereign from liberal legality's limits, scrutiny, and procedures. In keeping with the discounting of life fostered through the asymmetries of militarized imperialism, a duplicitous, bifurcated "law" becomes the necropolitical sovereign's tool, selectively imposed upon those with less material and symbolic power.

In addition to framing necropolitical law and the necropolitical sovereign's power to differentially assign law's applications, in his Remarks Obama grounds justice in the American political myths that frame America and Americans as innocent and exceptional, legitimately directing violence toward racialized, enemy Others. Section 3.4 discusses the enmeshed roles of affect and American political myth as necropolitical law's meaning-making container.

3.4 NECROPOLITICAL LAW, POLITICAL MYTH, AND THE THREE BODIES OF OBAMA

Affect has been a key weapon in the counterterror state's arsenal (Anker 2014; Masco 2014; Lubin 2021). This section demonstrates

---

[37] For a discussion of the ideology informing the category "terrorist," see Chapter 5.

[38] Richard Falk (2007) argues that the construction of national security as the primary concern of foreign policy, particularly during the administration of George W. Bush, has been facilitated by recruiting neoconservative legal specialists who typically "have a highly skeptical attitude about whether international law should even be treated as real law."

how, in keeping with the co-constitutions of law and culture (Cover 1983; Rosen 2006), Obama's Remarks constructs affective legitimacy, authority, and community for necropolitical law's discounting of life, conditioning the meanings of "justice" through deployments of political myth. Briefly, political myth is "the work on a common narrative by which the members of a social group (or society) ... make significance of their experience and deeds" (Bottici 2007: 133).[39] By providing "fundamental cognitive schemata for mapping the social world," political myth reduces "the complexity of social life to the relative simplicity of its narrative plot" (Bottici 2007: 179), thereby meeting the acute "need for a symbolic mediation of political experience" generated by the "complexity of modern societies" (Bottici 2007: 132). Importantly, political myth tends to frame issues to preclude certain responses, while encouraging responses that legitimize policy (Bottici 2007: 363). Most potently, political myth tends to be ubiquitous, invisible, and taken for granted, in part because these myths have long been in existence; imperceptibly shaping a community's understandings of itself in relation to political conditions, experiences, nation-making narratives, and social memory (Slotkin 1973; Bottici 2007: 364).

Political myth's shared meaning-making narratives generate the *affect of significance*, creating a sense of proximity, shared impact, and shared relevance between individuals and nation, between individuals and political events and experiences, and between individuals and other individuals who constitute the imagined community of nation (Bottici 2007: 179). Continually "(re)produced, (re)interpreted, and (re)transmitted," political myth is richly intertextual and efficient, in that fragments, symbols, and words evoke and recall "an entire body of work on a given myth" conveying meaning "beyond what is actually said" (Esch 2010: 362, 363). When it comes to American political myth, scholars point to the simultaneously explicit and implicit

---

[39] In locating political myth as a field, Bottici argues that dominant thinking in contemporary political philosophy, as epitomized by Rawls's *Theory of Justice* and Habermas's *Between Facts and Norms*, proceeds on the assumption that when it comes to political actors and the sphere of politics, "one can count on the rationality of the actors involved ... either as rationality with regard to ends and values, or as communicative rationality" (2007: 1). Such an assumption risks failing to account for a social reality in which "quite often, people seem to act on the basis of arational elements, ... powerful symbols and images of the world, which are not taken into account by a purely rational image of politics" (2007: 2).

hierarchies of race threading through and informing national narratives and political myth (e.g., Slotkin 1973, 1992, 2001, 2017; Fredrickson 1981; Kaplan 2002; McAlister 2005; Rodriquez 2010; Dunbar-Ortiz 2014).[40] Indeed, for Richard Hughes, the myth of White supremacy is the primary US political myth:

> assumptions of white supremacy are like the very air we breathe: they surround us, envelop us, and shape us, but do so in ways we seldom discern ... notions of white supremacy are so embedded into our common culture that most whites take them for granted, seldom reflecting on their pervasive presence, or assessing them for what they are.
>
> (Hughes 2018: 3)

Tensions and contradictions between political myth's assumptions of White supremacy and political myth's function of generating a nation-unifying affect rise to the surface in the figure and discourse of Obama, the United States' first non-White president. Discarding the liberal legal discourse at the forefront of his early presidency (Anderson and Wittes 2015), Obama turns to political myth in his Remarks to consolidate the necropolitical law that legitimizes the killing of bin Laden. In so doing, he demonstrates that just as liberal legality is marked by a doubling – always already the secret twin of a disavowed necropolitical law – so, too, is Obama's racialized identity marked by a doubling. As discussed below, consistent with modifications made to American political myth in the service of militarized imperialism, Obama represents himself as the embodiment of America's multiracial, multiethnic

---

[40] Illustrating both the primacy of White supremacy as political myth and the richly efficient and intertextual nature of political myth's invocations, Chapter 2's discussion of "patriot" as a keyword in American culture demonstrates how a single lexical item evokes an expansive system of meanings and a founding narrative of nation, infusing "patriot" with militarized, revolutionary, and racialized convictions as to the proper composition of the US and America's proper sovereignty and jurisdiction over planetary empire. Scholars attentive to the shadow side of American political myth note how these myths, rooted in Puritan New England colonies and interpretations of Christian text, have played a role in justifying America's founding violence, including the genocidal dispossession of indigenous peoples, the annexation of territory under Mexican and Spanish rule, and relatedly, the discriminatory treatment of Hispanic peoples (Lipset 1996; Madsen 1998; Dunbar-Ortiz 2014: 40–55; Hughes 2018). Additionally, consistent with the co-constituting reverberations between "home" and "abroad" marking nation-making and empire-building, American political myth animates domestic politics as well as foreign policy and imperialism (Lipset 1963; Slotkin 1973, 1992; Kaplan 2002; Johnson 2004; Judis 2005; McAlister 2005; Restad 2015).

democracy (Slotkin 2017; 2001), as well as the preeminent figure of military multiculturalism in its imperial realization (McAlister 2005; De Genova 2012). In this role, Obama reproduces and reauthorizes the logics and ideology of White supremacy underpinning the United States both as nation and as empire. One of the ways he does this is by characterizing the extrajudicial killing of bin Laden as justice, thereby echoing Bush and, like Bush, invoking the myth of the frontier.

3.4.1 Extrajudiciality and the Myth of the Frontier

Six days after the events of 9/11, Bush represented justice as extrajudicial vengeance (Bush 2001d).[41] Speaking to reporters, he named bin Laden as the "prime suspect" for the attacks, saying, "I want justice. ... There's an old poster out West that said: "Wanted, Dead or Alive." ... All I want, and America wants him brought to justice" (Bush 2001d). In naming bin Laden as the prime suspect then pronouncing the death sentence, relying on that "old poster out West" to convey the legitimacy and desirability of an extrajudicial killing, Bush was speaking the words of the necropolitical sovereign, declaring the power to take life and to do so on the basis of suspicion, not proof. He was also enacting law by fiat. In the process, Bush both drew on and revitalized the myth of the frontier. The myth of the frontier is "the conception of America as a wide-open land of unlimited opportunity for the strong, ambitious, self-reliant individual to thrust his way to the top" (Slotkin 1973: 5). Richard Slotkin's highly influential analysis on American political myth illuminates the myth of the frontier as a relentless driver of American culture,[42]

> In American mythogenesis the founding fathers were not those eighteenth-century gentlemen who composed a nation at Philadelphia. Rather, they were those who ... tore violently a nation from the wilderness – the rogues, adventurers and land-boomers; the

---

[41] While there are many other instances of "justice" being constructed as extrajudicial vengeance, for two early examples, see Bush (2001e), speaking to a joint meeting of Congress, "Whether we bring our enemies to justice or bring justice to our enemies, justice will be done"; and Bush (2001f): "We will direct every resource at our command to win the war against terrorists: every means of diplomacy, every tool of intelligence, every instrument of law enforcement, every financial influence. We will starve the terrorists of funding, turn them against each other, rout them out of their safe hiding places, and bring them to justice."

[42] Like Bottici, Slotkin emphasizes the unifying quality, cultural pervasiveness, and processual, continuous dynamism of myth (1973: 4).

> Indian fighters, traders, missionaries, explorers, and hunters who killed and were killed until they had mastered the wilderness; the settlers who came after, suffering hardship and Indian warfare for the sake of a sacred mission or a simple desire for land; and the Indians themselves, both as they were and as they appeared to the settlers, for whom they were the special demonic personification of the American wilderness.
>
> (1973: 4)

Enfolded within the myth of the frontier is a particular understanding of justice as frontier justice,[43] which is conditioned by situations "when law and order does not exist, as in the early western frontier" (Royster 1997: 9). In the face of this absence of law and order, "people are compelled to take justice into their own hands" (Royster 1997: 9). A second condition of possibility for frontier justice is when existing "law and order does not satisfy the needs of justice and can therefore be 'rightly' ignored or circumvented" (Royster 1997: 9). It is important to note that this myth of frontier justice is at odds with documented histories of active law enforcement at frontier sites (Hoefle 2004: 285). However, as signaled by Bush's language, notions of frontier justice rely heavily on popular culture's representations of American history and its engagements in war (Slotkin 1973, 2001, 2017). Additionally, the affect and social dynamics of frontier justice have been associated with the racial hatred and mob violence so central to lynching in US history (Waldrep 2002).

In the many characterizations of existing law as either absent or inadequate, and its repudiations of human rights, the Geneva Conventions, and conventional criminal law, the Bush administration's conduct of the War on Terror was marked by both of these strands of frontier justice (for a comprehensive account, see Abel 2018a, 2018b). It is surely no accident that, consistent with Bush's invocations of frontier justice, he was denigrated by critics as the

---

[43] The myth of the frontier is a widely intelligible myth in American culture and has been deployed by leaders and thinkers to justify American necropolitics both within and beyond the continent of North America from at least the 1890s, throughout the Cold War, and, as signified by Bush's call to frontier justice six days after the events of 9/11, into the War on Terror (Slotkin 1992; Jackson 2005; Dunbar-Ortiz 2014; Carney and Stuckey 2015). In referencing frontier justice, Bush is consistent with the "talismanic" invocations of the myth of the frontier that came to be associated with his predecessor, Ronald Reagan (Slotkin 1992: 4). And Reagan's particular mode of statecraft as stagecraft strongly influenced Bush's own highly staged statecraft (Rogin 1988, 1990; McBride 2006; Schill 2009).

president of "cowboy politics" (Renshon 2005). In recruiting frontier justice, Bush relies on the legitimizing affect of political myth to disregard liberal legality. It is not a trial that Bush seeks but a vengeance thinly cloaked as "justice."

Notably, despite Obama's conspicuous efforts to distinguish himself as the lawyer–president–commander-in-chief who would restore engagements with international institutions, treaty obligations, international law, and diplomacy (as discussed in Section 3.2), Obama extends the precedent set by Bush, likewise recruiting frontier myth by casting extrajudicial killing as justice. In the Remarks, when Obama says, "We were also united in our resolve to protect our nation and to bring those who committed this vicious attack to justice" and "finally, last week, I ... authorized an operation to get Osama bin Laden and bring him to justice," he, like Bush, renders absent the possibility that bringing bin Laden to justice requires capture followed by a trial. In short, when Obama, like Bush, affirms the standing of extrajudicial killing as the proper execution of justice, Obama relies on the pervasive legitimation of the myth of the frontier in American culture to do so.

One tension that arises from Obama's invocation of the myth of the frontier is that it valorizes and justifies racialized violence. For the early colonists, violence served to regenerate "their fortunes, their spirits, and the power of their church and nation" (Slotkin 1973: 5). And the frontier myth's continued expressions continue to be animated by an American conviction that it is "the means of violence" that secure national regeneration, such that "the myth of regeneration through violence became the structuring metaphor of the American experience" (Slotkin 1973: 5). Importantly, the regenerative violence embraced as properly American is strikingly necropolitical, including "prolonged and intensified slavery in the teeth of American democratic idealism" and the valorization of "men like Davy Crockett [who] became national heroes by defining national aspiration in terms of so many bears destroyed, so much land preempted, so many trees hacked down, so many Indians and Mexicans dead in the dust" (Slotkin 1973: 5).

As indexed by slavery and the slaughter of Indians and Mexicans cited by Slotkin, the myth of the frontier, like other American political myths, understood "America as essentially a white man's country" (Slotkin 2001: 470) and valorized the role of White men's violence in securing both Whiteness and the American nation, in the process discounting the lives of a range of racialized enemies (Slotkin 1973,

115

1992).[44] However, from 1943 an important shift was engineered through the medium of cultural text[45] to reconstitute the myth in the service of America's self-image as a nation participating in World War II. Even as the United States directed a marked viciousness toward its Japanese enemies in the Pacific theater – European enemies were not racialized in the same way (Dower 1986) – World War II became a precipitating condition for a "radical innovation in national mythology" (Slotkin 2017: 2). This radical innovation altered the essential Whiteness of American identity through "a myth of American nationality that remains vital in our political and cultural life: the idealized self-image of a multiethnic, multiracial democracy, hospitable to difference but united by a common sense of national belonging" (Slotkin

---

[44] As developed in Slotkin later volume, *Gunfighter Nation* (1992), the myth of the frontier has long been enmeshed with the racialized violence at the heart of savage war: "a mythic trope and an operative category of military doctrine" that is convinced of the impossibility of peaceful coexistence. In savage war, White Americans justify the drive to exterminate the enemy Other. This racialized enemy is always presumed to be savagely bloodthirsty, thus necessitating and justifying the extreme and annihilatory violence deployed by the White American (Slotkin 1992: 11, 12). Untrammeled violence is, the myth insists, the only way to defeat the racialized enemy Other. And in defeating these "savage" enemies, the heroic American man —embodiment of the nation—achieves a muscular, admirable spiritual regeneration at the levels of both individual and nation (Slotkin 1973; 1992). As convincingly demonstrated by numerous scholars, for subsequent generations of Americans a series of populations have become versions of the enemy Other to be hated, subjugated, and eliminated, and other sites—including the Philippines, Cuba, Mexico, Vietnam, Iraq, and Afghanistan—have become the frontier to be "torn violently" for the greater glory of America (e.g., Drinnon 1980; Drinnon 1980; Kaplan 2002; Hoefle 2004; Eperjesi 2005; Judis 2005; Dunbar-Ortiz 2014; Slotkin 2017).

[45] Slotkin notes that the genre of combat films that emerged in 1943 known as the "platoon movie," set out to craft "a vision of the kind of nation that Hollywood, acting as custodian of public myth, thought we should become. American nationality is symbolized by a multi-ethnic and multi-racial military unit, pitted against an enemy figured as racially monolithic," with America cast as "the paternal 'liberator' nation. ... These films explicitly address the central paradox of American nationality: the persistence of racial inequality and exclusion in a supposed democracy. Almost every movie platoon includes (among a range of ethnic types) a Jewish soldier from Brooklyn; but what is to us a cliché was, in 1943, an explicit rebuke of the anti-Semitism that was rampant in America through the 1930s and 1940s. Even more striking was the way these movies strained to include Black soldiers in on-screen platoons. The US Army in World War II was racially segregated. Hollywood deliberately set reality aside to create allegories of racial integration" (Slotkin 2017: 4).

2001: 469). As America's first non-White president, bearing the race identity African American, Obama stands as the seeming realization of a race-blind meritocracy, the perfect embodiment of that ideal multiethnic, multiracial democracy first imagined through World War II combat movies.

Indeed, scholars and analysts optimistically celebrated Obama's election to the presidency as signifying a "post-racial" turning point in American culture and politics. In addition, the range of ways in which Obama's own policies on race as well as declining conditions for African Americans over the course of his presidency punctured this myth (Taylor 2016), the optimism was unambiguously ruptured, of course, by the 2016 election of Trump and the rise of White supremacy over the four years of his presidency.[46] The hope buoyed by Obama's election was twofold: not only would Obama, as lawyer–president–commander-in-chief, repair the disdain for liberal legality that had characterized the Bush administration, but that, as a Christian African American with a Muslim name, descended of a Kenyan father and a White American mother, and raised in plural and cosmopolitan settings, this first Black president would – symbolically and substantively – repair the long-standing subjugation of African Americans and reverse the Islamophobia cultivated by the Bush administration. However, as signaled by a prominent speech entitled "A New Beginning," delivered just four months after he took office,[47] in the geopolitically significant site of Cairo, Obama's strategy for dealing with his racialized identity would be to gesturally nod toward it and then reinforce the dominant ideologies of the United States as both nation and as imperial power. Through this discursive and ideological strategy, "race" is acknowledged but in a token manner, and the discounting of life implicit to dominant US ideologies is reinscribed. In the process, Obama represented his rise to the United States' apex political/military office as evidence of American egalitarianism, standing before his audience as both the potential and the realization of the mythic American dream.

> Now, much has been made of the fact that an African American with the name Barack Hussein Obama could be elected President. But my

---

[46] Celebrating America's arrival at a desirable "post-racial" ideal has been somewhat reinvigorated by America's first African Asian vice president, Kamala Harris.

[47] And some five months before Obama was awarded the 2009 Nobel Peace Prize.

> personal story is not so unique. The dream of opportunity for all people
> has not come true for everyone in America, but its promise exists for all
> who come to our shores – and that includes nearly 7 million American
> Muslims in our country today who, by the way, enjoy incomes and
> educational levels that are higher than the American average.
> (Obama 2009)[48]

Later in the speech he delivered a mythic account of American race
history, papering over both the founding and the United States' continuing violence and inequality:

> For centuries, black people in America suffered the lash of the whip as
> slaves and the humiliation of segregation. But it was not violence that
> won full and equal rights. It was a peaceful and determined insistence
> upon the ideals at the center of America's founding.
>
> (Obama 2009)

Representing the United States as essentially and always just and
nonviolent, Obama's celebration of America's founding ideals reproduces dominant accounts by disavowing the discounting of life effected
on a genocidal scale through the United States' founding violence
(Dunbar-Ortiz 2014) and by a state designed as a "pro-slavery
democracy" (Mbembe 2019: 17). Similarly, his lyrical account of the
"full and equal rights" won by Black Americans again discounts life by
disavowing the necropolitical reality of persisting and violent inequalities experienced by, and directed at, Black Americans (some of which
were detailed in Chapter 1). Obama's Cairo address evidences his
adoption of that revised political myth launched through the genre of
World War II combat movies, idealizing the United States as the
world's exemplary multiethnic, multiracial democracy, in which difference thrives but is unproblematically united under a shared sense of
national belonging. Almost seventy years after World War II combat
movies remade "race" in the service of belligerent imperialism,
Obama – his embodiment, his discourse – again subsumes racial subordination to the overarching project of American imperialism. By "con-
nect[ing] racial difference to a story of US advancement" (Cobb 2015:
79), Obama's Cairo address adheres to prior moments in US nation-
making in which the "office of the president, a powerful extension of
the US state, appropriated black images and black citizenship over

---

[48] At obamawhitehouse.archives.gov/the-press-office/remarks-president-cairo-univer-
sity-6-04-09.

time, to suppress autonomous black freedom struggles and to promote less threatening racial narratives (or fictions)" (Cobb 2015: 65). As argued below, drawing on Melani McAlister, one of necropolitical law's guises becomes through Obama a disembedded account of racial diversity, such that non-White race identities become co-opted to the project of legitimizing American imperialism (McAlister 2005: 206).

3.4.2 Military Multiculturalism and Obama

American cultural texts have long featured narratives and images legitimizing and justifying American imperialism (Kaplan 2002; McAlister 2005; Lubin 2021; Slotkin 1973, 1992, 2001, 2017). The multiethnic variation on the frontier myth's theme of White nation (Slotkin 2001) discussed above is one instance of how the home/abroad co-constitutions of American identity have shown an adaptable plasticity, modifying American political myth in ways that subsume difference within the nation to the imperial project of necropolitics.

A further facet of necropolitics at home and abroad is discernible in the adaptations wrought seamlessly through the imperial spectacles marking the first Persian Gulf War. American culture's imperial spectacles have typically bestowed heroic visibility on militarized White male figures, while cultivating passivity in those cast as spectators, and rendering invisibly oppressed, racially Othered "foreign" populations (Kaplan 202: 106–20). Chapter 5's analysis of Trump's announcement of the killing of al-Baghdadi shows how, in keeping with key features of Kaplan's argument, Trump stages himself as the militarized White male hero so central to American spectacles of imperialism. With Obama however, his race identity adds a layer of complexity to the spectacle of imperialism. President Obama figures as male, certainly, and explicitly militarized because the president is also commander-in-chief, but how does the first Black president of the United States inflect and alter American spectacles of imperialism?

Melani McAlister's theorizing on military multiculturalism illuminates the layers and complexities through which the subordinations, racism, and necropolitical violence experienced by racialized minorities within the domestic sphere of the United States become subsumed to imperialism's belligerent nationalism. Consistent with popular culture's role in shaping American political myth and, in turn, conditioning US statecraft (e.g., Rogin 1988, 1990; McBride 2006), McAlister shows how news coverage in the first Persian Gulf War (August 1990 to February 1991) strategically constructed "the racial diversity of the new military" (2005: 250). Repeatedly, media's "predominant theme was that the US soldiers were a microcosm of the US population – a heterogeneous mixture of races and ethnicities" (McAlister 2005: 250). Papering over continuing fault-lines relating to race, gender, and sexuality in both the military and the nation, "images of the military took on a particular emotional investment" as "the self-representation of the nation, and thus the United States at the height of its reconstituted global power" (McAlister 2005: 250).[49]

It was in this context that "the preeminent soldier-statesman, the sign of the nation in its expansionist mode" came to be embodied by General Colin Powell, "the first African American chairman of the Joint Chiefs of Staff, ... perhaps the most respected public leader to emerge from the war" (McAlister 2005: 253). As president/commander-in-chief, Obama's race identity intensifies this embodied preeminence. Specifically(drawing on Kantorowicz), Obama's three non-White bodies – president, commander-in-chief, lawyer – far exceeded Colin Powell as sign and substance of the nation in its militarized, imperial, expansionist mode. By staging himself as the exemplar of America's multiracial meritocratic democracy, Obama reproduces the visual dynamics so central to the military's representations of itself in the first Gulf War. In the process, he perpetuates, for the War on Terror, the papering over of persistent racialized subordination in the domestic sphere of the United States, even as, in the figure and personification of the sovereign, he stages US militarized imperialism as legitimate and a-racial. In addition to the factor of race identity, this legitimacy is uniquely staged by Obama, in part because, by adroitly toggling between liberal legal discourse and the War-on-Terror script established by his predecessor, Obama delivers a far more sophisticated register for necropolitical law than Bush.[50]

---

[49] The "appropriate" multiculturalism of this newly diverse army became something of a foil to the inappropriate multiculturalism conservative forces saw as undermining college education, as well as socio-political life more broadly (McAlister 2005: 245–50).

[50] In addition to the Obama administration's articulations of a specifically legal framework for the War on Terror (Anderson and Wittes 2015; and Section 3.2 above), two years after the killing of bin Laden, Obama delivered a major policy speech calling for the United States to conduct itself in a manner that upholds the rule of law when addressing terrorism and providing parameters for new, seemingly rule-of-law–aligned policies for drone warfare. However, Obama—"The Drone Presidency" in David Cole's (2016) succinct assessment—oversaw significant

The Remarks offers one example of how Obama's dignity, race identity, and skillful melding of liberal legality and necropolitics imbue necropolitical law with gravitas, masking the annihilatory violence at work. As discussed below, in addition to fostering the American political myth of frontier justice, Obama justified the killing of bin Laden by relying on the myth of the chosen nation.

3.5 LAW, JUSTICE, AND THE CHOSEN NATION

American exceptionalism is encoded in Obama's opening words to the Remarks: "Tonight, I can report to the American people *and to the world* that the United States has conducted an operation that killed Osama bin Laden" (italics added). When Obama situates America and American action as inherently and necessarily global in impact,[51] there is a taken-for-granted quality in his assertion that legal-technical notions of sovereignty, as well as limits on state violence, do not apply to the United States. In the process, he articulates the myth of America as the chosen nation. This myth is characterized by three main ideas: first, the conviction that the United States is God's chosen nation, anointed to conduct "a special mission in the world" (Hughes 2018: 1); second, that this mission is a "calling" to transform the world" (Judis 2005: 1); and third, that "in carrying out this mission, the United States is representing the forces of good over evil" (Judis 2005: 2). The myth of the chosen nation is an expression of American exceptionalism.[52] Scholars attentive to the shadow side of American

expansions in the drone program. Spending on the War on Terror ballooned under his administration and, unsurprisingly, increased even more during the Trump administration. Alongside his faithful echoing of the War on Terror discourse established by the Bush administration, Obama's unique capacity for "speaking the law" (Anderson and Wittes 2015) and his apex political-military office illustrate the capacious continuities of military multiculturalism in American cultural life.

[51] This particular killing most certainly played out in a global theatre. References to the United States, Afghanistan, Pakistan, and the globe run throughout the Remarks.

[52] Richard Hughes describes the political myth of the chosen nation as "[a]mong the most powerful and persistent of all the myths that Americans invoke about themselves" and as "the idea that lies at the heart of American exceptionalism" (2018: 32). Judis points out that while a nation's self-authored conviction in its exceptional status and quality is not unique to the United States, the United States is unique in history because—unlike Britain, Nazi Germany, or the Soviet Union—it has yet to suffer a crushing setback to its hopes. Over the last three centuries, America has steadily risen in prosperity and power. As a result, successive generations have passed on the belief

political myth note how these myths, which are rooted in Puritan New England colonies and interpretations of Christian text, have played a role in justifying America's founding violence, including the genocidal dispossession of indigenous peoples, the annexation of territory under Mexican and Spanish rule, and, relatedly, the discriminatory treatment of Hispanic peoples (Lipset 1996; Madsen 1998; Dunbar-Ortiz 2014: 40–55; Hughes 2018).

Importantly, the religious, sacralizing underpinning for American political myth has crucial implications for law. This is because, in addition to narrative working as law's meaning-making container and vehicle (Cover 1983), law in general in the secular, modern nation-state signals its secular modernity by turning away from "God" and transcendence as authority, instead grounding its authority in the territorial space of "nation" (Fitzpatrick 2001: 107).[53] Summarizing scholarship on the co-constitutions of nation, narration, and secular modern law, Ruth Buchanan and Sundhya Pahuja write,

> A key shift that heralds modernity as a distinct period is, of course, the loss of external foundations or what is sometimes shorthanded as the "death of God" ... provok[ing] a crisis of authority such that institutions in modernity face the need to become self-founding, ... posit[ing] their sources of authority within the modern world (and often within themselves) rather than beyond the world in some transcendent source. ... Law and nation each hold themselves out to be autonomous, legitimate and authoritative; ... they narrate, or author [this authority] themselves. Law's narratives assert that the law is what the law says it is. And nations, too, must create themselves by narrating their own stories of origin.
>
> (2004: 142)

Notably, in the specific instance of the United States, a particular variation marks the self-authoring, self-authorizing narrative that ties

---

that the United States has a special role in the world (2004). In referring to the myth of the chosen nation, I adopt Judis's and Hughes's terminology. See Judis (2004), Hughes (2018), Jackson (2005: 35), and Lipset (1996).

[53] This seeming fixity in the territory of "nation" lends itself to the violence and expansion of imperialism, Fitzpatrick argues, because "law" also repeatedly posits itself as a force against savagery, such that "coherence is sought in nation through the excluding of what is thus other to it" in explicitly and implicitly racialized terms (2001: 125). The Euro-Atlantic discourses of the "civilizing mission," "development," and "human rights," for example, become grounds on which certain nations elevate themselves as exemplary lawful nations and authorize their imperialism (Fitzpatrick 2001).

law to that other self-authoring, self-authorizing concept, "nation." In the discursive and cultural formations of the United States, while "law" and "nation" do indeed refer to and find authority in each other, we find a subversion of secular modernity: the American narrative of law, nation, and authority constructs the United States as *itself* transcendent. And, as already illustrated by Obama's opening words and as further detailed in the analysis of his Remarks yet to come, the vehicle for this sacralizing self-transcendence is political myth. This US-as-transcendent quality evident in Obama's opening invocation of the myth of the chosen nation is reinforced in the closing of the Remarks, which asserts the chosen nation's mission-driven zeal:

> [T]oday's achievement [the killing of bin Laden] is a testament to the greatness of our country and the determination of the American people. . . . [W]e are once again reminded that America can do whatever we set our mind to. That is the story of our history, whether it's the pursuit of prosperity for our people, or the struggle for equality for all our citizens; our commitment to stand up for our values abroad, and our sacrifices to make the world a safer place. . . . [W]e can do these things not just because of wealth or power, but because of who we are: one nation, under God, indivisible, with liberty and justice for all.[54]

In claiming American innocence and virtue, Obama illustrates the profound continuities of necropolitical law in the long War on Terror. He echoes Woodrow Wilson's 1917 War Message to Congress,[55] where Wilson asserted how, in seeking "peace and justice" in the world, the United States had "no selfish ends to serve" other than making the world "safe for democracy."[56] And, in addition to the "truly voluminous

---

[54] In tracing the contestations between a secularism drawn from Enlightenment thought and religiosity as a founding value of society, Margulies highlights the manner in which the last six words of the Pledge of Allegiance, "with liberty and justice for all," written in 1892, reflect Enlightenment values. In contrast, "under God" was a very recent addition, added in the Cold War context of 1954 in an effort to distinguish the United States from "godless communism" (Margulies 2013: 24–25).

[55] In a telling illustration of the long durée informing the long War on Terror, Wilson's 1917 speech echoes James Madison's 1812 War Message to Congress, but, as highlighted in Chapter 2, Wilson adds the dimension of making the world safe for democracy absent from Madison's address; https://millercenter.org/the-presidency/presidential-speeches/june-1-1812-special-message-congress-foreign-policy-crisis-war.

[56] Announcing the severing of diplomatic relations with Germany and the United States' entry into World War I, Wilson said, "Our object now, as then, is to vindicate the principles of peace and justice in the life of the world. . . . The world

store of texts" recording the Bush administration's insistence that the War on Terror was being fought to save the world from a catastrophic threat to democracy (Jackson 2005: 16), eighty-six years after Wilson's justifications George W. Bush announced Operation Iraqi Freedom. In keeping with the Orwellian statecraft of doublespeak, Bush characterized the 2003 US invasion as "military operations to disarm Iraq," while insisting that these disarming operations were

> to free its people and to defend the world from grave danger. ... We have no ambition in Iraq, except to remove a threat and restore control of that country to its own people. ... Our nation enters this conflict reluctantly. ... We will pass through this time of peril and carry on the work of peace. We will defend our freedom. We will bring freedom to others.
>
> (Bush 2003)

In addition to echoing his predecessors, Obama's closing phrase repeats the closing line of the Pledge of Allegiance, explicitly characterizing the killing of bin Laden as an act of patriotism saturated with the virtues of "our sacrifices to make the world a safer place" and "liberty and justice for all." By reinvigorating the myth of the chosen nation ("we can do these things ... because of who we are: one nation, under God") and looking to political myth rather than liberal legality for the authority and legitimation of precedent, Obama presents the killing of bin Laden as an expression of the United States fulfilling its sacred mission. Liberal legality is displaced when an extrajudicial, extraterritorial act of state violence becomes emblematic of "the greatness of our country" in both the national arena ("prosperity for our people, ... equality for all our citizens") and the world ("our commitment to stand up for our values abroad and our sacrifices to make the world a safer place"). By casting extrajudicial, extraterritorial aggression as selfless, sacrificial, and ethically motivated, the assertion is that such acts of violence are (affectively, transcendentally) legitimate. The foundation of that legitimacy is not national or international doctrinal law, but the self-scripted ascendancy of the United States as the chosen nation, such that what "justice" means is brewed within the cultural container of political myth.

must be made safe for democracy"; at https://wwi.lib.byu.edu/index.php/Wilson%27s_War_Message_to_Congress.

3.5.1 The Political Myth of American Innocence

Justice is conditioned by American political myth in a further, related sense when Obama rehearses the entrenched notion of American innocence in relation to the 9/11 attacks:

> It was nearly 10 years ago that a bright September day was darkened by the worst attack on the American people in our history. The images of 9/11 are seared into our national memory—hijacked planes cutting through a cloudless September sky; the Twin Towers collapsing to the ground; black smoke billowing up from the Pentagon; the wreckage of Flight 93 in Shanksville, Pennsylvania, where the actions of heroic citizens saved even more heartbreak and destruction. ... The American people did not choose this fight. It came to our shores, and started with the senseless slaughter of our citizens.
>
> (Obama 2011)

Representing the 9/11 attacks as "an unprovoked and undeserved assault on an innocent and peaceful nation" (Jackson 2005: 54) – another pillar of war-on-terror discourse from the earliest moments after 9/11 (e.g., Silberstein 2002; Jackson 2005; Anker 2014) – amplifies myths of American innocence, disregards analysis of the role of "blowback" in American foreign policy (Johnson 2004), and legitimizes America's violence in the War on Terror.

In keeping with the "surprising level of consistency" marking the counterterror state's discourse (Jackson 2005: 20), Obama echoes Bush in re-narrating the attacks as "a wound on the body politic of the nation itself" (Jackson 2005: 32). In a speech marking the first anniversary of the 9/11 attacks, Bush spoke of "the images" having been "seared on our souls" (Bush 2002b). Nine years after this Bush metaphor, Obama says, "[t]he images of 9/11 are seared into our national memory." The word "seared" represents the attacks as a burning, violent, painful, and indelible scarring on America's national "soul" (Bush 2002) and "memory" (Obama 2011).

Obama's language is heavily affective in characterizing the nation's wounded body politic as an expression of its innocence. He invokes the senses of touch, smell, sight, and sound, alongside the affects of trauma, loss, and grief, with the repeated alliterative, plosive consonant k sounds (hijacked, cloudless, cutting) aurally reproducing the violence of that trauma. In addition to rehearsing the myth of American innocence, in casting America and Americans as permanently scarred victims, Obama's account revitalizes the "appeal to identity" strategically crafted by the counterterror state from the very onset of its war-on-terror discourse (Jackson 2005: 59). In its reliance on constructions of identity, the counterterror state has turned away from deliberative processes as a means for addressing social conflict. Instead, by casting terrorists as guilty, evil, barbaric, and inhuman, and America and its coalition partners as innocent, "heroic, decent and peaceful – the defenders of freedom" (Jackson 2005: 59), deliberative processes and critical engagements are rendered irrelevant. As part of this sidelining of deliberative processes and critical engagements, the role of American foreign policy and the failure of US leaders to heed the warnings of intelligence services that an al Qaeda attack on American soil was imminent escape scrutiny (Young 2003; Powers 2004). Narrating the attacks through the lens of identities depoliticizes and decontextualizes the events, and pathologizes the enemy (Silberstein 2002; Mamdani 2004; Jackson 2005; Asad 2007). In short, the myth of American innocence works with the identities cast by the counterterror state's discourse to legitimize the necropolitical discounting of life enacted in the killing of bin Laden, and in the War on Terror more broadly.

When Obama moves the narrative arc of the Remarks from the public, iconic images of 9/11 to the domestic spaces of "nation," he deploys a standard trope of imperial spectacles in American culture: the "notion of the nation as a home, as a domestic space" to call into being "its intimate opposition to the notion of the foreign" (Kaplan 2003: 59). In Obama's Remarks, the familial and very intimate experiences of loss become national and nation-making;

> And yet we know that the worst images are those that were unseen. . . .
> The empty seat at the dinner table. Children who were forced to grow
> up without their mother or their father. Parents who would never know
> the feeling of their child's embrace. Nearly 3,000 citizens taken from us,
> leaving a gaping hole in our hearts.

In addition to implicitly reinforcing the violent and exclusionary nationalism of the post-9/11 United States as "homeland" (Kaplan 2003) and affectively reinscribing the myth of American innocence, the lexical chain "forced . . . never . . . taken," culminating in the permanent "gaping hole in our heart," underlines the triple violence of death, unforeseeable death, and unforeseeable death on a large scale. Grief, shock, and loss are simultaneously public/private when represented as a civic embodiment bearing a single punctured heart. The affects of love, grief, and loss span and link the spheres of familial and national, such that the story of "nation" coheres around this felt, collectively embodied loss.

Additionally, by situating "home" and the sphere of the domestic as the site of the nation's loss, Obama figures both "nation" and "home" as that "arresting emblem" of modern nationalism, the "cenotaphs and tombs of Unknown Soldiers" (Anderson 1991: 8). The "empty seat at the dinner table," like the empty tomb of the Unknown Soldier, symbolizes the "colossal sacrifice" of nation-sacralizing death in war, symbolizing and expressing the "deep, horizontal comradeship" of imagined communities (Anderson 1991: 7). The Remarks becomes an expression of the "public ceremonial reverence" attaching to these empty spaces, an emptiness so influentially theorized by Anderson as "saturated with ghostly *national* imaginings" (1991: 8).

3.6 THE DOUBLE VIOLENCE OF LAW'S FRAGMENTARY ARCHIVE

Read against the grain, Obama's construction of the unseen "worst images" in domestic and familial terms – the empty spaces of heart and home – points to dynamics of erasure, disavowal and silencing so central to the double violence of law's archive (Mawani 2012). In the simultaneity of what law's records make present and render absent, power typically erases accounts of its excesses so as to legitimize the symbolic and material force of law (Mawani 2012). One instance of erasure embedded in Obama's Remarks relates to his characterization of 9/11 as "the worst attack on the American people in our history." At one level, emphasizing American ownership and experience of the tragedy and trauma of 9/11 ("Nearly 3,000 citizens taken from us") discounts the lives of foreign nationals who died in the attacks and sustains continuity between the Remarks and prior official rhetoric constructing America as a unique victim. Continual emphasis on America's unique victimhood bestows the politically valuable status of primary victim, thereby implicitly justifying the violence of war (Jackson 2005; Esch 2010).

Moreover, emphasizing America's unique victimhood is coherent with the counterterror state's strategic refusal to frame America's experience of terrorism in transnational terms. Rather than creating global community by situating the 9/11 attacks in the category of political violence also experienced by people in other countries, the counterterror state fostered the myth of the chosen nation through its (perhaps unexpected) variation on the exceptional victim (Kaplan 2003; Jackson 2005). In the process, as a fragment of law's archive, the Remarks records an American grievance while erasing from both the record and social memory American violence toward others.

Amy Kaplan makes a related point illuminating how keywords constructed for the War on Terror do much of this ideological work of erasure by offering a variation on the theme of American exceptionalism, which is historical exceptionalism. In the naming of the site of the World Trade Center attacks "ground zero,"[57] American innocence is retold and folded into a narrative of historical exceptionalism, into "almost an antinarrative that claims that the event was so unique and unprecedented as to transcend time and defy comparison or historical analysis" (Kaplan 2003: 56). Kaplan elaborates:

> Historical exceptionalism ... is intimately related to a long-standing tradition of American exceptionalism, a story about the nation's uniqueness in time and place. The historical exceptionalism implicit in the appellation "ground zero" is belied by the history of the term itself ... coined to describe the nuclear strikes on Hiroshima and Nagasaki. Yet the wholesale adoption of the name "ground zero" for the destruction in New York has not prompted any overt comparisons to Hiroshima and Nagasaki. September 11 was not compared to August 6. Instead the analogy we heard over and over again was to Pearl Harbor. ... The repeated overemphasis on the one event worked to disavow the obvious connections to the other, ... consigning this prior reference to historical amnesia.
>
> (Kaplan 2003: 56–57)

In her poignant response to September 11, novelist Barbara Kingsolver (2001) reminds readers that, three and a half years after the Japanese bombing of Pearl Harbor, "American planes bombed a plaza in Japan where men and women were going to work, where schoolchildren were playing, and more humans died at once than anyone thought possible. Seventy thousand in a minute. Imagine." Read together, Kingsolver and Kaplan remind us of a US tradition of discounting life through strategic, selective narratives of American imperialism in relation to the world. In the process, American innocence is fostered through historical amnesia.

---

[57] See also the discussion of "ground zero" in relation to the 2017 MOAB strike in Afghanistan in Chapter 6.

In the Remarks, Obama's reproduction of the Bush administration's account of the 9/11 attacks has the effect described by Kaplan; through repeated overemphasis of the dominant narrative, a series of problematic connections are disavowed. When Obama says, "And yet we know, the worst images are *unseen*," he retells the War on Terror so as to erase from law's official record a counternarrative of worst *seen* images, including, for example, images of routinized torture at Abu Ghraib. More profoundly erasing than the opaque black oblongs marking redactions in the torture memos, by simply not acknowledging these and other seen and unseen "worst images," Obama implicitly reproduces his February 2009 declaration that, under his administration, America was to be "post-torture."[58] The absences in Obama's narrative of nation in relation to torture in the War-on-Terror work to secure, yet again, American innocence (Razack 2012).

In keeping with the statecraft of erasure evident in the Remarks, the two primary visuals accompanying the text – Obama's video announcing bin Laden's death[59] and the familiar Situation Room photograph[60] – extend the narrative of American innocence and occlude the violence of America's necropolitical law.

3.6.1 Obama's Video Announcement

The video, first and foremost, conveys the legitimizing resonance attaching to a public declaration delivered by a head of state. Distinct from the secrecy and alarm attaching to Ford's 1974 disclosure that the United States had made a practice of assassinating foreign enemies (discussed above), Obama's public announcement celebrates and legitimizes state violence. Additionally, the video draws on the modalities of image and sound to foreground symbolic legitimacy, in part through aesthetic representations of order, long-held wealth, and sovereign power. For example, the room shows a pleasing symmetry in the twin lamps that flank the highly polished wood of the doors at the end of the corridor. An ornate chandelier casts a soft, golden light over all we see,

---

[58] In this address to Congress, a month after taking office, Obama said, "I can stand here tonight and say without exception or equivocation, America does not torture."

[59] Video of President Obama's announcement on bin Laden's death is available at www.youtube.com/watch?v=m-N3dJvhgPg. In general, major newspapers worldwide carried an image of Obama delivering this speech as the pictorial accompaniment to the report's text (Kennedy 2012: 265–66).

[60] The Situation Room photograph, www.flickr.com/photos/whitehouse/5680724572/in/album-72157626507626189/.

reflecting off the floors and walls. Associations with royalty are evoked by the red of Obama's tie, the red upholstery of the two gilded chairs in the frame, and the red of the carpet, all of which appear to be an identical shade of red, adding to the visual harmony of the scene. Not only is red a color with particular affective potency (Bertelsen and Murphie 2010: 138), the red of the carpet appears especially rich, especially royal, because it has a border of gold. And when the camera dwells on Obama's confident stride down the carpeted corridor, the plush richness of the carpet is also conveyed by the pin-drop silence that accompanies Obama's steps. In the silence that is broken only by Obama's voice, in the symmetries, colors, rich beauty, and golden light, there is the sense of a power that (apparently effortlessly) controls the world.

Although it was almost midnight at the time the Remarks was recorded, Obama looks impeccable in his suit. He shows no signs of the human need for sleep or of having performed as president and commander-in-chief through an especially fraught and demanding day. Echoing the political theology of the king's two bodies (Kantorowicz 1957),[61] Obama appears, delivering the Remarks, as both mortal and more than mortal in his remarkable but composed vitality. Indeed, in an overlapping sequence of events, especially telling of the co-constitutions of publicity and secrecy (Dean 2002), stagecraft and statecraft (Schill 2009) even as the raid was unfolding, Obama hosted the Annual White House Correspondents' Dinner, at which his wit and charm sparkled and entertained, and offered not a clue that the killing of bin Laden was underway (BBC 2011). Presumably, had the "operation" not succeeded, the attempted assassination would never have been disclosed.

Through the video's meticulous staging, Obama embodies a gravitas and certainty that surpasses human frailties. His more-than-mortal presentation is entirely in keeping with the room's evocations of wealth, power, and permanence. In short, the video illustrates how necropolitical law relies upon a range of cultural and semiotic modalities to assert authority and legitimacy. The staging and delivery of the Remarks disavow the transgression of liberal legality inherent to extra-judicial, extraterritorial killing. When the president makes a public

---

[61] In *The King's Two Bodies* (1957), Ernst H. Kantorowicz famously traces the historical problem posed by sovereignty embodied simultaneously in the immortal body politic and the very mortal body natural.

announcement from a setting that signifies authority and legitimacy, iconic images, public gesture, and celebratory declarations become the platform for an account of legitimate power that turns away from liberal legality even as it inscribes necropolitical law.

3.6.2 The Situation Room Photograph: Obscuring Law's Violence

The Situation Room photograph depicts Obama's national security team watching a screen we cannot see.[62] With the exception of the uniformed Brigadier General Webb, who is working on his laptop, this room full of powerful state actors watches the screen beyond the photograph with intense concentration and fixed expressions. In this image, the United States is pictured as omnipresent watcher, surveilling and managing territory beyond its borders. The image subsumes the world to a US sphere of action and control, with no suggestion that this planetary jurisdiction needs to be explained or justified. Extraterritorial power is seamlessly presented as the proper order of things.

In a striking parallel to the post-9/11 re-semanticization of "ground zero" (Kaplan 2003), the Situation Room photograph visually displaces the primary scene of violence. In representing "spectatorship and virtualization" (Kennedy 2012: 265) instead of the Abbottabad raid, the photograph captures a double paradox: first, as law's record, it simultaneously reveals and conceals a killing; and second, in spite of hyper-mediatization, we see *less* of law's violence.[63] The arresting power of the Situation Room photograph resides, in part, in the action and state actors we *imagine*, even as we gaze upon the suspense and stillness of the photograph.[64] Indeed, the suspense captured by the Situation Room photograph lent itself to early contestation as to what was actually unfolding in the room at the time the photograph was taken. As Liam Kennedy highlights, the "first media reports, supported by

---

[62] It is noteworthy that the Situation Room photograph depicts an especially masculine space: only two women are visible in a room otherwise populated by men. One of these women is Secretary of State Hillary Clinton, and her gesture, of a hand held over her mouth, is the most dramatic expression of an affective response from anyone in the image. The other woman, Audrey Tomason, Director for Counterterrorism, stands at the back of the room. Eight years later, when Trump disseminated a Situation Room photograph to accompany his announcement on the killing of al-Baghdadi, no women were present.

[63] I am grateful to Alejandra Azuero for this point.

[64] In *The Civil Contract of Photography* (2008), Ariella Azoulay calls for dynamic watching—injecting movement and time into the stillness of the photograph.

White House spin, stated that the president and his team were watching live footage of the killing of bin Laden. Under media scrutiny, this story quickly swerved after it was admitted that only a small portion of the video viewed was live at the scene" (2012: 263). The quick swerve in the story reveals the state's ready participation in misrepresentation, which is just one of the strands of necropolitical law informing this event.

In what it does show, the Situation Room photograph captures another major strand of necropolitical law: that the authority of state resides in a national security team rather than in a (peacetime) cabinet, an apex court, or law's public thingness. With the national security team center stage, the photograph reinscribes a post-9/11 militarized civil sphere in which secrecy and counterterror are privileged in governance (Lutz 2009; Masco 2014). The uniformed brigadier general, taking the seat usually occupied by the president (*Washington Post* 2011), potently signals the centrality of the military in the governance of our post-9/11 world. In the tense demeanors of the national security team, augmented by Clinton's gesture of concern – her hand held over her mouth – we see affect appropriate to liberal legality displayed: when lives are at stake, decisions and actions are informed not by untrammeled bloodlust but by intense concentration and a somber gravitas. Implicitly working to replace those worst seen images of Americans gleefully torturing detainees, the Situation Room photograph retrieves the myth of American innocence so that American violence is disavowed, even as it is being exercised.

A further representation of conduct appropriate to American innocence and liberal legality might be read into the photograph's apparent delivery of transparency. Even as it displaces the primary scene of violence, the Situation Room photograph appears to supply transparency – an attribute of law as public thing – by taking us into the immediacy and intimacy of the inner workings of state power. Liam Kennedy has characterized this move as the construction of *visibility* as a species of transparency and legitimacy (2012: 267). In appearing to deliver transparency by showing us an otherwise secret state space populated by clean, orderly, concerned people, mostly dressed for work in corporate settings, and taking their work very seriously, indeed, the violence of the killing of bin Laden is deflected, is rendered absent within the frame of the image. The image is thus of a piece with Obama's retelling of the War on Terror through erasures and disavowals of US violence and imperialism.

Some of the contradictions inherent to the coexistence of liberal legality and necropolitical law rose to the surface when the conservative group Judicial Watch filed Freedom of Information Act lawsuits against the US Department of Defense and the Central Intelligence Agency. Judicial Watch sought "all photographs and/or video recordings of Osama (Usama) bin Laden taken during and/or after the US military operation in Pakistan on or about May 1, 2011."[65] At both first instance[66] and on appeal,[67] the courts upheld the US government's position that legitimate national security interests barred public release of these images. The courts agreed with the state's assessment that America and Americans were safer if the killing and burial were not evidenced by images. At first instance, Judge James Boasberg said:

> A picture may be worth a thousand words. And perhaps moving pictures bear an even higher value. Yet in this case, verbal descriptions of the death and burial of Osama bin Laden will have to suffice, for this court will not order the release of anything more.
>
> (Mears 2012)

In the challenge to the state launched by Judicial Watch, there is a striking commonality between plaintiff and defendant in that the legality of the killing, in and of itself, goes unquestioned. This extraterritorial, extrajudicial killing is understood by both plaintiff and defendant as belonging to a register of post-9/11 violence which "creates its own interpretive conditions and so suspends ethical and legal conventions of response to its enactments" (Kennedy 2012: 265). Before the courts, Judicial Watch invokes the Freedom of Information Act and principles of democratic transparency, with no awareness of the underlying law at work: necropolitical law.

3.6.3 Captions, Capture, and Slippage

Captions are a key attribute of photographs (Azoulay 2010) relevant to the complexities of law's archive. In addition to facilitating administrative aspects of record keeping, captions tend to influence what we see on a first encounter with a photograph. With renewed viewings, a

---

[65] See www.judicialwatch.org/document-archive/foia-request-for-osama-bin-laden-photos/.

[66] *Judicial Watch, Inc. v U.S. Dep't. of Defense*, Civil Action No. 11-890 (JEB) (D.C.D.C. 2011). For a media report, see Mears (2012).

[67] See *Judicial Watch, Inc. v. U.S. Dep't. of Defense*, 715 F.3d 937 (D.C. Cir. 2013).

photograph may reveal bodies, objects, and representations that our caption-directed gaze initially dismisses (Azoulay 2010: 10). Captions, as well as the key terms linked to a photograph, frequently disseminate discursive categories and ways of seeing that serve state power (Azoulay 2010: 9; 2008: 16). The relationship between captions, photographs, and necropolitical law is of particular salience with the Situation Room photograph for three main reasons. First, this photograph is especially expressive of state management of media and publics because it was taken by the White House's official photographer, Pete Souza. Minimally mediated by nonstate sources, disseminated both through the White House Flickr website and major news media worldwide, this state-generated photograph depicting state elites in a highly secretive state space was assessed at one point as the most viewed image on the internet (Kennedy 2012: 265).

A second reason to highlight the relationship between captions, photographs, and state power is the unwieldy caption accompanying the Situation Room photograph that was originally given on the White House Flickr site: "President Obama and Vice President Joe Biden, along with members of the national security team, receive an update on the mission against Osama bin Laden in the Situation Room of the White House, May 1, 2011." The leaden, bureaucratic language of the official caption illustrates Azoulay's point that captions serve a clerical archival function while perpetuating state perspectives (Azoulay 2010:9; 2008:16).[68] In the almost parodic bureaucratese of the official caption, it is as if the weighty burden of truth and fact is carried by the sharp distinction between the official caption and the witty wordplay typical of captions found in the sphere of entertainment. Unsurprisingly, the unwieldy official caption has been discarded in common usage, as the image has come to be known as the Situation Room photograph (Kenney 2012: 262). This de facto caption speaks to the vitality of dialogic engagement between the spheres of officialdom and popular culture. Similar to the de facto re-naming of the Patriot Act, the Situation Room photograph was taken up and disseminated, enlivened in this way with a new, unofficial caption.

---

[68] Additionally, the unimaginative captions given to photographs on the White House Flickr site appear to extend the titling conventions reflected by the White House archive of speeches, in which bland description appears to be the norm.

As a shorthand, the unofficial caption also expresses US soft-power dominance in the global arena. In addition to its factual depictions, various imagined guises of the Situation Room as the material encapsulation of US global supremacy via networks of technology, intelligence, and military command, have featured in popular film and television worldwide.[69] With the photograph, as with popular cultural texts, the Situation Room becomes synecdochic, a part representing the whole that is the extensive fabric of US geopolitical power. The operative presumption is that a reference to "the Situation Room" needs no explanation, whereby this presumption of shared knowledge is itself an expression of the asymmetries of power shaping globalized media culture and the work of the imagination (Appadurai 1996).

As images, both Obama's video announcement and the Situation Room photograph show how, in the long War on Terror, the US state *curates* visuals designed to occlude the counterterror state's violence, in part by representing the United States as removed from violence but proximate to liberal legality's values, affects, and settings. As components of law's archive, these images are documents of law's double violence in the facets of "law's self-generating truth claims" through which "law cultivates its meanings and asserts its authority while at the same time concealing and sanctioning its material, originary, and ongoing violence" (Mawani 2012: 341). The double violence of law's archive, traceable in the co-constituting text of the state's representations *and* the raid, is simultaneously performed and concealed by the seductive surface of the beauty and order of the video and the displaced violence animating the Situation Room photograph. As contributions to law's archive, both of these images function as cultural precedent signifying authority, legitimate power, and a state properly protective of its besieged national community. Because the images conceal and sanction the material and ongoing violence of the raid and of the long War on Terror, it is only by reading against the grain that the visual and aural chaos and killing of the raid on bin Laden's compound can be disruptively inserted as part of this event, allowing the simultaneous absences and presences of necropolitical law to be recognized in law's incomplete and contested archive.

---

[69] TV critic Hank Stuever offers a useful discussion of television and film representations of the Situation Room (*Washington Post* 2011), www.washingtonpost.com/wp-srv/lifestyle/style/situation-room.html.

3.7 HEALING THE (CHOSEN) NATION: NARRATING JUSTICE

Straddling the ideological moves of repeated overemphasis, on the one hand, and deceptive narratives and images, on the other, the Remarks also demonstrates how Obama leaves unresolved the tension between competing myths of US identity – multiethnic civic community versus Whites-only frontier – by narrating a near-absence. In his idealized picture of "love of community and country," Obama chooses to minimally acknowledge (in a peripheral mention toward the end of the Remarks),[70] the post-9/11 violence inside the United States directed at "persons who appear to be 'Middle Eastern, Arab, or Muslim'" (Volpp 2002). As detailed in Chapter 2, US policy and practice has resulted in a fracturing of civic community, such that people perceived as "Middle Eastern, Arab, or Muslim" become "identified as terrorists, and disidentified as citizens" (Volpp 2002: 147). In the counterterror state's deliberate fostering of systemic racial profiling and necropolitical violence, the deep undercurrents of the myth of the frontier, premised on savage war against a fully dehumanized enemy and promising regeneration through violence (Slotkin 1973), are at work. At the same time, and consistent with his subsuming of American necropolitics into the American dream, so powerfully enacted in his 2009 Cairo address, in the Remarks Obama again minimizes the significance of these racialized attacks so as to narrate an account of how the United States has healed from the trauma of 9/11.

Given this insistence that the American people are united, loving, and neighborly, the killing of bin Laden becomes an opportunity to re-narrate the nation, minimizing the fractures of a racialized public and private violence such that nation, as loving community, becomes a healing trope. After all, "[c]onstructing a memory involves forgetting. Creating the narrative structure of a memory requires us to choose what to place in the story, and what to leave out" (Dudziak 2003: 213). Obama's decision to leave out almost completely the post-9/11 failures of domestic citizenship as a-racial is consistent with "the attempt by nationalist discourses persistently to produce the idea of the nation as a continuous narrative of national progress, the narcissism of self-generation, the primeval present of the *Volk*" (Bhabha 1990: 1).

---

[70] Toward the closing of the Remarks, Obama acknowledges that "the sense of unity that prevailed on 9/11 ... has, at times, frayed."

Obama's particular narration of nation is also significant in terms of narrating justice into being. Once again, Obama rehearses a trope established by Bush in 2001 in moving from recounting the healing nation to a cause-effect narrative of a justified war: "The American people did not choose this fight. It came to our shores, and started with the senseless slaughter of our citizens."[71] Strategically deploying a passive sentence construction to erase the role of the United States in founding and sustaining the War on Terror, Obama repeats the counterterror state's position that the War on Terror is a just war (McCarthy 2002) because, as he insists, it was embarked upon to protect those who matter, "our citizens, our friends, and our allies."

In directing the narrative from the motif of healing and civic community to the attainment of justice, the Remarks presents a particular subset of social actors as key: military, intelligence, and counterterrorism personnel. Obama says, "Tonight, we give thanks to the countless intelligence and counterterrorism professionals who've worked tirelessly to achieve this outcome." If the military has long been understood to be "the instrument of American patriotism" (Slotkin 2001: 477), the manner in which the categories "counterterrorism professionals" and "intelligence community" are situated alongside the military is surely significant. The term "spies" is not used, but it lurks beneath the surface of "counterterrorism professionals" and "intelligence community." In celebrating those who work in counterterrorism and intelligence, the Remarks firmly relocates "spies" from the shadowy realm of deception and treachery to the valorized realm of the heroic and virtuous. There is no acknowledgment of the shame and scandal attaching to the horrific abuses of (military, intelligence, and counterterrorism) power invoked by names like Abu Ghraib and Guantanamo.[72] Obama thereby re-erases from the fragmentary and

---

[71] See, for example, Bush's Address to the Nation on September 11, 2001: "The search is underway for those who were behind these evil acts. I have directed the full resources of our intelligence and law enforcement communities to find those responsible and to bring them to justice" (Bush 2001g).

[72] In contrast, it is noteworthy that, in a prominent speech he delivered at the National Defense University on May 23, 2013, Obama implicitly distinguished the conduct of the Bush presidency, which "us[ed] torture to interrogate our enemies, and detain[ed] individuals in a way that ran counter to the rule of law," from the strategies of his administration, which has "unequivocally banned torture, affirmed our commitment to civilian courts, worked to align our policies with the rule of law, and expanded our consultations with Congress." Toward the end of this

selective official archive of the counterterror state damning episodes
recording just how necropolitical the counterterror state's violence has
been. Extending the discounting of life so central – yet so hidden –
throughout the long War on Terror, the necropolitical law Obama
articulates buries, disguises, and conceals the counterterror state's
killing, maiming, and depoliticizing moves. Illustrating yet again the
potency of Cover's argument that law is co-constituted by narrative
(1983), the absented and tangentially acknowledged in Obama's
Remarks express a form of "collateral damage," in that the unacknowledged and diminished become the ghostly missing limbs of law's
archive, recording the disavowed and discounted victims of
American imperialism.

If for liberal legality, the category "law" represents state power that is
visible, scrutinized, and accountable, then a shift in the parameters of
legitimacy is effected when those who work in the hidden worlds of
counterterrorism and intelligence are publicly celebrated, even as their
exclusion from public scrutiny is understood as individual and national
virtue. The Remarks repeatedly celebrates military, counterterrorism,
and intelligence personnel for work that is tireless, heroic, painstaking,
courageous, skillful, professional, patriotic, and self-sacrificing. The
sacralizing language with which this new cast of justice actors (and their
work) is constructed provides an authority for "justice" that returns the
foundations of that authority to "nation." However, very specifically,
the justice constructed by the Remarks does not situate justice's authority in the secular, modern nation-state. Instead, the Remarks brings
justice into being by relying on the chosen nation, inscribing, as we
have seen, the United States as itself transcendent:

> Tonight, we give thanks to the countless intelligence and counterterror-
> ism professionals who've worked tirelessly to achieve this outcome. ...
> We give thanks for the men who carried out this operation, for they
> exemplify the professionalism, patriotism, and unparalleled courage of
> those who serve our country. ... [W]e are: one nation, under God,
> indivisible, with liberty and justice for all. ... May God bless you.
> And may God bless the United States of America.

Importantly, this sacralizing of the United States and of the personnel
who serve America – the military, intelligence, and counterterrorism

address, Obama said, "we commit to a process of closing GTMO, ... consistent with
our commitment to the rule of law" (Obama 2013).

personnel – again deploys affect (determination, sacrifice, courage, patriotism, service) within a rhetorical framework that recalls the cadence of a Christian sermon. As with the statement from Bush, Obama's Remarks demonstrates that America's president is, in addition to being commander-in-chief, also chaplain-in-chief (Silberstein 2002: 40–42). Obama's sacralizing language elevates the new justice actors to a space beyond scrutiny or knowability. They are invisible because of the (virtuous and self-sacrificing) nature of their work, and the justification for this invisibility is experienced as a feeling and in the manifestation of justice: "The American people do not see their work, nor know their names. But tonight, they feel the satisfaction of their work and the result of their pursuit of justice."

In short, justice is authorized by a shared feeling, an affective conviction in the United States as transcendent. In the process what is toppled is liberal legality. If law, in particular rule of law, scrutinizes power and requires accountability, then justice in the post-9/11 world of the Remarks resides in the production (and disposal) of dead bodies and in the feelings that are shared and bordered as uniquely American in ideological, territorial, and profoundly mythic terms.

3.8 CONCLUSION

If language and conduct embody the rules and values that are law (Davies 2002: 4), then a major announcement like Obama's Remarks cannot be dismissed as the empty rhetoric of a politician, nor can the manner in which bin Laden was killed be minimized as an exception. Law is embodied and enacted by the text of the Remarks and the text of this killing. It is a law that has uncoupled law and justice, celebrating secretive state actors and elevating an extrajudicial killing into an emblem of national virtue and international ascendancy. Together, the killing of bin Laden, the text of the Remarks, and the images accompanying this news reconfigured the very grounds of state legitimacy and valorized the discounting of life. Expressing this reconfiguration four and a half years after the event, the apparently extralegal killing of bin Laden took on a second life as a hyper-legal killing when the *New York Times* reported that, weeks before the Abbottabad raid, a secretive coterie of federal lawyers had engaged in "[s]tretching sparse precedents" to produce "rationales intended to overcome any legal obstacles" (Savage 2015). In five secret memos:

legal analysis offered the administration wide flexibility to send ground forces onto Pakistani soil without the country's consent, to explicitly authorize a lethal mission, to delay telling Congress until afterward, and to bury a wartime enemy at sea. By the end, one official said, the lawyers concluded that there was "clear and ample authority for the use of lethal force under US and international law.

(Savage 2015)

These memoranda were so intensely secret that "the White House would not let them [the four federal lawyers involved] consult aides or even the administration's top lawyer, Attorney General Eric H. Holder Jr." (Savage 2015). This stretching of sparse precedents in order to manufacture legal authority vividly illustrates Mawani's analysis about how, by

referencing statutes and judgments that came before and by determining which are apposite, law cultivates its meanings and asserts its authority while at the same time concealing and sanctioning its material, originary, and ongoing violence.

(Mawani 2012: 341)

Importantly, just as images of the killing and burial have been maintained as secret and inaccessible to publics, so, too, are these legal memoranda secret. And yet, demonstrating the role of publicity and deception in displacing law's public thingness and enacting necropolitical law, despite these many layers and sites of secrecy, the killing of bin Laden has taken on multiple afterlives, perpetuating its necropolitical law-making force. For example, in January 2016, almost five years after the bin Laden killing, in his State of the Union address, Obama invoked the killing of bin Laden as proof of "American determination [to] root out, hunt down, and destroy killers and fanatics who go after Americans," and he named others who had been targeted and would be targeted in the same way (Obama 2016). In that same month, Hillary Clinton provided "riveting" and "cinematic" accounts of her role in the 2011 killing of Osama bin Laden (Thrush 2016). A few months later, on the fifth anniversary of the bin Laden killing, "CNN's Peter Bergen was given unprecedented access to the White House to talk about this monumental mission and the war on terror with President Barack Obama" (Levine 2016).On that same day, the CIA marked the anniversary by "live tweeting" the raid, providing a blow-by-blow account, as if the raid were happening in that moment (Farrington 2016). And in the lead up to the November 2016 presidential election, images of the Situation Room photograph were a regular feature of the Clinton campaign visuals. When considered together with Trump's production of a Situation Room photograph to accompany his announcement of the killing of al-Baghdadi, the Obama photograph has taken on an iconic status as an image of necropolitical law, just as much a precedent as the extrajudicial killing and the burial at sea. And in 2021, when President Biden repeatedly invoked the killing of bin Laden as the delivery of "justice," Obama's 2011 Remarks and the associated images were collectively affirmed as canonical for the corpus of necropolitical law.

The enduring resonance of US political myth as law's cultural container – remaking vengeance as justice – is one way of explaining the widespread acceptance in the United States for the manner in which bin Laden and other "terrorists" have been killed and buried. Most crucially, the continuing significance of the myth of the frontier explains how violence directed at the dehumanized, savage, racially Other enemy serves US transcendence in two senses. First, this violence is in continuity with long-entrenched understandings of a "justice" that has no need for the institutions, processes, and actors of secular modernity's law. And second, this violence is "just" because it consolidates the nation, healing internal fractures by casting the shared affective significance of US political experience and myth as that which transcends law. Political myth, in short, makes sense of the enduring vitality of necropolitical law in the long War on Terror.

Chapter 4 shows how the October 2019 killing of ISIS leader Abu Bakr al-Baghdadi builds on the May 2011 killing of bin Laden. Obama's Remarks and the visuals generated by the Obama administration became templates for Trump's visual and verbal consolidations of necropolitical law. As texts of necropolitical law, both Obama's Remarks and Trump's announcement are coherent with a range of ways in which US state power continues to be exercised in a post-9/11 world, in which torture, detention without trial, and extrajudicial killings have come to be normalized as long as they occur in distant places upon the bodies of distant Others. If the essence of rule of law is contained in the fragile crucible of law's capacity to strive for an apartness from power and to use this (notionally) separate standing to scrutinize and limit power, then commonalities between Obama's three bodies – lawyer, president, commander-in-chief – and Trump's three bodies – businessman, president, commander-in-chief – illustrate how necropolitical law collapses and discards the separations of power central to the rule of law.

CHAPTER FOUR

THE KILLING OF AL-BAGHDADI

4.1 CONSOLIDATING NECROPOLITICAL LAW

On October 27, 2019, President Trump announced that Abu Bakr al-Baghdadi, the leader of ISIS, had been killed (Trump 2019). Technically, one might argue that al-Baghdadi killed himself. Pursued into a dead-end tunnel by attack dogs and US Special Forces, al-Baghdadi detonated a suicide vest, killing himself and two of his own children.[1] But if we consider the al-Baghdadi killing through the register of Trump's announcement – a register of achievement, celebration, and, indeed, of gloating – and in relation to a number of other recent killings designated "enemy" targets, then it seems fair to conclude that the killing was engineered by the United States. Chapter 4 analyzes the killing of al-Baghdadi as an illuminating example of how necropolitical law legitimizes and authorizes the discounting of life through the spectacular yet secretive killings that have become periodic markers of the long War on Terror.

Focusing on Trump's announcement, this chapter shows how the killing of al-Baghdadi, as text and event, builds on the killing of bin Laden (Chapter 3) to revitalize and consolidate necropolitical law. Tracing images, narratives, and arenas key to Trump's announcement, Chapter 4 argues that the al-Baghdadi killing re-inscribed the

---

[1] Although Trump said that Baghdadi had dragged three of his own children into the tunnel with him and that these three children had died when al-Baghdadi detonated his suicide vest, subsequent reports said that it was two rather than three children who died along with al-Baghdadi (Baldor and Burns 2019).

necropolitical separations that justify extrajudicial, extraterritorial killing and the discounting of certain lives as the desirable realization of "justice" in the long War on Terror. Specifically, by reinscribing and re-semanticizing the compound category "terrorist," by invoking established tropes and spectacles authorizing imperialism and racialized subordination, and by constructing new parameters for the sayable, Trump's announcement illustrates the role of a particular set of discourses, images, and affects in the corpus of necropolitical law.

Unlike Obama's announcement of the bin Laden killing, Trump's announcement about al-Baghdadi made more explicit use of tropes long associated with imperialism and racism (Section 4.2). Exploring the less-restrained Trump's characterization of al-Baghdadi as "savage" and a "monster," Section 4.2 also explores how Trump expanded these central tropes in the counterterror state's meaning-making project, first, through his celebration of Conan, a military dog that was slightly injured by the detonation of al-Baghdadi's suicide vest (Pengelly 2019), and, second, through his re-semanticization of "terrorist." In terms of visuals, Trump's statement on the al-Baghdadi killing was carefully staged, like Obama's announcement about bin Laden.[2] Newspapers, televisions, and websites worldwide carried the image of Trump standing at a lectern in the White House Diplomatic Room. As discussed in Section 4.3, with Trump standing in front of a portrait of George Washington, the image signaled how law as publicity recruits imperial spectacle, drawing on histories, traditions, and lineages of legitimacy to distract us from necropolitical law's dismantling of law as public thing.

Section 4.4 considers the dynamics of imperial spectacle in relation to Trump's pairing of the al-Baghdadi announcement with a press conference. Obama, in contrast, announced the bin Laden killing in the form of a speech recorded on video, broadcast on television and the internet, and reported by media worldwide. Departing from this precedent, Trump staged himself as the militarized, White male hero that has always been central to spectacles of imperialism in American culture (Kaplan 202). With assembled journalists enlisted into the role of deferential spectators, the press conference had the misleading appearance of a democratizing encounter between the president and "the people." Paradoxically, as spectacle, the same encounter worked in national and global audiences to de-democratize by cultivating the

---

[2] And the Trump Situation Room photograph immediately generated comparisons with its "historical twin," the Obama Situation Room photograph (Shaw 2019).

passivity of spectatorship alongside fascination with the superior killing and surveilling technologies of the counterterror state.

Section 4.5 analyzes how Trump, by speaking the previously unsayable, excavates a subterranean strand of necropolitical law. Trump did this in two ways. First, he amplified the explicitly commercial dimensions of necropolitical law's planetary jurisdiction by repeatedly asserting US entitlements to Syrian oil. Undoubtedly informed by the many decades of US discourse constructing Middle Eastern oil as an American national interest (McAlister 2005), Trump discards the guise of a virtuous US "imperial stewardship," thanks to which Middle Eastern oil is managed on behalf of all humanity (McAlister 2005: 41). Instead, consistent with Trump's statecraft of straight-talking anti-rhetoric rhetoric (Thompson 2016) and the exaltation of wealth, Trump states straightforwardly and repeatedly that the United States is entitled to Syrian oil, while noting the possibility that he might "make a deal" for the oil.[3]

Section 4.5 also analyzes how, by detailing al-Baghdadi's fear and torturous manner of death, Trump, as president and embodied voice of the state, lends the state's stamp of approval to public expressions of delight in the pain, suffering, and violent killing of a war-on-terror enemy. By speaking words that conjure images and evoke the affect of the raid, Trump brings into being, at the highest level of state discourse, the long War on Terror's celebration of violence upon the racially Othered body of the terrorist. Put differently, Trump augments spectacles of imperialism with an explicitly necropolitical visuality. Like the killing of bin Laden, and as traced in Chapter 3, this necropolitical visuality keeps official images of the raid secret, even as sensed, imagined scenes of enemy suffering are summoned into being behind our eyes. However, unlike the bin Laden killing and burial, in which it was left to *unofficial* entertainment media to supply the images of a terrorist being killed and buried at sea (Rajah 2016), Trump explicitly cultivates public, state-endorsed voyeurism in the death and suffering of enemies.

All in all, Trump's announcement both consolidates and expands necropolitical law's norms and relations. Amplifying the displacements of law as public thing through spectacle and publicity, his

---

[3] Specifically, in the course of taking questions from journalists, Trump said, "either we'll negotiate a deal with whoever is claiming it [the oil], if we think it's fair, or we will militarily stop them very quickly. . . . [W]hat I intend to do, perhaps, is make a deal with an Exxon Mobil or one of our great companies to go in there and do it properly; . . . we're protecting the oil. We're securing the oil. Now, that doesn't mean we don't make a deal at some point."

announcement was fundamentally a reiteration of established meanings and associations for that inextricably ideological and contested category "terrorist," and it is with an analysis of Trump's consolidations of "terrorist" that Chapter 4 begins.

4.2 TERRORISTS, DOGS, AND MONSTERS

The established contours of necropolitical law's identity category "terrorist" are front and center in Trump's prepared remarks:

> Last night, the United States brought the world's number one terrorist leader to justice. Abu Bakr al-Baghdadi is dead. He was the founder and leader of ISIS, the most ruthless and violent terror organization anywhere in the world. ... He died after running into a dead-end tunnel, whimpering and crying and screaming all the way. ... He reached the end of the tunnel, as our dogs chased him down. He ignited his vest, killing himself and the three children. His body was mutilated by the blast. ... The thug who tried so hard to intimidate others spent his last moments in utter fear, in total panic and dread, terrified of the American forces bearing down on him. ... Baghdadi was vicious and violent, and he died in a vicious and violent way, as a coward, running and crying. ... A brutal killer, one who has caused so much hardship and death, has violently been eliminated. ... He died like a dog. He died like a coward." (Trump 2019)[4]

Trump characterizes terrorists and al-Baghdadi as vicious, violent, cowardly, brutal, sick, depraved, savage, killers, and monsters. Ignoring the ideological move inherent to the category "terrorist" – a delegitimizing label imposed by one set of political actors upon another (Rubenstein 1987: 17; Pinfari 2019: 3–6; Li 2020: 25) – Trump's language echoes the tropes used by the counterterror state to narrate the 9/11 attacks as a story of good versus evil, with Americans cast as virtuous, heroic, and innocent victims, obliged to do battle with barbaric, inhuman terrorists (Jackson 2005: 47–51). Indeed, with astonishing consistency, Trump's language reproduces the language

---

[4] The excerpt quoted above is from Trump's prepared remarks. In the course of the press conference, while responding to journalists' questions, Trump went on to thrice repeat his characterization of al-Baghdadi as cowardly, again while denigrating al-Baghdadi for feeling and expressing fear: "he died like a dog, he died like a coward. He was whimpering, screaming, and crying. ... He didn't die a hero. He died a coward – crying, whimpering, screaming, and bringing three kids with him to die a certain death; ... he was screaming, crying, and whimpering. And he was scared out of his mind."

generated by key officials of the counterterror state from the global War on Terror's inaugural moments.[5]

The counterterror state draws on deeply embedded political myths and metanarratives evoking racialized fear, enmity, and hatred (e.g., Volpp 2002; Jackson 2005; Singh 2017). Circulated repeatedly to mobilize support for the War on Terror, these metanarratives and political myths function like reparative social glue (Bottici 2007: 179). As noted in Chapter 3, political myth is inherently ideological, and it tends to frame issues in a way that elicits the affective responses that legitimize policy (Bottici 2007: 363). Illustrating the ideological dominance, coherence, and success of the counterterror state's meaning-making project, Trump reproduces the metanarrative and political myth in which Americans are engaged in a battle for "justice" against barbaric, evil, terrorists; he augments this metanarrative by analogizing al-Baghdadi to a dog, then diminishing al-Baghdadi to less than an American dog.

4.2.1 Less than Human, Less than Dog

Toward the end of his prepared remarks, Trump characterized al-Baghdadi as having "died like a dog."[6] Then, less than three minutes into answering journalists' questions, Trump celebrated Conan, a military attack dog that was slightly wounded when al-Baghdadi triggered his suicide vest. Trump did so in a seeming response to a question about the role played by Russia in the al-Baghdadi raid:

---

[5] For example, on a Sunday afternoon, on September 16, 2001, President Bush gave a brief speech, after which he took questions from the press on the White House lawn, during which he characterized the war on terror as a crusade. While that statement inspired some controversy, none whatsoever attached to how, in the course of just thirteen minutes, Bush described terrorists as "evil" and "evil-doers" nine times. He also described terrorists as "barbaric" and accused them of enacting "barbarism." On September 24, 2001, when Attorney General John Ashcroft advocated for what was to become the Patriot Act before the House Committee on the Judiciary, he characterized terrorists as "evil" and "savage." And in a speech delivered on October 23, 2001, Vice President Dick Cheney characterized the US response to 9/11 as "a fight to save the civilized world. ... This is a struggle against evil." In January 2002, Defense Secretary Donald Rumsfeld described Guantanamo detainees as the "most dangerous, best trained, vicious killers on the face of the earth." In short, Trump reproduces and conforms to the discourse established by the Bush administration at the launching of the counterterror state's War on Terror.

[6] Consistent with Trump's rhetorical reliance on repetition, he characterized al-Baghdadi as having "died like a dog" once in his prepared remarks, then again in the course of answering journalists" questions. Trump also denigrates some of al-Baghdadi's subordinates as "frightened puppies."

Q: And when you told the Russians, you requested permission –

T: Our dog was hurt. Actually, the K-9 was hurt, went into the tunnel. But we lost nobody."

And later in the press conference, in another nonresponse to a question, Trump again highlighted the attack dog:

Q: Sir, just to pin down the timing a little bit better here: You got back to the White House around 4:30 yesterday afternoon. Did you immediately go to the Situation Room?

T: Well, I knew all about this for three days.

Q: Yes, sir.

T: Yeah. We thought, for three days, this is what was going to happen. It was actually – look, nobody was even hurt. Our K-9, as they call – I call it a dog, a beautiful dog, a talented dog – was injured and brought back. But we had no soldier injured.[7]

Four days later, on October 31, 2019, Trump tweeted a photograph of himself tying the blue satin ribbon of a medal of honor around Conan's neck. While the photograph was convincing, it had been doctored (Chokshi and Zraick 2019). The photo of Trump awarding a medal of honor to a retired army medic had been altered to replace the face and head of the man with those of a dog.

Trump's celebration of a military attack dog serves as a troubling foil for the lives discounted in the killing of al-Baghdadi, as well as in the long War on Terror more broadly. Given that one of the functions of law is to constitute community by constructing norms for the ordering of social relations, Trump's celebration of Conan nurtures an account of community in which American publics are encouraged to disregard and discount the lives of certain racialized Others, in part, by valorizing the life and well-being of a dog nationalized as American. The manner in which Trump remarks on the dog sub-textually performs another function, revealing the degree to which a highly asymmetrical battle unfolded to produce the deaths of al-Baghdadi and others:

T: … many of his [al-Baghdadi's] people were killed. And we'll announce the exact number over the next 24 hours. But many were killed. We lost nobody. Think of that. It's incredible.

---

[7] Trump referred a third time to the attack dog still later in the press conference: "It's incredible that nobody was killed – or hurt. We had nobody even hurt. And that's why the dog was so great."

Q: And when you told the Russians, you requested permission –
T: Our dog was hurt. Actually, the K-9 was hurt, went into the
    tunnel. But we lost nobody.

When Trump celebrates the "incredible" achievement of a raid in which "many" enemies died and all Americans – except for Conan – escaped unscathed, he legitimizes military engagements conducted in such a manner that American lives are minimally risked and enemy lives maximally discounted. Consistent with asymmetrical warfare that "degenerates into slaughter or hunting" (Chamayou 2015 [2013]: 91), in the annihilations effected by the long War on Terror's military and technological supremacy (Gusterson 2014; Chamayou 2015 [2013]) and the secrecy of the counterterror project, Conan, the only American to have sustained injury, becomes the only viable public emblem of valor (in addition, of course, to Trump, as discussed at Section 4.4 below).[8] For Vice President Pence, Conan stands in for the heroism of the special forces who conducted the raid (Harkins 2019). At a staged photo opportunity with Conan, as well as Pence and First Lady Melania, Trump informed reporters that the heroic dog had also been awarded a certificate and a plaque and that the medal was to be displayed at the White House (Harkins 2019). The medal so displayed, it seems, operates as a trophy, declaring by extension Trump's heroism as the commander-in-chief responsible for killing al-Baghdadi. Trump attends to Conan as a decoy of sorts, which strategically distracts audiences from the many uncounted human deaths.

In addition to a range of verbal and metaphorical tropes through which "terrorists" are dehumanized and despised (Jackson 2005; Pinfari 2019), necropolitical law's practices and places evidence how "terrorists" are rendered both less than human *and* less than American dogs. At Guantanamo, for example, official photographs circulating through the Department of Defense visually rendered "terrorists" as more animal than human, indeed, as looking like "giant bright orange flies" (Gregory 2006: 414). This rendering played a role in facilitating their "abusive and demeaning treatment" (Rochelle 2020: 152–53). So deplorable were conditions at Guantanamo that

---

[8] Long held notions of valor, Hugh Gusterson argues, involve reciprocity of risk. In the long War on Terror's distanced warfare, in which one side does not risk life or limb, these old notions of valor continue to surface (2014, 2015).

detainees demanded to have the same rights as dogs in the camp, or to have the same rights as iguanas living on the base. As some detainees said, they demanded "dog-rights" because a dog in the camp had a house, water, food, shade, and grass on which to exercise. ... [Detainees] abandoned ideas one has about human life to legally live better as "a dog."

(Zevnik 2011: 163)

Augmenting the more-animal-than-human strand of the long War on Terror's identity ascriptions for "terrorist" is the discursive construction of "terrorists" as monstrous nonhumans (Pinfari 2019). More wildly and savagely threatening than the well-trained obedience exemplified by Conan the attack dog, Trump's characterization of all "terrorists" as monsters captures the fear and terror we – Trump's audience – experience when confronted with inhuman beings engaging in frightening and unthinkable conduct beyond our control or management (Pinfari 2019: 13).

In celebrating Conan, while giving only glancing mention to the killing of others alongside al-Baghdadi, Trump reinforced the systemic discounting of life already in place in the long War on Terror. And while he forcefully and repeatedly rehearsed meanings for "terrorist" already scripted by necropolitics, Trump added new dimensions to the category that illustrate how "terrorist" has been re-semanticized to become an *identity* category rather than a lexical item designating a person who has enacted political violence. It is to these discounted lives and the re-semanticization of the inherently ideological category "terrorist" that I now turn.

4.2.2 Necropolitical Law's Martial Life Cycle

Alongside al-Baghdadi and his two children, from sixteen to twenty-one others were killed by US forces in the raid (Callimachi 2019). This lack of certainty as to the number of people killed suggests that the munitions used were of such force that bodies could not even be counted, let alone identified. The US military maintains that no civilians were harmed, although Syrian villagers in the vicinity of the operation report helicopter gunfire having killed two innocent civilians and injured a third (Estrin 2019). These media reports, given their peripheral and tentative accounting for others killed along with al-Baghdadi, illuminate a key conceptual move of necropolitical law, which is the erasure of the liberal legal distinction between civilians and combatants, and, relatedly, the counterterror state's disavowal of international law (e.g., Alston 2010; Scheppele 2013). This

149

erasure of the civilian/combatant distinction has been constructed in part by the counterterror state's generation of multiple new categories for those regarded through the war-on-terror optic as enemies. Such categories as "military-age male" and "children with possible hostile intent" are considered below. First, I want to consider "terrorist" in relation to necropolitical law's reconfiguration of basic principles of criminal law.

The counterterror state's new categories for enmity work to implement a strategic discarding of the principles, processes, actors, and institutions of criminal law. Historically, liberal democracies, including the United States, have treated "terrorism" as a crime, requiring the attendant legal processes and protections for the accused (Jansson 2019). Indeed, as recently as December 2001, the United States indicted Zacarias Moussaoui on a series of criminal charges, including "conspiracy to commit acts of terrorism transcending national boundaries."[9] Importantly, foundational principles of criminal law require that, before an individual may be found guilty and punished by the legal system, the law must find both that the individual has committed the criminal act and possessed an intention to do so (e.g., Hall 1960). The element of intention, in turn, gives rise to categories of exceptions. Those lacking adequate mental capacity, a child or a person with dementia, for example, cannot (in general) be found guilty of crime. And, typically, under liberal legality, it is an *individual* who is made to account for actions and intentions. As a rule, an individual who has no knowledge of or involvement in a crime, cannot be made criminally responsible by reason of mere biology or proximity. For example, I cannot be punished for the crime of a neighbor, relative, or colleague, unless I too have been criminally complicit in the commission of the crime.

The counterterror state's disavowal of both international law and criminal law is brought to the surface in Trump's announcement of the al-Baghdadi killing. As argued in Chapter 1, in discarding liberal legality, what the counterterror state generates is not a legal vacuum but an alternative legality: necropolitical law. Specifically, Trump's announcement of the killing of al-Baghdadi illustrates how the counterterror state, in turning away from criminal law and international law, engineered a necropolitical law of enmity by re-semanticizing "terrorist" into an identity category. Consider, for example, Trump's articulation of a significant expansion of "terrorist":

---

[9] At www.justice.gov/archives/ag/indictment-zacarias-moussaoui.

Baghdadi's demise demonstrates America's relentless pursuit of terrorist leaders, and our commitment to the enduring and total defeat of ISIS and other terrorist organizations. Our reach is very long. As you know, last month we announced that we recently killed Hamza bin Laden, the very violent son of Osama bin Laden, who was saying very bad things about people, about our country, about the world. He was the heir apparent to Al Qaeda. Terrorists who oppress and murder innocent people should never sleep soundly, knowing that we will completely destroy them. These savage monsters will not escape their fate – and they will not escape the final judgment of God.

(Trump 2019)

Trump's juxtaposition of the al-Baghdadi killing with the killing of Hamza bin Laden points to how the counterterror state might choose to execute "enemies" by extraterritorial, extrajudicial means for reasons of biology and imagined future possibilities. Reaching beyond the present and the actual into future possibilities that the counterterror state predicts, supposes, and *imagines* in such a way as to justify a present action, Trump's characterization of Hamza bin Laden as deserving of assassination for being Osama bin Laden's son and al Qaeda's heir apparent demonstrates how "terrorist" identity – an identity constructed and imposed by the state – translates into a death sentence. Trump tells us that Hamza bin Laden has been executed for being guilty of unspecified "very violent acts" and for saying unspecified "very bad things." By compounding the relational, racialized dimension of enmity with an instrumental distortion of the state of exception, the counterterror state produces a necropolitical justification for killing Hamza bin Laden. This is not law on the terms of liberal legality.

A further implication of "terrorist" identity is discernible in Trump's argument that al-Baghdadi *deserved* to die in a vicious and violent manner because he was a vicious and violent man. Trump said, "Baghdadi was vicious and violent, and he died in a vicious and violent way, as a coward, running and crying." Even as Trump, in making such an argument, displaces criminal law, he revitalizes the necropolitical penal ideologies traceable to pre-republican monarchies and to colonialism and slavery. These necropolitical penalties justified violent, spectacular, and publicly enacted punishment to instruct, terrorize, and deter (e.g., Fisch 1983; Foucault 1995 [1977]; Hartman 1997; Mbembe 2019; Yang 2003;). Indeed, Trump is explicit about valuing spectacular and demeaning punishment for its presumed instructive, deterrent potential:

[H]e died like a dog, he died like a coward. . . . And, frankly, I think it's something that should be brought out so that his followers and all of these young kids that want to leave various countries, including the United States, they should see how he died.

(Trump 2019)

Trump's inextricably necropolitical penal ideologies illustrate profound continuities between punishment past and present under necropolitical law.

4.2.3 When Children Are Cast as "Terrorists"

In addition to killing on the bases of racialized subordination, family relationships, and imagined future possibilities, the proliferation of US-scripted categories relating to "terrorist" illustrates the ever-expanding racialized population captured by "terrorist" as an identity category. In the lexicon of the US military, "terrorist" incorporates the category "military-age male," which is highly problematic in ascribing bodies perceived to be male and of and above the age of adolescence, as actual or potential terrorists and therefore, as legitimately killable (Turse 2013). Critical journalism and scholarship on drone warfare highlight how the "unconscious cultural assumptions" and "palpable hunger to attack" of drone operators (Gusterson 2016: 66) combine with the grainy images of drone surveillance – images "with a resolution equal to the legal definition of blindness for drivers" (Cockburn 2015: 200) – with often lethal consequences for civilians. With tragic frequency, the civilians killed include women, children, and civilian men (e.g., Cloud 2011; Turse 2013; Chamayou 2015 [2013]; Gusterson 2016; Scahill 2017). Moreover, "military-age male," in naming one attribute that is conventionally knowable – male gender – alongside an attribute that is countable – of military age – distracts us from the ideological and human components of perception that are at work in the category. Nor does the military actually determine the age or gender of an individual before deciding to apply the designation "military-age male." From afar, the "screen killing," resembling a video game, couples with notoriously imprecise low-resolution images to open the lethal space of "cognitive misinterpretations" (Gusterson 2016: 69–71). As an identity category, "military-age male" also situates Muslim inhabitants in certain parts of the world into a biological and cultural chronology of militarization and enmity. As category, it weaponizes the natural growth cycle of the male human being, rendering children into bodies born into a martial temporality and trajectory. It is the coming-of-age cycle for the war-on-terror mentality, discounting life through an imposed ideological inscription.[10]

The already fraught parameters and racialized chronology of "military-age male" have extended into another problematic category of terrorist identity constructed by the counterterror state: "children with possible hostile intent." This discombobulating category has resulted in the killings by rocket strike of a group of three boys aged eight, ten, and twelve, who according to their community, were collecting dung for household fuel (McVeigh 2012). *The Guardian* reports:

> The US military is facing fresh questions over its targeting policy in Afghanistan after a senior army officer suggested that troops were on the lookout for "children with potential hostile intent." In comments which legal experts and campaigners described as "deeply troubling," army Lt Col Marion Carrington told the Marine Corp Times that children, as well as "military-age males," had been identified as a potential threat because some were being used by the Taliban to assist in attacks against Afghan and coalition forces. "It kind of opens our aperture," said Carrington, whose unit, 1st Battalion, 508th Parachute Infantry Regiment, was assisting the Afghan police. "In addition to looking for military-age males, it's looking for children with potential hostile intent."
>
> (McVeigh 2012)

Predictably, US officials have a competing account of this particular strike. According to the United States, before they called for the rocket strike on what they describe as "suspected insurgents planting improvised explosive devices," marines had seen the children digging a hole in a dirt road and presumed that "the Taliban may have recruited the children to carry out the mission" (McVeigh 2012). There is a striking lack of clarity, embedding a distorting amplification of the counterterror state's securitized logic of preemption in "the Taliban *may* have." To preempt, after all, requires certainty and knowledge relating to that which is being preempted. Preemption is not equivalent to *speculation*. The children may have been digging for dung or they may have been planting improvised explosive devices (the possibility that they may have been at play does not surface), but the uncertainty is interpreted against them. In the process, a lexical slippage is traceable from

---

[10] I am grateful to Bill V. Mullen for this point.

"children" to "suspected insurgents" and "children with possible hostile intent." This tragic incident – by no means isolated (Turse 2013) – illustrates how, in necropolitical law, distortions and amplifications of the counterterror state's logic of preemption and the assignation of enmity on the basis of racialized bodies are ever expanding. The counterterror state presumes for itself the omniscience to discern "possible hostile intent" embodied by children who are not seen as playing, participating in the everyday work of the family, at least, not in the eyes of an occupying force driven by the logics of necropolitical law.

Additionally, in keeping with "a fundamental and oft-repeated US practice of viewing foreign people through the lenses of racial categories at home" (Kaplan 202: 10), this denial of childhood and innocence in the long War on Terror's overseas sites is consistent with the historically entrenched criminalization of African American children inside the United States, re-classifying dependency as delinquency, and refusing to recognize Black children as vulnerable or innocent (Agyepong 2018). Building on a study of how US adults perceive girls, Sally Nuamah (2019) notes that this socially embedded lens of criminalization animates a perceptual adultification: Black girls are viewed as adults from when they are as young as five, with the effect of stripping them of the presumptive innocence of childhood. Instead, these children are regarded "as essentially guilty adults" (Nuamah 2019: 61). Assumptions about actual or potential criminality also inform the hostile policing of African American children in schools, a policing that generates disproportionate rates of school suspensions and expulsions (e.g., Fenning and Rose 2007; Morris and Perry 2017; Welsh and Little 2018; Nuamah 2019; Paul and Araneo 2019). And the 2014 shooting of twelve-year-old Tamir Rice, a child carrying a toy gun in a Cleveland park who was killed by two adult police officers who were quick to shoot, quick to perceive him as dangerous and criminal, speaks to the racialized regime of perception at work in law enforcement (Andrews 2017: 295–98; Stone and Socia 2019; Miles 2020). Tragically, for children assigned certain identity categories, the denial of childhood and innocence connects and co-constitutes the necropolitics of the United States as nation to the necropolitics of the war-on-terror empire.

In *The Guardian*'s report, the metaphor "aperture" in the US military's discourse does significant cultural work, reproducing the counterterror state's misrepresentation as accurate and trustworthy of weapons that combine surveillance and killing technologies (Chamayou 2015

[2013]). Contrary to the counterterror state's misrepresentations, critical journalism and scholarship, and activist experience show again and again the deplorable lack of clarity and frequent (erroneous and careless) killing and maiming of civilians effected by drone warfare (e.g., Cloud 2011; Turse 2013; Chamayou 2015 [2013]; Gusterson 2016; Scahill 2017; Wilke 2017). When the US infantry officer "assisting the Afghan police" speaks of opening "our aperture," the alarming and genocidal implication is that all Afghan children are now suspects.

The lexical item "aperture," by naming a mechanical part, distracts us from the temporal convulsions and god-like omniscience being claimed in Carrington's statement. The military's assertion is that it is able to discern a state of mind – *potential* hostile *intent* – before it exists and before it has been acted on. The military's reading of "potential hostile intent" into everyday conduct, like collecting dung for household fuel, becomes sufficient grounds to kill children by rocket strike. The criminal law principle, requiring both a criminal act and a criminal intent, is obliterated by the necropolitical law of the counterterror state. Children, generally treated under law as a separate and protected category of actors, are no longer regarded as vulnerable or distinguishable from adults, or from the military's expansive perception-based age range for "military-age males." Rather like the five-year-old Black girls perceived as guilty adults (Nuamah 2019: 61), through the ever-widening, increasingly imprecise aperture of necropolitics, racialized subjects are made to *look* like actual or potential terrorists. It is a looking that recalls two limbs of the workings of power. First, states select "tunnel vision" to simplify "a complex and far more unwieldy reality," manufacturing projects of "legibility and simplification" in their management of populations (Scott 1998: 11). And second, "aperture" speaks to the well-noted historical and technological connections between cameras and weapons. Susan Sontag observes, "Ever since cameras were invented in 1839, photography has kept company with death" (2003: 24). And Etienne-Jules Mary's chronophotographic rifle, which both resembled and was inspired by a machine gun, was the precursor to the Lumières' moving picture camera (Virilio 1989: 15; Stahl 2010: 8). For the counterterror state's seeing, the apertures converge, facilitating the long War on Terror's optics of enmity.

Relatedly, critical scholarship on the role of aerial surveillance in the War on Terror shows how an epistemology encoded with "background assumptions and situated knowledges, including fantasies of race, risk,

and violence," mediates and conditions interpretations of aerial surveillance images, in the process *producing* "civilians" and "combatants"
through specific forms of professional vision (Wilke 2017: 1055). In
the epistemic and affective distortions of the counterterror state's
tunnel vision, the seeing of surveillance bleeds rapidly into necropolitical law's normative grounds for killing: the relation of enmity
(Mbembe 2019: 70). In short, when "enemy" is an ever-expanding
and imposed identity category, the counterterror state's ways of seeing
too easily lead to killing authorized by necropolitical law.

The next section analyzes the visual dimensions of the White House
Diplomatic Reception Room, Trump's choice of setting for his
announcement of the al-Baghdadi killing. This is the setting, I argue,
of an imperial spectacle, legitimizing necropolitical law through visual
claims to the traditions of US nation and empire-building as "virtue."
Visual aspects of the White House Diplomatic Room also disclose
necropolitical law's deeper histories and Euro-Atlantic ties.

4.3 NECROPOLITICAL LAW'S IMPERIAL SPECTACLES

Imperialism, Achille Mbembe notes, is and has long been a dynamic of
power and sovereignty that is inextricably racialized and necropolitical (2019). And the imperial spectacle, in addition to being impressive (Said 1987: 103), is designed to bestow heroic visibility on
militarized, male figures, while cultivating passivity in those cast as
spectators, and rendering oppressed, racially Othered "foreign" populations invisible (Kaplan 2002). Sections 4.3 and 4.4 analyze Trump's
announcement of the al-Baghdadi killing for visual and verbal imperial spectacles. Section 4.3 shows how this impressive spectacle, which
in being imperial was also necropolitical, was staged. The imperial
spectacle of Trump's announcement foregrounded the grandeur of the
office of president, and symbols of the United States, and US military
forces, against backgrounded images of deeper histories of Euro-
Atlantic necropolitics. In that they stage law as publicity while
occluding law as public thing, the images I discuss in this chapter
are versions of visuality co-constituting spectacle and secrecy that
accompany necropolitical law as analyzed in Chapter 3. In this chapter, I show how, in the process of announcing the killing of al-
Baghdadi, Trump staged himself as the militarized, White male hero
that has always been central to American spectacles of imperialism
(Kaplan 202: 106–20).

4.3.1 Trump and Washington

The image carried by newspapers and on screens around the world shows Trump standing at a lectern in a richly decorated White House Diplomatic Reception Room (e.g., Baker et al. 2019). On the wall just behind Trump is a portrait of the first US president, George Washington. As the bottom of the portrait is just about level with Trump's head, Washington's face appears to hover just above his shoulder. This visual line, explicitly linking Trump's image, person, office, and authority to that of Washington, in photography is nick-named a "halo shot."[11] A halo shot is so named because it is designed to generate the halo effect (Thorndike 1920), bestowing, through association, impression, or proximity, a perceptual and affective penumbra of exalted and admired qualities upon the photograph's primary subject. In this particular halo shot, Trump is bathed in the reflected glory of Washington's exalted status in US history, culture, and nation-making.[12]

George Washington, according to the unsurprisingly reverential account of the White House, was a gentleman skilled in the military arts, as well as a participant in Western expansion, having battled in some of the early skirmishes of what later became known as the French and Indian wars.[13] As commander-in-chief of the Continental Army, he was also a military hero in the nation-founding revolutionary war. Washington was also president of the Constitutional Convention.[14] As a revolutionary leader-warrior at the core of the US founding, Washington is represented in dominant narratives as a desirable symbol of the two bodies – head of state and commander-in-chief – of the US president.

---

[11] Psychologist Edward Thorndike's 1920 analysis of how perceptions of visible, physical attributes bleed into perceptions of traits such as intelligence and leadership has given rise to the popular use of "the halo effect," a concept that is also used in marketing. For an example of the halo effect in analysis of photography, see Reading the Pictures (2019).

[12] This exaltation is immediately conveyed by the naming of the US capital after this "founding father." In addition to the naming of universities and sub-state spaces after George Washington, other territorial spaces named for George Washington in the United States include the state of Washington and the many sites called Georgetown throughout the United States.

[13] At www.whitehouse.gov/about-the-white-house/presidents/george-washington/.

[14] At www.whitehouse.gov/about-the-white-house/presidents/george-washington/.

Roxanne Dunbar-Ortiz's critical reading of US history casts Washington as an unambiguously imperial and necropolitical actor, an important figure prior to his presidency in the wars through which the US appropriated land and exterminated populations and who pursued further extirpative wars to secure control of land and populations during his presidency (Dunbar-Ortiz 2014). Dunbar-Ortiz highlights a further significant commonality between Washington and Trump:

> The militaristic-capitalist powerhouse of the United States derives from real estate (which includes African bodies as well as appropriated land). It is apt that we once again have a real estate man for president, much like the first president, George Washington, whose fortune came mainly from his success speculating on unceded Indian lands.
>
> (2018: 55)

However, this dimly acknowledged history, alongside the widely received account of Washington as a great president, works to Trump's advantage, reminding media consumers, nationally and internationally, of the lineage of leadership underpinning Trump's 2019 moment. The association situates both men as variations on the American imperial spectacle of White, militarized, male heroes.

Basking in the halo effect of Washington's portrait, Trump stands flanked at the lectern by seven ceremonial flags, consistent with Trump's deliberate display of battle flags in the Oval Office, which is another departure from the practice of his predecessors (Fallows 2017). Trump appears to have chosen the US flag, reinforced by flags representing six national military institutions: the Army, Navy, Air Force, Marine Corps, Coast Guard, and, possibly, Space Force.[15] The tall flag poles, topped with gleaming, golden-hued bald eagles, appear on the level of the ceiling of the room, lifting the gaze and inspiring a sense of awe in the presence of such towering objects of ritual and reverence. The flags are carefully placed, standing protectively to the right and left of the presidential duo of Trump and Washington, while leaving the audience a clear line of vision for looking upon the speaking president. The flags' rich colors, the golden yellow tassels marking their ceremonial function, and the majestic ornamental bald eagles topping the flagstands all add a specifically *military* pageantry and visual grandeur to the setting. With this wall of flags standing visually like an honor guard, the

---

[15] It is possible that one of the seven flags is the ceremonial flag bearing the presidential seal. The way the flags are draped makes it a little hard to tell.

president asserted the primacy of his commander-in-chief embodiment, celebrating the armed forces as the key state actors of necropolitical law. He did not, for example, stand flanked by the justices of the Supreme Court.[16]

While the flags appear as props specific to the occasion, the striking wallpaper in the White House Diplomatic Reception Room has been a permanent feature since the early 1960s. In 1961 Jacqueline Kennedy had chosen the wallpaper when, as First Lady, she undertook to restore and decorate the White House (Cobb 2015). The wallpaper embellishes the thirty-six by twenty-six-foot oval facade of the Diplomatic Reception Room (Kelly 2017), effecting the spectacle and experience of a panorama. Panoramas, emerged in the 1780s, "linked to … the emergence of forms of entertainment that encouraged a stronger consciousness of national identity in an era of almost constant warfare and rapid colonization" (Kaplan 2018: 31). As elaborated in what follows, the national identity cultivated by the panoramic wallpaper occludes the violence that both founded and sustains the United States as a necropolitical power.

Officially titled Vues de l'Amerique du Nord (views of North America) and produced in 1834 by "one of France's most renowned wallpaper companies," Zuber et Cie, the wallpaper depicts a panoramic "series of five idealized, picturesque vignettes," showing details of clothing, infrastructure, and transportation placing the vignettes "within the time frame of the 1830s, during the heart of Andrew Jackson's American presidency" (Gohmann 2010: 2, 8).[17] This French-made wallpaper depicts "an Indian dance in Virginia, the thundering water at Niagara Falls, strollers on the Palisades of New York, military drills at West Point, and shipping docks in Boston Harbor" (Gohmann 2010: 3).[18] Viewed through the analytic lens of

---

[16] This setting appears to have been actively staged, in that the lectern and the many flags flanking Trump like an honor guard appear to have been brought in for the occasion. Other images of the room show that these flags, exalting both the state and institutions of state violence, are not a permanent feature of the room.

[17] "Idealized" because the designer, Deltil, had not traveled beyond France (Gohmann 2010: 6; Emlen 1997). Additionally, wallpaper historian Catherine Lynn notes that the depictions of Boston Harbor are not historically accurate representations of the harbor as it then was. Instead, in Deltil's depictions, "the foreground bears a close resemblance to waterside views of European ports"; see www.whitehousehistory.org/the-diplomatic-reception-rooms-historic-wallpaper.

[18] Deltil based his scenes on illustrations from a popular travel book, J. Milbert's, Picturesque Itinerary of the Hudson River and the Peripheral Parts of North America (1828). However, Deltil and his team "made dramatic alterations to Milbert's

necropolitics, and alert to necropolitics' animating dynamics of deception and separation (Mbembe 2019), the remarkable feature of the wallpaper is the falsity of representation with regard to social relations inside the United States. Despite the fact that "racial violence was an inextricable component of Andrew Jackson's presidency, exacted in his forceful "removal" of Native Americans to western territories and replicated in extralegal brutality against free African Americans" (Cobb 2015: 67), the wallpaper "represented a French fondness for Jacksonian America imagined through notions of racial diversity, industriousness, and democracy as a successful experiment" (Cobb 2015: 69). For example, the pictorial vignette of the Indian dance in Virginia was made highly improbable by the violent nature of American settler colonialism. The impossible scene of undisturbed indigenous Americans, resplendent in their feathered headdress, performing a ceremonial dance for an audience of fascinated and respectful White and Black Americans, flies in the face of a history in which, from the seventeenth and early eighteenth centuries, "successive generations of Americans, both soldiers and civilians, made the killing of Indian men, women, and children a defining element of their first military tradition and thereby part of a shared American identity" (Grenier 2005: 12). By 1834, the year in which the wallpaper was produced, the first colonial armies in Virginia had been engaged in a sustained and brutal extirpative war against indigenous populations for more than 200 years (Dunbar-Ortiz 2014: 60). And, Jasmine Cobb argues, by depicting "Black figures . . .[as] comparable to whites in terms of consumer power and socioeconomic status but . . . distinct from unrefined Native Americans" the new republic's inhabitants "exist within a racial hierarchy so that the well-off, well-dressed, spectacularly free persons of African descent seemed evolved compared to Native Americans and far removed from enslavement" (Cobb 2015: 70–71).

Frequently, this extirpative violence against indigenous populations took place under cover of law, as with the 1830 Indian Removal Act, passed by Congress even as "the US government held Cherokee leaders in jail and closed their printing press during negotiations with a few handpicked Cherokees, who provided the bogus signatures Jackson needed as cover for forced removal" (Dunbar-Ortiz 2014: 110). The law's 1830 cover for forced removal is echoed by the 2001 Patriot Act's

compositions by adding more figures, changing perspective angles, and updating costume and transportation" (Gohmann 2010: 7).

cover for the fear-generated removal of rights and protections, as discussed in Chapter 2. Liberal legality, we are reminded, has a deep and largely unacknowledged history of providing facades for necropolitical law.

In a similar vein of deception, the wallpaper's New York Palisades vignette depicts people harmoniously coexisting in a separate but equal social space. Three stylish, confident African Americans (as we would now name this race identity) stand in the foreground of the image, while elsewhere we see stylish, confident White Americans. There is no sense of racially segregated social and public spaces, or of the history of slavery laying the foundation for enduring disparities in class and the many structures and expressions of overt and covert racial hatred and violence. It is a mythic, utopian America that the wallpaper depicts.

Situating the wallpaper's 1834 French production in context, art historian Joanna Gohmann notes that it was "a product of a very specific time in France's July Monarchy,"[19] spanning 1830–1848. This was a period during which the wallpaper's idealized images of the United States "must be understood ... as an illustration of the French vision of a perfect, successful republican government" (Gohmann 2010: 19). With America imagined as "a working model for a republican government in which individual liberties were protected," this vision overlooked "American democracy's faults and contradictions, specifically racial inequality" (Gohmann 2010: 18). Gohmann explains:

> During this period in French history, "republican" denoted a political state in which power rests in the populous, rather than an absolute monarchy. Aspects of a republican government include political representation, equality before the law, and individual liberty; republicanism did not necessarily mean democracy. The revival of this particular political ideal and the attitudes surrounding the 1789 revolution suggests a simultaneous revival of eighteenth-century Americanism, a philosophical ideal common amongst French Revolutionaries. ... [who] believed that America represented the political future of France: a working republican system that protected individual liberty. Because

---

[19] "The July Monarchy (July 1830–February 1848) marks the reign of Louis Philippe I, the only French monarch to assume the throne as an immediate result of a popular uprising. In its early stages, the July Monarchy responded to the cries of "liberté, égalité, et fraternité," the same republican principles that Vues d'Amérique du Nord celebrates" (Gohmann 2010: 10).

of the attitudes of major political figures involved with the July Monarchy, the revival of the 1789 spirit, and the overall call for republicanism, America once again served as a political aspiration and ideal.

(2010: 10)

Even as it represented Blacks as "spectacularly free persons," the wallpaper "overlooked the proliferation of state laws and antiblack violence that inhibited free people's mobility in the United States" (Cobb 2015: 71).

In keeping with necropolitical law's coexistence with the egalitarian ideals of liberal legality and republicanism, even as the political elite of France's July Monarchy looked to America as the model republic, it was under the July Monarchy that the French state consolidated its colonial conquest of Algeria "in brutal fashion" (Andrews and Sessions 2015: 4). These were also the years during which "the United States increased its national domain by 70%, engaged in a bloody campaign of Indian removal, fought its first prolonged foreign war, wrested the Spanish borderlands from Mexico, and annexed Texas, Oregon, California, and New Mexico" (Kaplan 2002: 26). By featuring an idealized French impression of the new US nation, the wallpaper in the Diplomatic Reception Room occludes the necropolitical violence founding and sustaining the United States. By importing the July Monarchy's fantasies and installing them in the White House, the United States also renders visible profound continuities between the racialized imperialisms of Europe and the United States.

The necropolitical deception of the wallpaper is only bolstered by the White House Historical Association's acknowledgment of the unreality of the wallpaper's representations, in noting that Boston Harbor on the wallpaper looks more like European waterfronts of the time than it does like the Boston Harbor of the 1830s (Kelly 2017). But the White House Historical Association is silent on the improbable representations of race relations, thereby tacitly reproducing the occlusions and deceptions of the wallpaper relating to racialized violence. Cumulatively, the images and the source of the wallpaper, as well as the halo effect produced by the portrait of Washington, are reminders of imperial culture's backgrounded, deceptive, and normalized expressions. In short, the setting for Trump's announcement of the al-Baghdadi killing visually encodes the way, "[f]ar from leading to democracy's spread across the planet, the race for new lands opened onto a new law (nomos) of the Earth, the main characteristic of which was to establish war and race as history's two privileged sacraments" (Mbembe 2019: 6).

4.4 IMPERIAL SPECTACLES IN TRUMP'S STATECRAFT

I move now from the setting for Trump's announcement on the al-Baghdadi killing to a consideration of Trump's choice of discursive arena: a press conference.[20] Trump made his announcement on the al-Baghdadi killing at a televised press conference that he conducted on a Sunday morning.[21] The evening before, when the raid had been "successfully" concluded, his cryptic tweet, "Something very big has just happened!," functioned as a promotional message, advertising his news conference and preparing media for the task of disseminating "something big."[22] This section considers Trump's press conference as a media event staged to bolster necropolitical law's imperial spectacles with Trump presenting himself as the militarized, White male hero central to American cultures of imperialism (Kaplan 202).

Media events perform three major functions. They set agendas and drive news coverage, they generate large audiences, and they are "a critical strategy used by politicians" to construct and disseminate a favorable political image (Schill 2009: xv, xvi). Media events, Dan Schill argues, provide examples of "how political stagecraft influences statecraft" (2009: xvi). Augmenting the already complex operations of statecraft through stagecraft, with political campaigns and governing unfolding "in a mass-mediated democracy influenced largely by how newsmakers stage events for media and public consumption" (Schill 2009: xv), is the factor of Trump's energetic self-marketing "as always the best, the smartest, the most successful" (Kessler 2020: 25), practiced through his "many years posing as his own publicist" (Kessler 2020: 25). In other words, Trump's statecraft is informed by Trump the real estate tycoon and reality television star's career of self-aggrandizing self-promotion. Borrowing from his media-savvy predecessors (Rogin 1988),

---

[20] At the press conference, Trump delivered a prepared speech for about eight-and-a-half minutes then engaged with reporters for about forty minutes.

[21] Trump began speaking at 9:20 am, suggesting that the press conference was scheduled for 9 am. www.washingtonpost.com/politics/2019/10/28/trumps-news-conference-abu-bakr-al-baghdadis-death-annotated/.

[22] Trump's tweet also functioned, as Trump was to explain in the course of answering a reporter's question, "to notify you guys that you have something big this morning, so you wouldn't be out playing golf or tennis or otherwise being indisposed."

Trump turned a covert operation into a media spectacle while representing the imperial violence of a military operation as "a spectacular adventure" (McBride 2006: 257), illustrating, yet again, how "spectacle and secrecy support each other" (Rogin 1990: 99).

When it comes to the press conference as a staged media event, Trump's unique brand of presidential rhetoric and media relations needs to be considered in relation to the long-held and much-cherished notion of "the press" as an institution of American democracy. In this conception, the press is composed of independent, power-scrutinizing journalists who work to observe, investigate, analyze, and report on current events, in this way mediating between events and publics in the service of truth and fact. Oriented toward the "ideal goal" of making power accountable (Entman 2005: 48), media – particularly news journalism – serves as a public thing in Honig's terms: an accessible object held in common, anchoring and serving democracy (2017). As an event, a press conference is imbued with these legitimizing resonances. By attending press conferences and asking questions of authority, journalists are presumed to perform the role of "public-spirited surrogates for citizens" (Schudson and Tifft 2005: 31), generating the communicative content bridging between the powerful figures who make news and reading, viewing, mediatized citizen-consumer publics.

Importantly, however, against the abstractions of this ideal of "the press" as a fourth estate, journalism and "the press" in the United States must be contextualized with reference to three primary factors. First, journalism in the United States is far more complex than the essentializing label "the press" suggests (Schudson 2005: 1).[23] A second principal feature of American journalism has been "voluntary cooperation between state and media in time of conflict" (Schudson and Tifft 2005: 27), a cooperation established during World War II and extended more generally through the five decades of the Cold War (Zelizer 2018: 10). While this cooperation between state and media has occasionally been somewhat ruptured, Barbie Zelizer reads deeper continuities in

---

[23] Michael Schudson cautions, "[T]here are multiple types of American journalism, with multiple purposes, diverse audiences, and varying relationships to democracy. It is a mistake to identify American journalism exclusively with the dominant mainstream-television-network news and high-circulation metropolitan daily newspapers" (2005: 1).

state-media ideological complicities.[24] For Zelizer, "deep mnemonic cues about enemy formation, consolidated and entrenched during the Cold War" continue to operate today in the "distrust, polarization, negative stereotyping, black-and-white-thinking, aggression, deindividualization, and demonization ... fostering ethnic intolerance, racism, and political and religious fundamentalism," which undermine "US journalistic coverage of the Trump phenomenon" (Zelizer 2018: 9, 16). The binaried and reductive polemics of enemy formation require "clarity and simplicity, ... provoking anxiety over an imminent threat," and an instrumental deployment of that anxiety to upend civic values and permit the hitherto impermissible (Zelizer 2018: 9). The Cold War decades included the paranoid politics of McCarthyism (Hofstadter 1963) and fostered "long-standing journalistic conventions and practices" marked by "deference and moderation, which helped turn journalists into eager spokespeople for those in power" (Zelizer 2018: 11).

A third principal feature of "the press" in the United States, a feature with global reach and resonance, relates to the global scale of US media corporatization (Herman 1997). Independent, democracy-enhancing media was further undermined when the "conformity and homogeneity of the Cold War era" (Zelizer 2018: 16) was augmented by consolidations in interest between media corporations and political power (Herman and Chomsky 1988), with market forces playing "the most decisive role in transforming the delivery of news" (Hamilton 2005: 351). And yet, against this disheartening recent history of ideological complicity and of profit and power motives eclipsing journalistic and democratic ideals, scholars and activists assessing journalism and media in the Trump presidency express conviction in media's capacity to recover a free press (Benson 2019), in part by turning away from norms of competition to instead build the solidarity of professional collaboration (Russell 2019) and also by providing fact-checking so as to enable readers to assess the accuracy of reported news (Kessler 2020: xv). In other words, the ideological and economic complicities shaping contemporary media have undeniably undermined, but not obliterated, the orienting ideals animating media's capacity – like rule of law – to serve

---

[24] These ruptures were "the conflicts of the 1960s – Vietnam, the civil rights movement, the assassinations of President Kennedy, his brother Robert Kennedy, and the Reverend Martin Luther King Jr.," as well as the 1971 role of "the press" in exposing Watergate (Schudson and Tifft 2005: 31).

publics and democratic ideals by scrutinizing power and holding power accountable.

In short, a press conference is neither straightforwardly nor transparently a discursive encounter facilitating the delivery of news. With teams of public relations and communication officials skillfully deploying "proven political marketing tools" to create favorable media coverage for US presidents (Schill 2009: xii), the press conference on the al-Baghdadi killing is more usefully approached as an instance of imperial spectacle inflected by Trump's unique register of statecraft.

4.4.1 Trump as Hero

Visual aspects of the imperial spectacles staged by Trump's announcement were discussed in Section 4.3 above. Before considering the specifics of Trump's language, it is important to contextualize Trump's media relations. Consistent with a modality of statecraft that seeks rupture in the status quo and "an indictment of the establishment" (Bloomfield Jr. and Harvey 2017: 70), Trump has violated "virtually every rule of presidential messaging, decorum, and press management" (Benson 2018: 214). Trump has repeatedly denigrated the press as "dishonest" (Robinson 2018: 188), and he has delegitimized mainstream media by calling it "fake" (Caplan and Boyd 2018: 54) and the "enemy of the people" (Sugars 2019).[25] A businessman confident of his capacities to successfully market himself, Trump "effectively became his own press secretary" from the second year of his presidency (Kessler 2020: xvii). In addition to treating "any critical coverage as a personal threat" (Benson 2018: 214) during his presidency,

> Trump has restricted journalistic access to the White House in ways no other modern president has, seldom holding press conferences and limiting the number of on-camera press briefings by White House spokespeople, in addition to publicly castigating the news media as the enemy.

> (Mendelson 2018: 59)

---

[25] Stephanie Sugars tracks Trump's tweets to show how, from the moment of his candidacy to January 2019, they have been escalating in terms of content that is "critical, insinuating, condemning, or threatening" about media. She writes, "Nine percent of all original tweets during his candidacy contained negative rhetoric about the press, compared with 11 percent in his first two years in office. His rhetoric – increasingly targeting swaths of the press – appears to be escalating, first from the introduction of 'fake news' to 'opposition party' and his use of 'enemy of the people'" (Sugars 2019).

Trump's aversion to press conferences is evidenced by how compara-
tively few of them he has held.[26]

In addition to attacks on individual journalists, leading to their being
"harassed and doxed" (Ellerbeck 2016; Sugars 2019), Trump banned
certain news organizations from his reelection campaign events and
revoked the press passes of journalists he perceived as critical (Downie
Jr. 2020). In May 2019, the Trump administration enacted new regulations relating to the grounds on which press passes to the White House
would be issued. These rules

> give the Trump administration new levers with which to control the
> press corps. Some argue that access to the White House is already almost
> meaningless, since press briefings are few and far between (there hasn't
> been an on-camera briefing for 58 days, a new record) and what briefings
> there are often involve the White House press secretary and/or the
> president shutting down journalist questions and in many cases outright
> lying about various details of the administration's behavior or plans.
>
> (Ingram 2019)

In keeping with his hostility toward mainstream media and blatant
disregard for norms of public discourse, a notable feature of Trump's
statecraft is how he represents his embodied self as "truth" over and
above representation and record. As tracked by the *Washington Post*'s
fact-checker staff, in the three years from the day of his inauguration to
January 10, 2020 (Kessler et al. 2020), Trump generated 16,241 false or
misleading claims (Kessler 2020: x). It has been argued that Trump's
rhetorical style, "his tradition-shattering embrace of lurid rhetoric and
coarse insults" (Kessler 2020: vii), garners support among certain constituencies precisely because he violates norms of public discourse
(Conway, Repke, and Houck 2017). Denouncing "political correctness" (Chow 2016) as a way to present himself as the truthful alternative to career politicians has been a mainstay of Trump's mode
of statecraft.

Cumulatively then, Trump's curation of journalists attending his
press conferences, along with the well-entrenched alignments between
media corporations and political power discussed above, and as

---

[26] See also the figures compiled by the American Presidency Project on the number of
press conferences conducted by US Presidents from Coolidge (1923) to Trump
(through August 20, 2020). Trump, on average, conducts 1.81 press conferences a
month; see www.presidency.ucsb.edu/statistics/data/presidential-news-conferences.

complicated by Trump's contentious relationship with mainstream media and heavy reliance on Twitter, media over the course of his administration was eroded as a public thing. Instead of "the press" operating as a public thing, an object held in common, anchoring and serving democracy (Honig 2017), a press conference becomes a media event and an imperial spectacle: a platform for the staging of America's always superlative power and Donald Trump's always super-lative successes.[27]

4.4.2 Imperialism's Spectacular Speech

Mapping representations of US imperialism across genres and modal-ities of culture (including news and entertainment media, museum exhibitions, popular films, foreign policy, Supreme Court judgments, domestic manuals, and novels) and across time and space (including the American Revolution, the Spanish-American War, the Philippine-American War, the Civil War and Reconstruction, America's wars and encounters with Vietnam, the Middle East, Cuba, and Afghanistan), Amy Kaplan (2002) and Melani McAlister (2005) highlight narratives, images, actors, arenas, and roles called into being by US imperial spectacles. Typically, spectacles of American imperialism transport the resourceful, mobile, virile, heroic, White American male, skilled in battling the dangerous, racialized Other, to zones of wilderness, so that national and global audiences may witness, with admiration if not adoration, the desirable triumph of American virtue, valor, and expan-sionism. Consistent with the deceptive, depoliticizing effects of spec-tacle, which cultivates, rather than an engaged, informed citizenry, passive spectator-consumers (Debord 1967), imperial spectacles occlude and manage representations of American violence to reinscribe

---

[27] In the course of his press conference, Trump twice refers to himself in the third person. He once does so to characterize himself as possessing superlative technical brilliance, saying, "You know, these people [referring to 'terrorists'] are very smart. They're not into the use of cellphones anymore. They're not – they're very technic-ally brilliant. You know, they use the Internet better than almost anybody in the world, perhaps other than Donald Trump." In his second self-as-third-person refer-ence, Trump positions himself as a historical figure with a well-known biography, "If you read about the history of Donald Trump – I was a civilian. I had absolutely nothing to do with going into Iraq, and I was totally against it." In both instances, Trump, the businessman-president, might be seen as engaging in marketing and promotional advertising, citing his name as a brand for both technological and political brilliance.

America and Americans as virtuous and heroic and to cast audiences in the feminized role of approving, implicitly consenting, spectators (Rogin 1990; Kaplan 2002; McAlister 2005; McBride 2006).

Trump's announcement reproduces key elements of the imperial spectacle with a uniquely Trumpian twist: repeatedly, through his narrative and his shifting pronouns, Trump situates himself as both actor and audience.[28] In most instances, he represents himself in self-aggrandizing terms. As the White, male, militarized hero, Trump cast himself in a number of authoritative roles, including (1) president (e.g., "Capturing or killing Baghdadi has been the top national security priority of my administration"); (2) heroic, on-the-ground embodiment of the US military (e.g., "We were in the compound for approximately two hours"); (3) the counterterror state's exemplary commander-in-chief ("Baghdadi has been on the run for many years, long before I took office. But at my direction, as Commander-in-Chief of the United States, we obliterated his caliphate"); (4) the instinctive, *knowing*, superior political leader ("President Bush went in. I strongly disagreed with it, even though it wasn't my expertise at the time, but I had a – I have a very good instinct about things. They went in and I said, 'That's a tremendous mistake.' And there were no weapons of mass destruction. It turned out I was right."); (5) simultaneously the benevolent imperial leader and mindful protector of the well-being of US soldiers ("Turkey has lost thousands and thousands people from that safe zone. So they've always wanted that safe zone, for many years. I'm glad I was able to help them get it. But . . . I want our soldiers home or fighting something that's meaningful"); (6) a fiscally prudent leader ("But the United States taxpayer is not going to pay for the next 50 years. You see what Guantanamo costs. We're not going to pay tens of billions of dollars because we were good enough to capture people that want to go back to Germany, France, UK, and other parts of Europe"); (7) uniquely authorized to disparage institutions and individuals in US politics ("Washington leaks like I've never seen before. . . . [T]here's no country in the world that leaks like we do."); (8) the businessman-president-commander-in-chief adroitly toggling between roles (". . . that oil. We have taken it. . . . somebody else may claim it,

---

[28] As noted in Chapter 3, Obama's use of pronouns consistently referred to himself as either president or commander-in-chief, or as speaking on behalf of America and Americans. Obama did not situate himself as the heroic military actor on the ground, or as the enthralled spectator, in the same way that Trump did.

but either we'll negotiate a deal with whoever is claiming it, if we think it's fair, or we will militarily stop them very quickly."); (9) himself as one with and speaking for the United States (e.g., "Baghdadi's demise demonstrates America's relentless pursuit of terrorist leaders and our commitment to the enduring and total defeat of ISIS and other terrorist organizations."); (10) as embodying the world's most outstanding technological skills, referring this time to himself in the third person and thus deploying the naming-as-branding logic of marketing and advertising ("You know, they [terrorists] use the Internet better than almost anybody in the world, perhaps other than Donald Trump"); and (11) the prescient and superlatively successful author ("I think I wrote 12 books. All did very well. . . . The World Trade Center had not come down. I think it was about – if you check, it was about a year before the World Trade Center came down. And I'm saying to people, 'Take out Osama bin Laden,' that nobody ever heard of. Nobody ever heard of. I mean, al-Baghdadi everybody hears because he's built this monster for a long time. But nobody ever heard of Osama bin Laden until, really, the World Trade Center. But about a year – you'll have to check – a year, year and a half before the World Trade Center came down, the book came out. I was talking about Osama bin Laden. I said, 'You have to kill him. You have to take him out.' Nobody listened to me. And to this day, I get people coming up to me, and they said, 'You know what one of the most amazing things I've ever seen about you? Is that you predicted that Osama bin Laden had to be killed before he knocked down the World Trade Center.' It's true.").

Trump also shifts between pronouns to signify his dual roles of actor and audience. For example (1) simultaneously the endangered, military body and the spectator admiring military prowess (e.g., "We flew very, very low and very, very fast; . . . it was a very dangerous part. . . . We met with gunfire coming in. . . . These people are amazing. They had the gunfire terminated immediately, meaning they were shot from the airships."); (2) an enthralled spectator, exalted by his subordinates on the ground ("We were getting full reports on literally a minute-by-minute basis. 'Sir, we just broke in.' 'Sir, the wall is down.' 'Sir,' you know, 'we've captured.' 'Sir, two people are coming out right now.'"); (3) as simultaneously subject, object, and consumer of media and celebrity culture, picking his war-on-terror targets to maximize his own celebrity standing, quoting himself by way of creating an authentic record of the past ("Well, I'll tell you, from the first day I came to office – and now we're getting close to three years – I would say,

'Where's al-Baghdadi? I want al-Baghdadi.' And we would kill terrorist leaders, but they were names I never heard of. They were names that weren't recognizable and they weren't the big names. Some good ones, some important ones, but they weren't the big names. I kept saying, 'Where's al-Baghdadi?'").

Trump also refers to himself in the third person and cites to himself to establish himself as truth, authority, and celebrity ("If you read about the history of Donald Trump – I was a civilian. I had absolutely nothing to do with going into Iraq, and I was totally against it. But I always used to say, 'If they're going to go in. . . – nobody cared that much, but it got written about. 'If they're going to go in. . .' – I'm sure you've heard the statement, because I made it more than any human being alive."). With assembled journalists enlisted into the role of deferential but engaged spectators, the press conference *appears* to stage a democratizing encounter between the president and "the people." However, through the lens of imperial spectacle, the press conference can be seen as an instance of necropolitical culture's visuality, discounting lives by cultivating the passivity of spectatorship in national and global audiences, alongside fascination and awe for the superior killing and surveilling technologies of the counterterror state.

4.5 NECROPOLITICAL LAW AND THE SAYABLE

Transgression, as noted above, is a key modality of Trump's statecraft. Two strands of his al-Baghdadi announcement shape law's archive in a uniquely Trumpian, transgressive manner. First, he spoke repeatedly and explicitly about the national/imperial commercial advantage to the United States of commanding Syrian oil resources that had been under ISIS control (Section 4.5.1). And second, he dwelled upon the *manner* of al-Baghdadi's death and suffering (Section 4.5.2). Obama's announcement of the bin Laden killing (Chapter 3) offers a foil to Trump's announcement about al-Baghdadi, illustrating how Trump's detailing of the manner and affect of an enemy's death crosses a line into what has been called "war porn" (Section 4.5.2). And in explicitly exulting in control over Syrian oil, Trump also departs from past practice as elaborated in Section 4.5.1.

Departing from this norm of presidential discourse by delighting in an enemy's suffering and by making explicit the mutually constituting military-commercial dimensions of empire, Trump has rendered the unspeakable sayable, and the hidden visible. For Foucault, the archive is a system, "a whole set of relations that are peculiar to the discursive level," such that the archive is "first the law of what can be said," defining "at the outset *the system of its enunciability*" (2010 [1972]: 129). Drawing in part on Foucault, Renisa Mawani's important intervention has been to conceptualize law as archive, "a site from which law derives its meanings, authority, and legitimacy" (2012: 337). Through the lens of law as archive, it is not so much that Trump introduced a new note into the discursive system that is necropolitical law. Rather, he has excavated a subterranean, unspoken strand of law's archive relating to the discounting of life. In doing so, Trump mimics a discursive dynamic inherent to law's self-generating, self-authorizing texture. Some of these discursive dynamics of law as archive (Mawani 2012) were discussed in Chapter 2. The Patriot Act offers a straightforward instance of how law's co-constitutions with authority, sovereignty, violence, and documentation are expressed through the "self-generating qualities" (Mawani 2012: 341) of the Act's citational structures and its self-scripted planetary command. In privileging precedent, law refers to past discourse to selectively determine present relevance and utility, in the process remaking meaning while authorizing both the past and the sovereign's capacity to script law and law's meanings (Mawani 2012: 341; Goodman et al. 2014).

Engaging in the project of reading for law in cultural text illuminates a similar dynamic in Trump's discourse. By excavating a subterranean strand of the necropolitical sovereign's long-standing self-authorizing imperial violence, hatred of enemies, and extractive appropriation of resources, Trump is also referencing, reinterpreting, and remaking precedent. In the process, the symbolic and material force of the killing of al-Baghdadi and discounted Others constitute one part of law's archive on this matter. Additionally, by altering "the law of what can be said" (Foucault 1972 [2010]: 129), Trump authorizes a necropolitical set of meanings and relations, asserts his and the United States' authority, and sanctions violence that discounts life. In keeping with the traits of law as archive, Trump's seeming transgression articulates the "reciprocal and reinforcing violence of law as archive … highlight[ing] the preservation and destruction by which law generates the veracity of its own legality (Mawani 2012: 341).

4.5.1 Planetary Jurisdiction and Oil

Melani McAlister traces how constructing oil as a US national interest – even when that oil is in parts of the world other than the United

States – informs the "complex layering of cultural ... and social practices through which the Middle East is made significant to U.S. and global audiences" (2005: 2). She notes:

> For decades, beginning in the 1940s and intensifying after the oil crisis of the 1970s, narratives of a U.S. "national interest in oil" were present in everything from presidential statements to car advertisements ... By the time of the 1990–1991 Gulf War, when the United States led a multinational coalition to support Saudi Arabia and Kuwait against Iraq, oil was presumed, both by those who supported and those who opposed the war, to be a primary American interest and a motivation for U.S. policy.
>
> (2005:1)

Importantly, while the US national interest in oil has long been *presumed* to motivate US imperialism, previous presidents have crafted narratives of "benevolent supremacy," yoking US interest in oil to a moral discourse of US virtue in world affairs (McAlister 2005: 45–46). Benevolent supremacy justifies foreign policy and military action on more seemingly exalted grounds, for example, protecting America and its friends, saving democracy, disarming weapons of mass destruction, and ensuring peace (e.g., Bush 1991; Bush 2003). In a departure from past practice, in Trump's announcement there is a naked merging of the projects of imperial violence and imperial commerce. Notably, Trump does not mention oil in his prepared text, nor was he asked by the assembled journalists whether oil was a factor motivating the killing of al-Baghdadi. Instead, when responding to questions on two seemingly unrelated topics, Trump spoke at length about oil. Much of what he said was repetitive (see the excerpt quoted below on the flavor of the repetition), but despite Trump mentioning oil twenty-two times, none of the journalists present asked a follow-up question about the role oil had played in motivating the raid. Nor did any of the journalists question Trump's representation of Syrian oil as a US entitlement:

Q: Does this give you any pause by your decision to withdraw the troops?

T: No, I think it's great. ... We're out. But we are leaving soldiers to secure the oil. And we may have to fight for the oil. It's okay. Maybe somebody else wants the oil, in which case they have a hell of a fight. But there's massive amounts of oil. And we're securing it for a couple of reasons. Number one, it stops ISIS, because ISIS got tremendous wealth from that oil. We have taken it. It's secured. Number two – and again, somebody else may claim it, but either we'll negotiate a deal with whoever is claiming it, if we think it's fair, or we will militarily stop them very quickly. We have tremendous power in that part of the world. ...

Q: You mentioned that you met some – gotten to know some brilliant people along this process who really helped provide information and advice along the way. Is there anyone in particular, or would you like to give anyone credit for getting to this point today?

T: ... But where Lindsey and I totally agree is the oil. The oil is, you know, so valuable for many reasons. It fueled ISIS, number one. Number two, it helps the Kurds, because it's basically been taken away from the Kurds. They were able to live with that oil. And number three, it can help us because we should be able to take some also. And what I intend to do, perhaps, is make a deal with an Exxon Mobil or one of our great companies to go in there and do it properly. Right now, it's not big. It's big oil underground, but it's not big oil up top, and much of the machinery has been shot and dead. It's been through wars. But – and – and spread out the wealth. But, no, we're protecting the oil. We're securing the oil. Now, that doesn't mean we don't make a deal at some point. But I don't want to be – they're fighting for 1,000 years, they're fighting for centuries. I want to bring our soldiers back home. But I do want to secure the oil.

Despite Trump's emphasis on oil, media paid scant attention to Trump's assertion of a blatantly commercialized version of planetary jurisdiction. Framed by an imperialist assumption that the oil in this foreign territory was now America's to take or trade, Trump's narrative of the military and counterterror rationale for the raid – the importance of depriving ISIS of a primary source of income – pales in comparison to the repeated emphasis on the commercial dimensions. The benevolent supremacy and imperial stewardship couching prior US official discourse relating to Middle Eastern oil (McAlister 2005) is quite simply discarded. In saying the previously unsayable, Trump has recorded for necropolitical law's archive the explicitly commercial, deal-making dimensions of counterterror state's planetary jurisdiction. In doing so, he has excavated a subterranean strand of the "enunciative possibilities and impossibilities" (Foucault 1972 [2010]: 129) laid down by the discursive system on US imperialism.

Trump's transgressive articulation discloses the discounting of life accompanying and justifying US control and profit over Middle Eastern oil. Trump's language also discloses the profound success of the decades-long ideological and cultural project of constructing Middle Eastern oil as available for US appropriation, even as the Middle East is cast as the site and source of terrorism and military threat (McAlister 2005: 1–3). Trump departs from presidential traditions demarcating the sayable from the unsayable, in continuity with a tradition of US imperialism that understands oil as tied to overseas warring and the co-constitution of US domestic and imperial interests (McAlister 2005).

4.5.2 Necropolitical Law and War Porn

Trump's second noteworthy articulation of the previously unsayable is evident in Trump's insistent highlighting of al-Baghdadi's terrible end. He did so by positioning himself as a spectator well and truly enthralled with technologies of surveillance and lethality.[29] In response to the very first question asked during the press conference,[30] Trump said:

T: ... it was something really amazing to see. I got to watch it, along with General Milley, Vice President Pence, others, in the Situation Room. And we watched it so clearly.

Q: They had body cameras? Or how did you watch the –

T: Well, I don't want to say how, but we had absolutely perfect – as though you were watching a movie. It was – that – the technology there alone is really great.

When the killing of a war-on-terror enemy is likened to "watching a movie," the implication is that the viewing has yielded the thrills and pleasures of entertainment. At one level, Trump's spectatorship, along with his choice of words, conveys his voyeuristic pleasure in watching this person, and those around him, die. It is a form of pleasure also experienced by drone operators as they watch people die (Gusterson 2016: 63). The voyeurism of watching without being seen establishes "the dominance of the watcher over the watched" (Gusterson 2016:

---

[29] Ironically, while Trump makes repeated reference to ISIS's use of visual culture and technologies of publicity, deploring ISIS's use of orange suits, cages, and displays of brutal dominance over captives, he does so without seeming to realize how these visually index and mimic the counterterror state's treatment of detainees.

[30] The question asked of Trump was "When did you first hear that this was – operation was going to get started?"

63). The "structuring reality" of the watcher anticipating then celebrating the death and destruction of the watched has given rise to a genre of videos known as "war porn" and "drone porn" (Hussain 2013; Gusterson 2016: 63). In explicitly celebrating the pain and suffering experienced by al-Baghdadi, and in admiring the "great" technology that enabled him to watch the killing as if it were a movie, Trump – who is simultaneously audience, embodiment of the state, and president staging himself as the White, male, militarized hero of imperial spectacle – endorses this particular form of pleasure.

While, as media products, drone porn and war porn are very much of our present, they also reveal deeper histories at work. In tracing "the links between modernity and terror," Achille Mbembe points to how the guillotine, as a technology of killing, marked the emergence of "a new cultural sensibility ... in which the killing of the enemy of the state is an extension of play. More intimate, lurid, and leisurely forms of cruelty begin to take shape" (2019: 72–73). A strand of history closer to home informing Trump's voyeuristic pleasure in al-Baghdadi's death is captured by Saidiya Hartman's influential scholarship on the torture and subjection of slaves in nineteenth-century America. Deploring the casual circulation and reproduction of scenes of such torture, Hartman notes:

> [r]ather than inciting indignation, too often they immure us to pain by virtue of their familiarity; ... the theatrical language usually resorted to in describing these instances ... reinforce[s] the spectacular character of black suffering. What interests me is the way in which we are called upon to participate in such scenes. Are we witnesses who confirm the truth of what happened in the face of the world-destroying capacities of pain, the distortions of torture, the sheer unrepresentability of terror, and the repression of the dominant accounts? Or are we voyeurs fascinated with and repelled by exhibitions of terror and sufferance? ... Only more obscene than the brutality unleashed at the whipping post is the demand that this suffering be materialized and evidenced by the display of the tortured body or endless recitations of the ghastly and the terrible.
>
> (1987: 3–4)

The "more obscene" cultural sensibility of taking pleasure in the torture and killing of an enemy is also at work in the contemporary genre of visual media known as "militainment": "state violence translated into an object of pleasurable consumption ... [when it] is not of the distant or historical variety but rather an impending or current use of force, one directly relevant to the citizen's political life" (Stahl 2010: 6). As president, Trump's detailing of al-Baghdadi's fear and torturous manner of death lends the state's stamp of approval to public expressions of delight in the pain, suffering, and violent killing of a war-on-terror enemy. Trump's repetitive and transgressive language conjures up scenes of al-Baghdadi's torment and subjection, a version of the "endless recitations of the ghastly and the terrible" (Hartman 1987: 3). In the process, the necropolitical force of separation (Mbembe 2019: 1) is deepened, even as Trump discloses his eager participation in the workings of necropolitical power's "indifference to objective signs of cruelty" (Mbembe 2019: 38).

When, as president, Trump publicly dwells upon, with almost salacious delight, the suffering, distress, and intensity of violence experienced by enemies in the long War on Terror, the counterterror state signifies the degree to which "terrorists" are regarded, not as fellow human beings but as "a hateful and loathsome 'other' who can be killed and abused without remorse or regret" (Jackson 2005: 60).

> For both soldiers and wider society the common everyday language of human recognition and respect has to be replaced by the language of hate and fear; perceptions and emotions have to be profoundly altered so ordinary people can more easily countenance the deliberate infliction of suffering. There is no better way to achieve this than by replacing the language they ordinarily use with a new language of hate and fear based on powerful categories of identity: them and us, citizen and foreigner, civilized and savage, terrorist and soldier.
>
> (Jackson 2005: 60)

In other words, the killing of al-Baghdadi shows us that those designated "enemy" are situated beyond the bounds of conventional law and humanity. Framed instead through the logics of necropolitical law, the degree of their enmity, their monstrous savagery (borrowing Trump's language), is such that those around them may also be slaughtered and left uncounted and unidentified. Media and publics no longer ask, as they did when Osama bin Laden was killed – if US Special Forces can get close enough to kill, is there not the possibility of capture and a trial? That this question no longer gets asked is an omission pointing to the growing consolidation of necropolitical law.

Building on Chapter 4's discussion of the role played by imperial spectacles and the re-semanticization of "terrorist" in legitimizing necropolitical law, Chapter 5 addresses the necropolitical visuality of militainment in the 2016 film on drone warfare *Eye in the Sky* to illuminate popular culture's role in scripting us into being as spectator-consumers, while legitimizing the counterterror state's discounting of life through necropolitical law. Specifically, the film's gripping plot, stellar performances, and dazzling technology distract us, first, from the de-democratizing and dehumanizing concealments and erasures that accompany drone warfare and, second, from the remaking of lawful authority through a dramatization of the "responsibility to protect," which is a (highly contested) principle of international law. In the process, the film renders visible a particular set of actors, narratives, and questions while concealing and erasing others, thereby legitimizing drone warfare and valorizing its actors, institutions, practices, and technologies. As text *Eye in the Sky* is an instance of the "cultural sensibility ... in which killing the enemy of the state is an extension of play" (Mbembe 2019: 73). Given the official secrecy accompanying drone warfare and the film's convincing incorporation of fact into its fiction, *Eye in the Sky* becomes a compelling representation of the necessity of drone warfare as enacted by lawful military actors in the aim of securing civilians worldwide.

CHAPTER FIVE

NECROPOLITICAL LAW, NECROPOLITICAL CULTURE

Eye in the Sky

5.1 INTRODUCTION

On August 29, 2021, a US military drone strike blew up a vehicle in Kabul, which according to Defense Department officials was "laden with explosives" (Cooper and Schmitt 2021). Consistent with the counterterror state's logics of preemptive, anticipatory killing, a spokesman for US Central Command asserted that, with this strike, the United States had "eliminated an imminent threat to Hamid Karzai International Airport" posed by the same group that just two days earlier had conducted a suicide bombing at Kabul airport (Cooper and Schmitt 2021). However, as exposed a week later by a *New York Times* investigation, the strike killed at least ten innocent civilians, including seven children and a "completely harmless" aid worker.

> Almost everything senior defense officials asserted in the hours, and then days, and then weeks after the August 29 drone strike turned out to be false. The explosives the military claimed were loaded in the trunk of a white Toyota sedan struck by the drone's Hellfire missile were probably water bottles, and a secondary explosion in the courtyard in a densely populated Kabul neighborhood where the attack took place was probably a propane or gas tank, officials said.
>
> (Schmitt and Cooper 2021)

Disclosing the logics of drone warfare, this killing had been enacted and justified on the basis of "interpretive leaps," "framing moral judgments," and "narrative infilling" (Gusterson 2016: 66). These leaps expose the "unconscious cultural assumptions" through which "shards of visual information" combine with faulty intelligence to convince drone operators – not infrequently – to kill innocent civilians (Gusterson 2016: 66). From afar, this lethal cocktail of flawed intelligence, fragmentary images, and assumptions of enmity intoxicates those empowered to kill, such that water bottles are mistaken for explosives, an aid worker is cast as a "terrorist," based in part on the assumption that his boss's home looked like an ISIS safe house. If the *New York Times*'s investigative reporting had not challenged it, the counterterror state's false account would have captured and fixed law's record. This chapter examines the coconstitutions of law and culture through which drone warfare is legitimized as a key modality of American militarized imperialism's necropolitical law.

The asymmetry of drone warfare marks this form of weaponry as inextricably imperial (Chamayou 2015 [2013]).[1] Imperialism, Mbembe highlights, is always already necropolitical (2019), and as so influentially established by Frantz Fanon (1961; 1952) and Edward Said (1978; 1993), dominant culture justifies and authorizes imperialism, constituting hierarchies of racialized and exclusionary communities through oftennormalized relations and social formations of power, violence, and control. As a key strand of the fabric of the social, law has been exposed as the accomplice of imperialism's necropolitical violence (e.g., Fitzpatrick 1992; Anghie 2005; Comaroff and Comaroff 2007; Mawani 2012). When law and culture are approached as co-constituents (Cover 1983; Rosen 2006) and popular culture is recognized as a site for the "the production, interpretation, consumption, and circulation of legal meaning" (Sarat and Kearns 1998: 6), then the workings of law become discernible not only in the official texts of the state such as legislation, presidential announcements, and news media as analyzed in Chapters 2, 3, and 4 but also in entertainment media.

To demonstrate necropolitical law's legitimations in and through the cultural text that is entertainment media, Chapter 5 analyzes the 2015 Gavin Hood film on drone warfare, *Eye in the Sky*. As a text of necropolitical culture, *Eye* is an episode in the US state's broader project of eliciting popular consent for and acquiescence to the long War on Terror through entertainment media (Section 5.2). Section 5.3 describes the film's plot, examining the ways *Eye* expresses the concerns central to law's archive – law, violence, sovereignty, and authority. Section 5.4 shows how, by adhering to the key genre conventions of

---

[1] Chamayou characterizes drone warfare as structured by "necroethics" through the "quasi-invulnerability of the dominant camp" (Chamayou 2015 [2013]: 157).

the combat film, *Eye* valorizes militarized imperialism, while imparting knowledge about this relatively new form of warfare. At the same time, by drawing on the familiar genre of the combat film, *Eye* disseminates updated accounts of American political myth. Section 5.5 details *Eye's* legitimation of the controversial and neocolonial international law concept, responsibility to protect. In Section 5.6, because of the twinning of law and war in the film, I explore the work *Eye* does as a trial film, juridifying audiences and convincing us that we are informed, knowledgeable triers of the "facts" relating to drone warfare and counterterrorism. Section 5.7 analyzes how the spectatorship and virtualization central to *Eye* normalizes planetary jurisdiction, state surveillance, and preemptive violence, convincing us that the secrecy and asymmetry of drone warfare is necessary to our safety. As a whole, Chapter 5 reveals a sophisticated film playing a key and troubling role in the larger project of scripting and disseminating necropolitical law, thereby inducing popular consent for the discounting of life in the long War on Terror.

5.2 NECROPOLITICAL CULTURE

Attending to the co-constitutions of law and entertainment media becomes all the more important, given the centrality of visual and popular culture to the US state's project of eliciting popular consent for the long War on Terror (e.g., Koppes and Black 1990; Birkenstein, Froula, and Randell 2010; Stahl 2010; Masco 2014; Der Derian 2009). From at least 1927, the US military and Hollywood have been collaborators in the production of entertainment media (Lange 2018). During World War II the Office of War Information (OWI)

> hoped to capitalize on the artfulness of Hollywood and the susceptibility of movie audiences, "spellbound in the darkness," to insinuate its message into the minds of an unsuspecting public. As [OWI] Director Elmer Davis put it: "The easiest way to inject a propaganda idea into most people's minds is to let it go in through the medium of an entertainment picture when they do not realize they are being propagandized." Entertainment pictures could presumably reach a mass audience impervious to carefully reasoned writing. ... OWI prepared to manipulate cinema images in ways imperceptible to the public.
>
> (Koppes and Black 1990: 64)

From 1945, and the United States' nuclear bombing of Hiroshima and Nagasaki, "a broader aestheticizing of politics in support of increasing militarization and war" has been central to the US state's infrastructure for cultivating a fearful citizenry "through threat-based projection" (Masco 2014: 71, 14). Today, each branch of the armed forces has its own Hollywood liaison office (Lange 2018). While the US military justifies its close working relationship with Hollywood as motivated by a concern for "accuracy" and the protection of "sensitive information" (Lange 2018), scholars and critics point to long-standing dynamics of censorship, propaganda, and complicity designed to glorify, normalize, and legitimize American military imperialism (e.g., Koppes and Black 1990; Der Derian 2001; Suid 2002 [1978]; Slotkin 2001; Basinger 2003 [1986]; Robb 2004; Stahl 2010). In other words, the long War on Terror has systemically and structurally been accompanied by the generation of entertainment media justifying the discounting of the lives of racialized Others as the necessary means through which American lives and the American nation must be secured. It is this media that I call necropolitical culture.

One important modality for this broader aestheticizing of politics in support of militarism has been the combat film. A vital cultural platform for imagining America as legitimate in its belligerent patriotism and imperialism (Slotkin 2001), the emergence of combat films is traceable to World War II, when "a talented team of Hollywood directors and writers enlisted in the armed services and were assigned to the film units that created [documentary movies], including Frank Capra, John Huston, John Ford, George Stevens, and William Wyler" (Basinger 1998). Even though these were documentaries, "they contained their own kind of passionate storytelling" (Basinger 2003: 113). And of course, these filmmakers made war films both during and after the war, becoming part of an infrastructure that enmeshed Hollywood and the US state (Basinger 2003).

Jeanine Basinger's influential scholarship on the emergence of the combat film as a genre shows how the narrative and visual patterns of these World War II combat films transformed audiences into intimate and knowledgeable participants of that war. Exposed through the affect, images, sound, and narrative of film to war's technologies and perspectives, citizens became spectator-subject-consumers of the nation- and empire-securing ideological project of war (Basinger 2003 [1986]; Slotkin 2017, 2001;). As Basinger and Slotkin show, both during and after World War II, the genre of combat films introduced publics to war's technologies and dynamics, dissolving the line between "fact" and "fiction," while rehearsing and revitalizing American political myth. This melding of "fact" and "fiction" was achieved in part through the passionate storytelling animating war documentaries, but it also came from incorporating actual war footage into fictionalized representations (Basinger 2003). As technologies of war became more and more asymmetrical and spectacular, media representations of war have cultivated audiences to be fascinated with technology, such that, rather than "examine the legitimacy of military action," both news and entertainment media relating to war rely on technofetishism, "the worship of high-end weaponry, ... ascribing weapons an inherent virtue or beauty [and] positioning military hardware at the center of the television war drama" (Stahl 2010: 28).

It is in the tradition of American political myth and the war film to imagine apocalyptic and nation-destroying trauma. The war film

> concerns itself not only with history and battle, but also with the underlying issue of what it means to be an American. Here is a nation that [sometimes] seeks to whip its populace into patriotic fervor by showing them films based on *defeat*, not victory. ... We may be losers, but we never give up – and losers who never give up will finally win.
>
> (Basinger 2003: 31)

Basinger's examples of iconic defeats regarded as galvanizing for the future glories of American militarism include the Alamo, Valley Forge, and Custer's Last Stand (2003: 31). Put differently, the trope of glorifying momentary defeat as testament to the American national determination to fight and win reaches back into the founding moments of the United States – which, as I argued in Chapter 1, are simultaneously the founding moments of the long War on Terror. Rooted in this necropolitical past, the insistent memorializing of the 9/11 attacks is to be understood as the latest iteration of the long-established cultural trope of regarding defeat as the promise of future victory. The guarantee holds as long as America and Americans remain willing to go to war.

The place of the combat film in American popular culture and Masco's genealogy for how American visual culture imagines threat in order to foster militarization are expressions of what James Der Derian (2009) so memorably identifies as MIME-NET – the military-industrial-media-entertainment network.[2] Starkly put, MIME-NET is an all-encompassing necropolitical infrastructure, a socially pervasive, almost invisible (because normalized) engine of "the war machine"

---

[2] Der Derian traces the tentacular, manipulative, seductive, real, and hyperreal web of relations, media, and technologies informing our perceptions of, and disconnections from, contemporary war, attending, for example, to the way simulations and war-games *precede* the actual unfolding of events such that reality mimes hyperreality.

(Der Derian 2009: 254). Working in concert with the military, arms manufacturers, and "an aggressive American foreign policy," the entertainment industry "produces narratives that construct a sense of global insecurity ... [that justifies] the military" (Höglund and Willander 2017: 370). In this chapter, I approach *Eye*, an ostensibly fictional representation of drone warfare, as an instance of how, in the long War on Terror, cultural text represents the lawfulness of war.

Galvanizing the cultural infrastructures established from World War II (Basinger 2003; Masco 2014), the military–industrial–media–entertainment network took on a heightened and obvious expression in the 1991 Gulf War by virtue of the state's close management of media, the canny primetime staging of the war's launching, and the starring role played by the Patriot missile.[3] After 9/11 the symbiotic relationship (Suid 2002 [1978]) between the US military and media shifted from intimate to "incestuous," as something akin to a military coup over media unfolded (Der Derian 2009: 277). In addition to selectively embedding journalists, a "full-fledged infowar was also launched off the battlefield and in the home studios."

> Infowar, deployed after September 11 as the discontinuation of diplomacy by other means, became a force multiplier in Iraq, a weapon of destruction as well as persuasion and distraction. Lost in the hoopla over the stories and images streaming in from the dessert was the fact that the military had taken over the television studios. Retired general and flag officers exercised full spectrum dominance on cable and network TV as well as on commercial and public radio. (Der Derian 2009: 277)[4]

Consistent with the deception at the core of necropolitics (Mbembe 2019), this intensification of the military-industrial-media-entertainment network has been misrepresented as a fresh innovation, newly

---

[3] See discussion in Chapter 2.

[4] Infowar, in Der Derian's sense, is something of a catchall phrased used by the national security state to include communications, intelligence, surveillance, "smart" weapons, "multispectral sensors, real-time battlefield data ... networked commands, near real-time decision loops, just-in-time simulations ... deterritorialized forms of conflict, which use and target discourse of power – sign systems of belief, knowledge, representation – embedded in technologies of information. Broadly conceived, infowar is as old as Sun Tze's 'strategic factors' and as new as the armed forces' Joint Vision 2010's 'full spectrum dominance.' However, the new infowar is significantly different from past forms in the proliferation of networked computing and the use of high-resolution video. This makes possible new forms of control and governance" (2009: 118–19).

minted to meet the exigencies of the long War on Terror. Two months after the 9/11 attacks, news media reported:

> Top executives from Hollywood's movie studios, television networks, cinema operators and labor unions met for 90 minutes this morning with Karl Rove, senior adviser to President Bush, to discuss how the entertainment industry could cooperate in the war on terrorism and to begin setting up a structure to make it happen.
>
> (Lyman 2001)

In reality, as noted above, this "cooperation" had long been in place. From at least 1927, through World War II and the Cold War, an increasingly consolidated relationship between the state and media has accumulated and established a necropolitical culture: an infrastructure of images, affect, and narrative for a popular visual culture legitimizing and authorizing American militarized imperialism's discounting of life.

5.2.1 Drone Warfare and the Military–Industrial–Media–Entertainment Network

Despite the escalation and intensification of drone warfare over time, and despite the fact that we live in an era of visual culture, for those of us in the global North, drone warfare has become backgrounded, almost invisible (e.g., Hussain 2013; Chamayou 2015; Gusterson 2016). The backgrounding reflects in part the US state's careful management of how drone warfare is represented. In addition to the tentacular military-industrial-media-entertainment network (Der Derian 2009), the state's capacity to disproportionately manage representations of drone warfare is also a result of the amplified dynamics of secrecy, complexity, and unaccountable power characterizing the counterterror state (Masco 2014). Necropolitical law's operations in relation to drone warfare surfaced again in the public domain in November 2021, when the *New York Times* reported on the March 2019 killing of eighty people, mostly women and children, in Syria (Philipps and Schmitt 2021). The special operations unit in charge of the attack, combining drone warfare with airstrikes, was able to falsify records, force an evaluator out of his job, and manufacture claims of "imminent danger," in the aftermath of killing civilians on a scale amounting to a possible war crime (Philipps and Schmitt 2021). The *New York Times* investigation establishes how, "at nearly every step, the military made moves that concealed the catastrophic strike," while claiming to adhere to law and rules (Philipps and Schmitt 2021). March 2019, the moment of the catastrophe, was also the moment in which Trump summarily "revoked an Obama-era rule requiring an annual public report on US drone strikes, including civilian casualties" (Grossman 2019). In one researcher's assessment, the Trump revocation was an extension of the deceptions and fractured transparency of the notoriously imprecise counterterror state's reports (Grossman 2019). As spectator–consumer–publics, we are kept profoundly ignorant of the uncountable instances in which people falsely designated "enemy" have been killed and maimed in the possible war crimes executed and denied in the name of counterterror.

The complexity and secrecy of drone warfare relate, in part, to the fact that the US government runs two drone programs (Mayer 2009). One of them (the military's) is public and operates in recognized war zones. The second, however, is run in secret by the CIA. This covert program "is aimed at terror suspects around the world, including in countries where U.S. troops are not based." The CIA "declines to provide any information to the public about where it operates, how it selects targets, who is in charge, or how many people have been killed" (Mayer 2009). The March 2019 strike in Syria reveals that nested within this doubling of drone warfare as both public and secret, Task Force 9, operating "at a high level of secrecy," having killed large numbers of civilians, was able to claim that the killings were legal and justified. The "death toll was downplayed. Reports were delayed, sanitized and classified. United States-led coalition forces bulldozed the blast site. And top leaders were not notified" (Philipps and Schmitt 2021).

Necropolitical deception (Mbembe 2019) aligns with secrecy in the management of media on drone warfare, as is evident in the fractures and dissonances between what the state tells us and what we learn from scholars, investigative journalists, and activists. For example, between 2004 and 2010, an estimated 8,858–16,901 people were killed by US drone strikes.[5] In keeping with the racialized logics of necropolitics, these killings took place in Afghanistan, Pakistan, Somalia, and Yemen, discounting the lives of distant Brown and Black, primarily Muslim Others. Among these fatalities, from 910 to 2,200 were civilians, and 283 to 454 children, while a further uncounted number of

[5] See www.thebureauinvestigates.com/projects/drone-war.

people have been injured and maimed.[6] As the wide ranges of these estimates show, the United States does not disclose – and possibly does not track – the lives discounted by its asymmetrical killing technology. That the figures are such approximate estimates reflects the secrecy surrounding drone warfare. Updated tolls and closer estimates are hard to come by.

In official, state discourse, drones are repeatedly celebrated for being clean, precise, and surgical. According to Gregoire Chamayou, however, such declarations are meaningless without distinguishing between precision in terms of firing accuracy and the uncontainability of the radius measuring a munition's zone of killing and wounding:

> There is a crucial difference between hitting the target and hitting only the target. ... One cannot help wondering in what fictitious world killing an individual with an antitank missile that annihilates every living being within a radius of 15 meters, and wounds all those within a radius of 20 meters, can be reputed to be "more precise."
> (Chamayou 2015: 141–42)

Chamayou also points to the confusion between "the technical precision of the weapon and its capacity to discriminate in the choice of targets."

> The fact that your weapon enables you to destroy precisely whomever you wish does not mean that you are more capable of making out who is and who is not a legitimate target. The precision of the strike has no bearing on the pertinence of the targeting in the first place.
> (Chamayou 2015: 142–43)

The August 2021 killing of ten civilians in Afghanistan, described at the opening of this chapter, evidences the lethal precision accompanying drone warfare's frequent errors when it comes to discriminating targets. And when drones combine with other forms of aerial warfare, as in the March 2019 possible war crime in Syria, the scale and speed of killing are magnified. The acuity of Chamayou's analysis has been borne out not only by the November 2021 disclosures in the *New York Times* but also by the work of investigative journalist David Cloud (2011). Drawing on interviews and on transcripts of drone operations obtained through Freedom of Information Act requests, Cloud reconstructed a February 2010 operation in which the US Air

---

[6] See www.thebureauinvestigates.com/projects/drone-war.

Force launched an attack by drones and helicopters relying on drone surveillance. According to Afghan villagers, twenty-three civilians were killed in the attack, including three- and four-year-old children. The United States argues that only fifteen or maybe sixteen were killed, conceding that the victims were all civilians. In the transcripts Cloud obtained, the language the operators used (and the many expletives deleted by the government censor) show their eager anticipation to kill, the dynamics of hatred for a foreign Other, and a troubling dehumanizing of the victims (Cloud 2011; Chamayou 2015; Gusterson 2016). Additionally, contrary to representations of drones relaying high-resolution surveillance, drones tend to produce grainy images, where it is the interpretation of these unclear images that expresses the drone operators' "palpable hunger to attack" (Gusterson 2016: 70).

These realities of drone warfare must be borne in mind for the sake of the narrative tension and plot development in *Eye*, which in the film's penultimate moments lead us to witnessing the two primary forms of killing in drone warfare: targeted assassination and collateral damage. Liam Kennedy argues that the execution of violent state power "enacted as shock and awe, as high technological interventions in foreign terrains, with the use of drones" works in tandem with "collateral damage."

> [T]hese forms of violence are linked in the visual culture of perpetual war: in different yet closely related ways they signify the naturalization of preemptive violence as the right and might of the state. They also assert the powerful sovereignty of the state, for such violence creates its own interpretive conditions and so suspends the ethical and legal conventions of response to its enactments.
>
> (Kennedy 2012: 265)

For us as audiences – as mediatized spectator-consumers – of necropolitical culture, this chapter argues that by justifying preemptive violence and showing "Western" military actors to be ethical and humane, *Eye* reinscribes the dominant narratives and identities of the long War on Terror. And by showing us the global coordinates of a drone strike, *Eye* does more than assert "the powerful sovereignty of the state" (265); it asserts that *planetary* military sovereignty for the "West" is necessary to our security. In the process, *Eye's* narrative arc legitimizes drone warfare's enactments of necropolitical law. Before going into further detail about the film, however, a brief discussion of the relationship between necropolitical culture and state policy is called for.

5.2.2 Necropolitical Culture and Policy

The centrality of popular culture to necropolitical law has already been evidenced in this book in the naming of the Patriot Act (Chapter 2), the invocations of frontier justice (Chapter 3), and in the political myth marking the dominant tropes of the long War on Terror (Chapters 2 through 4). Richard Slotkin highlights a related instance of popular culture's imbrications with the state in policy-making in President Bush's elevation in January 2002, five months after the events of 9/11, of the 2001 Ridley Scott movie, *Black Hawk Down*, to the status of "official Washington's must-see movie." He screened the film at the White House for invited members of Congress, describing it to aides as a cautionary tale about how America had been wrong to hastily exit Somalia after eighteen American soldiers died in the 1993 raid on Mogadishu (Slotkin 2017: 1; Barry 2005).[7]

The film was based on the account of the UN-authorized US military raid by investigative journalist Mark Bowden. Ostensibly nonfiction, the book is written in a style more commonly associated with fiction, including an omniscient narrator operating in the style of a Tom Clancy page-turner.[8] Bowden is straightforward about his conviction that the US soldiers are heroic and morally exalted, detailing how his manner of writing is meant to capture "the undeniable nobility of military service" (2010: 358).

In the afterword to 2010 edition of *Black Hawk Down* (first published in 1999), Bowden reflects on the book's popular appeal and commercial success, as well as the promotional effects of the 2001 film. Situating his book in a pantheon of popular and critically acclaimed novels, films, and works of journalism, Bowden declares, "We can and ought to deplore war," even as he exalts American soldiers. Characterizing war as "an essential element of the human experience" (2010: 356), Bowden rehearses prominent tropes in the counterterror state's discourse:

---

[7] In keeping with the necropolitical logics that discount certain lives, there is no clarity as to how many Somalis died. Estimates range from 315 to 2000; Höglund and Willander (2017: 367).

[8] Discussing his goal to write "a story of brave men at war" (Bowden 2010: 358), Bowden's choice of authorial omniscience is consistent with his stance: "As a writer and a journalist, someone with an ambition to tell true stories with the emotion and intimacy of good fiction" (2010: 387).

> [E]vil exists. So long as men are both good and evil, inside themselves
> and in their actions in the world, there will be conflict. And when there
> are evil forces at work in the world ... good men and women will step
> forward to fight. ... The book sold and sold and sold and then that great
> movie was made and the book sold some more. ... I like to think that
> *Black Hawk Down* contributed to a sea change in America's attitude
> about war and about soldiers. The attacks of September 11, however,
> were the most dramatic change. Suddenly, Americans were reminded
> why they needed soldiers. In the years since, we've seen a steady stream
> of literary books and movies and TV shows that no longer strictly
> portray soldiers as sadists, stooges, victims, or lunatics. Today, even
> those who oppose the wars in Iraq or Afghanistan take pains to empha-
> size their respect for our troops. I have seen young men and women in
> combat fatigues get spontaneous standing ovations as they move
> through their airports, and it never fails to bring a tear to my eyes.
>
> (Bowden 2010: 358–59)

The "sea change" lauded by Bowden is, of course, linked to the broader
cultural project of amplified militarism and militarization after 9/11
(Lutz 2009). Considering the wide reach and popular appeal of movies,
it is important to note that Bowden's book was much more complex
than the Ridley Scott movie adaptation. In his book, despite his
explicit admiration for American soldiers, Bowden makes an effort to
contextualize the conflict historically, including incorporating to a
degree a Somali perspective as part of the complexity (Höglund and
Willander 2017: 373–74). Bowden also details a critical violation of
US military protocol that resulted in many (although uncounted)
Somali civilian victims (Höglund and Willander 2017: 373). The
movie, in contrast, abandons the book's efforts to supply context and
account for complexity. The movie

> celebrates the camaraderie, sacrifice, and heroism of the fighting soldier
> even as it depicts the deplorable brutality and even futility of war, ... [in
> the process] celebrat[ing] the culture of soldiers who embody laudable
> core values even in the face of harrowing danger and insurmountable
> odds. These narrative and cinematic elements invite viewers to release
> any dissonance they might feel at the prospect of supporting what
> soldiers do (make war when war is terrible). Ironically, such a construc-
> tion transforms ostensibly "anti-war" films into American pro-
> war propaganda.
>
> (Klein 2005: 428)

Within the broader frame of the military–industrial–media–entertainment network and the visual culture fostering militarization (Masco

190

2014; Der Derian 2009), in reaction to the American public's hostility to war following the Vietnam War, combat movies have played a significant role in recuperating the American political myth of the Good War. Combat movies disseminate narratives and images that constitute "a script for action" in which "heroes model a political response to crisis which the audience is invited to emulate – or at least consent to" (Slotkin 2017: 2). The already discounted lives of necropolitics are made to all but disappear through combat films' representations of righteous war as that which is unavoidable, "forced upon us, not chosen" (Slotkin 2017: 7). Bowden cites 9/11 as the event that reminded Americans "why they needed soldiers" (Bowden 2010: 359), and in doing so Bowden likewise reproduces the myth of the Good War. He also reproduces the political myth of American innocence by accepting counterterror state's discursive erasures of the military's ignoble role in torture, kidnapping, the killing of civilians, and human rights violations. As Sherene Razack (2012) highlights, popular cultural narratives that disavow the systemic, structural abuses of the War on Terror, work to erase accountability, reinforcing the violent imperialism that dehumanizes and discounts racialized lives. The disclosures regarding the Kabul drone attack in November 2021, some two and a half years after the killings of mostly civilians in the March 2019 airstrike in Syria (Philipps and Schmitt 2021), are a fresh reminder of the erasures of accountability built into necropolitical law.

In addition to participating in narrative erasures legitimizing American imperialism, Bowden's afterword, like the book and the movie based on it, demonstrates *Black Hawk Down*'s reproduction of what Elizabeth Anker (2014) theorizes as melodramatic political discourse, which casts

> politics, policies, and practices of citizenship within a moral economy that identifies the nation-state as a virtuous and innocent victim of villainous action. It locates goodness in the suffering of the nation, evil in its antagonists, and heroism in sovereign acts of war and global control coded as expressions of virtue. By evoking intense, visceral responses to wrenching injustices ... [melodramatic political discourse] suggests that the redemption of virtue obligates state power to exercise heroic retribution on the forces responsible for national injury.
> (Anker 2014: 2)

Anker demonstrates George W. Bush's mastery of melodramatic political discourse and the dominance of the register and genre of melodrama in the broader political discourse of the counterterror state.

Bowden's invocations of sentiment and his sacralizing of soldiers reproduce the counterterror state's register of melodramatic political discourse while legitimizing American militarism. Given that both the movie version of his book, and, according to his 2010 afterword, Bowden, participate ideologically and in terms of genre conventions in counterterror state discourse, it is unsurprising that Bush – the president who launched the War on Terror – celebrated the film, reading it as an instructive articulation of the need "to persist in the use of military force" (Slotkin 2017: 1). At the very highest levels of the counterterror state, then, popular culture has served as pedagogy and information. Law, too, must attend to this powerful social modality, by grappling with necropolitical culture's relationship to necropolitical law.

5.3   EYE IN THE SKY AND LAW'S ARCHIVE

In keeping with the irreducible reverberations between nation/empire, the combat films generated by the military–industrial–media–entertainment network emerging from the United States become in their status as cultural text simultaneously national and global. Through media, planetary jurisdiction for the United States is asserted when audiences worldwide become spectator–consumer–subjects, as Judith Butler notes, of a US-centric point of view (2010: xv). Put differently, entertainment media is part of what Mawani theorizes as law's archive, a globalized site dramatizing the enmeshed questions of law, violence, sovereignty, and authority (Mawani 2012). Questions of law, violence, sovereignty, and authority are inescapable features of the combat film, which invariably centers on "open displays of state power," interpellating citizens as "at once spectators, subjects and agents of state power" (Slotkin 2017: 2).

Within the broader field of necropolitical culture, given, first, the central role played by drone warfare in the War on Terror, and, second, the identification of entertainment media as a key site and modality through which affect, images, political myth, and narrative disseminate necropolitical law, entertainment media's representations of drone warfare are of critical interest. In particular, while another film on drone warfare, Good Kill (2014), represents the secrecy, unaccountability, and slaughter of civilians effected by drone warfare, particularly under the CIA, and numerous films made after 9/11 incorporate drones in their action and plots, Eye stands out from these other contemporary war films, in that in it law is a major driver of plot, action, and dialogue.

Before analyzing *Eye's* representations of law and of drone warfare as lawful, a description of the film is called for.

Eye in the Sky opens on a scene of familial warmth and domestic togetherness. Words on the bottom left corner of the screen inform us that the place is Kenya, and the time is 7:00 a.m. We are introduced to a little girl, Alia, in the outdoor space of her family's very simple home, a home that appears to have been built out of scavenged and somewhat makeshift materials. The space is adjacent to an outdoor oven. Alia's mother is setting bread into the oven with a baking peel. The parents have calm, loving demeanors and use endearments when speaking to the child. Alia stands next to her father, who is putting the finishing touches to a hoop that Alia receives with excitement. "Go play," her father instructs her. Alia spins and twirls inside the hoop with an entrancing, lyrical grace. Then the camera moves up and away to show us a jarring contrast: on the other side of the cinder block wall separating the family's compound from the street, men in camouflage uniforms stand in a jeep with a machine gun set on a tripod,[9] patrolling the neighborhood.

Mirroring the act of surveillance but discarding its brute militarism, and surpassing the limits of the human eye, the camera moves farther up, a scope and scale of vision that, as viewers, we understand to be the drone seeing, the eye in the sky for which the film is named. The aerial view induces us to identify with power (Stam 1992), drawing us into "an imperial gaze through which to map, understand, and ultimately know the expanding battlefields of the war" (Lubin 2021: 104), bestowing our vision with the all-seeing omniscience of a God's eye view.[10] On our screens, the panorama acquires an overlay: crosshairs. This aiming, framing visual device is again a signifier of the drone's

[9] The tripod – a piece of equipment common to photography and to war – visually invokes (at least) two associations: first, Susan Sontag's well-known assessment that "[e]ver since cameras were invented in 1839, photography has kept company with death" (2003: 24), and second, the history of film in which "[t]he precursor to the Lumieres' moving picture camera was Etienne-Jules Mary's chronophotographic rifle, which both resembled and was inspired by a machine gun (Stahl 2010: 8; Virilio 1989: 15)". The weapon on a tripod in these opening moments is visually echoed when, later in the film, a camera is set on a tripod for recording suicide videos of young men recruited to be al-Shabaab suicide bombers.

[10] Caren Kaplan (2018) offers a fresh and compelling discussion of the authority attaching to the view from above in relation to advances in technology. In general, the privileging of sight as "the sovereign sense" (Mitchell 2005: 265) is traceable to Aristotle's hierarchy of the senses.

seeing, which is precise, calibrating, *factual* because it is mechanical. Crosshairs are among the visual techniques through which our spectatorial eye is endowed "with the symbolic function of a weapon" (Stam 1992: 104). In this film, just as the drone is "an eye turned into a weapon" (Chamayou 2015: 11), our gaze too becomes weaponized. Together, the crosshairs, the patrolling soldiers, and their weapon show us that the loving, familial space of the home is precariously cheek-by-jowl with the battlefield. Consistent with the spatial logics of planetary jurisdiction, we are shown that the threat of terrorism is proximate to, if not embedded within, the spaces of civilian and domestic life, especially in the distant, dangerous, geography inhabited by the Other.

Eye's opening presages the film's compelling narrative tension. Alia, the child, is likely to become "collateral damage,"[11] should a missile be launched at a target close to her family's home. The target in question is a room occupied by terrorists loading suicide vests with explosives. If Alia is not risked (sacrificed?) and the terrorists conduct their planned suicide mission, at least eighty civilian deaths is the probable result. Against the urgency of a ticking-bomb scenario,[12] with Alia's life at stake, we watch elite, mid-, and low-ranking British, American, and Kenyan state actors – military and intelligence personnel, cabinet ministers, the British Attorney General, the Senior Legal Adviser to the US National Security Council – as the decision is made to authorize the killing. Consistent with the logics of necropolitical law, the plot renders the sovereign's power to take life – by killing terrorists and effecting collateral damage – as the only possible way of securing life for those of us who are not-terrorists.

After opening in Kenya, the film takes us to England, where we see a restless Colonel Katherine Powell waking at 4:15 a.m. She leaves her bedroom and goes into her study. On the cork noticeboard on the wall,

---

[11] The compound meanings of "collateral damage" are discussed in Chapter 1.

[12] The ticking-bomb scenario has been characterized as "one of the most vexing issues of the torture debate," a scenario that has been deployed to justify torture and the discarding of legal safeguards for suspects and detainees "when the public is in danger" (Lokaneeta 2011, 61). With *Eye*, there is a deft transplantation of the ticking-bomb scenario from the torture debate to the uncertainties surrounding the limits on (and scrutiny of) state power in drone warfare. This transplantation is troubling for the way it deploys fear and posits a state omniscience relating to the future. The arc of *Eye's* narrative legitimizes an expansive, secretive, state power in drone warfare through the compelling need to protect innocent publics by preventing the unfolding suicide bombings.

we see photos of a White woman in a hijab. When she opens her computer, we watch with her a newsclip that was sent to her earlier that morning. The clip shows al-Shabaab shooting and killing a bound, hooded, defenseless man, executed because they suspected him of being an undercover agent for British and Kenyan forces. The newsclip informs us, in a soundbite, of the context needed to understand the film: al-Shabaab is fighting for a particular version of Islamic rule in the horn of Africa and "bitterly resents the role of Kenya and Britain in propping up the Somali government." Powell makes her way to her headquarters in Northwood. Here, in a high-security basement room full of screens and computers operated by men and women in military uniforms, she commands a top-secret Anglo-American-Kenya joint mission to capture two British nationals who are al-Shabaab leaders: Susan Danford, also known as Ayesha al-Hady, and her husband, a British-Somali. Danford/al-Hady is the woman in a hijab on Powell's study wall. The capture mission is scheduled for that day because the British have reliable intel that Danford/al-Hady and her husband are meeting other al-Shabaab operatives in a safehouse in Nairobi.

From England, the film takes us to Creech Air Force Base in Nevada, where, seated inside an industrial-looking metal container in the middle of the desert, US drone pilot, Second Lieutenant Steve Watts, and sensor operator, Carrie Gershon, control the drone providing the aerial surveillance and potential lethality needed for the mission. Back in Kenya, we are shown armed forces in uniform, standing by to assist in the planned capture mission. We are also shown a man and a woman who are undercover intelligence operatives. The man, Jama Farah, is a Somali working with the Kenyans. Farah is a central player in the unfolding story.

The film returns us to England, where we are shown a meeting at the Cabinet Offices Briefing Room A. In the room, a screen relays the images from Powell's command center. Powell's military superior, Lieutenant General Benson is present, along with high-level British politicians and civil servants, including the government's highest-ranking lawyer, the Attorney General. In addition to moving among the three primary sites of action – Kenya, England, and Nevada in the United States – the film also shows us that drone warfare relies on a military-political web connecting Washington DC (where the Senior Legal Adviser to the US National Security Council calls in from the White House), Singapore (the British Foreign Secretary attends an event displaying and selling British-made armaments), Beijing (the US Secretary of State engaging in ping-pong diplomacy), and Hawaii, where the facial recognition unit relies on aerial surveillance to identify targets and confirm kills. In short, the film shows us how war, technology, and politics animate planetary jurisdiction.

Weaponized technology is foregrounded by the opening crosshairs, the drone's seeing, the command center in Northwood, Creech Air Force Base, the screen in the cabinet meeting room, and the fact that Powell issues orders and manages the operation across three continents. Augmenting this foregrounding of weaponized technology, we see Farah, the undercover agent, using fascinating surveillance technology – almost the stuff of science fiction or a Bond movie – as he controls a minuscule aerodynamic camera disguised as an insect. Farah skillfully navigates this insectothopter camera (Marsh 2017) into the otherwise unsurveillable room in which the al-Shabaab operatives are gathered. Also in the room are two young men – a British national and an American national whose Black bodies contextually signify their Muslim identities and sympathies for the al-Shabaab cause. These young men have just flown into Nairobi. We see them being met at the airport by al-Shabaab operatives and taken to the al-Shabaab territory, where Powell's targets, the British nationals, meet with these new arrivals and proceed to equip them to undertake the bombing. The insectothopter shows us that a camera has been set up for the young men, wearing vests strapped with explosives, to record videos of themselves before they go to their deaths. As audiences, we see both inside this room and inside the many other rooms in which images of preparations for suicide bombings are relayed. It is this image that accelerates the plot, prompting Powell to ask the politicians for authority to conduct a kill rather than capture mission. As a result of this twist in the plot – the imminent suicide bombing – and the absence of prior civilian, political authority to conduct a kill mission, a contestation around law ensues.

Because Powell has the authority for a capture rather than a kill mission, she turns first to the Army's legal counsel for clearance as to the legality of ordering the kill. True to negative stereotypes of lawyers, this legal counsel uses obfuscating and evasive language before telling Powell she should "refer up," by seeking permission from her superiors. From this moment onward, we see a series of lawyers, politicians, and senior British government officials pass the buck up the chain of command. In the process, adversarial arguments on questions of law, authority, responsibility, risk, and liability expose the lawyers, politicians, and government officials as self-interested and somewhat cowardly foils to the clear-thinking, clear-seeing military figures: Powell and her superior, Benson. For Powell and Benson, there is no doubt that the kill mission must proceed in order to preempt the probable suicide bombing. Senior US officials – the Secretary of State and the Senior Legal Adviser to the US National Security Council – likewise have no hesitation in insisting on a kill mission. It is the British civilian officials who hesitate and prevaricate.

While, for the debating British lawyers, politicians, and government officials, the legality of the killing centers on thinly disguised self-interest and a wariness around public and media critique, for Watts, the US drone pilot, the safety of the child, Alia, is of paramount concern. At the point in the plot when Powell receives the go-ahead from her political superiors for the kill mission, Alia is standing just outside the targeted building, selling the bread her mother has baked. The contestation on law rises in its pitch when Alia is at risk of becoming "collateral damage," especially because Watts challenges the order he is given, refusing to fire the Hellfire missile as long as Alia is inside the kill radius. Acutely aware of the time pressure caused by the imminent suicide bombing, Powell asks her Kenyan counterpart to direct Farah, the undercover agent and the one person actually on the ground in the zone controlled by al-Shabaab, to try and buy all of Alia's bread so Alia will move away. Farah buys the bread, but before he can get away, al-Shabaab militants recognize him as someone who works with the Kenyans and pursue him. Farah runs for his life, dropping the bread in the process. He is shot in the leg but manages to escape. In the meantime, Alia has picked up the bread and is again displaying it for sale. In hiding, with his wounded leg, Farah seeks out a boy, hands him money, instructing him to "run like the wind" and buy the bread. Desperately aware that he is putting this little boy at risk, Farah waits anxiously for the boy to return.

Obstructed by Watts's insistence that as the pilot in charge he has "the right" to refuse to fire his weapon, Powell has ordered her risk-assessment officer – a subordinate – to recalculate the collateral damage estimate adjusting the parameters to demonstrate a reduced risk of collateral damage to satisfy Watts's demand. Reluctantly, the subordinate obeys. As audiences, we see his reluctance and realize that an actuarial deception is being committed. Subject to the chain of command, this subordinate is not in a position to contest or refuse Powell's order. He manufactures the figures and calculations needed to compel

Watts's compliance. Watts is given the new calculation. He pushes the button that fires the Hellfire. Alia is killed and we witness the wordless despair of her parents.

In *Eye*, the various Anglo-American lawyers, politicians, and military personnel express competing values and understandings of law in relation to threats to life and security. Through this dramatized contestation, *Eye* appears to examine the legitimacy of military action and the impact of drone warfare. However, despite the sharp contestation around law characterizing much of the film's dialogue, the plot, characters, and affect legitimize the discounting of certain lives – terrorists, collateral damage – through a coded transcript of necropolitical law. This coding takes place in part through the familiar features of combat films and the familiar narratives, affect, and beliefs of American political myth. In other words, necropolitical law is coded through necropolitical culture. Section 5.4 details the conventions of the combat film and the recruitments of political myth in *Eye*'s depictions of drone warfare as lawful.

5.4 THE COMBAT FILM AND POLITICAL MYTH IN *EYE IN THE SKY*

The combat film, Basinger (2003) notes, has been an important modality through which audiences have acquired knowledge as to war, its specialist lexicon, its terrains (deserts, oceans, skies), and the vehicles and equipment needed to traverse spaces and secure lives. In keeping with the knowledge-disseminating attribute of combat films, *Eye* exposes audiences to the language, concepts, and equipment of drone warfare – kill lists, collateral damage estimates, missiles, and weaponized computers and cameras. The combat film has also been an important vehicle for the rearticulation of American political myth, reshaping myth to meet the exigencies of particular political moments (Slotkin 2001, 2017). The following summarizes some of the genre features of combat films (Basinger 2003), noting the reanimation of the American political myth typical of combat movies (Slotkin 2001; 2017) and evident in *Eye*:

- Hero: The role of hero is taken on by at least four characters in *Eye*: the woman in command of the operation, Colonel Katherine Powell (played by Helen Mirren); her superior, Lieutenant General Frank Benson (Alan Rickman); US drone pilot, Second Lieutenant Steve

Watts (Aaron Paul), and the person most at risk of death because of this military operation, Jama Farah (Barkhad Abdi), the Somali undercover field agent supporting Kenyan security forces. Within the complexities of the plot, what these four characters share is, first, that they are extensions of the counterterror state and, second, that they are all part of the military-security forces. In short, *Eye* positions both counterterrorism and the military as heroic.

- Military objective: As *Eye* opens, the military objective is to capture Susan Danford (alias Ayesha al-Hady), the British national who married a British-Somali and, with him, joined al-Shabaab. Once surveillance cameras show that Danford/al-Hady and her husband are involved in preparations for a suicide bombing, the military objective pivots from a capture to a kill mission. Framed by the urgency of a "ticking-bomb" scenario, the absence of prior civilian/ political authority for a kill mission precipitates the contestation around law that ensues.

- A "mixed" platoon: A distinctive feature of the World War II combat films is the platoon consisting of a group of mixed ethnic types, representing the multiracial, multiethnic unity of America when faced with a savage, racialized "foreign" enemy (Slotkin 2001; Basinger 2003). The "mixed" platoon was a cinematic device designed to shift the political myth away from America "as essentially a white man's country" more toward "a multiethnic, multiracial democracy" (Slotkin 2001: 470). During the 1991 Gulf War, women were conspicuously added to this visibly "mixed" platoon. By fronting women as warriors in the service of the co-constituted project of nation/empire, US representations of "military multiculturalism" expanded into a seeming "full female participation" (McAlister 2005: 250–59). In *Eye*, the "mixed" races and ethnicities of the characters[13] and the prominence of women warriors – both in the counterterror operation and as a "terrorist" – reconfigure the mixed platoon to rehearse the story of the War on Terror as a race and gender-neutral, individual and collective rights-advancing, global alliance, led by an Anglo-American partnership of the virtuous, fighting the irredeemably evil "terrorists." Against the military multiculturalism and full female participation of the

---

[13] In addition to the multiracial composition of characters inherent to a multinational military operation, the United States and British militaries are shown to be multiracial – emblematic microcosms of the mixed platoon.

"mixed" platoon, scenes through which al-Shabaab is shown to be repressive of girls and women and violently racially exclusionary become foils illuminating al-Shabaab's lack of desirable, liberal qualities and values.[14]

- Rescuing "natives": A genre convention of the combat film is the virtuous capacity of the mixed American platoon to defend and rescue helpless "natives" menaced by the savage enemy (Slotkin 2001). This genre feature is molded to the dominant narrative of the War on Terror, in that the mixed American platoon includes and embraces those affiliated with the state in the Anglo-American-Kenyan alliance. The menacing savage enemy is al-Shabaab. Consistent with the positioning of the "West" and its allies as rescuers (see discussion of responsibility to protect in Section 5.5 below), we see the US drone pilot Watts and the undercover agent Farah doing their best to defend and rescue Alia. Though Alia is killed, Eye convinces us that she has been sacrificed in a straightforward calculus of life: a minimum of eighty civilians would have died in the imminent suicide bombing had the targeted killing of the "terrorists" not taken place.

- Regeneration through violence: Combat films represent the spiritual and political regeneration of America and Americans achieved by destroying or subjugating the racialized enemy (Slotkin 2001; 2017). In Eye, the project of counterterrorism in its global dimensions is affirmed as virtuous and necessary, a contemporary variation on the myth of regeneration through violence (Slotkin 1973). Counterterrorism, with its technologies of preemptive killing and surveillance, its expansive and expensive technologies, and global networks of actors, is represented as justified, as is the regrettable loss of life through collateral damage. The Anglo-American alliance is depicted to be a critical partnership working with less effective states to protect these other states, and by extension the world.

---

[14] Against the closures of this representation of al-Shabaab, Mark Massoud's study of law and religion in Somalia describes how within al-Shabaab, understandings of Islam and shari'a were used "to justify extreme and often opposing ends. Some in al-Shabaab benefitted financially from piracy and terror, while others spoke out against piracy and terror as crimes that did not accord with God's will. Some in al-Shabaab instilled fear in those who did not support the organization, while others created space for people to work out their problems. In 2018, some al-Shabaab operatives were organizing suicide attacks, while others were instituting an environmental protection ban on single-use plastic bags" (2021: 303).

- A little mascot: The combat film generically features a little mascot – a small animal or a child – to signify the soldier's need to retain humanity and military discipline despite the insanity of war (Basinger 2003). In *Eye*, Alia is unambiguously the little mascot. We see the humanity and discipline of the soldier, specifically, US Air Force drone pilot Second Lieutenant Watts and his sensor operator, Carrie Gershon (played by Phoebe Fox), through their responses to Alia. Furthermore, both Watts and Gershon are beautiful young people. A man and a woman, they symbolically appear as Alia's parents because they care about her and try to protect her. Enchanted by Alia's grace and innocence as they watch her spinning in her hoop, it is their spotting of Alia's play that brings the child within the audience's gaze. Their response to Alia convinces us not just of their humanity but also that good, nurturing people populate the armed forces in the War on Terror. Humanity despite the insanity of war is demonstrated when Watts challenges the order to fire his missile. Watts demands an assurance that the collateral damage estimate show Alia to be within a zone of safety. In the contest between humanity and military discipline central to combat films, once Watts is given an estimate that satisfies him, military discipline triumphs and Watts obeys the order he is given.
- Actual battle zones and enemies: Genre conventions of the combat film represent action unfolding in actual battle zones against established enemies (Basinger 2003). *Eye* sets the on-the-ground battle in Kenya, representing al-Shabaab's militarized control of Kenyan territory and a cowed Somali refugee population, and its capacity to convince overseas Muslims to conduct suicide bombings targeting Kenyan populations. In keeping with the genre conventions of combat films, this context is indeed an actual battle zone involving conflict against established enemies. According to the US Council of Foreign Relations, from at least 2007, when al-Shabaab was ousted from Mogadishu by a US-backed Ethiopian invasion, it has been based in southern Somalia and in neighboring countries, including Kenya. From February 2008, the United States designated al-Shabaab a "foreign terrorist organization" (Felter et al. 2021).[15] Al-Shabaab has conducted suicide bombings in the Ugandan capital Kampala, killing more than seventy people (July 2010); is suspected

---

[15] See www.cfr.org/backgrounder/al-shabab.

of murdering and kidnapping British tourists and European aid workers in 2011; and in September 2013, in a siege lasting four days, took control of the premier shopping mall in the Kenyan capital Nairobi, killing sixty-seven people (Kron and Ibrahim 2010; Gettleman 2011; Howden 2013). In April 2015, al-Shabaab stormed a university campus in Kenya, killing a 147, most of whom were students (BBC 2015). In *Eye*, when the al-Shabaab militants are seen preparing to conduct a suicide bombing, this history and social memory of political violence directed at civilians is invoked.

In addition to actual battle zones and established enemies, *Eye* also relies on the authenticating affect of "fact" threading through the film in a range of ways: the actors playing Alia and her parents are actual Somali refugees (Military.Com 2016); Susan Danford's character is probably based on British national, Samantha Lewthwaite, characterized by the British tabloid press as "terror fugitive" and believed to be behind certain terrorist attacks in Kenya (Robinson 2016); director Gavin Hood and writer Guy Hibbert's numerous interviews with military officials inform the script (Manly 2016); the script draws on British procedure for drone strikes on its citizens detailed in *The Economist* and in leaked US secret documents published on the website The Intercept (Bowen n.d). Additionally, the Permanent Joint Headquarters in Northwood[16] and Creech Air Force Base[17] are actual UK and US military facilities; and *Eye*'s depictions of drones have been assessed as realistic, involving "a lot of cutting-edge tech" (McFarland 2016).[18] The invocations of actual military facilities and the assessment that the cutting-edge tech is realistic suggest that like other films of emerging out of the military-industrial-media-entertainment network, *Eye* has been made with the cooperation of state militaries.

---

[16] See www.gov.uk/government/groups/the-permanent-joint-headquarters.

[17] See www.creech.af.mil/.

[18] In 2009, Jane Mayer reported that the US government was planning "to commission hundreds more [drones], including new generations of tiny "nano" drones, which can fly after their prey like a killer bee through an open window" (Mayer 2009: 5). The implication of Mayer's report was that General Atomics Aeronautical Systems, a private company that manufactures the best known drones, the Predator and the Reaper, would also be manufacturing the tiny nano drone. With the release of *Eye* in 2016, the probable actual existence and deployments of the tiny drone augments the technofetishism so central to the film.

- Death: The threat and representation of death, especially for soldiers on the ground but also for those fighting from a mechanized remove (e.g., aircraft), is a core genre convention in the combat film. In *Eye*, while it is the al-Shabaab operatives and the child Alia who actually die, it is Jama Farah (played by Barkhad Abdi), the Somali agent working with the Anglo-American-Kenyan alliance, who is the person most at risk of death because he enters enemy territory. Additionally, consistent with evidence of post-traumatic stress disorder among drone pilots (Gusterson 2016), at the end of the film the pilot and sensor operator appear dazed – traumatized – walking corpses embodying a psychic death of sorts.
- Iconography of battle: Consistent with the combat film genre, *Eye* presents "the appropriate uniforms, equipment, and iconography of battle" (Basinger 2003: 22). And, in keeping with the strategic centering of killing technologies as a major draw of the war film (Stahl 2010), an important part of the visual enticement of *Eye* is the depiction of the new and fascinating equipment and technologies of drone warfare.
- In-group conflict: Combat films feature conflict within the group itself, not only conflict between the group and the established enemies. Through this in-group conflict, the military objective and leadership are challenged, and "the hero, who has usually had the objective forced on him, has to make a series of difficult (and unpopular) decisions" (Basinger 2003: 22, 15). The US drone pilot, Watts, is one expression of the hero. In-group conflict ensues when Watts challenges the order he is given. In-group conflict is also dramatized when, within the cluster of British military and political elites, the British commander of the operation, Colonel Powell, and her superior, Lieutenant General Benson, challenge the evasion of responsibility and decision-making of the lawyers and politicians. It is these two British military officers who, through the in-group conflict, make and enforce the difficult decision to conduct the preemptive killing that also kills the child.

5.5 RESPONSIBILITY TO PROTECT

Eye replicates the post-9/11 environment by discarding legal and judicial processes and institutions tied to liberal legality. Instead, it represents an alternative legal system. This legal system is necropolitical law, of course. Its social actors are those relevant to a militarized civil sphere

(Lutz 2009), and its dynamics are those of the counterterror state: secrecy and complexity (Masco 2014). *Eye* shows us that this necropolitical legal system is decidedly *not* a public thing (in Honig's terms), in that it unfolds in sites that exclude publics. Coherent with necropolitical law's focus on death-dealing, in *Eye* regulatory force lies with kill lists, rules of engagement, and collateral damage estimates. In this necropolitical legal system, it is military and counterterrorism personnel (not lawyers and certainly not politicians!) who can be trusted to be protective of innocence and ethical in their decision-making. In short, by representing necropolitical law, *Eye* convinces us that the experts able to meet the demands of contemporary security are military, technology, and counterterrorism experts.

In the Anglo-American-Kenyan alliance, *Eye* dramatizes a form of international administration "premised upon the separation of title to and control over territory in the decolonized world" (Orford 2011: 199). With the former British colony Kenya, the least powerful state in this alliance, *Eye* depicts and legitimizes the controversial international law concept, responsibility to protect:[19]

> Conceptually, the responsibility to protect asserts that the lawfulness of authority – both local and international – flows from the factual capacity and willingness to guarantee protection to the inhabitants of a territory. This argument for the lawfulness of authority does not prioritize self-determination, popular sovereignty, or other romantic or nationalist bases for determining who should have the power to govern in a particular territory. Rather, it asserts that authority, to be recognized and respected, must be effective in guaranteeing protection.
>
> (Orford 2012: 29)

In its depiction of an urgent desire to protect Alia while also protecting the probable eighty civilian victims of a double suicide bombing in Kenya, *Eye* represents a decolonized nation-state – Kenya – with responsibility-to-protect's triggering condition: the factual incapacity to guarantee protection to its inhabitants. And while the territory in which the targeted killing will take place is technically Kenya, Kenyan territorial sovereignty is fractured. Alia's family lives in a neighborhood controlled by extremists in which the only inhabitants we see appear to be either Somali refugees or al-Shabaab militants. Presumably, all who occupy the space are biologically, visibly, and culturally marked as

---

[19] With thanks to Shaun McVeigh for drawing my attention to this feature of the film.

somehow belonging such that outsiders are, by their very appearance, immediately identifiable as trespassers.

So stark is the territorial exclusion that the Kenyan army commander liaising with Colonel Powell instructs a Kenyan intelligence operative not to endanger himself by entering that space. At a point of entry as concrete as any walled and barbed-wired national border, the Kenyan intelligence agent, who has followed suspects from the airport to a pleasant Nairobi residential neighborhood, turns away the moment the suspects' car enters the al-Shabaab controlled area. When the newly arrived young men – one a US national, the other a UK national – and the known al-Shabaab leaders exit the car in the al-Shabaab-controlled area, drone surveillance reveals the British nationals who are the prime targets of Powell's initial capture mission. On spotting her targets, Colonel Powell immediately asks the Kenyan commander to find a way to "put a man on the ground." The man who is sent is Farah, a Somali working with Kenyan intelligence.

In keeping with the border that excludes Kenyans from this space, the manner in which those in control rule expresses a very specific relationship between territory, authority, and forms of law. Al-Shabaab's law, we are shown early in the film, takes the form of extra-legal executions: we watch, in the early moments of the film, a video clip of al-Shabaab shooting to death a bound intelligence agent. Al-Shabaab's law also takes certain extremist forms repressive of women. This extremism is conveyed in an early moment in the film in which we see a bustling marketplace. As if out of nowhere, a young woman's exposed wrist (her sleeves conceal three-quarters of her arm) is hit by a disciplining stick. The man policing the space and the woman is simultaneously interrogating and accusing, "Why aren't your wrists covered?" We are shown that he wears an army uniform, and the woman complies with his demand that she leave the public space of the market.

Coherent with this narrative strand on the repressive policing of women, a customer seeking Alia's father's bicycle-repair skills chastises him when she, a child intent on play, picks up her hoop and starts spinning in it. Immediately afraid, apologizing to the customer, her father stops her. Once the man is safely beyond the wall, her father issues a stern warning to Alia, exclaiming, "These people are fanatics. Never play in front of them!" One of the ways in which Alia's family is sympathetically portrayed to us (a "Western" audience) is that Alia's parents do what they can to give Alia an education, instructing her surreptitiously in their home, hiding her books under sofa cushions when there is a risk that the books might be seen by a stranger. In this territory, which is simultaneously Kenyan yet not Kenyan, as long as she is dressed in a certain way, Alia can safely be in public, as a girl and a child, to sell bread. But she cannot safely be seen playing, just as she cannot safely be seen to be acquiring literacy and numeracy.

Through the enforcement of certain forms of repression, and through the vigilance and violence of men – some armed and in uniform – we are shown that Kenyan territory harbors people who threaten the lives of Kenyans (the probable targets in the prospective shopping center suicide bombing), and people who in different ways threaten Alia's capacity to grow into the kind of adult who, as Nan Seuffert notes,[20] represents the hope for a liberal, democratic future. In short, the law at work in this territory is not Kenyan. In keeping with the logics of responsibility to protect, the lawfulness of international authority over this territory flows from the factual incapacity of the Kenyan state to "guarantee protection to the inhabitants of the territory" (Orford 2012: 29).

5.5.1 Women Who Lead, Women Who Serve

Crucially, however, just as responsibility to protect is inherently neo-colonial in its logics, ideology, and operations (Orford 2011), Alia's vulnerability also seems in troubling continuity with colonial ideologies. As a vulnerable, Brown, girl-child, Alia perpetuates the colonial justification of "white men saving brown women from brown men" (Spivak 1988: 297). Indeed, the post-9/11 context has "re-vitalised Orientalist tropes and representations of backward, oppressed and politically immature women in need of liberation and rescue through imperialist interventions" (Zine 2016: 21) even as certain American women, through a "specifically female freedom," have become signifiers of "the moral superiority of the United States" (McAlister 2005: 306).

Alia's sacrifice (she is the single instance of collateral damage that we are shown) draws attention to the roles assigned to women in this film. The operation is led by a woman, Colonel Powell, and the atypical terrorist, Susan Danford, is an English woman Powell has been pursuing for six years. At one level, these roles render race irrelevant, pitting English women against each other in a way that uses the vile terrorist as

---

[20] Paper on file with me.

a foil to the virtuous warrior. But to what extent do the roles of woman warrior and woman terrorist function to mask the patriarchal cultures and violence of two belligerent institutions: the army and extremist terrorism? Possibly, the leadership assigned to women works in *Eye* by "fram[ing] militarism to appeal to viewers historically the most resistant to the military: women" (Vavrus 2013: 92).

The casting of women as leaders takes on a second troubling dimension: in different ways, both Powell and Danford play a part in killing a girl-child.[21] Symbolically, does *Eye* suggest that women who lead are rendered somehow murderous? There is a troubling misogyny at work in the way Powell and Danford mirror each other as threats to Alia. Augmenting the tainting of women as leaders in *Eye* is the fact that Angela Northman, the parliamentary undersecretary of state responsible for Africa, is the only woman present in the cabinet briefing room, and it is she who speaks the single most cynical and power-serving sentiment uttered in this film. Bearing in mind that this is a film replete with self-serving utterances (primarily from politicians and lawyers), it is this one woman in the cabinet room who suggests that perhaps they (the decision-makers) should do nothing to prevent the suicide bombing. "Politically," she says, "I'd rather point to al-Shabaab as murderers of eighty people shopping than have to defend a drone attack by our forces that killed an innocent child." Her savvy assessment of what the Attorney General characterizes as "the propaganda war" leaves the room shocked and silent for a few moments.

In contrast to the women who lead, in *Eye* the women who serve (for example, Carrie Gershon, the sensor operator who works alongside Steve Watts in the Nevada Ground Control Station; Lucy Galvez, the woman who conducts the image analysis from Pearl Harbor; Alia's mother; the women who buy bread from Alia in the market) do not endanger life. Misogyny in *Eye* takes on a sinister but subtextual form, fronting women in power as emblems of a desirable gender equality, even as it suggests that power dehumanizes women. In summary, by establishing the failure of the Kenyan state to protect, first, its own population from suicide bombings and, second, girls and women from the misogyny of al-Shabaab, the stage is set for the (Western, imperial) rescuing mission under the rubric of responsibility to protect. Accordingly, under the terms of responsibility-to-protect's moral

---

[21] I am grateful to Shaun McVeigh for drawing my attention to this aspect of the film.

internationalism (Orford 2013), a British-led military and intelligence operation, in collaboration with the United States and Kenya, is a lawful expression of authority. In the fabric of jurisprudence woven by *Eye*, responsibility to protect becomes a convincing, compelling feature of the necropolitical law and planetary jurisdiction central to legitimizing the War on Terror.

5.6 NECROPOLITICAL LAW AS TRIAL FILM

The contestation on law woven through *Eye*'s plot and dialogue has prompted more than one critic to describe *Eye* as analogous to a courtroom drama (Jenkins 2016; Pyke 2016). The spectacle of something very like a courtroom drama is indeed generated in that *Eye* features lawyers,[22] hierarchies of authority,[23] rules of procedure,[24] and dynamics of adversarial argument in which precedent,[25] rights,[26] and law are invoked. Indeed, the centrality of law and adversarial argument to *Eye* affirms Carol J. Clover's insight that "the hegemonic status of

---

[22] The lawyers in the film are British Attorney General, the Senior Legal Adviser to the US National Security Council, and a British army lawyer with the rank of Captain. The contestation between these various state-affiliated lawyers distracts us from the absence of the voice of a nonstate lawyer in the role of defense counsel.

[23] Hierarchy is of course an entrenched feature of the common law. Hierarchies of authority are explicit with the film's military personnel but it is also striking that, in an ironic mirroring of the military chain of command, the lawyers and the politicians keep "referring up" in an effort to deflect responsibility and make others responsible for a difficult decision.

[24] These rules are dramatized as a core feature of military and counterterrorism operations. It is the sight of the suicide vests that precipitates the urgent debates around law because the mission's authority was for a capture rather than a targeted killing. Toward the film's end, we are reminded of law as bureaucracy and record keeping when Colonel Powell instructs her targeteer, "You will file your report as a 45% CDE, understood Sant?" And when the US drone pilot refuses to fire the weapon unless the collateral damage estimate is revised, his astonished superior asks (rhetorically!) what he is thinking by "throwing the rule book at a Colonel." The many constraining rules and procedures depict military violence as restrained and law-full.

[25] In the Cabinet Offices Briefing Room, the Parliamentary Under-Secretary of State Responsible for Africa asks, "Has there ever been a British-led drone attack on a city in a friendly country that is not at war? If not, how can we sanction it?"

[26] Lieutenant Watts, the US Air Force drone pilot in the Nevada container, relies on the language of rights in an effort not to risk Alia's life, saying, "Colonel Powell, ma'am, I am the pilot in command. I have the right to ask for the CDE [Collateral Damage Estimate] to be run again. I will not release my weapon until that happens."

American media and of English-language culture more generally" amplifies the "overwhelmingly Anglo-American phenomenon of the courtroom drama" into a globally recognizable narrative form in globalized
popular culture (1998a: 97, 98). Drawing on Tocqueville's argument
that the institution of the jury imbricates law and "the common
people," providing "a rhetorical and logical template that gives shape
to all manner of social forms above and beyond the court of law"
(1998a: 101), Clover highlights the "positioning of the film audience
as jury":

> [S]o fundamental is the adversarial jury trial in the American imaginary
> that ... [it turns up] as a ghost matrix with a life of its own above and
> beyond its source ... Not only in film and television drama, but in board
> games, interactive software, Internet tribunals, television game shows,
> and radio talk shows, we enact and reenact trials, in the process pos-
> itioning ourselves, as Tocqueville also appreciated, first, last, and always,
> as triers of fact.
>
> (Clover 1998a: 102)

For juridified audiences in the era of "the military-industrial-media-
entertainment network" (Der Derian 2009), the task of assessing "fact"
is a covertly managed, de-democratizing task. With film as trial stage-
managed to elicit a particular verdict, "the common people" need to be
aware of the military-industrial-media-entertainment network, and its
deployments of political myth, in order to engage critically in the
project of reading for law.

Despite its familiar liberal legal tropes, *Eye* departs from the standard
courtroom drama (Clover 1998b) in two important ways. First, in
addition to ourselves as juridified audience-witnesses, the role of "witness" is (primarily) scripted for machines. With our weaponized spectatorial eye (Stam 1992: 104; Stahl 2018) framed by a range of differently
marked crosshairs, we see what the various drones show us. Indeed, the
film's plot and pace are quickened when the tiny, discreet (and therefore fascinating) beetle-shaped drone reveals two suicide vests being
loaded with explosives. In *Eye*, what the drones show us operates like
the incontrovertible facticity of proof in a courtroom drama, a facticity
of seeing that distracts us from the questions that are, in Nasser
Hussain's words, eclipsed.

> [T]he accuracy of the drone's eye structures more than vision; it shapes
> how we think about, talk about, and evaluate a bombing. We focus in
> on the target, the moment of impact. We dispute how contained or

collateral the damage was, how many civilians died alongside the chosen target. These questions begin to eclipse all other questions about the global military apparatus that makes the strike possible or about civilian injury that goes beyond body counts.

(Hussain 2013)

The global military apparatus that makes the strike possible relates to the second key departure from the genre of courtroom drama: events do not unfold in a single courtroom. Instead, signifying the unbounded expanse of planetary jurisdiction, the "courtroom" is a technologically networked space across many global sites. Consistent with the neo-imperialism of responsibility to protect, the center of command is "the West" and the periphery is Kenya, Africa, with two sites for this networked courtroom in England. Colonel Powell runs the operation from Basement Three of the Permanent Joint Head Quarters in Northbrook. A room with no windows, Basement Three features a large wall of screens and a team of Colonel Powell's subordinates operating computers and electronic devices too complicated for us to understand. On the wall of screens, however, we see what they see on their various screens, as well as images relayed from other sites around the world. Everyone in this room wears an army uniform.

The second English "courtroom," mimicking perhaps a superior court, is the beautifully appointed Cabinet Offices Briefing Room A. This venue has the sinister acronym COBRA. Sunlight streams through large windows perpendicular to a wall equipped with a screen. Only one person in this room wears a uniform: Colonel Powell's superior, Lieutenant General Benson. Benson sits at the head of a conference table along with the Attorney General, the Minister of State for Foreign and Commonwealth Affairs, and Angela Northman, the Parliamentary Under-Secretary of State Responsible for Africa; the one woman in the room. On their wall of screens, these elite actors see the same images on the wall of screens in Colonel Powell's Basement Three room, images which include those relayed from drones managed by the US pilots sitting in the industrial-looking metal box in Nevada that is their ground control station. When the Senior Legal Adviser on the US National Security Council calls in from the White House, we see her on these walls of screens. When the British Foreign Secretary calls in from Singapore to ask, "Gentlemen, what action is being *legally* recommended?" we see him on these walls of screens too.

In spilling beyond the container of a courtroom, *Eye* dramatizes planetary jurisdiction. In connecting events and people across four continents – Africa, Europe, North America, and Asia – *Eye* shows us something of what this means. As a corollary of planetary jurisdiction, just as the military officers, politicians, and lawyers in the film invest trust in images on screens relayed from multiple places, our spectator-consumer sense of the total picture comes from watching. The single screen that we watch repeatedly multiplies into the film's many screens. *Eye* is a film that mirrors our act of watching such that the familiar tropes of liberal legality – adversarial argument relating to precedent and rights, lawyers invoking rules of procedure – become entwined with spectatorship and virtualization, as elaborated in Section 5.7 below.

5.7 SPECTATORSHIP, VIRTUALIZATION, AND NECROPOLITICAL LAW

Spectatorship and virtualization, Liam Kennedy (2012) highlights, are core to visual culture in our time of perpetual war. The spectatorship and virtualization of watching *Eye* is like looking into a befuddling set of many reflecting mirrors: we engage in spectatorship and virtualization; the film shows us others engaging in spectatorship and virtualization; and the film convinces us that a transnational technological network of spectatorship and virtualization is central to the functioning of a secretive form of warfare imperative to our safety. In *Eye*, these dynamics of spectatorship and virtualization combine with images – "the equivalent of an ammunition supply" in industrialized war (Virilio 1989: 1) – to render us subject to, and subjects of, the necropolitical culture accompanying necropolitical law.

Part of what dazzles us into a quiescent acceptance of necropolitical law is the message that the technological apparatus and nation-state alliances of drone warfare and the War on Terror are all too complex for any single, civilian, non-expert individual to comprehend. In its geographic scope alone, the film convinces us of a spatial and techno-logical complexity beyond our grasp. In short, technology's capacity to almost-instantaneously span space and time, alongside the dynamics of spectatorship and virtualization, becomes part of the enmeshments of law, and the military–industrial–media–entertainment network, condi-tioning *Eye*.

Notably, much of the critical acclaim for *Eye* centers on its repre-sentation of deliberation (Jenkins 2016; Manly 2016; Pyke 2016). This acclaim fails to notice that should these debates occur off-screen, between lawyers, politicians, and the military, we, as publics, would not be aware of them because the legal system of the counterterror state features secrecy as "a core tool" and "an ever-expanding practice" (Masco 2014: 128). With *Eye*, the explicitly jurisprudential script almost acts like a decoy. The characters' shared abhorrence for taking an innocent life and the consequent contestation around law, liability, and responsibility distract us from a larger discounting of life that the film participates in. One way in which we, as audiences, are distracted from the larger discourse of discounting life, is that, in the dynamics of spectatorship and virtualization, visibility stands in for transparency. As noted in Chapter 3's discussion of the Situation Room photograph, Liam Kennedy (2012) makes the point that visibility is strategically treated as a species of transparency, even as the counterterror state produces and disseminates an image revealing the undemocratic and nontransparent exercise of state power. This distinction between visibility and transparency points to a crucial difference between the courtroom trial and *Eye*: the courtroom is, in general, a public space. The visibility of events in a courtroom expresses the rule-of-law principle that law must have the capacity to scrutinize power and to hold power accountable. In *Eye*, however, law's visibility is recalibrated, through secrecy, in the service of national security. Privileging national security above accountability and transparency is, of course, a key move of necropolitical law.

If visibility stands in for transparency in the mainstream visual culture of the War on Terror, as Liam Kennedy has argued (2012), then it is important to note that part of the fascination of *Eye* is that it shows us what is otherwise hidden and secret. Conditioned by the broader secrecy of drone warfare, with the Basement Three command center, the cabinet briefing room, Creech Air Force Base, and the Image Analysis Unit, we enter highly secure state spaces from which publics are excluded. When Colonel Powell briefs the Americans, she instructs them that the mission is classified top secret. When the suicide vests become visible and Alia's proximity puts her at risk, the politicians demand assurances that secrecy will be maintained and that there is no risk of a video of the drone strike leaking and being posted on YouTube. As juridified audiences (Clover 1998a), when *Eye* shows us what is otherwise secret and hidden, it is as if we are made complicit. Equipped with new knowledge as to what drone warfare is "really" like, the narrative and affect of *Eye* – including the affect and thrill of being let in on secrets – are akin to what comes from being privileged to evaluate "the facts" in the film-as-trial.

In keeping with necropolitical culture's patterns and ideologies (Section 5.2), *Eye* inserts the events of the film into a conflict understood to be ongoing, the bearer of an inevitable momentum (Stahl 2010: 32). *Eye* also perpetuates the identities the United States has scripted for the War on Terror: terrorists are "evil, barbaric, and inhuman while America and its coalition partners are ... heroic, decent, and peaceful – the defenders of freedom" (Jackson 2005: 59).[27] In *Eye*, none of the state actors is portrayed as fueled by racism, righteous nationalist rage, or in the way of the Iraq War, by a heavy metal soundtrack (Pieslak 2009). Instead, with self-serving politicians and responsibility-avoiding lawyers as foils, the film portrays military and counterterrorism personnel as the most ethical, selfless, and heroic among the dramatis personae. Against the considerable body of scholarship and investigative journalism that shows how drone warfare engages a distancing, dehumanizing optic, the two young US Air Force officers in their Nevada ground station are shown to be humane and nurturing, intimately invested in protecting and saving Alia. Their virtual relationship with Alia, their care and concern for her, could not be more unlike the verbal violence and Islamophobic interpretive frames deployed by actual drone teams (Cloud 2011; Chamayou 2015; Gusterson 2016). In *Eye*, Colonel Powell, and her superior, General Benson, make the decision to conduct the strike despite the risk to Alia, because of the greater number of innocent lives at stake should they not preempt the suicide bombings. We are shown that, in having to make these decisions and operate the technologies to surveil and kill, thoughtful, likeable individuals are burdened and distressed. By the end of the film, the mission is accomplished, but there is no celebration.

In relation to necropolitical culture, a brief consideration of the soundscape of *Eye* offers a further revelatory detail on the role of deception in necropolitical culture's texts. In his influential essay, *A Phenomenology of Drone Strikes* (2013), Nasser Hussain draws attention to "the chronic and intense harm continuous strikes wage on communities." Consistent with the troubling silences and erasures that mark debates in the United States on drone warfare (Hussain 2013;

---

[27] Also of interest is the fact that *Eye* features in musician and artist David Byrne's installation on implicit bias. In National Public Radio's report on Byrne's installation, the role of race, religion, and dress in assumptions about terrorism are brought to the fore (Myrow 2017).

213

Masco 2014; Gusterson 2016), the soundscape of Eye does *not* include the "terrifying buzz of a distant propeller" heard by people on the ground when drones are visible (Rohde 2012). Instead, *Eye* portrays the surveilling, bomb-bearing drone as unobtrusively silent, while the smaller drones we see whirr and click so subtly as to be unnoticed by those who are being recorded and relayed. However, *Eye's* soundscape *does* feature a powerful moment of silence. Mirroring perhaps the fact that "[d]rones fire missiles that travel faster than the speed of sound [such that a] drone's victim never hears the missile that kills him" (Rohde 2012), when a missile strikes the room with the suicide bombers and their al-Shabaab handlers, we hear nothing but we *see* Alia falling to the ground, her parents rushing to look for her, embodying fear and grief. We see, in this striking silence, devastated bodies and buildings. For an intense few seconds, the film's sound is, eloquently, the sound of silence. In this silence, we witness Alia's parents' despair and experience our own wordless distress at the slaying of innocence.

The distress of the young US drone pilots and the concern of the UK elites to avoid the problem of killing Alia while also managing the imminent suicide bombings is entirely humanized by the film's images, narrative, and soundscape. What *Eye* conceals is the role of silence in facilitating an "aura of detachment ... [that] eases the ability to kill" (Hussain 2013) inherent to the drone's technology of sight without sound:

> In the case of drone strike footage, the lack of synchronic sound renders it a ghostly world in which the figures seem unalive, even before they are killed. The gaze hovers above in silence. The detachment that critics of drone operations worry about comes partially from the silence of the footage.
>
> (Hussain 2013)

In *Eye*, the soundscape's deceptive slippages discount the terror experienced by communities subject to drones. When this sonic deception is deployed alongside the authenticating affect of fact, *Eye* augments the distortions marking US-dominated perceptions of the nature of drone warfare. In *Eye's* jurisprudential texture, the responsibility to protect is taken seriously by an international administration populated by people who care. They care for the vulnerable child Alia, but also for us: the spectator-consumer. As audiences, we stand in for innocent, ignorant publics who might, like us, step into shopping centers in the course of a mundane weekend, vulnerable in their routines to death by terrorist attack. In the affective terrain of *Eye*, the secrecy and disproportionate power of that international counterterror administration seem legitimate and desirable.

In this chapter, I have argued that the arc of *Eye*'s narrative legitimizes an expansive, secretive necropolitical power exercised through drone warfare. Drone warfare is an especially de-democratizing technology of war, while the responsibility to protect renews and revitalizes neocolonial operations and ideologies of international executive rule. Within the dazzling expanse of planetary jurisdiction, spectacular technology becomes justifiable, if not *necessary*, in an archetypal battle between good and evil. Both law and the military are undone as public things when the film valorizes military and counterterrorism sites and personnel as responsible protectors of vulnerable global populations. In *Eye*, contemporary war's apparently borderless operations demarcate a form of planetary jurisdiction in which targeted killings and collateral damage must necessarily, justifiably, occur in distant places, upon distant, uncounted bodies.

In Chapter 6, the penultimate chapter of this book, I examine the United States' 2017 deployment of its most powerful nonnuclear weapon, the MOAB, in Afghanistan. Highlighting the secrecy and monologic texture of media reports on the MOAB strike, the incantations of "shock and awe" used to describe and characterize the strike, and the visual and verbal linking of the MOAB strike to America's 1945 nuclear bombings of Hiroshima, Chapter 6 builds on Chapter 5's discussion of how necropolitical culture's texts amplify public fear, cultivate public fascination with killing technology, and re-narrate American political myth to authorize, legitimize, and reanimate necropolitical law's discounting of life in the long War on Terror.

CHAPTER SIX

THE MOTHER OF ALL BOMBS

6.1 INTRODUCTION

In April 2017, the United States dropped its largest, most destructive, nonnuclear bomb, the Massive Ordinance Air Blast, or MOAB, in eastern Afghanistan. It was the first time the bomb had been used in combat.[1] Major global news corporations reproduced official US and Afghan representations – statements, photographs, and videos – to describe the weapon and its effects. The photographs and videos depicting the explosion showed aerial perspectives, dissected by cross-hairs centering on a billowing cloud rising from the ground (Cooper and Mashal). Beneath both still and moving images were appended captions naming the MOAB's "mushroom cloud" and emphasizing the bomb's "shock and awe" effect (e.g., Bergengruen 2017). The official images and words invited two key associations. The first was with the 2003 invasion of Iraq, when "shock and awe" was first disseminated through media as a desirable and effective defense strategy.[2] And, second, the images, narrative, and analogies linked the MOAB to another inaugural bombing conducted by the United States:

---

[1] While most reports rank the MOAB as the United States' largest nonnuclear weapon, it has also been described as the "second largest." In terms of destructive power, the MOAB is currently the most destructive nonnuclear weapon in the US arsenal (Klimas 2017).

[2] Section 6.4 addresses the discourse of "shock and awe" in the 2003 invasion of Iraq.

the dropping of the devastating atomic bomb on Hiroshima on August 6, 1945.[3]

Chapter 6 analyzes the 2017 MOAB strike, showing how the strike, Afghanistan as its site, and the intertextuality constructed between the MOAB and the nuclear bomb are together profoundly revealing of necropolitical law's ongoing discounting of life in the long War on Terror. Three key pillars of necropolitical law are evident in the MOAB strike and the accompanying public discourse; first, the discounting of life, both for citizens and for those designated "enemy," when the United States kills, and directs resources to killing; second, amplifications of the violence and instability inherent to law's archive when unrestrained militarized imperialism is actively engendered and passively acquiesced to by politicians, scholars, and publics (Mawani 2012: 338); and, third, the role of political myth and deception in the strategic dismantling of law's public thingness through images and narratives celebrating asymmetrical warfare and the large-scale discounting of life. In the process, through a cannily managed public discourse legitimizing and authorizing the killing of Others, citizen complicity with necropolitics is cultivated and the discounting of life through necropolitical law becomes more and more backgrounded and normalized.

Section 6.2 elaborates on how, in the narratives and images accompanying the MOAB strike, the United States dismantled law's public thingness, managing and distorting law's archive by controlling access to the bombing site and, by extension, controlling media and discourse. This controlled and managed discourse is animated, first, by a cultivation of technofetishism,[4] and, second, by a rhetorical move identified by Amy Kaplan (2003) as central to post-9/11 discourse. Through repeated overemphasis on that toward which the counter-terror state wishes to direct public attention, a selective disavowal and eclipsing of histories and peoples victimized by American imperialism's killing technologies has been effected. As Section 6.2 argues, by directing public attention to the specifics of the MOAB, while eclipsing the key issue of civilian deaths, the state rehearsed the political myth of American innocence and reenacted the authority, legitimacy, norms, and community of necropolitical law.

[3] The United States dropped the nuclear bomb on Nagasaki three days later, on August 9, 1945.
[4] Section 6.2's discussion of technofetishism builds on the introduction of the concept in Chapter 5.

Section 6.3 analyzes the graphic simulation of a MOAB attack directed at New York's Times Square to show how the MOAB strike participates in the conjunctures of necropolitical culture, necropolitical law, and the military–industrial–media–entertainment network. Specifically, images and narratives "amplifying official terror and public anxiety" (Masco 2014: 1), even when not directly produced by the counterterror state, are traceable to the state's long-term infrastructures and networks supporting a visual culture of existential terror. This networked infrastructure imagines and rehearses war as performative, preemptive, and perpetual, as well as asymmetrical and spectacular (Der Derain 2009; Masco 2014). Section 6.3 builds on Chapter 5's discussion of how necropolitical culture's texts amplify public fear to authorize and legitimize the necropolitical law informing the long War on Terror.

Section 6.4 analyzes "shock and awe" as ideology and enactment to demonstrate how, for necropolitical law, "shock and awe," is a keyword in the Raymond Williams sense. For Williams, keywords are compound and complex bearers of the values and powerful ideas shaping society, in that "the most active problems of meaning are always primarily embedded in actual relationships" (1983 [1976]: 22). Section 6.4 delves into some of the specific relations, values, and ideas carried by shock and awe exploring how the concept, by entwining military, policy, and political elites with corporate interests and the management of media and publics, illuminates some of the platforms and guises worn by the many-headed Hydra that is necropolitical law.

Section 6.5 shows how the 1945 nuclear devastation of Hiroshima and Nagasaki is a canonical precedent for "shock and awe," legitimizing the discounting of life through militarized imperialism. Excavating some of the parallels between this 1945 moment and the 2017 deployment of the MOAB, Section 6.5 details how, with both the nuclear bomb and the MOAB strike, the necropolitical attribute of deception has accompanied "innovations in the technology of murder . . . [that] aim at disposing of a large number of victims in a relatively short span of time" (Mbembe 2003: 19).

6.2 THE MOAB, MEDIA, AND KILLING AS "VIRTUE"

6.2.1 Strong and Wrong[5]

Reporting on the MOAB informs us that the GBU-43/B Massive Air Ordinance Blast is a more powerful version of the "daisy cutter" bomb

---

[5] This subheading is the title of Joni Mitchell's antiwar song repudiating "shock and awe," "Strong and Wrong" (2007).

that was used to instantly destroy large tracts of jungle in the Vietnam War (BBC 2017). At the time of the latter (November 1965–April 1975), "shock and awe" had yet to come into existence as a media-savvy military category, a shorthand inscribing necropolitical law (Cooper and Mashal 2017). Yet, almost fifty years after the Vietnam War, reporting on the 2017 MOAB strike tells us that, in addition to instantly clearing vast expanses of jungle in Vietnam, the daisy cutter bomb was "a psychological weapon, in that the loud sound and huge flash helped create 'shock and awe' in the enemy" (Miller 2017). Section 6.4 delves into the history, ideologies, and military–industrial–media–entertainment network relations of "shock and awe." Here in Section 6.2, however, the focus is on how media representations of the MOAB cultivate publics enthralled by the counterterror state's monopoly on large-scale killing.

The MOAB was initially designed and manufactured by the US Air Force[6] in 2003 for use in the Iraq War (Zachary 2008), a war that was explicitly *and deceptively* linked in the counterterror state's narrative to the events of 9/11 (Dower 2010: xxiii). A further layer of long War on Terror intertextuality lies in the MOAB's unfortunate nickname, the Mother of All Bombs. The expression, "mother of all [fill in the blank]," as a signifier of the definitively grandiose, entered popular American consciousness in 1990, with the first Gulf War, when Saddam Hussein promised to deliver "the mother of all battles" (Abadi 2017; Sylvester 2020: 23). Despite having been tested in the days leading up to the 2003 invasion of Iraq (Starr 2003), it was only twelve years later, in April 2017, that the bomb was first deployed, in Afghanistan, within the first hundred days of the Trump presidency.

The United States dropped the MOAB in Nangarhar Province in eastern Afghanistan, where, according to official US and Afghan statements, a complex of caves and tunnels housed about 800 Islamic State (ISIS) fighters and their cache of weapons (CNN 2017; Cooper and Mashal 2017). Given the force, depth, and radius of the MOAB's blast (described below), official estimates of the number of ISIS fighters killed by the MOAB were surprisingly low. These estimates opened at thirty-six on the day after the blast (Ackerman and Rasmussen 2017), increased to ninety-four two days later (Popalzai and Smith-Spark 2017), then were capped by US Secretary of Defense James Mattis

---

[6] The fact that it was designed and made in-house by the Air Force and not by the private, for-profit armaments industry, has been used to explain its seemingly low cost; www.businessinsider.com/real-cost-of-moab-mother-of-all-bombs-170-000-2017-4.

telling reporters, about a week after the explosion, that US troops would not be digging into the site to determine how many people may have been killed. He said, "Frankly digging into tunnels to count dead bodies is probably not a good use of our troops' time when they are chasing down the enemy that is still capable" (Sultan 2017). Official statements insisted that there were no civilian casualties (e.g., BBC 2017). Because ISIS has become notorious worldwide for its conduct of mass killings, torture, and shocking atrocities – including forcing Yezidi conversions to Islam, enslavement, and child abuse (e.g., Omarkhali 2016; Speckhard and Ellenberg 2020), by telling publics that only ISIS fighters died in the bombing, the United States legitimized its use of the MOAB as a weapon directed only at those who were already guilty of crimes that had placed them beyond human community.

A GPS-guided device, the MOAB is more than nine meters (thirty feet) in length and weighs 9800 kilograms (21,600 pounds), about 10,000 pounds larger than most bombs (Gunther 2017). Because it is a GPS-guided munition, the MOAB has been characterized as a "precision" weapon, but as the description below (in Section 6.2.2) of its impact and effects shows, the expansive and indiscriminate force of the MOAB is hardly "precise." Nor have been the cost estimates in dollar amounts. While the US military reports the cost of each MOAB to be about 170,000 dollars (Cooper and Mashal 2017), other sources cite 314 million (Harrington 2017; Silverstein and Dillon 2017) and 16 million (Latifi 2017). *The New Yorker*'s Robin Wright reports that the bomb itself costs 16 million dollars, and the related cost of developing the MOAB was 300 million (Wright 2017). In sequence, the military has first repudiated these figures running into the tens and hundreds of millions (Lockie 2017), then conceded that the official estimate of 170,000 dollars does not take into account the full set of costs incurred (Pawlyk 2017).

The coexistence of contested information and absence of data relating, first, to the number of victims killed in the attack and, second, to what should be a straightforward fact about the MOAB – its cost to the US taxpayer – are fragments capturing the discounting of life, both for citizens and for those designated "enemy," when the United States kills and directs resources to killing. The lack of data on that which is discrete and countable – money, lives – demonstrates the unstable and somewhat monologic texture of law's archive under conditions of militarized imperialism (Mawani 2012), with "truth," "news," and "fact" managed by the counterterror state in the service of discounting life. Further, when news media *appears* to deliver information and fails to highlight the constraints and conditions under which this "news" is managed by the counterterror state, publics are distracted from perceiving the strategic dismantling of law's public thingness. The *presence* of images and narratives authorizing and legitimizing asymmetrical warfare participates in the large-scale discounting of life by concealing the absences – independent journalism and critical interrogations of the bombing – underpinning the necropolitical law effected by the MOAB. In short, reporting on the MOAB illustrates some of the ways in which citizen complicity with necropolitics is managed and cultivated through an increasingly backgrounded and normalized necropolitical law.

The bombing also illustrates the workings of what James Der Derian identifies as "the military-industrial-media-entertainment network" (2009). In particular, values conventionally associated with the category "law" such as human rights, the prohibition on torture, and the protection of civilians in war are displaced through the military-industrial-media-entertainment network's near-seamless substitution of an alternative (necropolitical) set of values in which war, technology, and "total victory" are enmeshed as the epitome of "virtue" (Der Derian 2009). This new set of meanings and relations for "virtue" conditions "technofetishism" – Roger Stahl's concise neologism for what is produced when media representations of war cultivate citizen-spectator-audiences fascinated with technology such that, rather than "examine the legitimacy of military action," both news and entertainment media relating to war engender "the worship of high-end weaponry ... ascribing weapons an inherent virtue or beauty" (Stahl 2010: 28). Through technofetishism's fascination with military hardware, state "virtue" becomes the power to kill through asymmetrical, if not "absolutely unilateral," warfare (Brown 2005; Der Derian 2009; Stahl 2010; Chamayou 2015 [2013]: 13).

While technofetishism was unabashedly on display in the first Gulf War (Stahl 2010), in John Dower's assessment, a version of technofetishism informed the "terrible logic" impelling the decision to use the nuclear bomb against Japan in 1945, a logic which included conviction in

> scientific "sweetness" and technological imperatives – coupled with ... the technocratic kinetics of an enormous machinery of war – which combined to give both developing and deploying new weaponry a vigorous life of its own; ... the sheer exhilaration and aestheticism of unrestrained violence ... peculiarly compelling in an age of spectacular destructiveness; ... [and] "idealistic annihilation," whereby

> demonstrating the appalling destructiveness of an atomic bomb on real,
> human targets was rationalized as essential to preventing future war . . .
> [f]lattening combatants and noncombatants into a collective whole,
> rhetorically dehumanizing them.
>
> (Dower 2010: 223)

When asymmetrical warfare is exalted as war's "virtue," the "relation of reciprocity" at the heart of "the meta-legal principles that underpin the right to kill in war" (Chamayou 2015: 14, 17) is seamlessly displaced. Related ideals, concepts, and principles are also displaced, including legal doctrine relating to the proper conduct of war.[7] Through these sweeping displacements, necropolitical law is enacted, disseminated, and consolidated. In the process, *people* are de-centered, and killing technology becomes the featured celebrity and star of "the television war drama" (Stahl 2010: 28).[8] Through the lens of the military–industrial–media–entertainment network, technofetishism might be regarded as a contemporary expression of the necropolitical cultural sensibility "in which killing the enemy of the state is an extension of play" (Mbembe 2019: 73). This necropolitical sensibility is evident, for example, in how, when reporting on the MOAB strike, Fox News host Geraldo Rivera said, "One of my favorite things in the 16 years I've been here at Fox News is watching bombs drop on bad guys" (Szoldra 2017). The comment encapsulates the technofetishism through which killing enemies is legitimized, becoming a staple of the entertainment value of the necropolitical culture that accompanies and co-constitutes necropolitical law.

In keeping with the logics of technofetishism, the bomb's weight, dimensions, explosive mechanisms, and effects have been supplied by the military to the media in a manner that celebrates the momentous force of this "frankenbomb" (Pawlyk 2017). The somewhat lurid style of the British tabloid newspaper, the *Daily Mail*, exemplifies the technofetishism animating the military's disclosures.[9] After including a

---

[7] For a concise statement of these applicable legal principles, see Philip Alston (2010).

[8] As traced in Chapter 5, technofetishism is a facet of the military–industrial–media–entertainment network that engineers and sustains the post-9/11 wars through a distancing, dehumanizing optic (e.g., Chamayou 2015; Gusterson 2016; Kennedy 2012).

[9] To contextualize the *Daily Mail's* account, it is noteworthy that mainstream US and UK media offer less lurid but substantially similar detail on the MOAB deployment. For example, the MOAB's "principal effect is a massive blast over a huge area" (BBC 2017). And providing a soundbite describing the MOAB's effects, the CNN's military analyst drew on superlatives: "everybody underneath that thing is either obliterated, ears are bleeding or they're completely destroyed" (CNN 2017). In her qualitative and

bulleted subheading highlighting Trump's 2015 pledge, that if he became president he would "bomb the s**t out of ISIS," the *Daily Mail* described the MOAB and its effects:

> The GBU-43, also known as the Mother of All Bombs, or MOAB, unleashes a devastating fireball that incinerates and vaporizes anything within 30 feet upon detonation. In the milliseconds following the initial blast in Afghanistan, all the oxygen would have been forced out of the tunnels and for hundreds of feet around, literally sucking the life out of ISIS terrorists, suffocating them as their lungs imploded. Then, in a flash the fiery shockwave would have radiated outwards at the speed of sound for up to a mile, causing huge blunt force trauma injuries to anyone caught in its path, leveling buildings and trees. Ears would have been left bleeding and internal organs battered by the sheer force of the shockwave. The blast would also have caused many within two miles of the blast to lose their hearing. Anyone caught within the tunnels would have been crushed as the force of 19,000 pounds of highly complex explosives caused them to collapse on top of the ISIS terrorists. Those left alive would have been shocked and left in awe by the sight of a terrifying mushroom cloud – the psychological scars staying with them forever.
>
> (*Daily Mail* 2017)

Consistent with the counterterror state's claims as to who was killed, the *Daily Mail* is gleeful in detailing the torturous, gruesome *how* of that death. It is "only" "ISIS terrorists" who would have had the life sucked out of them. The loss of hearing suffered by "many within two miles of the blast" is not interrogated, neither is the impact and expanse of the "psychological scars" that would last "forever." In short, the *Daily Mail*'s report itself is a straightforward demonstration of necropolitical law's dehumanizing and discounting of enemy lives, as well as technofetishism's delight in killing technology.

Uncritical Citizens
In addition to fostering technofetishism as a way of legitimizing necropolitical law, media on the MOAB illustrates the related dimension of the affect of belligerent patriotism and political idealization. In her discussion of political idealization, Wendy Brown explores "the

quantitative analysis comparing US and English-media versus non-US media on the bombing, Judith Sylvester (2020) demonstrates that while non-US media generated some critical questioning of the bombing, US media was, in general, passive in reproducing official discourse.

relationship between citizenship, loyalty, and critique ... as they are configured by a time of crisis and by a liberal democratic state response to that crisis" (Brown 2005: 18). In exploring the psychoanalytic dimensions of the state-citizen relation, Brown focuses on "the place of *idealization* and *identification* in generating political fealty and conditioning the specific problem of dissent amid this fealty" (2005: 27; emphasis in original). Brown draws on Freud to explain the dynamics of collective political idealization typical of conventional patriotism.

> [I]ndividuals replace their natural rivalry toward one another with identification, an identification achieved by loving the same object ..., e.g., the image of the nation, or the power of the nation. ... However, the attachment ... produces two very significant, indeed troubling effects for democratic citizenship even as it binds citizens into a nation; first, the attachment achieved through idealization is likely to glory in the *power* of the nation, a power expressed in state action; second and relatedly, because individual ego ideals have been displaced onto the nation, citizenship and patriotism are rendered as both passive and uncritical adoration of this power. Power thus replaces democracy as the love object, and passivity, obeisance, and uncritical fealty replace active citizenship as the expression of love.
>
> (Brown 2005: 30; emphasis in original)

As illustrated by the excerpt from the *Daily Mail* above, glorying in power by deploying the obliterating weaponry of asymmetrical warfare is a dominant feature of the information supplied by the United States to media. Indeed, as is evident from reading between the lines of the description supplied by the United States, the force of the MOAB's blast is so ferociously devastating that bodies would have been too fragmented to be identified, let alone counted (Marks 2017; Osman 2017). And, as then secretary of defense Mattis made clear, the counterterror state did not consider counting the MOAB's victims a task worth undertaking.

6.2.2 Annihilating Civilians

Official US statements, as noted above, kept the focus away from victims and casualties, insisting that the area affected by the MOAB had been populated *only* by ISIS fighters so that the only victims of the MOAB were the ninety-four ISIS fighters (Popalzai and Smith-Spark 2017). However, Kabul-based journalist Ali Latifi (2017) notes that the terrain that was bombed is identified as home to 1.5 million people.[10] If, as CNN reports, "more than 3,000 families had fled the district in the past year or so since the militant group [ISIS] established its presence" (Popalzai and Smith-Spark, 2017), that still leaves many hundreds of thousands of civilians unaccounted for. The Afghan American Artists and Writers Association points out that the MOAB, which was "dropped on an Afghan town of almost 150,000 residents," needs to be recognized as a weapon of mass destruction (Popal et al. 2017). The Association's critique illuminates yet another instance of the counterterror state's deployment of the rhetorical move of implicitly disavowing its own culpability and violence by pointing to the recurring overemphasis on content that redirects attention to the master narrative of an imperiled American national security (Kaplan 2003). By *not* using the term "weapon of mass destruction" to describe the MOAB, the counterterror state distracts publics, yet again, from the history of America's deployments of weapons of mass destruction to terrorize and kill on a large and, indeed, indiscriminate scale.

Wazhmah Osman, a media and culture scholar familiar with the targeted region, also describes the region as populated by civilians:

> I know that the MOAB annihilated entire villages, but we heard nothing of that and part of the reason is because they completely quarantined that area. The US can claim such sovereignty over another country without any kind of international oversight where they can block this entire area from not only international journalists but even Afghanistan officials, ... so when they make claims, like only a handful of militants were killed, ... [i]t becomes very difficult to dispute.
>
> (Osman 2017)

Osman's points about the co-constitutions of territorial control, media control, and the distortions of what is and can be known direct us back to the fragilities of law's archive. For example, when mainstream news media reported that a schoolteacher and his young son had been identified as the only known civilian victims of the MOAB strike (Ackerman and Rasmussen 2017), questions immediately arise as to what happened to the other teachers and students and their families. If only ISIS fighters were killed in the strike, what did those ISIS fighters live on? Did ISIS fighters also farm and cultivate livestock and the land? It is the probable answers to these questions that make Osman's information all the more

---

[10] *The Guardian* reports on support for the MOAB strike from villagers who fled the area to escape the brutality of ISIS and now felt able to return (Rasmussen 2017a).

convincing, that "the MOAB annihilated entire villages"; it was a slaughter of civilians that "we heard nothing of" (Osman 2017).

Osman further notes that by characterizing the region as "remote" and occupied exclusively by ISIS fighters, the United States shows itself to be in troubling continuity with colonial ideologies depicting supposedly primitive places as bereft of life that counts, a variation on the (European imperialist) international law doctrine of terra nullius.[11] By extension, she points out, all inhabitants of multiple villages were designated as terrorists "just by virtue of living in those regions" (Osman 2017). Implicitly, in this conjuncture of first, terra nullius; second, "terrorists" as nonhumans; and, third, civilians as "collateral damage" profound continuities in the racialized, imperial, and necropolitical logics of the long War on Terror are evident. And because the force of the MOAB's explosion destroys bodies beyond recognition, the step of identifying the dead to contradict official accounts is lost irrevocably. In the decimation of bodies is an augmentation of the category "collateral damage" and the manner in which the latter discounts life by erasing people from law's record. If the sheer force of the powerful missiles used in drone warfare already made identifying and counting fatalities difficult (Gusterson 2016: 87), then "the inviolable principle of the equal dignity of all human lives" (Chamayou 2015 [2013]: 155) is completely undone by the MOAB's destructive intensity and spatial reach. Further, as discussed in Section 6.5, in the course of displacing the meta-legal right to life, the American political myth of regeneration through violence (Slotkin 1973) is re-animated.

Assessments by journalists and scholars echo Osman's concern over the information void (e.g., Mashal and Abed 2017; Sylvester 2020). Kabul-based journalist Ali Latifi was part of a group of journalists conducted by Afghan officials on a carefully managed visit near the site of the bombing:

> We finally reached a hilltop overlooking a green valley besides Asadkhel [the tiny village that had been the immediate target of the MOAB]. . . . Two hills obstructed view of the bombed area. American helicopters flew overhead. Three hours passed but we weren't allowed to proceed further. Officials spoke cheerfully of resounding success and precision of the operation. Yet every time we sought permission to visit the bombed

---

[11] As discussed in Chapters 1 and 5, colonialism and imperialism are inherently necropolitical.

area, they found excuses to keep us away: "The operation is ongoing!" "There are still Daesh"—Islamic State—"fighters on the loose!" "There are land mines!" and finally, "The area is being cleared!" "No civilians were hurt!" We weren't allowed anywhere near the bombed village. We were simply told that about 94 Islamic State fighters had been killed. In the end, "Madar-e Bamb-Ha" [the MOAB] became the star of a grotesque reality television show. We know how much it weighs, what it costs, its impact, its model number and its code name. We know nothing about the people it killed except they are supposed to be nameless, faceless, cave-dwelling Islamic State fighters. It was a loud blast, followed by a loud silence.

(Latifi 2017)

In Section 6.4, I argue that this "loud blast followed by a loud silence" expresses the US military tactic of shock and awe. While media constructions of "shock and awe" have tended to focus on images that "visually consecrate the destructive acts of war" (Butler 2010: xi), in operation the tactic also aims for the deliberate and strategic control of mediatized publics through "deception, disinformation, and misinformation."[12] But before turning to "shock and awe" itself as a concept, Section 6.3 considers media coverage of the MOAB strike in relation to the military–industrial–media–entertainment network (Der Derian 2009) and the specifically American visual cultural project of fostering existential terror (Masco 2014).

6.3 DISCOUNTING LIFE THROUGH HYPERREALITY

In addition to reporting on the extreme obliterating force of the MOAB in lurid and technofetishistic detail – vaporized bodies, crushed internal organs – the *Daily Mail* offered a graphic simulation of the effects of a MOAB strike targeting New York's Times Square. This simulation was reported in words and visuals depicting aerial maps of New York City, overlaid with four concentric circles radiating outward from the epicenter of Times Square.

This simulation deploys a key rhetorical move of the counterterror state's post-9/11 discourse: displacing and substituting *actual* victims in a way that amplifies the political myth of American innocence and

---

[12] *Shock and Awe* (1996, Chapter 2). As the online versions of the book oddly do not include page numbers, in my references I specify the chapters in which quotes are situated.

victimization (Kaplan 2003). As historian John Dower writes with reference to the 9/11 attacks:

> It is testimony to the impressive defense mechanisms of popular consciousness in general, and patriotism in particular, that most Americans managed to embrace the resurrected images of Ground Zero, the mushroom cloud, and shock and awe without giving much if any thought to the contradictions among them, or to the fact that it was the United States itself that, in the final five months of the war against Japan, perfected the policy and practice of destroying cities and enemy populations with weapons of mass destruction.
>
> (2010: 156)

Further, as Amy Kaplan notes, when Ground Zero becomes "a highly condensed and charged appellation that has come to represent the terrorist attacks on the World Trade Center" rather than the nuclear bombing of Hiroshima and Nagasaki, American historical exceptionalism is revitalized through a disavowal and eclipsing of the immense suffering unleashed by the United States on Japanese civilians (Kaplan 2003: 55–57). And when "disastrous failures of intelligence" (Dower 2010: xxi) were concealed by George W. Bush's Manichean explanations – "they hate us" and "they hate our freedoms" – American publics were victimized many times over.

At the most immediate level, US publics were victims of terrorist attacks. Mostly, however, US publics were displaced as victims of their own government. These displaced victimizations include, first, the US state's failures of intelligence in relation to the 9/11 attacks and the invasion of Iraq (e.g., Powers 2004; Scahill 2007; Dower 2010); second, public ignorance and incomprehension relating to the "blowback" generated by US foreign policy (Johnson 2004); and third, distortions in public discourse effected through "a directly politicized popular culture, which worked to imagine American national power in a global context" in relation to Middle East terrorism from at least 1972 (McAlister 2002: 440). The tragic actual attacks of 9/11 cannot be understood apart from these other factors, but the rhetorical move of displacing the *actual* victims of American policy and practice (domestic and global) and substituting mythic America and Americans as always already innocent and endangered perpetuates the cultures and ideologies that feed and sustain the long War on Terror.

In addition to rehearsing American innocence through the rhetorical move of displacing and substituting, the *Daily Mail*'s simulation implicitly restates American innocence and victimization by recalling the specifics of the 9/11 attacks directed at New York's World Trade Center. It also invites the cautions articulated by Masco (2014) and Der Derian (2009), according to which, in contemporary warfare, the imagined precedes the real. Tracing American national security culture in relation to "the domestic deployment of images of a ruined United States for ideological effect" (Masco 2014: 46), from the early moments of the nuclear bomb to the post-9/11 project of counterterror, Masco notes that "the specific symbols in the [9/11] attacks (the Pentagon and the tallest building in the New York skyline) were also used by the nuclear state for three generations as part of its strategy of emotional management" (73–75). He writes:

> [I]n the first decade of the nuclear age in the United States … the project of building the bomb and communicating its power to the world turned engineering ruins into a form of international theater. Nuclear explosions, matched with large-scale emergency responses, became a means of developing the bomb as well as of imagining nuclear warfare. … By the mid-1950s it was no longer a perverse exercise to imagine one's home and city devastated, on fire and in ruins; it had become a formidable public ritual—a core act of governance, technoscientific practice, and democratic participation.
>
> (Masco 2014: 45–46)

From this moment in the mid-1950s onward, "the development and circulation of a specific set of ideas and images about ultimate danger" (Masco 2014: 46), namely, the destruction of America, extended from the Cold War project of civil defense into the post-Cold War Hollywood films "repetitively enact[ing] the destruction of the nation on film, … all in the name of fun" (Masco 2014: 69). In his monograph, Masco reproduces an image of the Twin Towers under attack from the 1998 film, *Armageddon*. The eerie similarities between the 1998 fictional image and the shocking images broadcast on September 11, 2001, vividly illustrate that before the specifics of the 9/11 attacks were conceived by the attackers, they had been imagined, produced, and disseminated globally through American visual culture. It is this visual culture of imagining the violent end of America, Masco argues, that has provided the infrastructure for the War on Terror "as a campaign of emotional management … redirect[ing] but also reiterate[ing] the American assumptions about mass violence, technology, and democracy" (2014: 73). In imagining a MOAB attack on Times Square, the *Daily Mail* reiterated this fifty-year-old American state-designed "project to install and articulate the nation through contemplating its violent end"

(Masco 2014: 72), legitimizing the War on Terror by rehearsing a threat to the United States, while illustrating the inextricably global nature and reach of American cultural texts and imaginings.

Focusing on a related strand of American visual culture – the relationship between computer-simulated war games and the wars that actually unfold – Der Derain provokes us to consider the possibility that "simulations can precede and engender the reality of war that they were intended to model and prepare for" (2009: 15). Tracing connections between Saddam Hussein's Iraq and the United States, Der Derian notes that Iraq bought "a war game from the Washington military-consulting firm BDM International to use in its earlier war [1980] against Iran" (2009: 14). Similarly, at least two years before invading Kuwait, Iraq "was running computer simulations and war games for the invasion of Kuwait ... also purchased from a US firm" (2009: 14). In an uncanny near-inversion of reality and hyperreality, before the first Gulf War,

> [General] Schwarzkopf sponsored a highly significant computer-simulated command post exercise that was played in 1990, July 23 to 28 [Iraq invaded Kuwait in the first days of August 1990] ... under the code name of Exercise Internal Look '90. ... [A]pproximately 350 high-ranking members from each of the military services gathered at Eglin Air Force Base to war game. ... The trigger for the real-world scenario? An Iraqi invasion of Kuwait. The resulting contingency plan was the size of a large telephone book, and spelled out everything from the number of divisions required, to the number of casualties expected, and the best way to handle news media. Less than a week after the exercise was completed, the Iraqis actually invaded Kuwait. Schwarzkopf, according to his autobiography, found that his planners at Central Command kept mixing up the reports from Internal Look with the real thing.
>
> (Der Derian 2009: 14–15)

After presenting these conjunctures, Der Derian asks a series of rhetorical questions:

> Had the paradox of simulation moved from the surreal to the hyperreal? Was the [first] Gulf War the product of a U.S. war game designed to fight a war game bought by Iraq from a U.S. company? ... [I]s it possible that new—let us say digitally improved—simulations can precede and engender the reality of war that they were intended to model and prepare for?
>
> (2009: 15)

The answer would seem to be yes. The slippages between the virtual and the real traced by Der Derian's compelling analysis also evoke

W. E. B. Du Bois's argument about war's teleology. In "The Souls of White Folk" (1920), an essay he "reworked numerous times up to its final publication date" (*Monthly Review* editors 2003: 44), Du Bois grapples with the co-constitutions of race hatred and extractive imperialism. His writing and revisions were conditioned and contextualized by the World War II and the so-called Red Summer of 1919, in which "sixty-six black men and women, mostly in the rural South, were lynched while some 250 more died in urban riots in the North and the Arkansas Delta" (2003: 44). This is the essay in which Du Bois so famously asserts, "The cause of war is preparation for war" (2003 [1920]: 54). And if, in the lines quoted below, "America" replaces "Europe," then we have in Du Bois, an ancestral voice prophesying war:

> The cause of war is preparation for war: and of all that Europe has done in a century there is nothing that has equaled in energy, thought, and time her preparation for wholesale murder. The only adequate cause of this preparation was conquest and conquest, not in Europe, but primarily among the darker peoples of Asia and Africa; conquest, not for assimilation and uplift, but for commerce and degradation. For this, and this mainly, did Europe gird herself at frightful cost for war.
>
> (Du Bois 2003 [1920]: 55)

The discussions below of shock and awe and American interests in Afghanistan (Sections 6.4 and 6.5 and Chapter 7) demonstrate the applicability of Du Bois's analysis to the long War on Terror. For now, however, to develop the discussion of the relationship between reality, virtualization, and war suggested by Der Derian, I turn to the work of Iraqi-American artist, Michael Rakowitz, which adds a startling thread of further connection between American popular culture, necropolitical law, and the global reach of the military–industrial–media–entertainment network.[13] Highlighting the fascination Saddam Hussein and his son Uday had with George Lucas's *Star Wars* films, Rakowitz's art includes a remarkable mapping of how the *Star Wars* films shaped Iraqi military attire and conduct, as well as a public war monument. The monument in the shape of a victory arch inaugurated by Saddam Hussein in 1989 mimics "a poster of Darth Vader wielding crossed lightsabers for the *Star Wars* sequel The Empire Strikes Back"

---

[13] I was lucky enough to attend Rakowitz's memorable 2017 exhibition, "Backstroke of the West," at Chicago's Museum of Contemporary Art. Details of this exhibition are available at https://mcachicago.org/Exhibitions/2017/Michael-Rakowitz.

(Rakowitz 2009).[14] And Uday Hussein had uniforms designed for an elite Iraqi militia to resemble Darth Vader, including that iconic helmet, which, in its materials and construction, provided little protection for the troops wearing them (Stein 2011). Given the history of Saddam Hussein's connection to the United States – he had been the CIA's "hired gunman" in 1959 (Rakowitz 2009: 2),[15] and an important US ally, if not proxy, in the 1980–1988 Iran-Iraq war (McAlister 2002: 449; Young 2003: 23) – Rakowitz's art traces a cultural encounter between Iraq and the United States reverberating with colonial mimicry (Bhabha 1990) but also exposing the slippages between reality and hyperreality Der Derian draws attention to:

> The first Iraqi screening of *Star Wars* most likely took place in March of 1980, nearly three years after its original US release, at a private event attended by Saddam Hussein and his fifteen-year old son Uday in the auditorium of Ba'ath Party Headquarters in Baghdad, six months before the beginning of the Iran-Iraq war [September 1980]. ... In 1991, on the eve of the first Gulf War, the film's theme music trumpeted a mass of Iraqi soldiers as they marched underneath the victory arch for Iraqi TV cameras.
>
> (Rakowitz 2009: 5)

It is impossible not to link the 1991 staged and televised marching of Iraqi soldiers to the immediately recognizable soundtrack of *Star Wars* to Ronald Reagan's 1983 double naming of his Strategic Defense

---

[14] In the comic book *Strike the Empire Back* (2009: 10) and in his exhibitions, Rakowitz has rendered his own versions of the arch, drawing out the intertext between *Star Wars*, Saddam Hussein's Iraq, and questions of empire. The comic book rendition may be viewed at https://assets-production.mcachicago.org/media/attachments/. The 2010 version of the Victory Arch installation at London's Tate Modern may be viewed at http://www.artasiapacific.com/Magazine/78/TheSweetAndBitterRoadMichaelRakowitz.

[15] While scholars note the probable "indirect" role of the CIA in toppling the pro-Moscow Iraqi leader, Abdul Karim Qasim in 1963, they stop short of naming Saddam Hussein as the CIA's hired gunman in the botched 1959 assassination attempt on Qasim. However, given Hussein's later involvement with the CIA, particularly when it came to Hussein's use of lethal chemical weapons on Iranian troops in 1988 (Harris and Aid 2013), Rakowitz's version of history cannot be dismissed. Further, as Marilyn Young highlights, the United States has been a key ally of Saddam Hussein, encouraging and prolonging the 1980–1988 Iraq-Iran war and supplying Saddam Hussein with "the 'feeder stocks' for germ warfare" and supporting Iraq's then development of weapons of mass destruction (Young 2003: 23).

Initiative as also "Star Wars."[16] These global reverberations for *Star Wars*, like George W. Bush's elevation of the movie *Black Hawk Down* to pedagogy on the proper way to conduct militarized imperialism (Chapter 5), are reminders that American popular cultural texts emanate from the United States to circulate for global consumption. Sometimes, the fantasies of militarized dominance and empire animated by popular cultural texts may feed more than one leader's imaginings. These moments are reminders of law's co-constitutions with culture through the sometimes unexpected, often disregarded, dynamics and effects of a globalized popular mass consciousness.

6.4 SHOCK AND AWE IN THE LONG WAR ON TERROR

6.4.1 Manufacturing Consent for the Discounting of Life

The 2017 deployment of the MOAB demonstrates that, in the long War on Terror, the extrajudicial, extraterritorial killing of the enemy Other engages the indiscriminate, large-scale discounting of life associated with the terrorizing effects of what has come to be known as "shock and awe." Promoted to publics and the Pentagon as an "advanced concept" necessary to meet "future security needs" in the post-Cold War "new world order" (Alberts 1996), "shock and awe" is the sensationalizing label attached to a strategy of asymmetrical and annihilatory warfare, twinning the extreme physical destructive power of weaponry to the extreme psychological traumatization of adversaries (Ullman and Wade 1996). A key strand of shock and awe is the management of publics – enemies *and* citizens – through "deception, confusion, misinformation, and disinformation."[17] The formulation, dissemination, and celebration of shock and awe illustrate some of the echo-chamber effects through which militarized American imperialism has been scripted, enacted, and justified by elite social actors, who are simultaneously affiliated with the armed forces, policy circles, the profit-driven military, armaments, and security industries,

---

[16] *Star Wars* was the enormously successful 1977 Lucas film. At the time Reagan announced his version of Star Wars as a defense initiative, the sequels, *The Empire Strikes Back* (1980) and *The Return of the Jedi* (1983) had also become tremendous successes.

[17] Ullman et al. (1996). While this particular quote is from a chapter entitled, "Introduction to Rapid Dominance," there are a further seventeen citations to "deception" in the text of *Shock and Awe*. Most frequently, "deception" is conjoined to "misinformation and disinformation."

elite educational establishments, and, as we have already seen, the entertainment industry.[18]

"Shock and Awe" is the title of a Pentagon briefing paper coauthored by Vietnam War veteran Harlan K. Ullman[19] and former Department of Defense senior official James P. Wade,[20] along with a further three "contributing authors"[21] and informed by a participating "study group."[22] This briefing paper became a book published by the National Defense University, entitled *Shock and Awe: Achieving Rapid Dominance* (1996; hereafter *Shock and Awe*). The book's title and subtitle effectively summarize its contents. Briefly, as concept and strategy, Ullman and Wade present "shock and awe" as an all-

[18] See, for example, the descriptions of the Study Group members in the book, and the discussion below.

[19] Further detail on Ullman follows.

[20] In the book, Wade is described as a scientist, a West Point graduate, and infantry officer who "has held many senior positions in DOD, including head of Policy Planning, Assistant to SECDEF for Atomic Energy, Assistant Secretary for Acquisition, and Acting Head of Defense Research and Engineering."

[21] Three appendices to *Shock and Awe*, grouped as "Reflections of Three Former Commanders," are authored by a retired admiral and naval aviator, L. A. "Bud" Edney, described as Vietnam War veteran, whose "senior billets included Vice Chief of Naval Operations and Commander-in-Chief, Atlantic Command/Supreme Allied Commander, Atlantic ... [with] an advanced degree from Harvard and was a 1970 White House Fellow"; Fred M. Franks, a graduate of the National War College and a Gulf War veteran, "a retired Army general and a highly experienced combat armor officer, ... [with] two master's degrees from Columbia" (Franks is noted for co-authoring *Into the Storm, a Study in Command*, written with Tom Clancy to be published by G. P. Putnam's Sons in 1997); Charles A. Horner, a Gulf War veteran who had "commanded all allied air forces" in the Gulf War. A "retired Air Force general and a highly experienced combat fighter and attack pilot" who "now serves as consultant to government and industry." These brief biographies are set out toward the end of *Shock and Awe*.

[22] In addition to Ullman, Wade, and the three "former commanders," these study group members were Jonathan T. Howe, described as "a retired Navy admiral and both a submarine and surface warfare qualified officer. He has served as Deputy Assistant to the President for National Security Affairs, Deputy Chairman of NATO's Military Committee, Commander-in-Chief Allied Forces Southern Europe/CINC US Naval Forces Europe, and was Special Representative of the Secretary General of the UN to Somalia. He has a PhD from the Fletcher School of Law and Diplomacy and currently heads a charitable foundation." And Keith Brendley, described as "a Vice President with Defense Group Inc. He was formerly with Sarcos Research Corporation, RAND, System Planning Corporation and NASA, Ames Research Center. He holds mechanical engineering degrees from the University of Illinois (B.S.) and the University of Maryland (M.S.)." These brief biographies are set out toward the end of *Shock and Awe*.

encompassing regime of control imposed through "rapid dominance" to render the imagined future adversary "impotent" as a means to securing "our strategic policy ends."[23] In *Shock and Awe*, America's global military preeminence ("destroying, defeating, or neutralizing the adversary's military capability") (Introduction to Rapid Dominance) is acknowledged and assessed as necessary but insufficient to condition and create the desired goal of "shock and awe" through "rapid dominance."[24] "Rapid dominance," Ullman and Wade postulate, delivers total control, including "the elusive goal of destroying the adversary's will to resist before, during, and after battle."[25] The goal of destroying an adversary's will *before* battle authorizes and legitimizes the preemptive violence of killing, wounding, and terrorizing that has been such a sustained feature of the counterterror state's conduct of the War on Terror. This goal of complete and totalizing control over *will* also legitimizes extreme and expansive violence, as disclosed by *Shock and Awe*'s references to a mythic account of feudal China (see Section 6.4.2) and to Hiroshima (Section 6.5).

Relatedly, if the goal is to destroy an adversary's will *before* battle, that would entail the adversary being defined and determined, not by present and actual conduct but by expansive swathes of territory, as well as by racialized logics embedded in classification, anticipation, projection, interpretation, and assumption (Gusterson 2016; Wilke 2017). In the necropolitical sovereignty that renders as "enemy" all civilian populations – even the elderly, children, and the unborn (Sherwin 1995: 1086) – the battlefield, as well as valid military targets, are unilaterally defined and determined by the contours of American "national security interests,"[26] not by principles of human rights or legal doctrine relating to the conduct of war. The troubling military categories – "unarmed enemy combatant," "military-age male," and "child with possible hostile intent" – alongside the uncounted, undisclosed killing and wounding swept under the obfuscations of "collateral damage," are versions of Ullman and Wade's legitimizing of the doctrine of

---

[23] Ullman et al. (1996), Introduction to Rapid Dominance.

[24] *Shock and Awe*'s rhetoric of alarm and imminent danger resulting from possible cuts to the defense budget was echoed a year later in the Project for a New American Century's 1997 Statement of Principles. As traced in this chapter, Cheney and Rumsfeld, two key signatories to this PNAC statement, were also advocates for shock and awe as a military strategy.

[25] Ullman et al. (1996), Prologue.   [26] Ullman et al. (1996), Chapter 3.

"destroying the adversary's will to resist before, during, and after battle."[27] Additionally, in *Shock and Awe*, "the production, application, and analysis of information by peaceful means for peaceful ends," as Der Derian highlights, is discarded (2009: 256). The project of destroying, preventing, and preempting the adversary's *will* also bestows a God-like omniscience to see and know that which is not necessarily visible or present. Consistent with the teleology for war Du Bois (1920) identifies, the *Shock and Awe* focuses on destroying will "before, during, and after" legitimizes and authorizes perpetual war. The temporality of "before, during, and after" can never cease because the future, as Masco (2014) notes, cannot be fully known or secured. Enemies are thus cast as perpetual, guaranteeing the necropolitics of "today's planetary-scale renewal of the relation of enmity" (Mbembe 2019: 1).

Despite its problematic analysis, repetitive content, and disregard for scholarly conventions of argument, *Shock and Awe* is presented as a "study" conducted by Defense Group Inc. (DGI).[28] Coauthor Wade founded DGI in 1986,[29] after holding "many senior positions in the Pentagon" (Correll 2003). He was also DGI's chair and CEO.[30] Wade's obituary details a career path illuminating the politics, networks, and relations of the military-industrial complex informing *Shock and Awe*:

> Dr. Wade, graduated from the United States Military Academy (B.S., 1953) and the University of Virginia (M.S., 1959; Ph.D., 1961). He served in a variety of airborne infantry command and staff positions while in active duty until 1968 when he joined the Department of Defense and continued in the reserves until 1998. From 1968 through 1986 he held various positions in the Department of Defense under presidents Johnson, Nixon, Ford, Carter and Reagan. . . . After his time

---

[27] Ullman et al. (1996), Prologue.

[28] This information is included in Wade's brief biography toward the end of *Shock and Awe*. According to its LinkedIn page, "DGI is a veteran-owned, small business specializing in defense, homeland security, combating weapons of mass destruction (WMDs), intelligence analysis, and information technology. Their personnel are expert in scientific and engineering disciplines, with extensive practical experience in military and intelligence endeavors. DGI provides program management, scientific and technical expertise, modeling and simulation analyses, assessments and forecasts of threats and associated technology and administrative support services, information technology development and integration services, system architecture design and analyses, and experimentation, training and exercise planning."

[29] See www.legacy.com/us/obituaries/washingtonpost/name/james-wade-obituary?pid=184652600.

[30] See www.bloomberg.com/profile/company/4474771Z:US.

at the DOD, in 1986, Dr. Wade founded Defense Group Incorporated and served as its President, Chairman and CEO. In 2003, working with the United States National Defense University Institute for National Strategic Studies he coauthored Shock & Awe, an influential book on modern military strategy.

(*Washington Post* 2013)

Coauthor Ullman's professional history and relations further illustrate the very lively operations of the military-industrial complex in its political, ideological, media, educational, and private sector enmeshments. Ullman is a graduate of the US Naval Academy, with advanced degrees in International Relations from the Fletcher School of Law and Diplomacy at Tufts University; he taught military strategy at the National War College – his former students include one-time secretary of state, Colin Powell[31] – and he founded and chairs a consultancy, the Killowen Group, that "provides advisory services to high-level government and business leaders." Ullman also "chairs high-technology firms CNIGuard Ltd"[32] (a company "serving Iraq") and CNIGuard Inc., both of which operate in the somewhat opaquely named "infrastructure industry." Infrastructure is an important category in *Shock and Awe*, in that Ullman and Wade repeatedly assert that a key feature of shock and

---

[31] Colin Powell, who met Ullman at the National War College, heaped praise on him in his autobiography, My American Journey (2003). "A teacher who raised my vision several levels was Harlan Ullman, a Navy lieutenant commander who taught military strategy," Powell wrote. "So far, I had known men of action but few who were also authentic intellectuals. Ullman was that rarity, a scholar in uniform, a line officer qualified for command at sea, also possessed of one of the best, most provocative minds I have ever encountered" (Powell and Persico 2003: 207, 208).

[32] On Ullman, see https://about.me/ullmanharlan. According to its website, CNIGuard Ltd "is a high technology firm delivering infrastructure protection and asset management solutions to the energy, electricity, water, transportation and other vital sectors. In an era of Big Data and the Industrial Internet of Things (IIOT), through our Sensorcore platform, CNIGuard solutions enable the monetization of data in three key ways: Our products provide real-time monitoring of vital national infrastructure to detect, safeguard and prevent human interference (such as vandalism or theft) or disruptive acts of nature resulting in cost-effective solutions and considerable savings in minimizing damage. Data can be used for preventive maintenance and early detection of problems; improving efficiency and effectiveness of the infrastructure; and monetization of data that our solutions collect. Our products enable linking numerous independent sensors into a single coherent system increasing effectiveness and efficiency"; www.environmental-expert.com/companies/cniguard-ltd-39584. See also www.environmental-expert.com/water-wastewater/water-asset-management/companies/serving-iraq.

awe is the targeting and destruction of enemy infrastructure. They use "infrastructure" both in the conventional sense of "traditionally vulnerable targets such as ports, roads, and other infrastructure,"[33] but also in a more expansive sense. For example, key to the strategy is that all attacks on enemy targets would

> be complemented by deception, disinformation, surveillance, targeting, and killing. "Pulse" weapons would be used to disarm and actively deceive the enemy through disrupting and attacking all aspects of the adversary's electronics, information, and C4I[34] infrastructure. It is this "lay down" of total power across all areas in rapid and simultaneous actions that would impose the Shock and Awe.[35]

Ullman and Wade's attention to the need to destroy infrastructure in order to achieve shock and awe cannot be segregated from Ullman's involvement in industries and businesses relating to infrastructure. Ullman also "sits on the advisory board of I.E.-SPS," a company producing material for "accelerated bridge construction"[36] and "SPS US, a business that manufactures a new material that is as revolutionary to steel as iron was to wood; and sits on the boards of two publicly traded investment funds."[37]

Ullman is also senior advisor to the Atlantic Council, an elite institution rooted in the Cold War.[38] The Council's access to power and

---

[33] Ullman et al. (1996), Chapter 3.

[34] C4I stands for command, control, communications, computers, and intelligence systems.

[35] Ullman et al. (1996), Chapter 3.

[36] I.E. appears to stand for Intelligent Engineering and SPS for Sandwich Plate System. "The Sandwich Plate System (SPS) is a composite material of two metal plates bonded together with a polyurethane core. It is a proprietary product marketed by IE-SPS and used in the civil engineering, maritime, offshore, and military fields"; see https://abc-utc.fiu.edu/resources/implemented-advanced-technologies/sandwich-plate-system-sps/.

[37] At https://about.me/ullmanharlan.

[38] On its website, the Atlantic Council describes itself thus: "For nearly sixty years, the Atlantic Council has pursued the mission that we have now boiled down to a few words: 'Shaping the global future together.' In short, we see our role as advancing and advocating constructive U.S. leadership in the world alongside friends and allies. Within a few years of the signing of the North Atlantic Treaty in 1949, voluntary organizations emerged in the member countries of the Alliance to promote public understanding and support for the policies and institutions that would build collective security and peace. This international network of citizens' associations was bound together formally in 1954 with the creation of the Atlantic Treaty

influence is signaled by how, in 1988, it organized a "major international conference" featuring "speeches by President Reagan, then-presidential candidate Michael Dukakis, Zbigniew Brzezinski, Jeanne Kirkpatrick, Colin Powell, and Brent Scowcroft."[39] The Atlantic Council also shows a keen awareness of the role of mass media in the shaping of public opinion:

> Throughout the 1960s, the Council produced a series of reports on the state of public opinion towards Alliance member countries and sought to actively educate the public about the need for engagement in international affairs through television commercials (starring Bob Hope), an academic journal, and its newsletter.[40]

Further elite offices Ullman has held include Advisor to Supreme Allied Commander Europe and Commander of US European Command, and Senior Advisor, Atlantic Council and Business Executives for National Security.[41] In addition to authoring "many books on foreign policy, strategy, and security,"[42] Ullman is a prolific producer of op-eds, having "written more than 500 columns for United Press International, Inc., the most recent of which called for a new version of the 1933 Glass-Steagall Act and stricter regulation of financial weapons of mass destruction."[43] In his professional biography, in terms that implicitly recognize the co-constituting effects of nation/empire, Ullman is described as

> widely recognized both in the United States and abroad as a global thought leader and highly innovative strategic thinker whose advice is sought by businesses and governments at the highest levels. For three decades Dr. Ullman has played an active role in the formulation of

Association. In 1961, former Secretaries of State Dean Acheson and Christian Herter, with Will Clayton, William Foster, Theodore Achilles and other distinguished Americans, recommended the consolidation of the U.S. citizens groups supporting the Atlantic Alliance into the Atlantic Council of the United States. . . . Since its inception, the Council has administered programs to examine political and economic as well as security issues, and to cover Asia, the Americas and other regions in addition to Europe. All its programs are, however, based on the conviction that a healthy transatlantic relationship is fundamental to progress in organizing a strong international system"; www.atlanticcouncil.org/about/history/.

[39] At www.atlanticcouncil.org/about/history/.
[40] At www.atlanticcouncil.org/about/history/.
[41] See www.jiaponline.org/2015/03/monday-in-washington-march-16-2015.html.
[42] At https://about.me/ullmanharlan.   [43] At https://about.me/ullmanharlan.

national security policy in Washington, NATO and foreign capitals of Europe, the Middle East, South Asia and the Far East.[44]

In 2003, when shock and awe came into prominence as the military strategy shaping the invasion of Iraq, Ullman was frequently quoted in the media on the concept he coauthored and was awarded the sardonic moniker, "the Dr Strangelove of the Iraq War" (Von Drehle 2003). These brief sketches of the professional paths of the principal authors of *Shock and Awe* illustrate the vested interests of the military-industrial complex. Flying in the face of sacralized notions of the military as patriotic "service," these biographies suggest that Ullman and Wade entrepreneurially reengineered their military experience and policy networks in the service of personal gain. These career paths also demonstrate that rule-of-law principles relating to the obligation to avoid conflicts of interest and the fiduciary duty of those in public service to serve the *public*, not themselves, are rescripted by necropolitical law.

According to a history of "shock and awe" as defense concept traced by *Air Force Magazine*, Donald Rumsfeld (Secretary of Defense to both Ford, 1975–1977, and George W. Bush, 2001–2006) "was a rump member of the original shock-and-awe group, so he knew about the concept" (Correll 2003, quoting Ullman). From at least 1996, then, and certainly by 1999, Rumsfeld was "one of the early supporters of Shock and Awe":

> Rumsfeld used the expression in an April 1999 statement to CNN [three years after *Shock and Awe* had been published], criticizing the strategy for the air war in Serbia as insufficiently forceful. "There is always a risk in gradualism," Rumsfeld said. "It pacifies the hesitant and the tentative. What it doesn't do is shock, and awe, and alter the calculations of the people you're dealing with." In October 1999, Rumsfeld joined three other former Secretaries of Defense, Harold Brown, Frank C. Carlucci, and James R. Schlesinger, in commending Shock and Awe to William S. Cohen, who was then Secretary of Defense.
>
> (Correll 2003)

The role of Rumsfeld is discussed further below. Here, to keep the focus on the marketing of "shock and awe," the term came into further prominence from January 24, 2003, two months in advance of the aerial bombardments that would launch the invasion of Iraq in

---

[44] See www.huffpost.com/author/dr-harlan-k-ullman.

March that year, when unnamed Pentagon officials told CBS that a "shock-and-awe" battle plan would involve "airstrikes so devastating they would leave Saddam's soldiers unable or unwilling to fight" (Chan 2003). The opening missile attacks would be on an unprecedented scale of "between 300 and 400 cruise missiles at targets in Iraq, ... more than number that were launched during the entire 40 days of the first Gulf War" (Chan 2003). To follow up on this opening, the second day of the invasion would again see the US-led coalition launching 300 to 400 cruise missiles, leaving Baghdad completely beleaguered (Chan 2003). As CBS and other media reported:

> "We want them to quit. We want them not to fight," says Harlan Ullman, one of the authors of the Shock and Awe concept which relies on large numbers of precision guided weapons. "So that you have this simultaneous effect, rather like the nuclear weapons at Hiroshima, not taking days or weeks but in minutes," says Ullman. In the first Gulf War, 10 percent of the weapons were precision guided. In this war 80 percent will be precision guided.
>
> (Chan 2003)

Hiroshima as the precedent and analogy of the shock-and-awe strategy is discussed below in Section 6.5, and the deception inherent in characterizing powerful ordnances as "precise" was addressed in Section 6.2. For now, to keep the focus on the dissemination of the concept through the mediatized account of the Iraq invasion, it is important to highlight the role of *repetition* as a key discursive strategy. On March 17, 2003, in his televised Address to the Nation on Iraq, President George W. Bush lamented Iraq's "deep hatred of America and our friends," alluding to shock and awe when he said, "the only way to reduce the harm and duration of war is to apply the full force and might of our military, and we are prepared to do so."[45] On March 19,

---

[45] In this speech, Bush asserted as a certainty that Iraq had weapons of mass destruction that threated America and the world and that Iraq had "aided, trained, and harbored terrorists, including operatives of Al Qaida. The danger is clear: using chemical, biological or, one day, nuclear weapons obtained with the help of Iraq, the terrorists could fulfill their stated ambitions and kill thousands or hundreds of thousands of innocent people in our country or any other. The United States and other nations did nothing to deserve or invite this threat. But we will do everything to defeat it. Instead of drifting along toward tragedy, we will set a course toward safety. Before the day of horror can come, before it is too late to act, this danger will be removed. The United States of America has the sovereign authority to use force in assuring its own national security" (March 17, 2003), 277–79; www.govinfo.gov/

2003, the United States conducted a stealthy night raid on "a senior Iraqi leadership compound."[46] At a Pentagon news briefing the next day, the day before the United States launched its aerial bombardments, Rumsfeld repeated Bush's narrative of American innocence and Iraqi evil from three days earlier, also alluding to shock and awe: "What will follow will not be a repeat of any other conflict. It will be of a force and a scope and a scale that has been beyond what has been seen before" (Rumsfeld 2003).[47]

In a crucial and strategic management of public discourse, the accounts of Shock and Awe as a military operation (formally Operation Iraqi Freedom) delivered by experts, leaders, and media have consistently absented the book Shock and Awe's legitimation of the key necropolitical attribute of deception. Despite the fact that Ullman and Wade repeatedly assert, throughout the book, that "deception, disinformation, and misinformation are crucial aspects of waging war,"[48] media has compliantly followed the lead set by military and political elites and failed to notice the centrality of deception to Shock and Awe the document, while excusing the deception of the military practice in operation. For example, media invocations of "shock and awe" in the 2017 MOAB strike do not reflect the reality that in the invasion of Iraq, the inaugural moment of shock and awe as an actual military strategy,[49] the promised Iraqi weapons of mass destruction were never found.

content/pkg/PPP-2003-book1/pdf/PPP-2003-book1-doc-pg277.pdf. By July 2004, the links between Al Qaida and Iraq and the much-touted Iraqi weapons of mass destruction had been exposed as lies; see "Report of the Select Committee on Intelligence on the US Intelligence Community's Prewar Intelligence Assessments on Iraq." Marilyn Young draws attention to how the declared war on terrorism began in August 1998, under Clinton. In mid-December 1998, Clinton "launched a particularly heavy series of raids" on Iraq, prophesying, "mark my words, he will develop weapons of mass destruction. He will deploy them, and he will use them" (Young 2003: 11).

[46] At https://transcripts.cnn.com/show/se/date/2003-03-20/segment/08.

[47] Both Bush and Rumsfeld also instructed Iraqi forces not to destroy the oil wells, characterizing oil as "a source of wealth that belongs to the Iraqi people" (Bush 2003: 278) needed for post-war Iraqi rebuilding (Rumsfeld 2003).

[48] This quote is from the penultimate paragraph of Chapter 2, Shock and Awe. "Deception" is valorized at least seventeen times throughout Shock and Awe.

[49] John Dower (2010) highlights that "shock and awe" is a rebranding of the heavy aerial bombardments of urban centers deployed, in violation of the Geneva Conventions, in World War II.

6.4.2   Deception and the Enemy Within

On the surface of Ullman and Wade's argument, "deception, disinformation, and misinformation" are directed at the foreign enemy. However, keenly aware of "information war" and "information warfare,"[50] Ullman and Wade could not possibly have imagined that impenetrable borders existed between nation/empire or friend/enemy, in terms of the mass-mediatized dissemination of news. Indeed, Ullman and Wade demonstrate their awareness of the multiple audiences addressed by "shock and awe," writing, "When the video results of these attacks [deploying shock-and-awe tactics] are broadcast in real time worldwide on CNN, the positive impact on coalition support and negative impact on potential threat support can be decisive."[51] In other words, the deception, disinformation, and misinformation consumed by enemy publics are, of necessity, also the deception, disinformation, and misinformation directed at and consumed by domestic publics. Indeed, as Chalmers Johnson highlights, it is not only the US publics but US political elites at the highest levels who are subject to a carefully managed deception and disinformation relating to US foreign policy and practice (2004: ix).[52]

Consistent with their goal of "total dominance," as part of the larger project of ensuring the "total" nature of "shock and awe,"[53] in *Shock and Awe* Ullman and Wade identify US domestic media, domestic political processes, domestic democratic contestation, and domestic public opinion as facets of the enemy within. For example, in the process of justifying the need for shock and awe in a post-Cold War world, they argue:

> The other major shortcoming of a force-on-force or a platform-on-platform attrition basis is that with declining numbers of worthy and well enough equipped adversaries against whom to apply this doctrine, justifying it to a questioning Congress and public will prove more difficult.[54]

[50] These terms occur at least nine times throughout *Shock and Awe*.

[51] Ullman et al. (1996), Chapter 3.

[52] Also notable, and as detailed in Chapter 3 of this book, when the memo on the legality of killing Osama bin Laden was prepared, it was kept secret from the government's top legal officer, Attorney General Eric Holder (Savage 2015).

[53] For example, "[t]otal mastery achieved at extraordinary speed and across tactical, strategic, and political levels will destroy the will to resist"; "Introduction to Rapid Dominance," *Shock and Awe*.

[54] Ullman et al. (1996), Chapter 2.

And:

> Today, the First Armored Division, the principal American unit serving in Bosnia is, in essence, the same force that fought so well in *Desert Storm* and, for the bulk of the Cold War ... These are also operations that, because of intense, instantaneous media coverage, can have huge domestic political impact especially if events go wrong.
>
> (Ullman et al. 1996, Introduction to Rapid Dominance)

These related difficulties of "instantaneous media coverage," leading to the problem of justifying military action to "a questioning Congress and public" are ones Ullman and Wade seek to eliminate. Thus, for example, to authorize and legitimize their argument that "shock and awe through rapid dominance" must replace the Cold War approach of "defense through mobilization," "political limits" are characterized as obstacles to the desirable and necessary total, rapid victory of physical and psychological control:

> It was not by accident that this Cold War concept of defense through mobilization was similar to the strategy that won the Second World War and the literal ability of ultimately overwhelming the enemy using the massive application of force, technology, and associated firepower. Two decades later, Vietnam exposed the frailty of this approach of dependence on massive application of firepower especially when political limits were placed on applying that firepower.[55]

Disregarding evidence of how the United States engaged in horrific practices of asymmetrical warfare, including routine torture and "confirmed atrocities" (Nelson 2008) on a genocidal scale during the Vietnam War,[56] Ullman and Wade's references to the Vietnam War encapsulate the susceptibilities of law's archive to power (Mawani 2012). In addition to turning a blind eye to the genocidal discounting of the lives of an estimated 3.1 million (Spector 2021) Vietnamese soldiers and civilians who were killed,[57] Ullman and Wade also discount the lives of the United States' own citizen-troops. Among these

---

[55] Ullman et al. (1996), Chapter 1.

[56] In 1967, philosopher Bertrand Russell established an unofficial inquiry into US war crimes in Vietnam. See Duffett (1968). For a useful summary and discussion, see Marcos Zunino (2016).

[57] Civilians in neighboring Cambodia and Laos were also identified as victims of the war in a range of ways, including the "unlawful treatment of prisoners" and the United States' use of "prohibited weapons" (Zunino 2016: 215).

discounted American lives are an estimated 58,220 US military fatalities,[58] with further uncounted numbers of veterans affected by the Department of Defense formulated "tactical herbicide" Agent Orange (Young and Cecil 2011), and by suicides linked to either physical wounds sustained during the war or to post-traumatic stress (e.g., Bullman et al. 2019; Bullman and Kang 2011). When Ullman and Wade write, "Vietnam exposed the frailty of this approach of dependence on massive application of firepower especially when political limits were placed on applying that firepower," the implication is that firepower directed at the enemy must be without limits – a covert yet core pillar of the necropolitical law accompanying the necropolitical sovereign's power to *take* life in the long War on Terror.

6.4.3 Law in the Hands of the Iraq War's Dr. Strangelove

Ullman and Wade's necropolitical ideology affirms Der Derian's analysis showing that, for the United States, total victory has become the only valid "virtue" of contemporary war (2009). Re-making state "virtue" into total militarized victory is at the heart of necropolitical law's contemporary displacements of liberal legal rules and principles relating to the conduct of war. Augmenting the covert and subtextual assertions of necropolitical law, neither *Shock and Awe* the document nor shock and awe the mediatized practice contain any explicit references to categories belonging to the web of meanings connected with "peace," such as "democracy," "justice," or "human rights." Alongside these absences, *Shock and Awe's* few references to "law" (discussed below), must be understood in relation to the book's repeated celebration of entrepreneurship and "free markets,"[59] alongside Ullman and Wade's repeated signs of frustration with the machinery of state. Demonstrating the ideological convergences between neoliberalism and neoconservatism that make for a specifically American political "nightmare" (Brown 2006), the "law" invoked by Ullman and Wade bears no connection to democracy or peace. The public things that

---

[58] At www.archives.gov/research/military/vietnam-war/casualty-statistics.

[59] With no apparent sense of the contradictions articulated by their yoking of "U.S. national security interests" to "the democratic community of states," Ullman and Wade write, "[t]he top priority of Rapid Dominance should be to deter, alter, or affect those actions that are either unacceptable to U.S. national security interests or endanger the democratic community of states and access to free markets" (Ullman et al. 1996, Chapter 3).

facilitate democracy through constellation and contestation (Honig 2017) are implicitly denigrated, not merely by the valorization of "deception, disinformation, and misinformation" but also through a celebration of the private sector defense industry in contrast to the frustrations of government.

For example, Shock and Awe presents its advocacy of producing shock and awe through rapid dominance as desirable "external thinking, removed from the bureaucratic pressures and demands, . . . essential to stimulating and sustaining innovation."[60] For Ullman and Wade, commerce and innovation are unambiguously desirable, but they are also nongovernmental and nationalistic: "the American commercial-industrial base is undergoing profound change propelled largely by the entrepreneurial nature of the free enterprise system and the American personality."[61] Celebrating the speed of innovation evident in market competition, Shock and Awe regrets that these "positive trends are not matched yet in the defense-industrial base."[62] It recommends

> learning to harness private sector advances in technology-related products. It must also be understood that only the United States among all states and nations has the vastness and breadth of resources and commercial capability to undertake the full exploitation of this revolutionary potential.[63]

By repeatedly celebrating the private sector and innovation as uniquely American strengths to be harnessed to the profit-driven defense industry, the military as service – epitomized by the sacralizing "patriot" called into being by the Patriot Act, for example – is, quite simply, erased, even as the foundation is laid for augmentations of the military-industrial complex.

In its explicit sense "law" for Ullman and Wade takes on two impoverished, highly limited meanings consistent with a coded necro-political law. First, "law" is the militarized imperial policing of "law enforcement" in "non-traditional Operations Other Than War."[64] Consistent with the militarization of civic domains (Lutz 2009),

---

[60] Ullman et al., Prologue.   [61] Ullman et al., Prologue.
[62] Ullman and Wade et al., Prologue.   [63] Ullman et al., Prologue.
[64] "It is clear that these so-called gray areas involving nontraditional Operations Other Than War (OOTW) and law enforcement tasks are growing and pose difficult problems and challenges to American military forces, especially when and where the use of force may be inappropriate or simply may not work. The expansion of the role of UN forces to nation-building in Somalia and its subsequent failure comes to

Ullman and Wade's citations to "law" in this sense of militarized policing convert "law" to a handmaiden of US militarized imperialism, in which the calls for interagency "trust" and "cooperation" appear to be guises for US global control:

> These same techniques [for controlling the information highway] also apply to law enforcement agencies targeting international crime and drug cartels using the highway. Closer interagency cooperations and coordination between military and law enforcement activities and capabilities must be established. Experience with the military involvement in the drug war revealed considerable cultural differences between these organizations. . . . The required trust and confidence for sharing sensitive information and support between these agencies and the military needs to be developed further. . . . Some laws may need to be changed. War in Cyberspace does not recognize domestic or foreign boundaries. In this environment the subjects of Information Warfare and Information In Warfare take on new meaning and require focused development.[65]

The voluminous changes to US legislation effected by the Patriot Act, along with the globalized regulatory, blacklisting, and security regimes effected hot on the heels of 9/11 through UN Security Council resolutions (detailed in Chapter 2), implement the changes in law that Ullman and Wade call for.

The second manner in which "law" features in *Shock and Awe* is in a passing but approving reference to the reformed regulatory order for the department of defense spelled out by the Reagan-era Goldwater-Nichols Act.[66] The Act was precipitated by the Iran hostage crisis (Locher 2017: 83), which unfolded from November 1979 to January 1981, a crisis that contributed to Reagan's electoral success in the presidential elections of November 1980. The controversial and contested Goldwater-Nichols Act (Locher 2017: 84), was designed to "remedy . . . [the] chronic service parochialism hamper[ing] the efficient functioning of the Joint Chiefs of Staff (JCS)" (Godin 2005) by

---

mind as an example of this danger" (Ullman et al. 1996, Introduction to Rapid Dominance.

[65] Ullman et al (1996), Chapter 3.

[66] "Third, because of significant changes in law and organization regarding the military, particularly the Goldwater-Nichols Act, and through a willingness to examine alternatives, the Department of Defense has actively sought new ideas and concepts" (Ullman et al. 1996, Chapter 1).

centralizing authority in two key figures, the secretary of defense, and the chairman of the Joint Chiefs of Staff:

> Under the act's provisions, the secretary of defense alone, rather than each of the individual civilian service secretaries, was authorized to act as the president's principal civilian source of military counsel from the Pentagon. ... The most extensive organizational alterations that stemmed from the 1986 legislation affected the Joint Chiefs of Staff and its chairman. Section 151(b) stipulated that the chairman was to serve as the principal military adviser to the president, National Security Council, and the secretary of defense. ... In addition to advising these high-ranking civilian authorities, Section 153(a) charged the chairman with directing military strategy, planning and preparing potential military responses, and assessing defense budget needs. ... The Army chief of staff, chief of naval operations, Air Force chief of staff, and Marine Corps commandant retained their roles as military advisers in the JCS; however, the Goldwater-Nichols Act placed unprecedented constraints on their access to their civilian superiors.
>
> (Godin 2005)

Along with Ullman and Wade, other key figures who approve of the 1986 Goldwater–Nichols Act and its centralization and concentration of authority in the secretary of defense and the chairman of the Joint Chiefs of Staff are Richard Cheney and Colin Powell (Godin 2005). Colin Powell was "the first JCS chairman to fully exercise the powers granted under the act" (Godin 2005). Powell was chairman of the JCS under the first George Bush, from 1989 to 1993. Cheney was the very first wielder of the concentrations of power in the secretary of defense scripted by the Goldwater-Nichols Act (Godin 2005). Not only was Cheney secretary of defense to the first George Bush, he was also vice president to the second George Bush from 2001 to 2009, and a "close ally" of twice secretary of defense, Rumsfeld (Scahill 2007: xv). Rumsfeld's early involvement in and support for shock and awe was noted above.

Relatedly, the question arises as to whether this support for the strategy at the very highest levels of US state power, along with the cast of actors involved, might help explain the blinkers worn by the George W. Bush administration in regard to the risks posed by al Qaeda and Osama bin Laden:

> In the nine months before September 11 the White House officer charged with worrying about terrorism, Richard Clarke, found it impossible to get the full attention of high officials with warnings about al-

Qaeda because the administration had a different agenda in mind—building a super-expensive, space-based anti-missile defense system. Critics of the Bush version of the Star Wars plan said the reasons for that had died with the cold war; terrorism was the danger facing America in the first years of the twenty-first century. The 9/11 Commission reported that Clarke, the CIA, and others had warned the administration as many as forty times of the threat posed by Osama bin Laden, but that is not what the administration wanted to hear, and it did not hear it.

(Powers 2004)

In light of this massive neglect on the part of the Bush administration to take seriously its own intelligence services, the War on Terror might be seen as expressing three key dynamics in necropolitical law's post-9/11 discounting of life. First, the "inner order" of the US state appears to have regarded "shock and awe" as providing a telos and "magic" of sorts, with the phrase "incanted by the inner order to transform the indeterminacies and complexities of policy, intelligence, and war" into the total victory delivered by rapid dominance (Der Derian 2009: 271). Second, the rush to war after the events of 9/11 may articulate a version of the politics of distraction – a variation on the theme of the deception so central to necropolitical law. By way of the spectacular and belligerent action of invading, first, Afghanistan, then Iraq, traumatized and fearful US publics were distracted from asking about their leaders' failures, accountability, and responsibility. And, third, this politics of distraction also worked seamlessly with the US "crisis of sovereignty" evident in the dismantling of public things effected by neoliberal governance, a dismantling that was well entrenched by the late 1990s (Lowe 2010: 230; Honig 2017). By the late 1990s:

> [t]he state increasingly lost legitimacy as it abandoned any role as a guardian of social welfare, and its functions became more disaggregated. Rather than broadening social or economic enfranchisement, the state struggled to maintain its legitimacy by exerting legal, policing, and military controls over migrant workers, poor communities of color, and other territories. The September 2001 attacks on the World Trade Center provided the conditions for the US government to imagine a "solution" to this crisis of sovereignty through a national project of war in Afghanistan and occupation of Iraq. . . . [F]rom the outset, the US war in Iraq appeared to many to have been an attempt to occupy the oil-rich region in order to resolve the much longer-standing crisis in US sovereignty.

(Lowe 2010: 231)

These three strands – shock and awe as an unstoppable, driving telos; war as distraction; and the necropolitical sovereign's legitimacy through war-making (directed at enemies both domestic and foreign) – are reminders of the complex weave of necropolitical law's expressions through the co-constitutions of nation.

With the 2017 MOAB deployment, the cultivation of technofetishism accompanies a reanimation of the origin story, affects, and identities scripted by the Bush administration for the War on Terror. In the meantime, the endless, unwinnable project of counter-terror, discounting life while channeling vast resources into "super-expensive" weapons (Powers 2004), has flourished. Who then is profiting from these super-expensive weapons? The Watergate scandal encouraged publics to follow the money. Of course, when it came to Watergate, Nixon's corruption was exposed by investigative journalists Bob Woodward and Carl Bernstein in 1972. The scandal unfolded prior to the intensified corporatization of media under Reagan (Chiappinelli et al. 2007: 986) and media's deepening complicities with and susceptibilities to power. Corporatized media's enmeshments with political power resulted in a barely discernible machinery for what Herman and Chomsky famously identified as the manufacturing of consent (1988). And as detailed in Chapter 5 in this book, the workings and relations of corporatized media in the (notionally separate) civic sphere have been augmented by the even closer management of media in the military sphere from at least the 1991 Gulf War onward. That cherished conviction in the freedom of the press might more accurately be re-framed as yet another American political myth (Bennet 2003; Ehrlich 2005). And certainly, as pointed out above, for Ullman and Wade, controlling media through "deception, disinformation, and misinformation" is a major factor in the delivery of "shock and awe" and ensuring American national interests.

Bearing in mind that Cheney was the very first secretary of defense to enjoy the concentrations of power effected by the Goldwater-Nichols Act (Godin 2005), it becomes fruitful to trace some of that money trail. In 1993, before Cheney departed as secretary of defense under the first President Bush,

> Cheney commissioned a study from a division of the company he would eventually head, Halliburton, on how to quickly privatize the military bureaucracy. Almost overnight, Halliburton would create an industry for itself servicing U.S. military operations abroad with seemingly

infinite profit potential. . . . In the ensuing eight years of governance by Bill Clinton, Cheney worked at the influential neoconservative think tank the American Enterprise Institute, which led the charge for an accelerated privatization of the government and the military. By 1995, Cheyney was at the helm of Halliburton building what would become the U.S. government's single largest defense contractor.

(Scahill 2007: xvi)

Halliburton is "a supplier of technology and services to the oil and gas industries."[67] Cheney was "a major force behind the decision" to invade and occupy Iraq in 2003 (Dower 2010: 91). Both Cheney and Halliburton have been named as major war profiteers, obscenely enriched by the 2003 invasion of Iraq (e.g., Greenwald 2006; Jacobs 2006; Scahill 2007). Within days of the launching of the Shock and Awe invasion of Iraq, the US online publication *AsianWeek* reported:

[T]wo stories about wartime profiteering that slipped under the radar last week while the networks were awed by the bombing campaigns reveal that Iraqi freedom may not be the only imperative for Bush Administration officials. The *Washington Post* reported on March 11 that the Bush administration was preparing to award non-competitive bid contracts to a few giant American construction companies worth hundreds of millions of dollars. Citing the need for speed and the state of emergency, companies such as Vice President Cheney's former firm, Halliburton Co., will get an inside track on rebuilding roads, oil wells, and other infrastructure in post-war Iraq. Meanwhile, the *New York Times* reports that Richard Perle, advisor to Secretary of War Donald Rumsfeld and head of the official Defense Policy Board, has been retained by Global Crossing, the bankrupt telecommunications company, to help overcome Pentagon resistance to the proposed sale of the company's assets to a joint venture involving a Hong Kong billionaire. Global Crossing has agreed to pay Perle $725,000, with $600,000 of that contingent on government approval of the sale. Whether the Iraqis are lying awake in their beds at night shocked and awed, we do not know at this time. But, once the facts get out about Perle, Halliburton and the other wartime profiteers—whose self-interest contrasts starkly with the self-sacrifice of young soldiers who are being asked to put their lives on the line, I am sure that many Americans will find themselves shocked and disgusted.

(Nash 2003)

---

[67] See www.britannica.com/biography/Dick-Cheney.

Tellingly, this article exposing processes involving persons in what many would perceive as corruption, unlike the Watergate scandal, was not making headlines in a major daily like the *Washington Post*. Instead, the shock and disgust at war profiteering was brought to light in a San Francisco-based weekly newspaper primarily read by an Asian American community.[68] Nor has post-9/11 war profiteering emerged as a political scandal the way Watergate did. Tragically for all, except the war profiteers, and as the MOAB deployment illustrates, a stupefied public's attention continues to be trained on "shock and awe" rather than following the money. Bearing in mind that Ullman and Wade themselves move in elite military and policy circles and that close Cheney ally Rumsfeld (Scahill 2007: xv) was an enthusiastic promoter of shock and awe to others within these same circles (Correll 2003), it is important to perceive in *Shock and Awe*'s valorizations of "the uniquely American ability" to integrate "strategy, technology, and the genuine quest for innovation,"[69] an exaltation of the military-industrial complex that authorizes and legitimizes the pursuit of profit over and above the valuing of life.

For some, the 1986 Goldwater-Nichols Act is implicated in the failures of intelligence precipitating the 2003 invasion of Iraq:

> Critics of the bill ... observe that by increasing the military advising authority of the defense secretary and JCS chairman, the legislation insulated the president from the viewpoints of the military chiefs and the individual civilian service secretaries. In its Senate Intelligence Report, released in July 2004, the Senate Intelligence Committee revealed that the military advice presented to Pres. George W. Bush about the existence of weapons of mass destruction in Iraq was based on faulty information, indicating that the quality of military advice provided to the president remain points of interest into the 21st century.
>
> (Godin 2005)

Thus, in Ullman and Wade's approving citation to the Goldwater-Nichols Act, alongside their references to "law" as militarized imperial policing, an ideological containment of law's other meanings – including meanings suspicious of power and insisting on power's accountability – are disclosed. In their insistence on total control, law does not exist as a public thing for Ullman and Wade. Instead, "deception, disinformation, and misinformation are crucial aspects of waging

---

[68] At www.loc.gov/item/2010254005/.   [69] Ullman et al. 1996, Prologue.

war . . . This is more than denial or deception. It is control in the fullest sense of the word."[70] To summarize, the exercise of interrogating the presence and absence of the category "law" in *Shock and Awe* points to how, for Ullman and Wade, total control is the "virtue" that authorizes and legitimizes the "infowar" of "shock and awe" (Der Derian 2009: 272). And this infowar is waged on every front, in the process dismantling law as public thing while deceiving and convincing *all* concerned – domestic and foreign.

6.4.4 "Shock and Awe" as Necropolitical Law's Keyword

In the 2003 war in Iraq, the counterterror state's management of media content was already discernible in the first aerial bombardments on March 21, 2003, which were broadcast on live television, the correspondents instructing watching publics that "[t]his is shock and awe" (Correll 2003). The next day, a story in the *Washington Post* traced the global parroting effected by contemporary news media, reporting on a worldwide database of news reports that "reveals a few dozen uses of the phrase in January, a couple of hundred in February and early March, and more than 600 in the past week" (Von Drehle 2003). Three days after the United States launched its invasion of Iraq (Cohn 2003), General Tommy Franks again invoked the phrase, repeating the content delivered by the Pentagon to the media some eight weeks earlier.[71] So effective was the repetition of this expression – "short, catchy, ideal for television" – that by the end of summer of 2003:

> Shock and Awe had become a cliche, applied in situations ranging from the box office boom of "The Matrix Reloaded" to a ninth inning home run by San Francisco Giants slugger Barry Bonds to (by political activist Tom Hayden) Arnold Schwarzenegger's announcement that he would run for governor of California.
>
> (Correll 2003)

Unsurprisingly, "shock and awe" has also been taken up in popular culture, featuring in the lyrics of more than 160 songs,[72] including

---

[70] Ullman et al. 1996, Chapter 2.
[71] He said, "This will be a campaign unlike any other in history. A campaign characterized by shock, by surprise, by flexibility, but the employment of precise munitions on a scale never before seen, and by the application of overwhelming force."
[72] See www.lyrics.com/lyrics/shock%20and%20awe.

songs protesting war,[73] and, more reflective of the "puerile arrogance" of the term (Young 2003: 28), in video games glorifying war.[74] At the risk of stating the obvious, the branding, marketized, computer game sensibility in the expression "shock and awe," casting national and global publics as spectator-consumer-audiences susceptible to violence as titillation, feeds into the depoliticizing logics of spectacle and the enmeshments of the military–industrial–media–entertainment network (Der Derian 2009). In 2003, profit-making entities seized upon the currency of "shock and awe":

> Sony applied for a trademark on Shock and Awe to use as the title of a video game, but dropped the application in embarrassment when it was discovered by the news media. Others sought to trademark Shock and Awe for pesticides and herbicides, barbecue sauce, and fireworks displays.
>
> (Correll 2003)

This unfolding, from the 1996 Pentagon briefing paper, to the 2003 headlines celebrating "shock and awe," to the frequency and fluency with which media reports on the 2017 MOAB strike cited to "shock and awe," demonstrates the consolidation of "shock and awe" as a keyword in the Raymond Williams sense, as a compound category calling up values, feelings, and "important ideas" through which a "temporarily dominant group may try to enforce its own uses as 'correct'" (1983 [1976]: 11). War, Williams notes, structures our experience of time through intensities of change, facilitating "unusually rapid and conscious" shifts in the values, "formations and distributions of energy and interests" embedded in and signified by keywords (1983 [1973]: 11–12). As keyword, "shock and awe" reconfigures our citizen-spectator sense of what war is, how war is fought, and how war is legitimized, imbuing authority and legitimacy in asymmetrical, if not annihilatory, military violence. Total and obliterating power, as Der Derian writes, becomes the distorted "virtue" of the " "virtuous war" (2009). By casting annihilatory warfare as the bearer of a desirable "virtue," law's function of creating community through enactments of norms, authority, and legitimacy is fulfilled. In the process, law's other virtues, such as

---

[73] For example, Patti Smith's "Radio Baghdad" (2004), Neil Young's "Shock and Awe" (2006), and Joni Mitchell's "Strong and Wrong" (2007).

[74] At www.imdb.com/title/tt2152841/ and https://tvtropes.org/pmwiki/pmwiki.php/ShockAndAwe/VideoGames.

accountability, prohibitions on torture, protections of human rights and civilians – these virtues are displaced. Virtuous war (Der Derian 2009) is yet another strand in the fabric of necropolitical law's discounting of life.

6.4.5 Always War, Never Peace

Shock and Awe was presented to the Pentagon in 1996, just seven years after the December 1989 fall of the Berlin Wall heralding the end of the Cold War and almost five years before the 9/11 attacks. As the *Shock and Awe* study group collectively acknowledged, "It is, of course, clear that US military forces are currently the most capable in the world and are likely to remain so for a long time to come."[75] With reduced defense spending in sight due to the end of the Cold War, the book conveniently argued that existing military doctrine and defense concepts were overly reliant on Cold War logics and infrastructures. Animating the alternatives presented in *Shock and Awe* is not a present or foreseeable war or enemy, but, as Masco (2014) highlights, the national security state's affect of *future*-oriented fear.

> In both relative and absolute terms, since the end of World War II, the military strength and capability of the United States have never been greater. Yet this condition of virtual military superiority has created a paradox. Absent a massive threat or massive security challenge, it is not clear that this military advantage can (always) be translated into concrete political terms that advance American interests.[76]

In addition to normalizing and legitimizing American militarized imperialism,[77] this brief excerpt illustrates a central analytic move in the *Shock and Awe* argument: war/security/American interests (the terms are used interchangeably) are abstracted from the present and from material realities, then invariably re-situated in a future constructed as risk-ridden and fearful. This toggling between the abstract and the actual is also used to displace "law" in the sense of "rule-of-law" liberal legal values, constructing instead, a subtextual necropolitical law by foregrounding and valorizing winning without regard for the lives of citizens and enemy Others.

---

[75] Ullman et al. (1996), Prologue.   [76] Ullman et al. (1996), Chapter 1.

[77] As Masco writes, "each iteration of the national security state announces itself through acts of normalization and naturalization" (2014: 10).

While toggling between the actual and the imagined – always authoritatively insisting that the future must be a site of danger – Ullman and Wade conjoin the vocabulary of manufacturing and efficiency to the language of affect. For Ullman and Wade, "shock and awe" delivers the "outputs" of "intimidation and compliance ... by the threat of use or by the actual application of our alternative force package [shock and awe]."[78] To illustrate these desired "outputs," Ullman and Wade draw on history and media,

> One recalls from old photographs and movie or television screens, the comatose and glazed expressions of survivors of the great bombardments of World War I and the attendant horrors and death of trench warfare. These images and expressions of shock transcend race, culture, and history. Indeed, TV coverage of *Desert Storm* vividly portrayed Iraqi soldiers registering these effects of battlefield Shock and Awe.[79]

Ullman and Wade demonstrate their awareness of visual culture and global media as platforms for instructing publics on the co-constitutions of military power and discounted lives. The discounted lives of barely alive, comatose survivors are part of what they promise to deliver through "shock and awe." By way of specificity, Ullman and Wade offer a typology of shock and awe, discussing "nine examples representing differing historical types, variants, and characteristics of Shock and Awe."[80] The excerpt below shows how Ullman and Wade's cryptic discussion positions the apocryphal as instructive "history." In the process, Ullman and Wade script necropolitical law by covertly celebrating the necropolitical sovereign's power to take life.

> The fifth example is named after the Chinese philosopher-warrior, Sun Tzu. The "Sun Tzu" example is based on selective, instant decapitation of military or societal targets to achieve Shock and Awe. ... Sun Tzu was brought before Ho Lu, the King of Wu, who had read all of Sun Tzu's thirteen chapters on war and proposed a test of Sun's military skills. Ho asked if the rules applied to women. When the answer was yes, the king challenged Sun Tzu to turn the royal concubines into a marching troop. The concubines merely laughed at Sun Tzu until he had the head cut off the head concubine. The ladies still could not bring themselves to take the master's orders seriously. So, Sun Tzu had the

[78] Ullman et al. (1996), Chapter 2.   [79] Ullman et al. (1996), Chapter 2.
[80] Ullman et al. (1996), Chapter 2.

head cut off a second concubine. From that point on, so the story goes, the ladies learned to march with the precision of a drill team.

The objectives of this example are to achieve Shock and Awe and hence compliance or capitulation through very selective, utterly brutal and ruthless, and rapid application of force to intimidate. The fundamental values or lives are the principal targets and the aim is to convince the majority that resistance is futile by targeting and harming the few. Both society and the military are the targets. In a sense, Sun Tzu attempts to achieve Hiroshima levels of Shock and Awe but through far more selective and informed targeting. Decapitation is merely one instrument. This model can easily fall outside the cultural heritage and values of the U.S. for it to be useful without major refinement. Shutting down an adversary's ability to "see" or to communicate is another variant but without many historical examples to show useful wartime applications.[81]

The weight of Ullman and Wade's words rests on the "success" of decapitation as a technique of "shock and awe." Even as we read the account, we are shocked, the better to be instructed on its effectiveness. Their cryptic closing lines leave open the possibilities of "major refinement" to spectacular decapitation, targeting "fundamental values or lives" in order to "convince the majority that resistance is futile." Decapitation takes on a further dimension in terms of targeting and killing demonized enemy leaders – the *head* of the monstrous beast. As noted above, when US officials first announced the MOAB strike, there was no mention of casualties. The next day it said that thirty-six ISIS fighters, including one commander, had been killed (CBS 2017). And three days after the strike, Afghan officials[82] announced that the number ISIS fighters killed by the MOAB had "jumped to 94, including four commanders" (Popalzai and Smith-Spark 2017). Bearing in mind the improbability of identifying and counting bodies discussed above (Section 6.2), these "jumps" in numbers, and the announcement that commanders – heads – had been severed from the body of ISIS, appear to be a version of the Sun Tzu example.

Furthermore, it is impossible not to wonder whether the hooding of Guantanamo detainees – a symbolic decapitation – is a version of this "major refinement" Ullman and Wade open the door to. At

---

[81] Ullman et al. (1996), Chapter 2.

[82] As an invaded and occupied state, these notionally Afghan officials were very probably the mouthpiece of the United States.

Guantanamo, as well as possibly at a range of other black sites, hooding has accompanied a range of sensory and communicative deprivations, augmented by the use of light and sound to torment, if not torture, detainees (e.g., Smith 2008; Couch 2013). Cumulatively, the counter-terror state's treatment of detainees is a chilling realization of how "[s]hutting down an adversary's ability to 'see' or to communicate is another variant [of decapitation]." It is almost as if, through the near-decapitation techniques accompanying extraordinary rendition, detention without trial, and torture, the counterterror state has sought to correct the lack of "historical examples to show useful wartime applications" through its shock and awe "innovations."

In a further assessment of the shortcomings with the Sun Tzu example, Ullman and Wade are again cryptic, "[i]t is questionable that a decision to employ American force this ruthlessly in quasi- or real assassination will ever be made by the U.S."[83] Significantly, they leave the question open. Ullman and Wade do not exclude the Sun Tzu example on the basis of incommensurability, that the law and politics of fifth-century BC feudal China cannot possibly have a bearing on how the contemporary US state conducts its power. Rather than delimit "examples" on the foundational basis of "rule of law" – attending to how societies manage the asymmetry of power between sovereign and subject, foregrounding individual rights and limits on state power – the story of Sun Tzu's decapitation of the emperor's concubines is told to seed possibilities for "shock and awe" through unanswered questions relating to contemporary "major refinements" for realizing this "model."

6.5 HIROSHIMA AND NAGASAKI AS SHOCK AND AWE'S PRECEDENT

As noted above (Sections 6.1 and 6.2), media discourse explicitly linked the MOAB's "shock and awe" to the 1945 nuclear bombing of Hiroshima and Nagasaki. In turn, and as illustrated by the *Daily Mail*'s simulation of a MOAB attack on Times Square, "the connection between September 11 and Hiroshima was locked in place when politicians and the media almost immediately baptized the ravaged site of the World Trade Center's twin towers 'Ground Zero'" (Dower 2010:

---

[83] Ullman et al. (1996), Chapter 2.

152). In *Shock and Awe*, the nuclear devastation of these Japanese cities is "glorified" (Dower 2010: 154) as both "legacy"[84] and as exemplary precedent, turning "Hiroshima as code for horror on its head" (Dower 2010: 154). This is how Ullman and Wade glorify, to borrow Dower's assessment, the shocking devastation of nuclear bombing:

> Theoretically, the magnitude of Shock and Awe Rapid Dominance seeks to impose (in extreme cases) is the non-nuclear equivalent of the impact that the atomic weapons dropped on Hiroshima and Nagasaki had on the Japanese. The Japanese were prepared for suicidal resistance until both nuclear bombs were used. The impact of those weapons was sufficient to transform both the mindset of the average Japanese citizen and the outlook of the leadership through this condition of Shock and Awe. The Japanese simply could not comprehend the destructive power carried by a single airplane. This incomprehension produced a state of awe.[85]

As this excerpt illustrates, for Ullman and Wade, "awe" is a cipher for extreme trauma. Crucially, "suicidal resistance" is presented as an unacceptable challenge to the necropolitical sovereign's power to take life. Under necropolitical law's planetary jurisdiction, no subject is permitted to be sovereign over her or his own life. If suicide is an expression of resistance, then the necropolitical sovereign must assert a corrective, punitive control by *taking* life on an unprecedented scale, while also effecting large-scale *collective* trauma upon survivors.[86]

In addition to this assertion of necropolitical sovereignty, Ullman and Wade's discussion of Hiroshima and Nagasaki as "the second example" of shock and awe does not acknowledge the asymmetries of scale and differences in targeting that sharply distinguish nuclear bombing and "suicidal resistance" as two forms of death dealing. In

---

[84] Ullman et al. (1996), Introduction to Rapid Dominance. Instead of the exaltation of "legacy," alternative characterizations of the nuclear bombing of Hiroshima and Nagasaki might include, for example, delegitimizing signifiers of shame and criminality, such as crimes against humanity or war crimes.

[85] Ullman et al. (1996), Introduction to Rapid Dominance.

[86] As argued by Jeffrey C. Alexander, the individual trauma model is inadequate for addressing collective cultural trauma which "occurs when members of a collectivity feel they have been subjected to a horrendous event that leaves indelible marks upon their group consciousness, marking their memories forever and changing their future identity in fundamental and irrevocable ways" (2004: 1). Alexander points out how, at the level of the collective, trauma is discursively constructed and disseminated through media (2004: 89).

the notorious World War II suicide (or kamikaze) bombings, like a sinister prequel to the 9/11 attacks, "[m]ost kamikaze planes were ordinary fighters or light bombers, usually loaded with bombs and extra gasoline tanks before being flown deliberately to crash into their targets."[87] Typically, these targets were enemy ships.[88] In contrast, the nuclear bombing of Hiroshima and Nagasaki targeted civilians in urban settings, and did so, Talal Asad notes, "without any warning and with no opportunity for civilian escape" (2007: 66). The suicidal resistance of kamikaze attacks is estimated to have killed close to 5,000 US sailors and wounded 5,000 more.[89] If life counts, then the scale of death dealing by "suicidal resistance" is but a fraction of the estimated "150,000 to 200,000 Japanese civilians, mostly old men, women, and children" killed by the 1945 nuclear bombs dropped on Japan (Sherwin 1995: 1086).

Ullman and Wade's discussion of Hiroshima and Nagasaki anticipates the public discourse of the War on Terror, through which suicide bombing has been constructed as a horrific and cruel atrocity and the counterterror state's asymmetrical warfare and death dealing has been constructed as necessary and justified militant action in response (Asad 2007). The authors indirectly dismiss the critique, according to which dropping the nuclear bomb on Nagasaki three days after the first bomb devastated Hiroshima was gratuitous violence, by asserting that "both" Hiroshima and Nagasaki needed to be bombed to dismantle Japanese resistance.[90] The MOAB, the United States' most powerful nonnuclear weapon, is anticipated in Ullman and Wade's "theoretical" search for "the nonnuclear equivalent" of the 1945 nuclear bomb.[91] And as noted above, media on the MOAB strike invariably included comparisons between the MOAB and the nuclear bomb.

In Ullman and Wade's account, the nuclear bombing of Hiroshima and Nagasaki becomes a cause-and-effect story in which "shock and awe" is the cause effecting the *transformation* of Japanese resistance into capitulation. Their word choice – "transform" – is illuminating. They describe the annihilation of Japanese resistance through asymmetrical

---

[87] See www.britannica.com/topic/kamikaze.
[88] See www.britannica.com/topic/kamikaze.
[89] "John Chapman and the Kamikaze Attack," www.pbs.org/wgbh/americanexperi ence/features/pacific-john-chapman/.
[90] Ullman et al. (1996), Introduction to Rapid Dominance.
[91] Ullman et al. (1996), Introduction to Rapid Dominance.

warfare, but they do so by spinning extreme destruction as "transform-ation"; they legitimize *winning* while minimizing the discounting of Japanese life. For Ullman and Wade, Japanese "incomprehension" is a desirable effect of "shock and awe," erasing the possibility that "incom-prehension" was also attributable to the experience of inhumanity on a previously unknown scale. There is no acknowledgment that, at the time the bombs were dropped, negotiations had been underway for conditions of surrender (Sherwin 1995; Dower 2010: 222). Also absent from Ullman and Wade's telling is any sense that the nuclear bombings of Hiroshima and Nagasaki constitute, in some assessments, the crime of genocide (Marcoń 2011).

Advocating consistently for the privatization of defense as the best way to foster innovations in military strategy, Ullman and Wade present "shock and awe" as a bold innovation that was necessary to sustain American military primacy. However, noting the old wine in new bottles quality of "shock and awe," Dower points to the combin-ation of military violence with "psychological warfare" (2010: xxiii) World War II, when the saturation firebombing of "congested cities" was "the onset of an epoch in which slaughter from the air became routine" (2010: 222). And, in tracing continuities between the Cold War state and the counterterror state, Masco shows how the seemingly new military doctrine of "shock and awe" is a repackaging of the threat issued to Japan on July 26, 1945, via the Potsdam Declaration,[92] that unless Japan surrendered unconditionally, "prompt and utter destruc-tion" would follow. Ten days before delivering this threat "the first nuclear bomb was detonated secretly in New Mexico" (Masco 2014: 213, note 5). Like a prequel to the technofetishism that celebrates, indeed, *sacralizes* killing technology, Robert Oppenheimer, the lead

---

[92] On May 7, 1945, Germany formally surrendered to the Western allies, and on May 9 to the USSR. From July 17 to August 2, 1945, the Potsdam Conference was convened by the heads of the Allied governments (Churchill, then Attlee from July 26, Stalin, Truman) and the Potsdam Declaration was issued in the names of the leaders and the people of the United States, China, and Great Britain. In addition to the discussion of the administration of Germany, the governments still fighting Japan (the United States, United Kingdom, and China) wrote a declaration announcing terms of unconditional surrender for Japan. The Potsdam Declaration included provisions about disarmament, occupation, and territorial sovereignty, but did not mention the emperor. The Japanese government initially rejected the declaration outright, but later agreed to it after the atomic bombs were dropped and the Soviet Union had invaded Japanese territory. Some have theorized that the declaration's final threat referenced the atomic bomb.

physicist and principal architect of the nuclear bomb, code-named the test Trinity, in troubling homage to John Donne's 1633 sonnet of muscular metaphysical struggle with "three-person'd God" whose "force" would "break, blow, burn and make me new."[93] The nuclear bomb's destructive force did, indeed, "break, blow, burn" but only to effect death, alongside enduring toxicity and harm; this was not the renewal through faith that Donne writes about, unless, consistent with the political myth of regeneration through violence, it is *American* spiritual/imperial potency that was and is made new by violence toward those "dark of skin and seemingly dark of mind" (Slotkin 2000 [1973]: 18; Du Bois 2003 [1920]: 52).

6.5.1 Necropolitical Law's Precedent

For former Afghan president Hamid Kharzai, the MOAB strike was "not the war on terror but the inhuman and most brutal misuse of our country as testing ground for new and dangerous weapons" (BBC 2017). The condemnation articulated by Kharzai and others points to a historical precedent.[94] In 1945, when the United States used a new and most powerful weapon for the first time, it used it on an enemy that, like ISIS, was the distant, racialized, evil Other. In other words, for necropolitical law, the nuclear bombing of Hiroshima and Nagasaki is a key – if not canonical – precedent authorizing the MOAB strike. In addition to the explicit assertion of the relationship between the nuclear bomb and the MOAB – the MOAB has been consistently described as the United States' most powerful nonnuclear weapon – the images of the MOAB's mushroom cloud, and the references to Ground Zero, are further signifiers of continuities in necropolitical law's authority, community, and scripts of legitimacy from 1945 to 2017.

When Hiroshima and Nagasaki were nuclear bombed, the United States exercised enormous control over media, concealing from publics the truly devastating nature and extent of the bombs' force and effects (Sherwin 1995; Marcon 2011). While Ullman and Wade do not acknowledge this deception through control of media, in *Shock and*

---

[93] See www.energy.gov/lm/doe-history/manhattan-project-background-information-and-preservation-work/manhattan-project-1.

[94] In addition to the International Crisis Group, and Latifi and Osman (whose critique is discussed in this chapter), the mayor of Achin, the province in which the bomb was dropped, questioned the need "for such a large-scale strike against a relatively small militant group" (Rasmussen 2017).

Awe they do assert the need to replicate this feature of the US management of the 1945 nuclear bombing, arguing that in war "deception, confusion, misinformation, and disinformation, perhaps in massive amounts, must be employed."[95] In 1945, when the United States dropped the nuclear bomb on Japan, it justified its action on the grounds that it would "save American lives by ending the war as quickly as possible" (Sherwin 1995: 1085; Dower 2010: 222). However, the United States had other, undeclared motives for using the nuclear bomb, including the technofetishism detailed above in Section 6.2. Partly because of the chilling effects of the Cold War and partly because of "the long delay before the relevant documents because available to historians," these undeclared motives remained hidden for decades, such that state "spin" became the received account in "a classic case of a historical narrative shaped by government insiders to serve their view of the national interests" (Sherwin 1995: 1085). Martin Sherwin writes:

> Ending the war quickly was certainly one motive for using the atomic bombs. But other motives promoted, reinforced, and perhaps even overtook the one put forward by [Secretary of War] Stimson[96] These included: (1) the hope that the bomb(s) would curb Stalin's ambitions in Eastern Europe and the Far East; (2) the pressure that senior Manhattan Project administrators felt to justify the money, materials, and talent spent to build atomic bombs; (3) the momentum to use these new weapons created by the strategy of urban bombing; and (4) the desire to avenge Pearl Harbor and the ghastly treatment of American prisoners of war.
>
> (Sherwin 1995: 1086)

With the MOAB, seventy-two years after the bombing of Hiroshima and Nagasaki, troubling parallels abound. First, just as the nuclear bomb was meant to intimidate Stalin, some analysts have seen in the MOAB strike a "disproportionate" show of strength, staged as a warning message directed at regional and international adversaries (Kumar 2017).[97] In particular, enemies with actual or potential nuclear

---

[95] Ullman et al. (1996), Introduction to Rapid Dominance.

[96] Henry L. Stimson was secretary of war from 1940 to 1945. Sherwin describes him as chief "spin doctor" of the history of the atomic bomb (1995: 1085).

[97] Support for the argument that the MOAB strike was staged as a warning to watching enemies is bolstered by reports that in February 2017 "the top U.S. commander in Afghanistan, Army General John Nicholson, told a Congressional committee that ISIS-K had lost about a third of its fighters and two-thirds of its territory during the last year to drone strikes and Special Forces operations. More

weaponry, such as Iran and North Korea, are meant to be instructed by the MOAB strike, that the United States has "bunker-buster" bombs able to "strike against underground nuclear facilities" (Klimas 2017). Second, while, at this point in time, it is impossible to know if the US Air Force has been under pressure to justify the money, materials, and talent channeled into the MOAB, what is immediately discernible is the military-industrial-media-entertainment network. Specifically, in addition to the technofetishism of focusing on the MOAB in tandem with the discursive near-erasure of victims, pro-Trump media was "elated" by the bombing, welcoming it as an early instance of Trump making good on his election promises (Sylvester 2020: 26). On the Fox News morning show, "the hosts could barely contain their enthusiasm for the strike," celebrating MOAB explosion as "freedom" (Szoldra 2017). If the mass and distanced killing of enemies through asymmetrical warfare becomes the image of freedom, then it is the community, authority, and legitimacy of necropolitical law that is inculcated in watching publics.

Further demonstrating the co-constitutions of nation/empire, the MOAB was represented less as an annihilating attack on people than as a media spectacle, staged for audiences and constituencies both inside the United States and globally. As Senator Lindsey Graham, a South Carolina Republican, tweeted, "I hope America's adversaries are watching & now understand there's a new sheriff [Trump] in town" (Starr and Browne 2017). Some of the world watching this "new sheriff" registered its alarm. Within the same week that the MOAB was dropped, cruise missiles were launched at a Syrian airbase "in retaliation for Syrian president Bashar al-Assad's chemical attack on his own civilians," drawing the admiration of well-known media figures – both for the weapon and for Trump's leadership (Hartung 2017).[98] On the same day that the Pentagon announced the MOAB strike, the Pentagon disclosed in a separate statement the mistaken

---

than a hundred additional fighters, including two leaders, have been killed this month [April 2017]" (Wright 2017).

[98] William Hartung notes, "The first strike – the launching of cruise missiles at a Syrian airbase in retaliation for Syrian President Bashar al-Assad's chemical attack on his own civilians – drew praise from unlikely suspects. These included MSNBC's Brian Williams, who described the attack and the weapons used to carry it out as 'beautiful,' and CNN's Fareed Zakaria, a longtime Trump critic and foreign policy analyst, who suggested that the strike finally certified Trump's status as a real live president."

killing of eighteen Syrian allies in an airstrike in Syria directed at ISIS (Cooper and Mashal 2017). Together with mistaken strikes earlier that month in Iraq and Syria that had "killed or wounded scores of civilians,"[99] this killing of Syrian allies was "the third American-led airstrike in a month that may have killed civilians or allies" (Cooper and Mashal 2017). Airwars, a not-for-profit transparency organization that tracks civilian harm in conflict zones, reported that "civilian deaths had risen sixfold in Syria, with more than 350 killed last month [March 2017] alone" (Cooper and Mashal 2017). For Airwars, this steep rise in civilian death was an indicator that, under Trump, US battlefield rules had been amended, "placing civilians at greater risk of harm" (Cooper and Mashal 2017). In short, the pressure that had built up to the deployment of the MOAB in April 2017 may have had more to do with Trump's statecraft of seizing the headlines to stage himself, America, and the US military as "the greatest,"(Cooper and Mashal 2017) while deploying the politics of distraction (Hartung 2017). In William Hartung's assessment, the sequence of, first, the cruise missiles launched at the Syrian airbase, second, the MOAB strike, and, third, sending US naval ships toward the Korean peninsula – all within a week – evidence "a formula for distracting the public and the media from his troubles at home: from allegations of collusion with Russia during the 2016 election to his failure at pushing through his most cherished domestic initiatives" (2017).

To return to the parallels between the history and politics of the 1945 nuclear bombing and the 2017 MOAB, in uncovering the United States' undisclosed motives for using the nuclear bomb against Japan, Sherwin highlights how the World War II strategy of urban bombing created a "momentum," pressing toward the use of the nuclear bomb (Sherwin 1995: 1086). In parallel, momentum relating to warfare in a terrain of caves and tunnels is discernible in the military's accounts of how and why, despite the already tremendously asymmetrical encounter between the United States and its enemies, the MOAB was called for:

> Islamic State fighters in Afghanistan "are using I.E.D.s, bunkers and tunnels to thicken their defense," said Gen. John W. Nicholson Jr., the

---

[99] In a telling expression of the discounting of life through the implicit application of the category "collateral damage," the Syrian fighters who were allies are counted and countable, whereas "civilians" are discounted through the imprecision of "scores."

United States commander there, referring to improvised explosive devices. "This is the right munition to reduce these obstacles and maintain the momentum of our offensive."

(Cooper and Mashal 2017)

A thickening defense, the presence of obstacles, and impeded momentum aggregate into "resistance" in *Shock and Awe*'s terms, and "shock and awe" sets out to completely destroy existing resistance and prevent resistance in the future (Ullman and Wade 1996).

A fourth parallel: in the 1945 nuclear attacks on Japan, the United States was motivated by "the desire to avenge Pearl Harbor and the ghastly treatment of American prisoners of war" (Sherwin 1995: 1086). Similarly, in the post-9/11 wars, vengeance has certainly been cast as a key element of "justice," as noted in Chapters 3 and 4, as well as in *Discounting Life*'s concluding chapter. And ISIS, as highlighted by Trump (Chapter 4), has handed out spectacularly ghastly treatment of its prisoners, American and otherwise. The enthusiasm of Trump's fan base for the MOAB bombing, celebrating the MOAB's mushroom cloud as "freedom" and a desirable expression of patriotism (Szoldra 2017; Sylvester 2020), alongside Lindsey Graham's invocation of frontier justice ("there's a new sheriff in town") point to the strike having been interpreted by certain US constituencies as an appropriate act of vengeance. Further, some news reports noted that, in the week leading up to the MOAB – the first week of April 2017 – one "American special forces soldier was killed fighting [ISIS] militants" (BBC 2017). Staff Sergeant Mark De Alencar, "a Green Beret and a father of five" was "the first US combat death in Afghanistan" in the course of that year when he was killed (Wright 2017). In addition to the implication that some degree of punitive vengeance informed the decision to deploy the MOAB, media on the MOAB strike disclose the distinction between the lives that count – American forces, American allies – and those that don't: civilians and enemies. In the process, Tom Englehardt's analysis is affirmed, that in the post-9/11 wars, the deaths that are in substance *collateral* are those of the combatants. "Civilian deaths," he emphasizes, "are now the central fact, the very essence of war. Not seeing that means not seeing war" (Englehardt 2007). And, of course, when it comes to the MOAB strike, the images and information fed to the media have been precisely about the *not* seeing of the discounted lives of the long War on Terror.

Chapter 7 draws together the threads of this book's arguments through a consideration of Biden's April and August 2021 announcements on US troop withdrawals from Afghanistan. In these speeches,

Biden rehearsed the familiar moves of co-constituting nation/empire, the familial and the political, to authorize and legitimize American imperial violence. In the process, he discarded and implicitly disavowed legal doctrine. Instead of conventional law, political myths of American exceptionalism, American innocence, and frontier justice animated Biden's narrative of authority, legitimacy, and community. With American political myth doing the work of law, imperial violence directed at distant, racialized Others reconstituted America as a community of power identified with asymmetrical violence as the lawful delivery of national security. Chapter 7 shows how Biden's account of the withdrawal operates as a text of necropolitical law, authorizing American imperial power expressed through the unbounded right to kill as the properly protective, and necessarily ongoing, project of the long War on Terror.

NECROPOLITICAL LAW AND ENDLESS WAR

7.1 THE THREE BODIES OF THE FATHER–PRESIDENT–COMMANDER-IN-CHIEF

In April 2021 President Biden announced the withdrawal of US troops from Afghanistan, saying he wanted them all "home" by September 11, 2021 (Biden 2021a). Mourning and sacralizing "the exact number of American troops killed in Iraq and Afghanistan," Biden reminded us that his "late son, Beau, was deployed to Iraq," making him "the first President in 40 years who knows what it means to have a child serving in a warzone." Biden's invocations of his son Beau, his lamenting of American fatalities, together with his frequent references to "home" and "homeland," cast him as a fatherly, protective figure, a president caring for and suffering with the nation, and one uniquely authorized by personal loss to redirect foreign policy. Images of Biden following his statement showed him standing with his head bowed reverentially and sorrowfully among the white tombstones of the Arlington National Cemetery, the nation's military cemetery, performing his sense of loss, both personal and presidential.

In this speech, as in other moments of the long War on Terror, US state discourse was co-constituting nation/empire, the familial and the political, to authorize and legitimize the discounting of life.[1] Indeed, in

---

[1] To recapitulate arguments traced throughout this book, I draw, first, on Amy Kaplan's field-shaping argument of "how dominant representations of national identity at home are informed and deformed by the anarchic encounters of empire, even as those same representations displace and disavow imperialism" (2002: 16). And

key public speeches delivered after the events of September 11, President Bush linked "the spectacle of mourning and the political resolve for warfare . . . in ways that presented war as the only salve for loss and mourning" (Lubin 2021: 27). Consistent with Bush's weaving together of mourning, militarism, and necropolitical law, Biden discarded and implicitly disavowed legal doctrine regulating violence in international contexts, such as laws of war, as well as many of law's conventional sites, processes, actors, and values, such as courts, trials, lawyers and judges, due process, and human rights. Offering political myth, concern for the nation, and a US-Taliban agreement as the converging grounds for the 2021 withdrawal, Biden reiterated the necropolitical sovereign's power to take life.

In this concluding chapter, I show how Biden's account of the US withdrawal from Afghanistan operates as a text of necropolitical law, deploying deception, narratives of enmity, and statements elevating American political myths into legitimizing grounds for state action. In particular, the myths of American exceptionalism, American innocence, frontier justice, and the discourse of American national interests become the grounds of necropolitical law. Section 7.2 analyzes the plural and paradoxical temporalities and sovereignties that are woven together with deception into a legitimation of the US withdrawal. Section 7.3 analyzes Biden's selective recognition of law in the form of the US-Taliban agreement and his selective accounting for the lives lost in the war on terror. Section 7.4 examines how "American national interests" relate to the profit-seeking of powerful corporations in Afghanistan, demonstrating the co-constitutions of law and war as tools in the service of private-sector enrichment and extractive imperialism. This section also considers the role played by Zalmay Khalilzad, an individual who exemplifies the global networks, influence, and interests of individuals that come together into the military-industrial complex. Section 7.5 analyzes the necropolitical law expressed through Biden's August 2021 statements defending the withdrawal, blaming the Afghans for the rapid Taliban takeover, and enacting vengeance as necropolitical law's delivery of justice. In total, my argument in this

second, on Melani McAlister's analysis of how cultural and political texts relating to the Iran hostage crisis fostered nationalist discourse identifying the nation-state "with the private sphere that it was said to protect," such that "counterterrorism or military force could be undertaken for the sake of something identified as private—love, the family, revenge" (2005: 233).

concluding chapter highlights how, consistent with the other moments this book has traced, post-9/11 US discourse legitimizes, authorizes, and perpetuates necropolitical law's discounting of life in an unending war on terror.

7.2 NECROPOLITICAL LAW'S CODED TEXTS

On April 14, 2021, announcing the withdrawal of US troops from Afghanistan, President Biden drew attention to the fact that he was delivering his speech from "the same spot where . . . President George W. Bush informed our nation that the United States military had begun strikes on terrorist training camps in Afghanistan" (Biden 2021a). In noting this continuity across time and place, Biden invoked the medieval political theology of the two bodies of the king: the ruler's mortal body corporeal and the state's immortal body politic (Kantorowicz 1957). Specifically naming two presidents as two (corporeal) bodies speaking to and for the immortal United States had the subtle effect of narrating the mythic temporality of a United States before and beyond the time of the present. Superficially, however, Biden was scripting a temporality of beginnings and endings, explicitly linking the 2001 launching of the global war on terror (Bush) to its apparent 2021 closing (Biden), at least with reference to Afghanistan. In terms of the shifting, layered, and plural temporalities of American exceptionalism, which include distinguishing the United States from Europe in terms of histories of monarchical rule (Pease 2007), and asserting 9/11 as a moment of inauguration and rupture, a remaking of history (Dudziak 2003), Biden's opening words invoke American exceptionalism to selectively suture recent and ongoing national trauma to the restoration of an imagined, perpetual, and timeless national body politic.

Re-stating the political myth of American innocence, and re-sacralizing the spaces and victims of the 9/11 attacks, Biden also narrated a temporality of heroic, nation-protecting rapid response in the way the United States launched its war in Afghanistan:

> [T]he United States military had begun strikes on terrorist training camps in Afghanistan . . . just weeks after the terrorist attack on our nation that killed 2,977 innocent souls, that turned Lower Manhattan into a disaster area, destroyed parts of the Pentagon, and made hallowed ground of a field in Shanksville, Pennsylvania, and sparked an American promise that we would "never forget."
>
> (Biden 2021a)

Biden's invocation here of "never forget" reproduces the counterterror state's discursive move of appropriating language associated with other moments in history and eclipsing those prior moments through repeated overemphasis on American victimization (Kaplan 2003: 56–57). "Never forget" as a shorthand for 9/11 illustrates how an injunction once strongly associated with memorializing the Holocaust was appropriated to a particularly American "narrative of historical exceptionalism ... claim[ing] that the event was so unique and unprecedented as to transcend time and defy comparison or historical analysis" (Kaplan 2003: 56). One crucial effect of this historical exceptionalism is the augmenting of "a historic weakness of U.S. security policy and scholarship to consider relevant comparative experience" (Brysk 2007: 3).

In addition to this assertion of American historical exceptionalism, the dynamic of deception features as a key necropolitical move in that, by telling the story of a protective, pro-active US response to the 9/11 attacks, Biden leaves out the 1998 missile attacks directed at al Qaeda training camps in Afghanistan, a camp "well known to the United States because it had originally been set up to train the same people to fight against the Soviet Union" (Young 2003: 10). He likewise left out the approximately forty warnings conveyed by US intelligence services to the Bush administration in 2001 about probable and imminent al Qaeda–engineered terrorist attacks on US soil (Scahill 2013: 21). In parallel, just as Bush ignored intelligence warnings and assessments in 2001, so, too, throughout the summer of 2021, Biden appears to have disregarded "classified assessments by American spy agencies" warning of the likelihood of "a Taliban takeover of Afghanistan and ... the rapid collapse of the Afghan military" (Mazzetti et al. 2021). Biden also leaves out the disclosures of the 2019 Afghanistan Papers, revealing extreme corruption and incompetence at the very highest levels of US government in relation to the military occupation of Afghanistan (Whitlock 2019; Thomas 2020).

Instead, by rehearsing the Bush administration's account of the 9/11 attacks as "some diabolical deception that came like a bolt from the blue" (Jackson 2005: 43), Biden re-narrated American innocence and trauma, thereby re-identifying terrorists as evil, irrational, social actors, bent on attacking a blameless America. Biden's strategically crafted narrative insisted that the United States invaded Afghanistan solely to achieve the twinned purposes of ensuring future US national security and avenging the 9/11 attacks. Departing from Bush's insistent yoking of al Qaeda and the Taliban (Bush 2002a),[2] Biden foregrounded al Qaeda as the enemy and minimized the risk posed to the United States by the Taliban, authorizing necropolitical law's re-making of justice as vengeance:

> We went to Afghanistan in 2001 to root out al Qaeda, to prevent future terrorist attacks against the United States planned from Afghanistan. Our objective was clear. The cause was just. . . . We delivered justice to bin Laden a decade ago.
>
> (Biden 2021a)

In keeping with necropolitical law's reliance on deception, Biden glossed over a highly significant detail – bin Laden was killed in Pakistan, not Afghanistan. Biden's blurring of the details served to re-vitalize the racialized American imperial gaze that treats certain non-White peoples as fungible. As highlighted in Chapter 2, Leti Volpp (2002) has traced how, in the United States, that capacious and heterogenous post-9/11 identity category – persons who appear to be "Middle Eastern, Arab, or Muslim" – has led to the disidentification of citizens and their reidentification as terrorists. Similarly, in rendering Afghanistan and Pakistan fungible, Biden cast populations in Central and South Asia as terrorists, as opposed to rights-bearing human beings and citizens with claims to protection by their own governments and by international law. Biden's slippage between Afghanistan and Pakistan also normalized necropolitical law's planetary jurisdiction. Implicitly reproducing colonialism's racialized designations of "enemy" as "the manifestation of evil that threatens civilization" (Saito 2010: 235), he asserts that as necropolitical sovereign, the United States is empowered to track, target, and kill the enemy, no matter where in the world that enemy might be.

Even while asserting America's planetary jurisdiction to enact necropolitical law, Biden toggled paradoxically between imperial and national sovereignties, nodding toward national sovereignty for

---

[2] In his April 2002 address to the Virginia Military Institute, which was widely reported in media, Bush delivered a speech detailing America's role in Afghanistan. He repeatedly yoked al Qaeda and the Taliban. He also said, "we help the Afghan people recover from the Taliban rule. And as we do so, we find mounting horror, evidence of horror. In the Hazarajat region, the Red Cross has found signs of massacres committed by the Taliban last year, victims who lie in mass graves. This is the legacy of the first regime to fall in the war against terror. These mass graves are a reminder of the kind of enemy we have fought and have defeated. And they are the kind of evil we continue to fight" (Bush 2002a).

Afghanistan in the conventional sense ("only the Afghans have the right and responsibility to lead their country), while reiterating the United States' planetary jurisdiction ("We went to Afghanistan in 2001 to root out al Qaeda, to prevent future terrorist attacks against the United States planned from Afghanistan"). In re-stating America's planetary jurisdiction, Biden injected new life into the war on terror even as he seemed to be taking steps to contain it:

> Over the past 20 years, the threat [of terrorism] has become more dispersed, metastasizing around the globe: al-Shabaab in Somalia; al Qaeda in the Arabian Peninsula; al-Nusra in Syria; ISIS attempting to create a califit [caliphate] in Syria and Iraq, and establishing affiliates in multiple countries in Africa and Asia. ... [S]ignificant terrorist threats ... [are found] in Africa, Europe, the Middle East, and elsewhere.
>
> (Biden 2021a)

In Biden's announcement, fundamental categories in conventional liberal understandings of law – including nation-state sovereignty and jurisdiction, due process, and citizen rights – dissolve into necropolitical law's contingencies and asymmetries. In the process, it is the necropolitical sovereign's right to take life that is asserted and upheld.

7.3   AN HONORABLE AMERICA

In addition to rooting out al Qaeda and killing bin Laden as the legitimizing authority for invading and occupying Afghanistan, Biden offered two further reasons for the troop withdrawal. First was a February 2020 agreement negotiated by the Trump administration, which, as Neta Crawford (2021) emphasizes, was a bilateral agreement between the United States and the Taliban, pointedly excluding the Afghan government. Biden said, "When I came to office, I inherited a diplomatic agreement, duly negotiated between the government of the United States and the Taliban, that all US forces would be out of Afghanistan by May 1, 2021" (2021a). Notably, Biden considered himself and the US government bound by this Trump-brokered agreement, while not being bound at all by George W. Bush's promises to deliver "true peace" to Afghanistan with development assistance along the lines of the Marshall Plan for postwar Europe.[3] Also notable is the

---

[3] In his address to the Virginia Military Institute, Bush said, "We know that true peace will only be achieved when we give the Afghan people the means to achieve their own aspirations. Peace—peace will be achieved by helping Afghanistan develop its

Orwellian doublespeak in the language of sovereignty naming the parties to the US-Taliban agreement, "Agreement for Bringing Peace to Afghanistan between the Islamic Emirate of Afghanistan which is not recognized by the United States as a state and is known as the Taliban and the United States of America."[4] In addition to eclipsing the role of the United States in bringing war rather than peace to Afghanistan from at least 1979 (Mackenzie 1998; Pilger 2021), this language deceives and doubles in a second way. At the level of the literal, these words permit the United States to disavow any recognition of the Taliban as a state power. But at the level of metapragmatics, the language, the fact of the agreement, and the text as an artifact of diplomacy binding upon the United States, disclose the substance of US recognition of the Taliban as Afghanistan's de facto government. Or, more cynically, this document discloses the US decision to situate the Taliban as its new proxy or partner in the governing of Afghanistan as its client state. According to at least one analyst, the US withdrawal from Afghanistan was motivated by the US recognition that the Taliban is the social actor best placed to protect the proposed pipeline discussed in Section 7.4 below (Dennett 2021).

In identifying this agreement as the legal text binding him and the United States, Biden discards law's humanitarian principles and the obligations of the United States, in its capacity as an occupying sovereign, to care for and protect vulnerable Afghan populations. And in departing from Bush's insistent yoking of al Qaeda and the Taliban as evil terrorists, Biden implicitly re-categorizes the Taliban as "not-terrorists." As part of his assertion of the binding legality of the agreement with the Taliban, Biden characterizes the United States as honorable and reliable in the conduct of foreign affairs ("It is perhaps not what I would

---

own stable government. Peace will be achieved by helping Afghanistan train and develop its own national army. And peace will be achieved through an education system for boys and girls which works. We're working hard in Afghanistan. We're clearing minefields. We're rebuilding roads. We're improving medical care. And we will work to help Afghanistan to develop an economy that can feed its people without feeding the world's demand for drugs. ... By helping to build an Afghanistan that is free from this evil and is a better place in which to live, we are working in the best traditions of George Marshall. Marshall knew that our military victory against enemies in World War II had to be followed by a moral victory that resulted in better lives for individual human beings" (Bush 2002a).

[4] At www.state.gov/wp-content/uploads/2020/02/Agreement-For-Bringing-Peace-to-Afghanistan-02.29.20.pdf.

have negotiated myself, but it was an agreement made by the United States government, and that means something"). In short, by citing this agreement as valid and binding, Biden engages that key move of necropolitical law: selectively subjecting peoples to law's violence while withholding law's putative obligations to protect and nurture life.

In keeping with discounting the lives of racialized Others as a central driver of necropolitical law, Biden enumerated a quite specific selective accounting of life that counts:

> For the past 12 years, ever since I became Vice President, I've carried with me a card that reminds me of the exact number of American troops killed in Iraq and Afghanistan. That exact number, not an approximation or rounded-off number—because every one of those dead are sacred human beings who left behind entire families. An exact accounting of every single solitary one needs to be had. As of the day—today, there are two hundred and forty—2,488 [2,448] U.S. troops and personnel who have died in Operation Enduring Freedom and Operation Freedom's Sentinel—our Afghanistan conflicts. 20,722 have been wounded.
>
> (Biden 2021a)

Omitted from Biden's accounting of "sacred human beings who left behind entire families" are the estimated "100,000 Afghans (many of them non-combatants)" who died under the US occupation and the wounding of "three times that number" (Ali 2021). The necropolitical law of American imperialism erases from law's record the lives of those who are non-American victims of American militarized imperialism. It is a selective accounting in service of a deceptive facticity: by centering American victims, American innocence is secured even as American imperial violence is eclipsed and disavowed. This is a re-deployment of the discursive move animating American historical exceptionalism, as identified by Amy Kaplan (2003) in her analysis of how the post-9/11 re-semanticization of "ground zero" twinned repeated overemphasis on Americans as victims to the erasure of America's victimization of Others.

7.4   AMERICAN NATIONAL INTERESTS

In April 2021, Biden stated a further reason for the troop withdrawal. He argued that withdrawing troops from Afghanistan was "in keeping ... with our national interests." The language of American national interests has routinely included claims to Middle Eastern oil (McAlister 2005). With the 9/11 attacks, discourses that had hitherto centered on the Middle East – linking oil, Islam, and the threat of terrorism – have expanded to include Muslim-majority regions of Europe, Asia, and Africa. In the process, the post-9/11 area studies category, Greater Middle East,[5] works to subsume and reconfigure Afghanistan according to culturally constructed American understandings of the Middle East, evoking deep discursive associations between American "national interests," including an embattled national security tied to oil and American cultural constructions of terrorism and Islam (McAlister 2005).

In his April 2021 announcement, while invoking American "national interests," Biden did not acknowledge the role of oil and natural gas as a probable factor in the decision to invade and occupy Afghanistan. However, pointing to how post–Cold War US conduct reflects a shift to the construction of "a balanced world" as one dominated by the blatantly aggressive exercise of "exclusive American power," Marilyn Young traces some of the connections between US militarized imperialism, the US oil industry, and post-9/11 "profit-taking" (2003: 18, 24):

> In 1998 the vice president of Unocal, an energy giant with close ties to the Bush family, described his vision of a "new Silk road" to the House Committee on International Relations: a 1,040-mile long oil pipeline beginning in northern Turkmenistan and running through Afghanistan to a terminal on the Pakistan coast. ... War has made all Unocal's wishes accessible.
>
> (Young 2003: 24)

Other scholars, and investigative journalists, have traced and noted Unocal-CIA collaborations supporting the Taliban throughout the 1990s, sometimes via US allies Saudi Arabia and Pakistan (Ahady 1998; Coll 2018; Mackenzie 1998; Rashid 1998; Dennett 2020). Consultants employed by Unocal include former secretary of state Henry Kissinger (Ottaway and Morgan 1998), and it is known that in the 1990s, "Unocal officials were briefed extensively by US intelligence analysts" (Mackenzie 1998: 97). In June 1996, when the Senate Committee on Foreign Relations conducted hearings under the rubric, "Afghanistan: Is There Hope for Peace?" (Brown 1998), the "most

---

[5] The first use of this new area studies category appears to be in Harlan Ullman's *Unfinished Business: Afghanistan, the Middle East, and Beyond—Defusing the Dangers That Threaten America's Security* (2002). See Chapter 6, where Ullman is identified as a figure who embodies the military-industrial complex, with elite connections and influence in US policy, military, and defense education and industry circles.

memorable presentation was not by an Afghan but by Marty Miller, the UNOCAL Vice President in charge of the proposed Afghan pipeline project" (Mackenzie 1998: 96). When the Taliban took Kabul in 1996, "another UNOCAL official would applaud the arrival of the Taliban in Kabul and speak glowingly about the immediate prospects of doing business with them" (Mackenzie 1998: 97).

In the 1998 testimony to the House Committee noted by Young, Unocal Vice President of International Relations John Maresca disclosed the continuing logics of colonialism by describing Central Asia as territory with underutilized resources (Maresca 1998). Characterizing post-Soviet Central Asia in these terms is a version of the European imperial international law doctrine of terra nullius, referring to supposedly empty or underutilized land that has long justified – and clearly continues to justify – imperial appropriations in which land, labor, and resources are converted into the legally cognizable property of Western imperial law (Anghie 2006). Terra nullius surfaces repeatedly in post-9/11 American discourse on Afghanistan (Osman 2017). In addition to urging active US involvement in the former Soviet bloc in his testimony, the Unocal vice president sought a very specific change to legislation: the "repeal or removal of Section 907 of the Freedom Support Act." This oil executive's attention to legislation speaks to the enmeshments of law, war, private-sector enrichment, and continuing colonial logics animating US foreign policy relating to Central and South Asia in the post-Soviet era.

The 1992 F.R.E.E.D.O.M. Support Act, signed into law by President George H. W. Bush, is problematically freighted with an ideological yoking of "freedom" and "democracy" to "open markets." "Freedom," Biden reminded us in April 2021, is the United States' preferred cipher for legitimizing and authorizing militarized imperialism: the United States named the Afghan conflicts "Operation Enduring Freedom and Operation Freedom's Sentinel."[6] In the 1992 legislation, F.R.E.E.D.O.M. is a bacronym for "Freedom for Russia and Emerging Eurasian Democracies and Open Markets." The section 907 that Maresca sought to undo had been lobbied for by the Armenian

---

[6] Operation Enduring Freedom was launched on September 11, 2001, and declared concluded in December 2014, to be succeeded by Operation Freedom's Sentinel, in Secretary of Defense Chuck Hagel's words, to "help secure and build upon the hard-fought gains of the last 13 years." Statement by Secretary of Defense Chuck Hagel on Operation Enduring Freedom and Operation Freedom's Sentinel, December 28, 2014.

National Committee of America (ANCA 2001). Motivated by Armenian-Americans alert to the racialized discounting of life effected by the state of Azerbaijan, section 907 prevents US aid to "the Government of Azerbaijan until ... the Government of Azerbaijan [takes] demonstrable steps to cease all blockades and other offensive uses of force against Armenia and Nagorno-Karabakh" (ANCA 2001). On October 24, 2001, some five weeks after the 9/11 attacks, President George W. Bush was legislatively authorized to waive section 907 of the F.R.E.E.D.O.M. Support Act in the name of counterterror,[7] and by January 2002 he had done so.[8] By May 2002, a mere eight months after the United States invaded Afghanistan, global media reported that "Afghanistan hopes to strike a deal later this month to build a $2bn pipeline through the country to take gas from energy-rich Turkmenistan to Pakistan and India" (BBC 2002). This was the pipeline described in 1996 by Unocal to the Senate (Brown 1998: 143). Relatedly, in the few months between the events of 9/11 and the end of 2001, George W. Bush had appointed a former Unocal aide, Afghan-born Zalmay Khalilzad, to be his special envoy to Afghanistan as "a representative to the Afghan people as they seek to consolidate a new order, reconstruct their country and free it from al-Qaida and Taliban control."[9] It is worth taking a moment to detail Khalilzad's professional biography because this former Unocal executive was, along with Cheney and Rumsfeld, a signatory to the 1997 Statement of Principles issued by the neoconservative Project for the New American Century (PNAC). In the post-Cold War moment of 1996, PNAC advocated for "perpetual military readiness" (Lubin 2021: 12), and like *Shock and Awe* (Chapter 6), its 1997 statement of principles is characterized by "linking militarism and national culture

---

[7] Public Law 107-115: Foreign Operations, Export Financing, and Related Programs Appropriations Act, 2002, section 599 (6) (b), reads, "The President may waive section 907 of the FREEDOM Support Act if he determines and certifies to the Committees on Appropriations that to do so (1) is necessary to support United States efforts to counter terrorism; or (2) is necessary to support the operational readiness of United States Armed Forces or coalition partners to counter terrorism." At www .govinfo.gov/content/pkg/BILLS-107hr2506eas/pdf/BILLS-107hr2506eas.pdf.

[8] In May 2021, the Biden administration, like its predecessors, extended the waiver first put in place by the George W. Bush government (*Federal Register* 2021).

[9] "President Names Special Envoy for Afghanistan," Statement by the Deputy Press Secretary (December 31, 2001), https://georgewbush-whitehouse.archives.gov/ news/releases/2001/12/20011231-1.html; https://www.sourcewatch.org/index.php/ Zalmay_Khalilzad#Private_Career.

and economy" (Lubin 2021: 12). Khalilzad is also former US ambassador to the UN and Iraq,[10] former US permanent representative to the UN,[11] and the person who "led 18 months of talks between the US and the Taliban in 2018–19 that resulted in the withdrawal agreement" (Al Jazeera 2021). In 2018 and 2021, the Trump and Biden administrations retained Khalilzad as US Special Envoy to Afghanistan (DeYoung 2021). Khalilzad stepped down from this post in mid-October 2021 (DeYoung 2021). And, like the coauthors of *Shock and Awe* discussed in Chapter 6, Khalilzad is the embodiment of the enmeshments that exist among elite government and policy circles, institutions of higher education, and the profit-motivated military-industrial complex.

Employed in the Reagan and both Bush administrations, Khalilzad's career was detailed in the 2001 Bush administration's press statement on his appointment as special envoy, listing high-level appointments in these administrations and noting inner-circle influence through the military-strategy–focused organization, the RAND Corporation:

> Dr. Khalilzad headed the Bush-Cheney Transition team for the Department of Defense and has been a Counselor to Secretary of Defense Donald Rumsfeld. Between 1993 and 1999, Dr. Khalilzad was Director of the Strategy, Doctrine and Force Structure program for RAND's Project Air Force. While with RAND, he founded the Center for Middle Eastern Studies. Between 1991 and 1992, Dr. Khalilzad served as Assistant Under Secretary of Defense for Policy Planning. He also served as a senior political scientist at RAND and an associate professor at the University of California at San Diego in 1989 and 1991. From 1985 to 1989 at the Department of State, Dr. Khalilzad served as Special Advisor to the Under Secretary of State for Political Affairs, advising on the Iran-Iraq War and the Soviet War in Afghanistan.[12] From 1979 to 1989, Dr. Khalilzad was an Assistant Professor of Political Science at Columbia University. Dr. Khalilzad holds a Ph.D. from the University of Chicago (1979).
>
> (Office of the Press Secretary 2001)

---

[10] Khalilzad was appointed US Ambassador to the UN (2004–2005) and US Ambassador to Iraq from 2005 to 2007 by George W. Bush.

[11] At https://web.archive.org/web/20181122112728/; www.state.gov/r/pa/ei/biog/287479.htm.

[12] Given that former mujahideen are believed to have constituted the core of what later became the Taliban (Katzman 2009), it is noteworthy that it was in September 1986, during Khalilzad's time in the Reagan administration, that the US equipped and trained "the mujahedeen with shoulder-held anti-aircraft Stinger missiles,

Like Harlan Ullman (Chapter 6), Khalilzad founded and headed a consultancy (his current level of official involvement is unclear). This consultancy, Gryphon, describes itself in neoliberal terms as focused on "markets" in the Middle East and Central Asia as well as "promising emerging and frontier markets worldwide, including the Balkans, Eastern Europe and the Caribbean" (Gryphon-Partners.com). Gryphon assures customers that "[o]ur team and partnerships reflect the political, economic, financial, security, energy, trade, legal and regional skills and capabilities required for clients to become comfortable and to succeed in these attractive yet complex markets." Like Ullman, Khalilzad had been on the boards of numerous influential organizations, including the

> National Endowment for Democracy, America Abroad Media, the Center for the National Interest, ... the Atlantic Council, the American University of Kurdistan, and the American University of Afghanistan. He was also a counselor at the Center for Strategic and International Studies and a member of the Council on Foreign Relations and the editorial board of the National Interest magazine.[13]

In his April 27, 2021, testimony to US Senate Foreign Relations Committee some two weeks after Biden announced the troop withdrawal, Khalilzad substantially reproduced the content of Biden's announcement, repeating the assertion in the agreement with the Taliban that the United States had only invaded Afghanistan to "root out al Qaeda there" and bring "its infamous leader Osama bin Laden ... to justice," and declaring "[t]he President determined that it was not in our national interest to maintain U.S. troops in Afghanistan" (Khalilzad 2021). Anticipating Biden's August 2021 narrative of undeserving Afghans, Khalilzad said, "In the end, however, it will be up to the Afghans to seize their opportunities. Our troops deserve to come home."

This brief sketch of Khalilzad's biography – specifically, his links traversing the oil industry, government, and the military-industrial complex – suggests that just as oil, Islam, and the threat of terrorism converged in the adoption of "the war against terrorism ... [as] the theoretical structure that supported the Reagan-Bush military buildup

---

which turns the course of the war. Soviets begin negotiating withdrawal" (Katzman 2009; AP 2021).

[13] At https://2017-2021.state.gov/biographies/zalmay-khalilzad/index.html.

and the determined assertion of U.S. political and military hegemony in the Middle East" (McAlister 2005: 199), so too, the post-9/11 iteration of the global War on Terror, its focus on Afghanistan and then Iraq, have much to do with determinations of US "national interests" as code for an American foreign policy driven by the interests and profits of the US oil industry. In short, American "national interests" in Biden's April 2021 announcement may appear to be about caring for the lives of American troops and personnel and seeing to American national security against terrorism, but these concerns are deceptively imbricated in the long history of America turning to violence against other nations to secure the extractive colonialism and profit-taking of powerful American corporations.

7.5 BLAMING AFGHANS

In the wake of Biden's April 2021 announcement that the troops would be "home" by the twentieth anniversary of 9/11, news media in August 2021 were awash with reports of a chaotic US withdrawal and a speedy Taliban takeover of Afghanistan's major centers of population, and indeed, by August 15, 2021, the Taliban had control of the capital Kabul. The speed of the Taliban's takeover has been explained in terms of the major role played by private military contractors. Of course, because Biden's April 2021 announcement was crafted to sacralize America and American troops in the exalted pursuit of national security and a thinly disguised pursuit of vengeance as justice, no mention was made of the private military contractors, a striking omission given January 2021 estimates that "[t]he Pentagon employs more than seven contractors for every service member in Afghanistan" (Lawrence 2021). By mid-August 2021, as the world was captivated by news of the turmoil in Afghanistan, military analysts pointed to how the departure of private military contractors left Afghans vulnerable to the Taliban. The United States had structured the Afghan army in such a way that the "Afghans had relied on contractors for everything from training and gear mainten-ance to preparing them for intelligence gathering and close air support in their battles against Taliban fighters" (Detsch 2021).

On August 16, the day after the Taliban took over in Kabul, Biden said in a speech justifying his decision to withdraw American troops:

> I stand squarely behind my decision. After 20 years, I've learned the hard way that there was never a good time to withdraw U.S. forces. . . . We planned for every contingency.

But I always promised the American people that I will be straight with you. The truth is: This did unfold more quickly than we had anticipated. So what's happened? Afghanistan political leaders gave up and fled the country. The Afghan military collapsed, sometimes without trying to fight.

(Biden 2021b)

Absenting the role of private military contractors from this "straight" and "true" explanation enabled Biden to infantilize and denigrate Afghans as somehow unteachable and lacking in moral fiber; the Other as the "half-devil and half child" of Du Bois (2003 [1920]: 52):

We gave them every tool they could need. We paid their salaries, provided for the maintenance of their air force—something the Taliban doesn't have. Taliban does not have an air force. We provided close air support. We gave them every chance to determine their own future. What we could not provide them was the will to fight for that future.

(Biden 2021b)

Deploying key tropes of orientalism, Biden depicts Afghans as inferior to Americans. Afghans, in Biden's account, personify a passivity that approximates the "silent indifference," "feminine penetrability," and "supine malleability" that featured in nineteenth-century European portrayals of the East (Said 1978: 206). The orientalism in Biden's racialized imperial discourse also discloses the Orientalist myth of the "lazy native" (Alatas 1977).[14]

Biden's narrative of blame that faults Afghan leaders and the Afghan military for abandoning their people eclipses a history of American involvement in Afghanistan reaching back to 1979 when, "unknown to the American people and Congress, Carter authorised a $500 million 'covert action' program to overthrow Afghanistan's first secular, progressive government. ... The $500 million bought, bribed and armed a group of tribal and religious zealots known as the *mujahedin*" (Pilger 2021). Taken together, the sums funneled through the CIA by the

---

[14] Published a year before Said's *Orientalism*, Syed Hussein Alatas's *The Myth of the Lazy Native: A Study of the Image of the Malays, Filipinos and Javanese from the 16th to the 20th Century and Its Function in the Ideology of Colonial Capitalism* (1977) examined Western scholarship on Southeast Asia to show how images and notions of "the indolent, dull, backward and treacherous native" (1977: 8) served colonial capitalism and ideology by legitimizing structural dependency among colonized subjects.

Carter and Reagan administrations "to support the Afghan resistance" amounted to three billion dollars (Mackenzie 1998: 94). In 1983, Reagan met with mujahideen leaders at the White House, valorizing them as "freedom fighters" (AP 2021). As noted above, the Taliban, like the mujahideen, were covertly backed by the United States. Given George W. Bush's vehement vilification of the Taliban as "evil" to legitimize the American invasion, Biden's eclipsing of an inconvenient history provides another instance in which the political myth of American innocence in all matters relating to foreign policy is asserted, while Afghans forces are paternalistically denigrated as lacking in the will to fight:

> American troops cannot and should not be fighting in a war and dying in a war that Afghan forces are not willing to fight for themselves. We spent over a trillion dollars. We trained and equipped an Afghan military force of some 300,000 strong—incredibly well equipped.
>
> (Biden 2021b)

However, it is to be noted that this spending Biden flags of US taxpayer dollars represented a disinvestment in the lives of US citizens, even as it disinvested in the lives of Afghans. Tariq Ali's evaluation of the US occupation is worth quoting at length:

> In one of the poorest countries of the world, billions[15] were spent annually on air-conditioning the barracks that housed US soldiers and officers, while food and clothing were regularly flown in from bases in Qatar, Saudi Arabia and Kuwait. ... The low wages paid to Afghan security services could not convince them to fight against their countrymen. ... During the Taliban years, opium production was strictly monitored. Since the US invasion it has increased dramatically, and now accounts for 90% of the global heroin market ... Trillions have been made in profits and shared between the Afghan sectors that serviced the occupation. Western officers were handsomely paid off to enable the trade. One in ten young Afghans are now opium addicts. Figures for NATO forces are unavailable. ... Despite repeated requests from journalists and campaigners, no reliable figures have been released on the sex-work industry that grew to service the occupying armies. Nor

---

[15] Ali's article includes a hyperlink to an NPR report citing a former Pentagon official saying that the US military spends $20.2 billion annually on air conditioning in Iraq and Afghanistan. "That's more than NASA's budget. It's more than BP has paid so far for damage from the Gulf oil spill. It's what the G-8 has pledged to help foster new democracies in Egypt and Tunisia" (NPR 2011).

are there credible rape statistics—although US soldiers frequently used sexual violence against "terror suspects," raped Afghan civilians and green-lighted child abuse by allied militias. During the Yugoslav civil war, prostitution multiplied and the region became a centre for sex trafficking. UN involvement in this profitable business was well-documented. In Afghanistan, the full details are yet to emerge.

(Ali 2021)

For Biden, moreover, the omission of these grounded realities in favor of detailing American imperial virtue extends to an additional important omission: consistent with the logics of colonial capitalism (Alatas 1977), these gifts of empire were structured to create *dependent* subject populations, while enriching private defense corporations. The Afghan army was designed to fail in the absence of the private military contractors (Detsch 2021). Necropolitical law, we are shown yet again, relies on deception and the myth of American innocence to conceal from American publics the full extent of American imperialism's discounting of life, in part through valuing American private-sector profit-taking above life.

7.6 VENGEANCE AS JUSTICE

On August 26, 2021, a suicide bombing at Kabul's airport killed thirteen US service members. As dictated by necropolitical law's discounting of the racialized Other, Biden's swift condemnation, and his valorization of vengeance – he said, "We will hunt you down and make you pay" (Burns et al. 2021) – focused on the thirteen American lives taken, and rendered peripheral the at least 169 Afghans killed in that attack (Baldor and Burns 2021). These thirteen were the first US service members killed in Afghanistan since February 2020. Indeed, for the "U.S. military, it was a day with more deaths than any other since 2011" (Shear 2021), a statistic affirming Tom Engelhardt's insight that it is not civilian but combatant deaths that are "collateral" in the contemporary wars (2007).

The day after the suicide bombing, media reports noted that one of the thirteen US service members killed, Lance Corporal Rylee McCollum, a twenty-year-old US Marine, had been "a baby on 9/11" (Healy and Philipps 2021). The late Lance Corporal McCollum had also been a husband, and the couple's first child was due to be born three weeks from the date of the suicide bombing. The co-constituting dynamics of nation/empire, the enmeshments of the intimate sphere of family and the public domain of the national-political, so much at the forefront of Biden's April 2021 announcement, were re-inscribed through the biography of this young victim, mourned as a son, a husband, and a father-to-be.

Consistent with necropolitical law's staging of extraterritorial, extrajudicial revenge killings as justice, the United States responded to the airport bombing by attempting to stage a drone attack on a suspected ISIS terrorist:

> Acting swiftly on President Joe Biden's promise to retaliate for the deadly suicide bombing at Kabul airport, the U.S. military said it killed a member of the Islamic State group's Afghanistan affiliate with a drone strike in the group's eastern stronghold.
>
> (Baldor and Burns 2021)

Three days later, media reported that the retaliatory drone strike that supposedly killed the ISIS-K planner of the airport bombing had instead killed a family of ten civilians, including seven children (Sidhu et al. 2021). Prior to the reports of civilian deaths, media inscribed authority in the necropolitical sovereign, and legitimacy in the affect of vengeance, in the care it took identifying the persons and processes according to which this revenge killing was lawful, even while noting their uncertainty as to the identity of the targeted individual "believed to be involved in planning attacks against the United States in Kabul":

> Biden authorized the drone strike and it was ordered by Defense Secretary Lloyd Austin, a defense official said, speaking on condition of anonymity to provide details not yet publicly announced. It was not immediately clear whether the targeted IS member was directly involved in Thursday's airport attack.
>
> (Baldor and Burns 2021)

The questions prompted here are threefold. First, if US military intelligence was able to identify and kill the "terrorists" it knew to be responsible for planning and executing attacks on Afghan civilians and US service members, why was the US unable to take action that would have prevented these attacks in the first place? Second, why is the US state not held responsible, by publics and media, for its failures to protect Afghan civilians, as well US service personnel and Afghan allies, by effecting an orderly withdrawal? And third, when US foreign policy is at the root of the political violence called "terrorism" (Young 2003: 10; Johnson 2004; Wright 2021), why is it not under scrutiny for being a failed policy, and therefore subject to radical revision?

Instead of these questions rising to the surface of discussion, with the August 26, 2021, bombing of Kabul airport, what shaped public discourse was "the national narrative of victimization and longed for revenge," as established previously in the Iran hostage crisis from November 1979 to January 1981 (McAlister 2005: 198–99). The August 2021 discourse of vengeance and rapid US reprisals, when considered together with the incompetence and corruption unveiled by the 2019 Afghanistan Papers and the absence of any initiative to revamp foreign policy, suggests that the US state's delivery of revenge killings is part of a politics of distraction and deception central to the staging of necropolitical law. Indeed, the rapid delivery of this revenge killing disclosed the continuing infrastructure for clandestine CIA operations in Afghanistan (Mazzetti et al. 2021). By exiting officially, while retaining its CIA infrastructure for surveillance and killing, the United States amplifies necropolitical law's secrecy and unaccountability. Put differently, the manner of the US exit from Afghanistan authorizes and legitimizes the discounting of Afghan life through an extension of secretive and asymmetrical warfare, with further obstructions to public disclosure and state accountability.

Necropolitical law, I have argued, accompanies, authorizes, and legitimizes American militarized imperialism. Even as the United States staged its withdrawal from Afghanistan, the narratives, images, and affect disseminated through news media have legitimized the killing of Others, while instructing US publics to care about and count the lives of US troops but not of Afghan civilians. The key necropolitical dynamic of deception has concealed the US state's failures to attend to warnings delivered by its own intelligence services, while re-animating myths justifying American violence toward racialized Others. The role of oil companies and alliances between US corporations, the CIA, and the Taliban are also missing from dominant public discourse of the war on terror, consistent with myths of American innocence that continue to legitimize and authorize American violence on a planetary scale through the unending long War on Terror.

7.7 NECROPOLITICAL LAW IN THE UNENDING LONG WAR ON TERROR

In November 2021, the *New York Times* reported on a March 2019 massacre of civilians in Syria, in which an airstrike involving surveillance drones and jets dropped three bombs "without warning" on "a large crowd of women and children" (Philipps and Schmitt 2021). Totaling four and half thousand pounds in weight, the bombs killed an estimated eighty people. The *Times* reports the military being aware of the possibility that a war crime had been committed with the strike, while, from the moment the killings took place, the military engaged in concerted efforts to conceal what had happened and absolve the killers:

> The Baghuz strike was one of the largest civilian casualty incidents of the war against the Islamic State, but it has never been publicly acknowledged by the U.S. military. The details, reported here for the first time, show that the death toll was almost immediately apparent to military officials. A legal officer flagged the strike as a possible war crime that required an investigation. But at nearly every step, the military made moves that concealed the catastrophic strike. The death toll was downplayed. Reports were delayed, sanitized and classified. United States-led coalition forces bulldozed the blast site. And top leaders were not notified.
>
> (Philipps and Schmitt 2021)

In keeping with necropolitical law's tactical deployments of a gestural legality, the *Times* details a process involving rules, procedures, investigations, and reports and explains how all these mechanisms of regulation and accountability designed to protect civilians went along with so much deception, secrecy, and denial of wrongdoing. In the process, even as law's record was falsified and law as public thing was dismantled, the discounting of enemy life, including civilians, was reaffirmed as the overarching norm and value of the war on terror.

An example of the way the military's gestural legality works primarily to occlude necropolitical law is how the category "self-defense" has been re-semanticized. While "military lawyers were embedded with strike teams to ensure that targeting complied with the law of armed conflict . . . to identify military targets and minimize civilian harm," the special operations unit responsible for the March 2019 massacre was frequently allowed to claim "imminent danger" and "self-defense" as justifications for a strike (Philipps and Schmitt 2021):

> The rules allowed U.S. troops and local allies to invoke [self-defense] when facing not just direct enemy fire, but anyone displaying "hostile intent." . . . Under that definition, something as mundane as a car driving miles from friendly forces could in some cases be targeted. The task force interpreted the rules broadly.
>
> (Philipps and Schmitt 2021)

In the lexicon of the long War on Terror then, an attack, a stance of aggression, a weapon, a display of hostility in any sense – none of this is required to precipitate the justification of "self-defense" for killing enemy Others. Instead, consistent with how "the state of exception and the relation of enmity have become the normative basis of the right to kill" (Mbembe 2019: 70), a necropolitical presumption permits the US military and its allies to swiftly kill people engaging in everyday conduct, such as moving from one place to another in a car. Or, as in the March 2019 instance, women and children huddling in a group by a river bank (Phillips and Schmitt 2021). It is the human being designated as enemy, not merely the enemy soldier, that the necropolitical sovereign seeks to annihilate. No action is required on the part of that person to precipitate necropolitical law's justification of killing.

Further illustrating how necropolitical law re-semanticizes key definitions, categories, and classifications to legitimize killing, the news report sets out the military's account of "justice":

> This week, after the *New York Times* sent its findings to U.S. Central Command, which oversaw the air war in Syria, the command acknowledged the strikes for the first time, saying 80 people were killed but the airstrikes were justified. It said the bombs killed 16 fighters and four civilians. As for the other 60 people killed, the statement said it was not clear that they were civilians, in part because women and children in the Islamic State sometimes took up arms.
>
> (Philipps and Schmitt 2021)

The deception entailed in these definitional evasions – sorting, counting, and classifying women and children into "16 fighters," "four civilians," and sixty people who were conceivably fighters – is compounded by the circumstance that "the military teams making those assessments [of victims] were not equipped to make an accurate count ... because the personnel doing the counting did not investigate on the ground and often based their findings on how many dead civilians they could definitively identify from aerial footage of the rubble" (Philipps and Schmitt 2021). Just as the force of the MOAB made counting and identifying victims impossible and the military declared the activity a waste of its time (Chapter 6), the military's performance of an actuarial counting of life extends the deceptions of necropolitical law. Crucially, the presence of doubt and lack of clarity ("it was not clear that they were civilians") turn into a presumption of guilt and enmity with lethal effects for women and children. While, in other moments, the United States has condemned the Islamic State for brutally victimizing the less powerful, including women and children (Chapter 4), in this instance, the US military declares its right to kill on the basis of mere speculative enmity. In the process, the extreme asymmetry of the warfare and weaponry directed at killing civilians becomes further backgrounded and normalized.

In April 2021, announcing the US withdrawal from Afghanistan, Biden asserted America's planetary jurisdiction. The "threat to our homeland from over the horizon," he said, "has become more dispersed, metastasizing around the globe" (Biden 2021a). Promising at the same time to keep the United States safe from terrorism, he said, "it's time to end the forever war" (Biden 2021a). And as noted earlier, the August 29, 2021, vengeful and wrongful killing of civilians – including seven children – as the United States exited Afghanistan, demonstrated the continuing US exercise of the power to take life over that territory.

That wrongful August 2021 killing in Afghanistan only came to light because of the *New York Times*'s investigative journalism. Similarly, the November 2021 report in the *Times* of the deaths of eighty people in Syria in a possible war crime discloses the military's capacity to conduct such killings, then conceal, deny, and justify its conduct. Significantly, the two and a half years that elapsed between the airstrike in Syria and the *New York Times* report point to how the long War on Terror shows every sign of continuing forever. As for the March 2019 killings in Syria:

> The details of the strikes were pieced together by the *New York Times* over months from confidential documents and descriptions of classified reports, as well as interviews with personnel directly involved, and officials with top secret security clearances who discussed the incident on the condition that they not be named.
>
> (Philipps and Schmitt 2021)

If a secretive, rule-breaking special operations task force was able to kill civilians with impunity, then enjoy the backing and protection of the military to conceal, condone, and legitimize that killing (Philipps and Schmitt 2021), how many more such killings remain to be exhumed in yet further evidence of the discounting of life in the unending war on terror? Equally troubling is the fact that publics and leaders have not been galvanized into shock and national self-examination, as for example, they were with the 1968 My Lai massacre. In that case, too, the killing of unarmed civilians that had been concealed by the US military was revealed by the press, and from "the initial media revelations in November 1969 to the immediate aftermath of Calley's court-martial in the spring of 1971, the killings at My Lai were one of the most prominent items of American national discourse" (Oliver 2003: 248). In contrast, the prominent press reports of the wrongful killings of civilians in both the vengeful August 2021 drone attack in Afghanistan and the March 2019 killing of women and children in Syria have not precipitated an American national discourse examining its conduct of the long War on Terror. Like the loud silence that followed the deafening MOAB blast (Latifi 2017), this absence of public attention to these wrongful killings points to the troubling consolidations of necropolitical law – at some level, there is widespread public acceptance for necropolitical law's norms and practices for the discounting of life, particularly when the discounted life belongs to the distant, racialized Other. The war on terror's narrative of existential crisis, cultivating citizen acquiescence for vengeance and asymmetrical war, are structures underpinning this silence.

By reading *for* law across the sites, genres, and modalities that contain us in the co-constitutions of culture and law, I have excavated the often-hidden transcript of necropolitical law, showing how necropolitical law fosters death, not life, by scripting authority and legitimacy for the United States in its wielding of violent, asymmetrical power. Necropolitical law discounts life for US citizens and for people around the world, disinvesting from life, social empowerment, and democratic contestation while directing resources to killing, to slow violence, and to dismantling law as public thing. When the state amplifies secrecy, conceals its violence, controls media, and lies to publics, law's archive is repeatedly fractured, further undermining law as public thing.

Discounting Life shows the diffuse yet coherent operations of necropolitical law, sometimes through subterranean, seemingly a-legal forces, including American political myth, affect, spectacle, and images. In tandem with these other-than-rational dynamics for necropolitical law, the latter also works by reconfiguring liberal legality, including the presumption of planetary jurisdiction, the counterterror state's near-complete seizing of law archive, and an ongoing dismantling of law's public thingness. In the process, the values, community, and authority inherent to categories that are part of law's compound lexicon, such as human rights, due process, civilian, transparency, accountability, and justice have been displaced or re-semanticized. By grappling with these processes and by recognizing the necropolitical law that authorizes them, we become equipped, as thinking, feeling, questioning citizen-subjects, to interrupt and dismantle the ongoing discounting life that feeds and sustains the unending long War on Terror. The hope that I hold to is that by seeing necropolitical law at work, we might begin to effect its dismantling, thereby re-valuing life and law, and life *in* law as one way to nurture conscious, critical engagements that might contribute to an end to the discounting of life.

Mourning the Long War on Terror, by Damien Cruz

REFERENCES

Abadi, Mark. 2017. "The Phrase 'Mother of All Bombs' Has a Long History in the Middle East." *Business Insider*, April 13, 2017. www.businessinsider .com/what-does-mother-of-all-bombs-mean-iraq-saddam-hussein-2017-4? r=US&IR=T.

Abanes, Richard. 1996. *American Militias: Rebellion, Racism, & Religion*. Downers Grove, IL: InterVarsity Press.

ABC News. 2015. "This Week' Transcript." *ABC News*, December 6, 2015. https://abcnews.go.com/Politics/week-transcript-hillary-clinton-jeb-bush/ story?id=35596885.

Abel, Richard L. 2018a. *Law's Trials: The Performance of Legal Institutions in the US "War on Terror."* Cambridge: Cambridge University Press.

Abel, Richard L. 2018b. *Law's Wars: The Fate of the Rule of Law in the US "War on Terror."* Cambridge: Cambridge University Press.

ABP News. 2016. "Big Revelation: Osama bin Laden Is Still Alive and Living in Disguise." YouTube video, 15:08. www.youtube.com/ watch?v=oGPatAC_TTc.

Ackerman, Spencer, and Sune Engel Rasmussen. 2017. "36 Isis Militants Killed in US 'Mother of All Bombs' Attack, Afghan Ministry Says." *The Guardian*, April 14, 2017. www.theguardian.com/world/2017/apr/ 13/us-military-drops-non-nuclear-bomb-afghanistan-islamic-state.

ACLU. n.d. "Surveillance under the Patriot Act." ACLU, accessed August 24, 2021. www.aclu.org/issues/national-security/privacy-and-surveillance/ surveillance-under-patriot-act.

Agamben, Giorgio. [1995] 1998. *Homo Sacer: Sovereign Power and Bare Life*. Translated by Daniel Heller-Roazen. Stanford, CA: Stanford University Press.

Agamben, Giorgio. 2005. *State of Exception*. Chicago: University of Chicago Press.

Agamben, Giorgio. 2010. *The Sacrament of Language: An Archaeology of the Oath*. Translated by A. Kotsko. Palo Alto, CA: Stanford University Press.

Agyepong, Tera Eva. 2018. *The Criminalization of Black Children: Race, Gender, and Delinquency in Chicago's Juvenile Justice System, 1899–1945*. Chapel Hill: The University of North Carolina Press.

Ahady, Anwar-ul-haq. 1998. "Saudi Arabia, Iran and the Conflict in Afghanistan." In *Fundamentalism Reborn? Afghanistan and the Taliban*, edited by William Maley. New York: New York University Press, 117-34.

Aikins, Matthieu, and Najim Rahim. 2021. "Afghanistan Live Updates: Children Killed in US Drone Strike, Family Says." *New York Times*, August 30, 2021. www.nytimes.com/live/2021/08/30/world/afghanistan-news.

Airwars. n.d. "Who We Are." Airways, accessed October 13, 2021. https://airwars.org/about/team/.

Al Jazeera. 2020. "Yemen al-Qaeda Leader al-Rimi Killed in US Operation, Says Trump." *Al Jazeera*, February 7, 2020. www.aljazeera.com/news/2020/2/7/yemen-al-qaeda-leader-al-rimi-killed-in-us-operation-says-trump.

Al Jazeera. 2021. "US Envoy Khalilzad Defends Afghan Peace Chances as Violence Rises." *Al Jazeera*, April 27, 2021. www.aljazeera.com/news/2021/4/27/khalilzad-defends-afghan-peace-before-sceptical-us-lawmakers.

Alatas, Syed Hussein. 1977. *The Myth of the Lazy Native: A Study of the Image of the Malays, Filipinos and Javanese from the 16th to the 20th Century and Its Function in the Ideology of Colonial Capitalism*. London: Frank Cass & Co.

Alberts, David S. 1996. Foreword to *Shock and Awe: Achieving Rapid Dominance*, by Harlan K. Ullman and James P. Wade, v–vi. Washington, DC: The Center for Advanced Concepts and Technology.

Alexander, Jeffrey C. 2004. "Toward a Theory of Cultural Trauma." In *Cultural Trauma and Collective Identity*, edited by Jeffrey C. Alexander, Ron Eyerman, Bernhard Giesen, Neil J. Smelser, and Piotr Sztompka, 1–30. Berkeley, CA: University of California Press.

Alexander, Michelle. 2010. *The New Jim Crow: Mass Incarceration in the Age of Colorblindness*. New York: The New Press.

Ali, Tariq. 2021. "Debacle in Afghanistan." *New Left Review*, August 16, 2021. https://newleftreview.org/sidecar/posts/debacle-in-afghanistan?fbclid=IwAR0rXwNtwMLhFyb1hhEv2GuZfuH6b01iSJEV1hhdtAGCy9ARMIcV5LPV7HU.

Alston, Phillip G. 2010. Report on the Special Rapporteur on Extrajudicial, Summary, or Arbitrary Executions, Addendum: Study on Targeted Killings. UN Human Rights Council. www.refworld.org/docid/4c0767ff2.html.

Althusser, Louis. 1968. "Philosophy as a Revolutionary Weapon." Interview by Maria Antonietta Macciocchi. *New Left Review* 1 (64): 1–7.

Althusser, Louis. 1971. "Ideology and Ideological State Apparatuses." In *Lenin and Philosophy and Other Essays*. London, New Left Books, 85–126.

Anderson, Benedict. [1983] 2006. *Imagined Communities: Reflections on the Origin and Spread of Nationalism*. London and New York: Verso.

Anderson, Benedict. 1991. *Imagined Communities: Reflections on the Origin and Spread of Nationalism*. London: Verso.

Anderson, Kenneth, and Benjamin Wittes. 2015. *Speaking the Law: The Obama Administration's Addresses on National Security Law*. Stanford, CA: Hoover Institution Press, Stanford University.

Andrews, Christopher. 1996. *For the President's Eyes Only: Secret Intelligence and the American Presidency from Washington to Bush*. New York: HarperCollins.

Andrews, Theresa. 2017. "Tamir Rice Shooting in Cleveland." In *The Use and Abuse of Police Power in America: Historical Milestones and Current Controversies*, edited by Gina Robertiello, 295–98. Santa Barbara, CA: ABC-CLIO.

Andrews, Naomi J., and Jennifer E. Sessions. 2015. "The Politics of Empire in Post-Revolutionary France." *French Politics, Culture & Society* 33 (1): 1–10.

Anghie, Antony. 2005. *Imperialism, Sovereignty and the Making of International Law*. Cambridge: Cambridge University Press.

Anghie, Antony. 2006. "The Evolution of International Law: Colonial and Postcolonial Realities." *Third World Quarterly* 27 (5): 739–53.

Anker, Elisabeth R. 2014. *Orgies of Feeling: Melodrama and the Politics of Freedom*. Durham, NC: Duke University Press.

AP 2021. "A Timeline of More Than 40 Years of War in Afghanistan." *The Associated Press*. July 2, 2021. https://apnews.com/article/joe-biden-islamic-state-group-afghanistan-europe-middle-east-70451c485d46908ef5c6a83a1de9f0f6.

Appadurai, Arjun. 1996. *Modernity at Large: Cultural Dimensions of Globalization*. Minneapolis: University of Minnesota Press.

Armenian National Committee of America. 2002. "President Bush Waives Section 907: Action Opens Door to Military Aid to the Azerbaijani." ANCA, January 25, 2002. https://anca.org/press-release/president-bush-waives-section-907/.

Asad, Talal. 2007. *On Suicide Bombing*. New York: Columbia University Press.

Asia Policy Point. 2015. "Monday in Washington, March 16, 2015." Asia Policy Point. www.jiaponline.org/2015/03/monday-in-washington-march-16-2015.html.

Atlantic Council. n.d. "Since 1961." Atlantic Council, accessed October 13, 2021. www.atlanticcouncil.org/about/history/.

Azoulay, Ariella. 2008. *The Civil Contract of Photography*. New York: Zone Books.

Azoulay, Ariella. 2010. "What is a Photograph? What is Photography?" *Philosophy of Photography* 1 (1): 9–13. DOI: https://doi.org/10.1386/pop.1.1.9/7.

Bakalian, Anny, and Mehdi Bozorgmehr. 2009. *Backlash 9/11: Middle Eastern and Muslim Americans Respond*. Berkeley, CA: University of California Press.

Baker, Peter, Eric Schmitt, and Helene Cooper. 2019. "ISIS Leader al-Baghdadi is Dead, Trump Says." *New York Times*, October 27, 2019. www.nytimes.com/2019/10/27/us/politics/isis-leader-al-baghdadi-dead.html.

Baldor, Lolita C., and Robert Burns. 2021. "U.S. airstrike targets Islamic State member in Afghanistan." *AP News*, August 28, 2021. https://apnews .com/article/asia-pacific-evacuations-kabul-islamic-state-group-7f146c8ae 5d9e9ab225025527e421226.

Baldor, Lolita, and Robert Burns. 2019. "Pentagon releases new details on al-Baghdadi raid." *AP News*, https://apnews.com/article/politics-middle-east-ap-top-news-religion-abu-bakr-al-baghdadi-20641c6233dd403dba52 d512d149fc02.

Baldor, Lolita C., and Robert Burns. 2021. "U.S. airstrike targets Islamic State member in Afghanistan." *AP News*, August 28, 2021. https://apnews .com/article/asia-pacific-evacuations-kabul-islamic-state-group-7f146c8ae5d9e9ab225025527e421226.

Ball, Howard. 2004. *The USA Patriot Act of 2001: Balancing Civil Liberties and National Security: A Reference Handbook*. Santa Barbara, CA: ABC-CLIO.

Banks, William C. 2015. "Regulating Drones: Are Targeted Killings by Drones Outside Traditional Battlefields Legal?" In *Drone Wars: Transforming Conflict, Law, and Policy*, edited by Peter L. Bergen and Daniel Rothenberg, 129–59. Cambridge: Cambridge University Press.

Banvard, Joseph. 1876. *Soldiers and Patriots of the American Revolution*. Boston: D. Lothrop & Co.

Barry, John. 2005. "War of Nerves." *Newsweek*, July 3, 2005. www.newsweek .com/war-nerves-121397.

Barthes, Roland. [1964] 1977. "Rhetoric of the Image." In *Image-Music-Text*, 32–51. New York: Hill and Wang.

Basinger, Jeanine. [1986] 2003. *The World War II Combat Film: Anatomy of a Genre*. Middletown, CT: Wesleyan University Press.

Basinger, Jeanine. 1998. "Translating War: The Combat Film Genre and Saving Private Ryan." *Perspectives on History*, October 1, 1998. www .historians.org/publications-and-directories/perspectives-on-history/octo ber-1998/translating-war-the-combat-film-genre-and-saving-private-ryan.

Basu, Moni. 2016. "15 years after 9/11, Sikhs Still Victims of Anti-Muslim Hate Crimes." *CNN*, September 15, 2016. www.cnn.com/2016/09/15/us/ sikh-hate-crime-victims/index.html.

Baxi, Upendra. 2004. "The Rule of Law in India: Theory and Practice." In *Asian Discourses on the Rule of Law*, edited by Randall Peerenboom. London: Routledge, 318–39.

Bayoumi, Moustafa. 2015. *This Muslim American Life: Dispatches from the War on Terror*. New York: New York University Press.

BBC News. 2002. "Afghanistan plans gas pipeline." May 13, 2002. http://news .bbc.co.uk/1/hi/business/1984459.stm.

BBC News. 2004. "Profile: Richard Clarke." March 22, 2004. https://news.bbc .co.uk/2/hi/americas/3559087.stm.

BBC News. 2011. "Barack Obama mocks Donald Trump at White House dinner." May 1, 2011. www.bbc.com/news/world-us-canada-13251819.

BBC News. 2015. "Kenya attack: 147 dead in Garissa University assault." April 3, 2015. www.bbc.com/news/world-africa-32169080.

BBC News. 2017. "MOAB Strike: US Bombing of IS in Afghanistan 'Killed Dozens.'" April 14, 2017. www.bbc.com/news/world-asia-39598046.

BBC News. 2017. "MOAB strike: 90 IS Fighters Killed in Afghanistan." April 15, 2017. www.bbc.co.uk/news/world-asia-39607213.

BBC News. 2020a. "Breonna Taylor: Lawsuit after US Health Worker Shot Dead By Police." May 13, 2020. www.bbc.com/news/world-us-canada-52646460.

BBC News. 2020b. "Ahmaud Arbery: What Do We Know about the Case?" June 5, 2020. www.bbc.com/news/world-us-canada-52623151.

Belew, Kathleen. 2018. *Bring the War Home: The White Power Movement and Paramilitary America.* Cambridge, MA: Harvard University Press.

Bellow, Gary, and Martha Minow. 1996. *Law Stories.* Ann Arbor: University of Michigan Press.

Benjamin, Walter. [1921] 1996. "Critique of Violence." In *Walter Benjamin: Selected Writings, Volume 1, 1913-1926*, edited by Marcus Bullock and Michael W. Jennings, 236–52. Cambridge, MA: Belknap Press.

Bennett, W. Lance. 2003. *News: Politics of Illusion.* 5th ed. New York: Pearson Longman.

Ben-Porath, Sigal. 2006. *Citizenship under Fire. Democratic Education in Times of Conflict.* Princeton, NJ: Princeton University Press.

Ben-Porath, Sigal. 2011. "Wartime Citizenship: An Argument for Shared Fate." *Ethnicities* 11 (3): 313–25. DOI: https://doi.org/10.1177% 2F1468796811407845.

Benson, Rodney. 2018. "The Case for Campaign Journalism." In *Trump and the Media*, edited by Pablo J. Boczkowski and Zizi Papacharissi, 213–20. Cambridge, MA: The MIT Press.

Benson, Rodney. 2019. "Paywalls and Public Knowledge: How Can Journalism Provide Quality News for Everyone?" *Journalism* 20 (1): 146–49. DOI: https://doi.org/10.1177%2F1464884918806733.

Berg, Manfred. 2011. *Popular Justice: A History of Lynching in America.* Lanham, MA: Rowman & Littlefield Publishing Group.

Bergen, Peter L., and Daniel Rothenberg, eds. 2015. *Drone Wars: Transforming Conflict, Law, and Policy.* Cambridge: Cambridge University Press.

Bergen, Peter L., and Jennifer Rowland. 2015. "World of Drones." In *Drone Wars: Transforming Conflict, Law, and Policy*, edited by Peter L. Bergen and Daniel Rothenberg, 300–42. Cambridge: Cambridge University Press.

Bernstein, Anya. 2013. "The Hidden Costs of Terrorist Watch Lists." *Buffalo Law Review* 61 (3): 461–535.

Bertelsen, Lone, and Andrew Murphie. 2010. "An Ethics of Everyday Infinities and Powers: Félix Guattari on Affect and the Refrain." In *The Affect Theory Reader*, edited by Melissa Gregg and Gregory J. Seigworth. Durham, NC: Duke University Press.

Bevins, Vincent. 2020. *The Jakarta Method: Washington's Anticommunity Crusade and the Mass Murder Program that Shaped Our World*. New York: PublicAffairs.

Bhabha, Homi K. 1990. "Introduction: Narrating the Nation." In *Nation and Narration*, edited by Homi K. Bhabha, 1–7. London: Routledge.

Bhatia, Vijay K., Nicola Langton, and Jane Lung. 2004. "Legal Discourse: Opportunities and Threats for Corpus Linguistics." In *Discourse in the Professions: Perspectives from Corpus Linguistics* edited by Ulla Connor and Thomas A Upton, 203–31. Philadelphia, PA: John Benjamins.

Biden, Joseph R. 2021a. "Remarks by President Biden on the Way Forward in Afghanistan" (speech). *The White House*. www.whitehouse.gov/briefing-room/speeches-remarks/2021/04/14/remarks-by-president-biden-on-the-way-forward-in-afghanistan/.

Biden, Joseph R. 2021b. "Remarks by President Biden on the End of the War in Afghanistan" (speech). *The White House*. www.whitehouse.gov/briefing-room/speeches-remarks/2021/08/31/remarks-by-president-biden-on-the-end-of-the-war-in-afghanistan/.

Birkenstein, Jeff, Anna Froula, and Karen Randell. 2010. *Reframing 9/11: Film, Popular Culture, and the War on Terror*. New York: Continuum.

Blinken, Antony J. 2021. "Extension of Waiver of Section 907 of the Freedom Support Act with Respect to Assistance to the Government of Azerbaijan." *State Department*, April 23, 2021. www.federalregister.gov/documents/2021/05/04/2021-09259/extension-of-waiver-of-section-907-of-the-freedom-support-act-with-respect-to-assistance-to-the.

Blommaert, Jan, and Chris Bulcaen. 2000. "Critical Discourse Analysis." *Annual Review of Anthropology* 29: 447–66.

Bloomberg. n.d. "Defense Group Inc." Accessed on October 13, 2021. www.bloomberg.com/profile/company/4474771Z:US.

Bloomfield, Steve. 2008. "Somalia: The World's Forgotten Catastrophe." *Independent*, February 9, 2008. www.independent.co.uk/news/world/africa/somalia-the-world-s-forgotten-catastrophe-778225.html.

Bloomfield Jr., Lincoln P., and Tom Harvey. 2017. "A Strategy for the Age of Trump." *The National Interest*, August 20, 2017. https://nationalinterest.org/feature/strategy-the-age-trump-21963.

Boston Athletic Association. n.d "Boston Marathon History." Accessed on January 8, 2022. https://web.archive.org/web/20140424013642/http://216.235.243.43/races/boston-marathon/boston-marathon-history.aspx.

Bottici, Chiara. 2007. *A Philosophy of Political Myth*. New York: Cambridge University Press.

Bowden, Mark. 2010 [1999]. *Black Hawk Down: A Story of Modern War*. New York: Grove Press.

Bowen, Peter. n.d. "The Kill Chain: From Terrorist to Targeted Drone Attack." *Bleecker Street*. https://bleeckerstreetmedia.com/editorial/eye inthesky-chain-of-command.

Box Office Mojo. n.d. "Domestic Box Office for 1992." n.d. Accessed August 27, 2021. www.boxofficemojo.com/year/1992/.

Brennan, John O. 2012. "The Efficacy and Ethics of U.S. Counterterrorism Strategy." *Wilson Center*. www.wilsoncenter.org/event/the-efficacy-and-ethics-us-counterterrorism-strategy.

Briggs, Charles L, and Richard Bauman. 1992. "Gender, Intertextuality, and Social Power." *Journal of Linguistic Anthropology* 2 (2): 131–72.

Brooks, Peter and Paul D. Gewirtz. 1996. *Law's Stories: Narrative and Rhetoric in the Law*. New Haven, CT: Yale University Press.

Brown, Hank. 1998. *Afghanistan - Is There Hope for Peace?: Hearings Before the Committee on Foreign Relations, U.S. Senate*. Collingdale, PA: Diane Publishing Company.

Brown, Wendy. 2005. "Political Idealization and Its Discontents." In *Edgework: Critical Essays on Knowledge and Politics*, 22–36. Princeton, NJ: Princeton University Press.

Brown, Wendy. 2006. "American Nightmare: Neoliberalism, Neoconservatism, and De-Democratization." *Political Theory* 34 (6): 690–714. DOI: https://doi.org/10.1177/0090591706293016.

Brown, Michelle Lynn. 2010. "Bleeding for the Mother(Land): Reading Testimonial Bodies in Nuruddin Farah's Maps." *Research in African Literatures* 41 (4): 125–43. Bloomington, IN: Indiana University Press. DOI: https://doi.org/10.2979/RAL.2010.41.4.125.

Brysk, Alison. 2007. "Human Rights and National Insecurity." In *National Insecurity and Human Rights: Democracies Debate Counterterrorism*, edited by Alison Brysk and Gershom Shafir, 1–13. Berkeley, CA: University of California Press.

Buchanan, Ruth, and Sundhya Pahuja. 2004. "Law, Nation, and (Imagined) International Communities." *Law, Text, Culture* 8: 137–66.

Bullman, T. A., and H. K. Kang. 2011. "The risk of suicide among wounded Vietnam veterans." *American Journal of Public Health* 86 (5): 662–67. DOI: https://doi.org/10.2105/AJPH.86.5.662.

Bullman, Tim, Aaron Schneiderman, and Jaimie L. Gradus. 2019. "Relative Importance of Posttraumatic Stress Disorder and Depression in Predicting Risk of Suicide amonga Cohort of Vietnam Veterans." *Suicide and Life-Threatening Behavior* 49 (3): 838–45. DOI: https://doi.org/10.1111/sltb.12482.

Bumiller, Elisabeth. 2009. "U.S. Lifts Photo Ban on Military Coffins." *New York Times*, December 7, 2009, www.nytimes.com/2009/02/27/world/americas/27iht-photos.1.20479953.html.

Bunch, Will. 2008. "Obama Would Ask His AG to 'Immediately Review' Potential Crimes in Bush White House." *The Philadelphia Inquirer*, April 15, 2008. www.inquirer.com/philly/blogs/attytood/ Barack_on_torture.html.

Burns, Robert. 2021. "Biden Says Another Attack in Afghanistan 'Highly Likely' over Weekend; Airstrike Kills 2 in ISIS-K." *ABC7*, August 29, 2021. https://abc7chicago.com/politics/us-airstrike-in-afghani stan-targets-islamic-state-member/10982347/.

Burns, Robert, Darlene Superville, and Matthew Lee. 2021. "Biden Vows to Avenge Kabul Airport Attack Deaths in Emotional Speech." *ABC7*, August 27, 2021. https://abc7.com/biden-afghanistan-speech-kabul-air port-attack-address/10979952/.

Burns, Robert, and Lolita C. Baldor. 2021. "Retaliatory US Airstrike Kills Two 'ISIS-K Planners' in Afghanistan." *NBC Chicago*, August 28, 2021. www.nbcchicago.com/news/national-international/another-kabul-terror-attack-likely-president-biden-advised/2600266/.

Bush, George H. W. 1990a. "February 8, 1990: Address on Iraq's Invasion of Kuwait" (speech). *Miller Center of Public Affairs, University of Virginia*. Transcript and audio recording, 11:18. https://millercenter.org/the-presi dency/presidential-speeches/august-8-1990-address-iraqs-invasion-kuwait.

Bush, George H. W. 1990b. "National Security Directive 45." *The White House*. https://bush41library.tamu.edu/files/nsd/nsd45.pdf.

Bush, George H. W. 1991. "February 27, 1991: Address on the End of the Gulf War" (speech). *Miller Center of Public Affairs, University of Virginia*. Transcript and audio recording, 6:51. https://millercenter.org/the-presi dency/presidential-speeches/february-27-1991-address-end-gulf-war.

Bush, George W. 2001a. "President Bush" (speech). September 12, 2001. *PBS NewsHour*. www.pbs.org/newshour/world/terrorism-july-dec01-bush_speech_9-12.

Bush, George W. 2001b. "Remarks by the President Upon Arrival" (speech). September 16, 2001. *The White House*. https://georgewbush-whitehouse .archives.gov/news/releases/2001/09/20010916-2.html.

Bush, George W. 2001c. "President Signs Anti-Terrorism Bill" (speech). October 26, 2001. *The White House*. https://georgewbush-whitehouse .archives.gov/news/releases/2001/10/20011026-5.html

Bush, George W. 2001d. "Bush: 'There's No rules'" (speech). September 17, 2001. *CNN*. http://edition.cnn.com/2001/US/09/17/gen.bush.transcript/.

Bush, George W. 2001e. "Address Before a Joint Session of the Congress on the United States Response to the Terrorist Attacks of September 11 September 20, 2001" (speech). In *Administration of George W Bush*, 2001. www.govinfo.gov/content/pkg/WCPD-2001-09-24/pdf/WCPD-2001-09-24-Pg1347.pdf.

Bush, George W. 2001f. "Executive Order Freezing Terrorists' Assets" (speech). September 24, 2001. *Washington Post*. www.washingtonpost.com/wp-srv/nation/specials/attacked/transcripts/bush092401.html.

Bush, George W. 2001g. "Address to the Nation on the Terrorist Attacks" (speech). September 11 2001. In *Public Papers of the Presidents of the United States: George W. Bush (2001, Book II)*: 1099–1100. www.govinfo.gov/content/pkg/PPP-2001-book2/html/PPP-2001-book2-doc-pg1099.htm.

Bush, George W. 2001h. "Presidential Address to the Nation" (speech). October 7, 2001. *The White House*. https://georgewbush-whitehouse.archives.gov/news/releases/2001/10/20011007-8.html.

Bush, George W. 2001i. "US Bush Address" (speech). AP, September 20, 2001. http://www.aparchive.com/metadata/youtube/54ac73f6bd644d0c8b0e66f35a91f819.

Bush, George W. 2002a. "President Outlines War Effort" (speech). April 17, 2002. *The White House*. https://georgewbush-whitehouse.archives.gov/news/releases/2002/04/20020417-1.html.

Bush, George W. 2002b. "President's Remarks to the Nation" (speech). September 11, 2002. *The White House*. https://georgewbush-whitehouse.archives.gov/news/releases/2002/09/20020911-3.html.

Bush, George W. 2003. "President Bush Addresses the Nation" (speech). March 19 2003. *The White House*. https://georgewbush-whitehouse.archives.gov/news/releases/2003/03/20030319-17.html.

Bush, George W. 2003. "Address to the Nation on Iraq" (speech). March 17, 2003. In *Public Papers of the Presidents of the United States: George W. Bush (2003, Book I)* www.govinfo.gov/content/pkg/PPP-2003-book1/pdf/PPP-2003-book1-doc-pg277.pdf.

Bush, George W. 2006. "Address on the Creation of Military Commissions to Try Suspected Terrorists" (speech). September 6, 2006. In *Selected Speeches of President George W Bush 2001-2008*, 409–23. https://georgewbush-whitehouse.archives.gov/infocus/bushrecord/documents/Selected_Speeches_George_W_Bush.pdf.

Bush, George W. 2021. "9/11 Address to the Nation." *American Rhetoric*. Delivered on September 11, 2001. www.americanrhetoric.com/speeches/gwbush911addresstothenation.htm.

Butler, Judith. 2010. *Frames of War*. New York: Verso.

Callimachi, Rukmini. 2019. "ISIS Leader Paid Rival for Protection but Was Betrayed by His Own." *New York Times*, October 27, 2019. www.nytimes.com/2019/10/30/world/middleeast/isis-leader-al-baghdadi.html

Candlin, Christopher. 1989. "General Editor's Preface." In Norman Fairclough, *Language and Power*. London, England: Longman, vi-x.

Canestaro, Nathan. 2003. "American Law and Policy on Assassinations of Foreign Leaders: The Practicality of Maintaining the Status Quo." *Boston College International and Comparative Law Review*, 26 (1), 1–34.

Cape Fear Community College Libraries. 2014. "Black Lives Matter: Race, Policing, and Protest." Updated on September 7, 2021. https://libguides .cfcc.edu/Black-Lives-Matter.

Caplan, Robyn, and danah boyd. 2018. "Who's Playing Who? Media Manipulation in the Era of Trump." In *Trump and the Media*, edited by Pablo J. Boczkowski and Zizi Papacharissi, 49–58. Cambridge, MA: The MIT Press.

Carney, Zoë Hess, and Mary E. Stuckey. 2015. "The World as the American Frontier: Racialized Presidential War Rhetoric." *The Southern Communication Journal* 80 (3): 163–88. DOI: https://doi.org/10.1080/ 1041794X.2015.1043139.

Carson, Thomas L. 2010. *Lying and Deception: Theory and Practice*. Oxford: Oxford University Press.

CBS News. 2017. "U.S. commander explains use of 'mother of all bombs' in Afghanistan." April 14, 2017. www.cbsnews.com/news/us-afghanistan-moab-mother-of-all-bombs-isis-right-weapon-against-right-target/.

Chamayou, Grégoire. [2013] 2015. *A Theory of the Drone*. Translated by Janet Lloyd. New York: New Press.

Chan, Sue. 2003. "Iraq Faces Massive U.S. Missile Barrage." *CBS News*, January 24, 2003. www.cbsnews.com/news/iraq-faces-massive-us-missile-barrage/.

Cheesman, Nick. 2018. "Rule-of-Law Ethnography." *Annual Review of Law and Social Science* 14 (1): 167–84. Annual Reviews. DOI: https://doi.org/ 10.1146/annurev-lawsocsci-101317-030900.

Chesney, Robert M. 2014. "Beyond the Battlefield, beyond Al Qaeda: The Destabilizing Legal Architecture of Counterterrorism." *Michigan Law Review* 112: 163–224.

Chiappinelli, Eric, Adam Candeub, Jeffrey Chester, and Lawrence Soley. 2007. "The Corporatization of Communication." *Seattle University Law Review* 30 (4): 959–89.

Chimene-Weiss, Sara, Sol Eppel, Jeremy Feigenbaum, Seth Motel, Ingrid Pangandoyon, and Michael D'Ortenzio. n.d. "Documents." *Understanding the Iran-Contra Affairs*. www.brown.edu/Research/ Understanding_the_Iran_Contra_Affair/documents.php.

Chokshi, Niraj and Karen Zraick. 2019. "Trump Tweets Faked Photo of Hero Dog Getting a Medal," *New York Times*, October 30, 2019, www.nytimes .com/2019/10/30/us/politics/trump-dog.html.

Chotiner, Isaac. 2021. "How America Failed in Afghanistan." *The New Yorker*, August 15, 2021. www.newyorker.com/news/q-and-a/how-amer ica-failed-in-afghanistan.

Chow, Kat. 2016. "'Politically Correct': The Phrase Has Gone From Wisdom To Weapon." *NPR*, December 14, 2016. www.npr.org/sections/codes witch/2016/12/14/505324427/politically-correct-the-phrase-has-gone-from-wisdom-to-weapon?t=1631402550626.

Church, George J. 1990. "The Gulf: Saddam in the Cross Hairs." *Time Magazine*, October 8, 1990. http://content.time.com/time/subscriber/art icle/0,33009,971331,00.html.

Cloud, David S. 2011. "Anatomy of an Afghan War Tragedy." *Los Angeles Times*, April 10, 2011. www.latimes.com/archives/la-xpm-2011-apr-10-la-fg-afghanistan-drone-20110410-story.html.

Clover, Carol J. 1998a. "Law and the Order of Popular Culture." In *Law in the Domains of Culture*, edited by Austin Sarat and Thomas R. Kearns, 92–120. Ann Arbor, MI: University of Michigan Press.

Clover, Carol J. 1998b. "'God Bless Juries!'" In *Reconfiguring American Film Genres History and Theory*, edited by Nick Browne, 255–77. Berkeley, CA: University of California Press.

Coombe, Rosemary. 1998. "Contingent Articulations: A Critical Cultural Studies of Law." In *Law in the Domains of Culture*, edited by Austin Sarat and Thomas R. Kearns, 21–64. Ann Arbor, MI: University of Michigan Press.

CNN. 2001. "Bush: 'There's No Rules.'" September 17, 2001, www.cnn.com/2001/US/09/17/gen.bush.transcript/.

CNN. 2013. "Death of Osama bin Laden Fast Facts." www.cnn.com/2013/09/09/world/death-of-osama-bin-laden-fast-facts/index.html.

CNN. 2015. "State of the Union with Jake Tapper." December 6, 2015, https://cnnpressroom.blogs.cnn.com/2015/12/06/rubio-but-there-are-over-700000-americans-on-some-watch-list-or-anotherand-thats-the-problem/.

CNN. 2020. "Death of Osama bin Laden Fast Facts." Updated April 27, 2021. www.cnn.com/2013/09/09/world/death-of-osama-bin-laden-fast-facts/index.html.

CNN Newsroom. 2017. "ISIS Base Annihilated By Moab Strike, Say Afghan Officials; Us Sending Dozens More Troops To Somalia; Us Watching North Korea Closely On Major Holiday; Sources Say Uk And European Intel Intercepted Contacts Between Trump Associates And Russia; Chemical Attacks Is 100 Percent Fabrication Says Bashar Al-Assad; Cia Director Slams Wikileaks As Hostile to the US." CNN, April 14, 2017, 03:00 ET. https://transcripts.cnn.com/show/cnr/date/2017-04-14/segment/20.

Cobb, Jasmine Nicole. 2015. "A More Perfect Union: Black Freedoms, White Houses." *Public Culture* 28 (1): 63–87.

Cockburn, Andrew. 2015. *Kill Chain: The Rise of the High-tech Assassins*. New York: Picador.

Cohn, Laura. 2003. "Tommy Franks Takes the Stage – Finally." *Bloomberg*, March 23, 2003. www.bloomberg.com/news/articles/2003-03-22/tommy-franks-takes-the-stage-finally.

Cole, David. 2010. "What to Do About Guantánamo?" *The New York Review*, October 14, 2010. www.nybooks.com/articles/2010/10/14/what-do-about-guantanamo/?pagination=false.

Cole, David. 2016. "The Drone Presidency." *The New York Review* 63 (13): 19. www.nybooks.com/articles/2016/08/18/the-drone-presidency/.

Coll, Steve. 2018. *Directorate S: The C.I.A. and America's Secret Wars in Afghanistan and Pakistan, 2001-2016.* New York: Penguin Press.

Comaroff, Jean, and John Comaroff. 2007. "Law and disorder in the post-colony." *Social Anthropology* 15 (2): 133–52. DOI: https://doi.org/10.1111/j.0964-0282.2007.00010.x.

Committee on the Judiciary. 2009. "Reining in the Imperial Presidency: Lessons and Recommendations Relating to the Presidency of George W. Bush." https://fas.org/irp/congress/2009_rpt/imperial.pdf.

Conetta, Carl. 2004. *"Disappearing the Dead: Iraq, Afghanistan, and the Idea of a 'New Warfare.'"* Cambridge, MA: Commonwealth Institute Center for International Policy.

Constable, Marianne. 2005. *Just Silences: The Limits and Possibilities of Modern Law.* Princeton, NJ: Princeton University Press.

Conway, Lucian Gideon, Meredith A. Repke, and Shannan C. Houck. 2017. "Donald Trump as a Cultural Revolt against Perceived Communication Restriction: Priming Political Correctness Norms Causes More Trump Support." *Journal of Social and Political Psychology* 5 (1): 244–59. DOI: https://doi.org/10.5964/jspp.v5i1.732.

Conyers, John, Jr. 2009. Foreword to "Reining in the Imperial Presidency: Lessons and Recommendations Relating to the Presidency of George W. Bush." https://irp.fas.org/congress/2009_rpt/imperial.pdf.

Cooper, Helene, and Mujib Mashal. 2017. "U.S. Drops 'Mother of All Bombs' on ISIS Caves in Afghanistan." *New York Times*, April 13, 2017. www.nytimes.com/2017/04/13/world/asia/moab-mother-of-all-bombs-afghanistan.html.

Cooper, Helene, and Eric Schmitt. 2021. "U.S. Strikes Explosive-Laden Vehicle in Kabul." *New York Times*, August 29, 2021. www.nytimes.com/2021/08/29/us/politics/us-strike-kabul-airport.html.

Corbin, Jane. 2015. "Have We Been Told the Truth about bin Laden's Death?" *BBC News*, June 17, 2015. www.bbc.com/news/world-middle-east-33152315.

Correll, John T. 2003. "What Happened to Shock and Awe?" *Air Force Magazine*, November 1, 2003. www.airforcemag.com/article/1103shock/.

Couch, Stuart. 2013. "Torture at Guantánamo: Lt. Col. Stuart Couch on His Refusal to Prosecute Abused Prisoner." Interview by Juan González and Amy Goodman. *Democracy Now!*, February 22, 2013. www.democracynow.org/2013/2/22/torture_at_guantanamo_lt_col_stuart?autostart=true.

Council on Foreign Relations. n.d. "The U.S. War in Afghanistan." Updated August 2021. www.cfr.org/timeline/us-war-afghanistan.

Cover, Robert M. 1983. "The Supreme Court: 1982 Term —Foreword: Nomos and Narrative." *Harvard Law Review* 97 (1): 4–69. Cambridge,

MA: Harvard Law Review Association. DOI: https://doi.org/10.2307/1340787.

Cover, Robert M. 1986. "Violence and the Word." *The Yale Law Journal* 95 (8), July 1, 1986: 1601–29. New Haven, CT. DOI: https://doi.org/10.2307/796468.

Crawford, Neta. 2021. "The Afghan Army Didn't Just Fold: Having Already Sacrificed Greatly, They Chose to Spare Their Country the Costs of Further War." *Daily News*, August 17, 2021. www.nydailynews.com/opinion/ny-oped-the-afghan-military-didnt-just-fold-20210817-b7dglnnt2jasphhlw7svz2ouvq-story.html.

Cribb, Robert, ed. 1990. *The Indonesian Killings of 1965-66: Studies from Java and Bali.* Melbourne, Australia. Centre of Southeast Asian Studies, Monash University.

Cribb, Robert. 2001. "Genocide in Indonesia, 1965-1966." *Journal of Genocide Research*, 3 (2): 219–39. DOI: https://doi.org/10.1080/713677655.

Cronin, Bruce, and Ian Hurd, eds. 2008. *The UN Security Council and the Politics of International Authority.* New York: Routledge.

Dailymail.com Reporter. 2017. "How the Mother of All Bombs Kills People: Vaporized Bodies, Crushed Internal Organs and Suffocated to Death… While Anyone Who Survives is Left Psychologically Scarred for Life." *Daily Mail*, April 14, 2017. www.dailymail.co.uk/news/article-4410796/How-Mother-Bombs-kills-people-MOAB-s-effect.html.

Darian-Smith, Eve. 2013. *Laws and Societies in Global Contexts: Contemporary Approaches.* Cambridge: Cambridge University Press.

Davies, Margaret. 2002. *Asking the Law Question: The Dissolution of Legal Theory.* 2nd ed. Sydney: Law Book Co.

Davies, Margaret. 2017. *Law Unlimited: Materialism, Pluralism, and Legal Theory.* Abingdon, Oxon: Routledge, an imprint of the Taylor & Francis Group.

De Genova, Nicholas. 2012. "The 'War on Terror' as Racial Crisis: Homeland Security, Obama, and Racial (Trans)Formations." In *Racial Formation in the Twenty-First Century*, edited by Daniel HoSang, Oneka LaBennett, and Laura Pulido. Berkeley, CA: University of California Press.

De Goede, Marieke, and Gavin Sullivan. 2015. "The Politics of Security Lists." *Environment and Planning D: Society and Space* 34 (1): 67–88. DOI: https://doi.org/10.1177%2F0263775815599309.

Dean, Jodi. 2001. "Publicity's Secret." *Political Theory* 29 (5): 624–50. Los Angeles, CA: SAGE Publications. DOI: https://doi.org/10.1177/0090591701029005002.

Dean, Jodi. 2002. *Publicity's Secret: How Technoculture Capitalizes on Democracy.* Ithaca, NY: Cornell University Press.

Dean, Jodi. 2005. "Communicative Capitalism: Circulation and the Foreclosure of Politics." *Cultural Politics* 1 (1): 51–74. Biggleswade, England: Berg Publishers. https://doi.org/10.2752/174321905778054845.

Debord, Guy. [1967] 1977. *Society of the Spectacle*. Detroit: Black & Red.

Dennett, Charlotte. 2020. *The Crash of Flight 3804: A Lost Spy, a Daughter's Quest, and the Deadly Politics of the Great Game for Oil*. White River Junction, VT: Chelsea Green Publishing.

Dennett, Charlotte. 2021. "The Missing Link to the War in Afghanistan." *Toward Freedom*, May 12, 2021. https://towardfreedom.org/story/archives/asia-archives/the-missing-link-to-the-war-in-afghanistan/.

Der Derian, James. 2009. *Virtuous War: Mapping the Military-Industrial Media-Entertainment Network*. 2nd ed. New York: Routledge.

Derounian, Avedis. 1941. "America First Meeting – Manhattan Center." In *The U.S. Antifascism Reader*, edited by Bill V. Mullen and Christopher Vials, 134–38. London and New York: Verso.

Derrida, Jacques. 1992. "Force of Law: The 'Mystical Foundation of Authority'." In *Deconstruction and the Possibility of Justice*, edited by Drucilla Cornell, Michel Rosenfeld, and David Gray. New York: Routledge.

Detsch, Jack. 2021. "Departure of Private Contractors Was a Turning Point in Afghan Military's Collapse." *Foreign Policy*, August 16, 2021. https://foreignpolicy.com/2021/08/16/afghanistan-military-collapse-private-contractors/.

Devji, Faisal. 2008. *The Terrorist in Search of Humanity: Militant Islam and Global Politics*. New York: Columbia University Press.

DeYoung, Karen. 2021. "Zalmay Khalilzad, Special Envoy to Afghanistan, Resigns." *Washington Post*, October 18, 2021. www.washingtonpost.com/national-security/zalmay-khalilzad-afghanistan-envoy-resigns/2021/10/18/030b0168-304c-11ec-93e2-dba2c2c11851_story.html.

Diab, Robert. 2015. *The Harbinger Theory: How the Post-9/11 Emergency Became Permanent and the Case for Reform*. New York: Oxford University Press.

Dicey, Albert V. 1959. *Introduction to the Study of the Law of the Constitution*. 10th ed. London: Macmillan.

Diplomatic Security Service. 2019. "1993 World Trade Center Bombing." At www.state.gov/1993-world-trade-center-bombing/.

Dower, John W. 1986. *War without Mercy: Race and Power in the Pacific War*. New York: Pantheon Books.

Dower, John W. 2010. *Cultures of War: Pearl Harbor, Hiroshima, 9-11, Iraq*. New York: W. W. Norton; New York: New Press.

Downie Jr., Leonard. 2020. *The Trump Administration and the Media: Attacks on Press Credibility Endanger US Democracy and Global Press Freedom*. Committee to Protect Journalists. https://cpj.org/wp-content/uploads/2020/04/cpj_usa_2020.pdf.

Drinnon, Richard. 1980. *Facing West: The Metaphysics of Indian-Hating and Empire-Building*. Minneapolis, MN: University of Minnesota Press.

Du Bois, W. E. B. [1920] 2003. "The Souls of White Folk." *Monthly Review* 55 (6): 44–58. DOI: https://doi.org/10.14452/MR-055-06-2003-10_6.

Dudziak, Mary L. 2003. "Introduction." In *September 11 in History: A Watershed Moment?* edited by Mary L. Dudziak, 1–9. Durham, NC: Duke University Press.

Dudziak, Mary L. 2003. "Afterword: Remembering September 11." In *September 11 in History: A Watershed Moment?* edited by Mary L. Dudziak, 212–15. Durham, NC: Duke University Press.

Dudziak, Mary. 2010. "Law, War, and the History of Time." *California Law Review* 98 (5): 1669–709.

Dudziak, Mary. 2012. *War Time: An Idea, Its History, Its Consequences.* Oxford, England: Oxford University Press.

Dudziak, Mary. 2015. "Targeted Killings and Secret Law: Drones and the Atrophy of Political Restraints on the War Power." In *Drones and the Future of Armed Conflict: Ethical, and Strategic Implications.* Chicago: The University of Chicago Press.

Duffett, John, ed. 1968. "Against the Crime of Silence: Proceedings of the Russell International War Crimes Tribunal, Stockholm, Copenhagen." *International War Crimes Tribunal.* New York: Bertrand Russell Peace Foundation.

Dunbar-Ortiz, Roxanne. 2014. *An Indigenous Peoples' History of the United States.* Boston, MA: Beacon Press.

Dunbar-Ortiz, Roxanne. 2018. *Loaded: A Disarming History of the Second Amendment.* San Francisco, NC: City Lights Books.

Edmondson, Catie. 2019. "House Panel's Assent Gives Life to Effort to End 9/11 Military Authorization." *New York Times,* May 22, 2019. www .nytimes.com/2019/05/22/us/politics/authorization-military-force-congress.html.

Ehrlich, Matthew C. 2005. "Shattered Glass, Movies, and the Free Press Myth." *The Journal of Communication Inquiry* 29 (2): 103–18. DOI: https://doi.org/10.1177%2F0196859904272741.

Ellerbeck, Alexandra. 2016. "Why Trump's insults of Journalists Must Be Taken Seriously." *CPJ,* May 18, 2016. https://cpj.org/2016/05/why-trumps-insults-of-journalists-must-be-taken-se/.

Emlen, Robert P. 1997. "Imagining America in 1834: Zuber's Scenic Wallpaper 'Vues d'Amérique Du Nord.'" *Winterthur Portfolio* 32 (2/3): 189–210. http://www.jstor.org/stable/1215172.

Engel, David M., and Barbara Yngvesson. 1984. "Mapping Difficult Terrain: 'Legal Culture,' 'Legal Consciousness,' and Other Hazards for the Intrepid Explorer." *Law and Policy* 6 (3): 299–307. Oxford: Blackwell Publishing Ltd.

Engelhardt, Tom. [1992] 1994. "The Gulf War as Total Television." In *Seeing through the Media: The Persian Gulf War,* edited by Susan Jeffords and Lauren Rabinovitz. New Brunswick, NJ: Rutgers University Press, 81–96.

Engelhardt, Tom. 2007. "Collateral Damage and the 'Incident' at Haditha." *CLCWEB: Comparative Literature and Culture* 9 (1). Ashland: Purdue University. DOI: https://doi.org/10.7771/1481-4374.1015.

Entman, Robert M. 2005. "The Nature and Sources of News." In *The Press*, edited by Geneva Overholser and Kathleen Hall Jamieson, 48–65. Oxford: Oxford University Press.

Entous, Adam, and Evan Osnos. 2020. "Qassam Suleimani and How Nations Decide to Kill." *The New Yorker*, February 3, 2020. www.newyorker.com/magazine/2020/02/10/qassem-suleimani-and-how-nations-decide-to-kill.

Environmental XPRT. n.d. "CNIguard Ltd." Accessed October 13, 2021. www.environmental-expert.com/companies/cniguard-ltd-39584.

Environmental XPRT. n.d. "Water Asset Management Companies (Water and Wastewater) serving Iraq." Accessed October 13, 2021. www .environmental-expert.com/water-wastewater/water-asset-management/companies/serving-iraq.

Eperjesi, John R. 2005. *The Imperialist Imaginary: Visions of Asia and the Pacific in American Culture*. Hanover, NH: Dartmouth College Press.

Esch, Joanne. 2010. "Legitimizing the 'War on Terror': Political Myth in Official-Level Rhetoric." *Political Psychology* 31 (3): 357–91. DOI: https://doi.org/10.1111/j.1467-9221.2010.00762.x.

Estrin, Daniel. 2019. "Syrians Say Innocent Civilians Were Killed in U.S. Raid on Abu Bakr Al-Baghdadi." *NPR*, December 3, 2019. www.npr.org/2019/12/03/784553329/syrians-say-innocent-civilians-were-killed-in-u-s-raid-on-abu-bakr-al-baghdadi?t=1631229639684.

Ewick, Patricia and Susan S. Silbey. 1992. "Conformity, Contestation, and Resistance: An Account of Legal Consciousness." *New England Law Review* 26 (3): 731. Boston, MA: New England School of Law.

Ewick, Patricia, and Susan S. Silbey. 1998. *The Common Place of Law: Stories From Everyday Life*. Chicago: University of Chicago Press.

Fairclough, Norman. 1989. *Language and Power*. London, England: Longman.

Falk, Richard. 2007. "Encroaching on the Rule of Law: Post 9/11 Policies within the United States." *National Insecurity and Human Rights: Democracies Debate Counterterrorism*: 14–36. Berkeley, CA: University of California Press.

Fallows, James. 2017. "Donald Trump's Telling Change to the Oval Office." *The Atlantic*, August 25, 2017. www.theatlantic.com/politics/archive/2017/08/spot-the-difference-oval-office-edition/538008/.

Fanon, Frantz. [1952] 2021. *Black Skin, White Masks*. Translated by Richard Philcox. London: Penguin Modern Classics.

Fanon, Frantz. [1961] 2004. *The Wretched of the Earth*. Translated by Richard Philcox. New York: Grove Press.

Farivar, Cyrus. 2014. "The executive order that led to mass spying, as told by NSA alumni." *Ars Technica*, August 28, 2014. https://arstechnica.com/

tech-policy/2014/08/a-twisted-history-how-a-reagan-era-executive-order-led-to-mass-spying/.

Farrington, Dana. 2016. "CIA 'Live Tweets' Bin Laden Raid on 5th Anniversary." *NPR*, May 2, 2016. www.npr.org/sections/thetwo-way/2016/05/02/476438422/cia-live-tweets-bin-laden-raid-on-5th-anniversary.

Farris, Sara R. 2017. *In the Name of Women's Rights: The Rise of Femonationalism*. Durham, NC: Duke University Press.

Felter, Claire, Jonathan Masters, and Mohammed A. Sergie. 2021. "Al-Shabab." *Council on Foreign Relations*, May 19, 2021. www.cfr.org/back grounder/al-shabab.

Fenning, Pamela, and Jennifer Rose. 2007. "Overrepresentation of African American Students in Exclusionary Discipline: The Role of School Policy." *Urban Education* 42 (6): 536–59. DOI: https://doi.org/10.1177%2F0042085907305039.

Fisch, Jörg. 1983. *Cheap Lives and Dear Limbs: The British Transformation of the Bengal Criminal Law, 1769-1817*. Wiesbaden: Franz Steiner Verklag.

Fitzpatrick, Peter. 1992. *The Mythology of Modern Law*. London: Routledge.

Fitzpatrick, Peter. 2001. *Modernism and the Grounds of Law*. Cambridge: Cambridge University Press.

Florida International University Accelerated Bridge Construction University Transportation Center. n.d. "Sandwich Plate System (SPS)." Accessed October 13, 2021. https://abc-utc.fiu.edu/resources/implemented-advanced-technologies/sandwich-plate-system-sps/.

Flowerdew, John, and John E. Richardson. 2018. *The Routledge Handbook of Critical Discourse Studies*. London, England: Routledge.

Foucault, Michel. [1972] 2010. *The Archeology of Knowledge*. New York: Vintage Books.

Foucault, Michel. [1977] 1995. *Discipline and Punish: The Birth of the Prison*. New York: Vintage Books.

Foucault, Michel. 2003. *Society Must Be Defended*. London: Penguin.

Foucault, Michel. [2004] 2007. *Security, Territory, Population*. Basingstoke: Palgrave Macmillan.

Fox News. 2017. "What is the MOAB?" April 13, 2017. www.foxnews.com/politics/what-is-the-moab.

Fraenkel, Ernst. 1941. *The Dual State; A Contribution to the Theory of Dictatorship*. New York: Oxford University Press.

Franke-Ruta, Garance. 2013. "All the Previous Declarations of War." *The Atlantic*, August 31, 2013. www.theatlantic.com/politics/archive/2013/08/all-the-previous-declarations-of-war/279246/.

Fredrickson, George M. 1981. *White Supremacy: A Comparative Study in American and South African History*. New York: Oxford University Press.

Freeman, Michael, ed. 2004. *Law and Popular Culture*. Oxford: Oxford University Press.

Friedersdorf, Conor. 2013. "The Audacity of Eric Holder's Letter Admitting Team ObamaKilled 4 Americans." *The Atlantic*, May 22, 2013. www .theatlantic.com/politics/archive/2013/05/the-audacity-of-eric-holders-letter-admitting-team-obama-killed-4-americans/276145/.

Friedman, Lawrence M. 2015. *The Big Trial: Law as Public Spectacle*. Lawrence, KS: University Press of Kansas.

Gervais, Bryan T, and Irwin L Morris. 2018. *Reactionary Republicanism: How the Tea Party in the House Paved the Way for Trump's Victory*. New York: Oxford University Press.

Gettleman, Jeffrey. 2011. "Gunmen Seize 2 Aid Workers near Kenya-Somalia Border." *New York Times*, October 13, 2011. www.nytimes.com/2011/10/14/world/africa/kidnappers-again-target-europeans-in-kenya.html.

Gilbert, Emily. 2015. "The Gift of War: Cash, Counterinsurgency, and 'Collateral Damage'." *Security Dialogue* 46 (5): 403–21. DOI: https://doi .org/10.1177/0967010615592111.

Godin, Jason. 2005. "Goldwater-Nichols Act." In *Encyclopedia of War & American Society*, edited by Peter Karsten. Thousand Oaks, CA: SAGE.

Gohmann, Joanna M. 2010. "A Republican Mirage: Zuber Et Cie's Vues D'amérique Du Nord." Master's thesis, University of North Carolina at Chapel Hill. DOI: https://doi.org/10.17615/pgn9-1n41.

Gonzales, Richard. 2019. "Head of U.S. Central Command Says ISIS Leader Baghdadi Buried At Sea." *NPR*, October 30, 2019. www.npr.org/2019/10/30/774617578/head-of-u-s-central-command-says-isis-leader-bagh dadi-buried-at-sea.

Goodman, J. E., M. Tomlinson, and J. B. Richland. 2014. "Citational Practices: Knowledge, Personhood, and Subjectivity." *Annual Review of Anthropology*, 43 (1): 449–63.

Goodstein, Laurie, and Tamar Lewin. 2001. "A Nation CBenged: Violence and Harassment; Victims of Mistaken Identity, Sikhs Pay a Price for Turbans." *New York Times*, September 19, 2001. www.nytimes.com/2001/09/19/us/nation-challenged-violence-harassment-victims-mis taken-identity-sikhs-pay-price.html.

Gorta, William J. 2001. "Missing - or Hiding? - Mystery of NYPD Cadet from Pakistan." *New York Post*, October 12, 2001. https://nypost.com/2001/10/12/missing-or-hiding-mystery-of-nypd-cadet-from-pakistan/.

Greenhouse, Carol J. 2019. "Legal Pluralism." *Anthropology*. Oxford University Press. DOI: https://doi.org/10.1093/OBO/9780199766567-0217.

Greenhouse, Carol J., and Christina L. Davis. 2020. *Landscapes of Law: Practicing Sovereignty in Transnational Terrain*. Philadelphia, PA: University of Pennsylvania Press.

Greenwald, Robert, dir. 2006. *Iraq for Sale: The War Profiteers*. Culver City, CA: Brave New Films.

Gregory, Derek. 2006. "The Black Flag: Guantánamo Bay and the Space of Exception." *Geografiska Annaler: Series B, Human Geography* 88 (4): 405–27.

Grenier, John. 2005. *The First Way of War: American War Making on the Frontier, 1607-1814*. New York: Cambridge University Press.

Grossman, Nicholas. 2019. "Trump Cancels Drone Strike Civilian Casualty Report: Does It Matter?" *War on the Rocks*, April 2, 2019. https://warontherocks.com/2019/04/trump-cancels-drone-strike-civilian-casualty-report-does-it-matter/.

Gryphon Partners. n.d. "About Us." Accessed October 13, 2021. www.gryphon-partners.com/about-us/.

Guardian Staff. 2019. "Trump Tweets Fake Photo of Isis Raid Dog, and Appears to Declassify Its Name." *The Guardian*, October 31, 2019. www.theguardian.com/us-news/2019/oct/30/trump-latest-news-tweet-dog-isis.

Gunneflo, Markus. 2016. *Targeted Killing: A Legal and Political History*. New York: Cambridge University Press.

Gunther, Brad. 2017. "MOAB Has Only Been Dropped in One Other Place - Northwest Florida." *WKRG*, April 13, 2017. www.wkrg.com/news/moab-has-only-been-dropped-in-one-other-place-northwest-florida/867760231/.

Gusterson, Hugh. 2014. "Toward an Anthropology of Drones: Remaking Space, Time, and Valor in Combat." In *The American Way of Bombing: Changing Ethical and Legal Norms, From Flying Fortresses to Drones*, edited by Matthew Evangelista and Henry Shue. Ithaca, NY: Cornell University Press.

Gusterson, Hugh. 2016. *Drone: Remote Control Warfare*. Cambridge, MA: The MIT Press.

Hage, Ghassan. 2006. "Warring Societies (and Intellectuals)." *Transforming Cultures eJournal* 1 (1). http://epress.lib.uts.edu.au/journals/TfC.

Hall, Jerome. 1960. *General Principles of Criminal Law*. Indianapolis, IN: Bobbs-Merrill Company.

Hall, Stuart. 1980. "Cultural Studies: Two Paradigms." *Media, Culture & Society* 2 (1): 57–72.

Hall, Stuart. 1997. "Introduction." In *Representation: Cultural representations and signifying practices*, edited by Stuart Hall. Sage Publications, Inc: Open University Press.

Hamilton, James T. 2005. "The Market and the Media." In *The Press*, edited by Geneva Overholser and Kathleen Hall Jamieson, 351–71. Oxford: Oxford University Press.

Hansen, Thomas Blom, and Finn Stepputat. 2005. *Sovereign Bodies: Citizens, Migrants, and States in the Postcolonial World*. Princeton, NJ: Princeton University Press.

Hansen, Thomas Blom, and Finn Stepputat. 2006. "Sovereignty Revisited." *Annual Review of Anthropology* 35 (1): 295–315. DOI: https://doi.org/10.1146/annurev.anthro.35.081705.123317.

Harding, Luke, and Ben Doherty. 2021. "Kabul Airport: Footage Appears to Show Afghans Falling from Plane after Takeoff." *The Guardian*, August 16, 2021. www.theguardian.com/world/2021/aug/16/kabul-airport-chaos-and-panic-as-afghans-and-foreigners-attempt-to-flee-the-capital.

Hardt, Michael, and Antonio Negri. 2004. *Multitude: War and Democracy in the Age of Empire*. New York: Penguin Press.

Harkins, Gina. 2019. "Trump Awards Conan the Hero Special Forces Dog a Medal at the White House." *Military.com*, November 25, 2019. www.military.com/daily-news/2019/11/25/trump-awards-conan-hero-special-forces-dog-medal-white-house.html.

Harrington, Rebecca. 2017. "Here's how much the 'mother of all bombs' the US just dropped on ISIS in Afghanistan actually cost." *Business Insider*, April 13, 2017. www.businessinsider.com/how-much-does-moab-bomb-cost-mother-of-all-bombs-2017-4?r=US&IR=T.

Harris, Shane, and Matthew M. Aid. 2013. "Exclusive: CIA Files Provide America Helped Saddam as He Gassed Iran." *Foreign Policy*, August 26, 2013. https://foreignpolicy.com/2013/08/26/exclusive-cia-files-prove-america-helped-saddam-as-he-gassed-iran/.

Hartman, Saidiya. 1997. *Scenes of Subjection: Terror, Slavery, and Self-Making in Nineteenth-Century America*. New York: Oxford University Press.

Hartung, William D. 2017. "Trump Bombings: The Mother of All Distractions?" *CNN*, April 14, 2017. https://edition.cnn.com/2017/04/14/opinions/trumps-erratic-bombings-hartung/index.html.

Hauser, Christine. 2016. "20 Marines Face Discipline after Muslim Recruit's Death is Ruled a Suicide" *New York Times*, September 9, 2016, www.nytimes.com/2016/09/10/us/marine-corps-raheel-siddiqui.html.

Healy, Jack, and Dave Philipps. 2021. "He was a baby on 9/11. Now He's One of the Last Casualties of America's Longest War." *New York Times*, August 29, 2021. www.nytimes.com/2021/08/27/world/asia/marine-killed.html.

Heidenrich, John G. 1993. "The Gulf War: How Many Iraqis Died?" *Foreign Policy* 90: 108–25.

Helsel, Phil. 2020. "White House Says U.S. Killed Qassim al-Rimi, Leader of al-Qaeda in Yemen." *NBC News*, February 6, 2020. www.nbcnews.com/news/world/white-house-says-u-s-killed-qassim-al-rimi-leader-n1132076.

Herman, Edward S., and Noam Chomsky. 1988. *Manufacturing Consent: The Political Economy of the Mass Media*. New York: Pantheon Books.

Herman, Edward S., and Robert W. McChesney. 1997. *The Global Media: The New Missionaries of Corporate Capitalism*. London: Cassell.

Hersh, Seymour M. 1974. "Huge C.I.A. Operation Reported in U.S. against Antiwar Forces, Other Dissidents in Nixon Years." *New York Times*, December 22, 1974. www.nytimes.com/1974/12/22/archives/huge-cia-operation-reported-in-u-s-against-antiwar-forces-other.html.

Hersh, Seymour M. 2016. *The Killing of Osama Bin Laden.* London: Verso.

History.com Editors. 2010. "U.S.-Led Attack on Afghanistan Begins." *History*, published on July 20, 2010, updated on October 6, 2020. www.history.com/this-day-in-history/u-s-led-attack-on-afghanistan-begins.

Hoefle, Scott William. 2004. "Bitter Harvest: The Frontier Legacy of US Internal Violence and Belligerent Imperialism." *Critique of Anthropology* 24 (3): 277–300. DOI: https://doi.org/10.1177/0308275X04045422.

Hofstadter, Richard. 1963. *Anti-Intellectualism in American Life.* New York: Knopf.

Höglund, Johan, and Martin Willander. 2017. "Black Hawk-Down: Adaptation and the Military- Entertainment Complex." *Culture Unbound: Journal of Current Cultural Research* 9 (3): 365–89. DOI: https://doi.org/10.3384/cu.2000.1525.1793365.

Homeland Security. 2015. "Creation of the Department of Homeland Security." September 24, 2015. www.dhs.gov/creation-department-homeland-security.

Honig, Bonnie. 2003. *Democracy and the Foreigner.* Princeton NJ: Princeton University Press.

Honig, Bonnie. 2009. *Emergency Politics: Paradox, Law, Democracy.* Princeton, NJ: Princeton University Press.

Honig, Bonnie. 2015. "Public Things: Jonathan Lear's 'Radical Hope', Lars von Trier's 'Melancholia', and the Democratic Need." *Political Research Quarterly* 68 (3). DOI: https://doi.org/10.1177/1065912915594464.

Honig, Bonnie. 2017. *Public Things: Democracy in Disrepair.* Ist ed. New York: Fordham University Press.

Hosang, Daniel M., Oneka LaBennett, and Laura Pulido, eds. 2012. Racial Formation in the Twenty-First *Century*. Berkeley, CA: University of California Press.

Howden, Daniel. 2013. "Terror in Nairobi: the Full Story behind al-Shabaab's Mall Attack." *The Guardian*, October 4, 2013. www.theguardian.com/world/2013/oct/04/westgate-mall-attacks-kenya.

Huey, John, and Nancy J Perry. 1991. "War: The Future of Arms." *Fortune* 123 (4): 34.

HuffPost. n.d. "Dr. Harlan K. Ullman." Accessed October 13, 2021. www.huffpost.com/author/dr-harlan-k-ullman.

Hughes, Richard T. 2018. *Myths America Lives By: White Supremacy and the Stories That Give Us Meaning.* 2nd ed. Urbana, IL: University of Illinois Press.

Hussain, Nasser. 2003. *The Jurisprudence of Emergency: Colonialism and the Rule of Law*. Ann Arbor, MI: University of Michigan Press.

Hussain, Nasser. 2007. "Beyond Norm and Exception: Guantánamo." *Critical Inquiry* 33 (4), 734–53

Hussain, Nasser. 2013. "The Sound of Terror: Phenomenology of a Drone Strike." *Boston Review*, October 14, 2013. https://bostonreview.net/world/hussain-drone-phenomenology.

Ignatius, David. 2016. "Obama's Tenure Ends with a Turf War over Killing Terrorists." *Washington Post*, December 8, 2016. www.washingtonpost.com/opinions/obamas-tenure-ends-with-a-turf-war-over-killing-terrorists/2016/12/08/b3c371d8-bd84-11e6-91ee-1adddfe36cbe_story.html.

IMDb. n.d. "Shock and Awe." Accessed October 13, 2021. www.imdb.com/title/tt2152841/.

Ingraham, Christopher. 2014. "The United States is in a State of Emergency - 30 of Them, in Fact." *Washington Post*, November 19, 2014. www.washingtonpost.com/news/wonk/wp/2014/11/19/the-united-states-is-in-a-state-of-emergency-30-of-them-in-fact/.

Ingram, Mathew. 2019. "White House Revokes Press Passes for Dozens of Journalists." *Columbia Journalism Review*, May 9, 2019. www.cjr.org/the_media_today/white-house-press-passes.php.

Jackson, Richard. 2005. *Writing the War on Terrorism: Language, Politics, and Counter-Terrorism*. Manchester: Manchester University Press.

Jacobs, Rick. 2006. "Halliburton and Cheney: War Profiteers in Chief Fight to Keep Their Wallets Fat." *Huffpost*, September 17, 2006. www.huffpost.com/entry/halliburton-and-cheney-wa_b_29635.

Jacquard, Roland. 2002. *In the Name of Osama Bin Laden: Global Terrorism and the Bin Laden Brotherhood*. Durham, NC: Duke University Press.

Jansson, Julia. 2020. *Terrorism, Criminal Law and Politics: The Decline of the Political Offence Exception to Extradition*. Abingdon, Oxon: Routledge.

Jayasuriya, Kanishka. 1999. "Globalization, Law, and the Transformation of Sovereignty: The Emergence of Global Regulatory Governance." *Indiana Journal of Global Legal Studies* 6 (2): 425–55.

Jayasuriya, Kanishka. 2001. "The Exception Becomes the Norm: Law and Regimes of Exception in East Asia." *Asian-Pacific Law & Policy Journal* 2 (1): 108–24.

Jeffords, Susan. 1993. "The Patriot System, or Managerial Heroism." In *Cultures of United States Imperialism*, edited by Amy Kaplan and Donald E. Pease. Durham, NC: Duke University Press.

Jeffords, Susan, and Lauren Rabinovitz. 1994. *Seeing through the Media: The Persian Gulf War*. New Brunswick, NJ: Rutgers University Press.

Jenkins, Brian Michael. 1984. "Combatting Terrorism Becomes a War". Santa Monica, CA: The Rand Corporation. https://www.rand.org/pubs/papers/P6988.html.

Jenkins, Mark. 2016. "A War Seen in Unnerving Close-Up from 'Eye in the Sky'." *KQED*, March 18, 2016. www.kqed.org/arts/11412346/a-war-seen-in-unnerving-close-up-from-eye-in-the-sky.

Johns, Fleur. 2005. "Guantánamo Bay and the Annihilation of the Exception." *European Journal of International Law* 16 (4): 613–35. DOI: https://doi.org/10.1093/ejil/chi135.

Johns, Fleur. 2013. *Non-Legality in International Law: Unruly Law*. Cambridge: Cambridge University Press.

Johnson, Boyd M., III. 1992. "Executive Order 12,333: The Permissibility of an American Assassination of a Foreign Leader." *Cornell International Law Journal* 25 (2): 401–35.

Johnson, Chalmers. 2004. *Blowback: The Costs and Consequences of American Empire*. New York: Henry Holt.

Jones, Terry. 2001. "Why Grammar is the First Casualty of War." *The Telegraph*, December 1, 2001. www.telegraph.co.uk/news/uknews/1364012/Why-grammar-is-the-first-casualty-of-war.html.

Judis, John B. 2004. *The Folly of Empire: What George W. Bush Could Learn From Theodore Roosevelt and Woodrow Wilson*. New York: Scribner.

Judis, John B. 2005. "The Chosen Nation: The Influence of Religion on U.S. Foreign Policy." *Carnegie Endowment for International Peace*. http://carnegieendowment.org/files/PB37.judis.FINAL.pdf.

Kahn, Paul W. 1999. *The Cultural Study of Law: Reconstructing Legal Scholarship*. Chicago, IL: University of Chicago Press.

Kantorowicz, Ernst Hartwig. 1957. *The King's Two Bodies: A Study in Mediaeval Political Theology*. Princeton, NJ: Princeton University Press.

Kaplan, Amy. 1993. "'Left Alone with America': The Absence of Empire in the Study of American Culture." In *Cultures of United States Imperialism*, edited by Amy Kaplan and Donald E. Pease, 3–21. Durham, NC: Duke University Press.

Kaplan, Amy. 2002. *The Anarchy of Empire in the Making of US Culture*. Cambridge, MA: Harvard University Press.

Kaplan, Amy. 2003. "Homeland Insecurities: Some Reflections on Language and Space." *Radical History Review* 85 (1): 82–93.

Kaplan, Amy. 2005. "Where is Guantánamo?" *American Quarterly* 57 (3), September 1, 2005: 831–58. College Park, MD: Johns Hopkins University Press. https://doi.org/10.1353/aq.2005.0048.

Kaplan, Amy. 2018. *Our American Israel: The Story of an Entangled Alliance*. Cambridge, MA: Harvard University Press.

Kaplan, Caren. 2018. *Aerial Aftermaths*. Raleigh, NC: Duke University Press.

Karpf, David. 2019. "We All Stand Together or We Fall Apart: On the Need for an Adversarial Press in the Age of Trump" in *Trump and the Media*, edited by Pablo Boczkowski and Zizi Papacharissi, 221–28. Cambridge, MA: MIT Press.

Katzman, Kenneth. 2009. "Afghanistan: Post Taliban Governance, Security, and U.S. Policy. *Congressional Research Service*, July 20, 2009. www.everycrsreport .com/files/20090720_RL30588_a8fd7425406c1b1588a258b6fa1dda8ee10d16 3d.pdf.

Keller, Jared. 2017. "New Satellite Photos Suggest the 'Mother of All Bombs' Did Its Job in Afghanistan." *Task & Purpose*, April 21, 2017. https:// taskandpurpose.com/news/moab-afghanistan-photos/.

Kellner, Douglas. 1992. "U.S. Television, the Crisis of Democracy, and the Persian Gulf War." In *Media, Crisis, and Democracy*, edited by Mark Raboy and Bernard Dagenais, 44–62. London: Sage.

Kellner, Douglas. 2003. *Media Spectacle*. London: Routledge.

Kellner, Douglas. 2007. "Bushspeak and the Politics of Lying: Presidential Rhetoric in the "War on Terror." *Presidential Studies Quarterly* 37 (4): 633–45.

Kelly, Mary Louise. 2016. "When the U.S. Military Strikes, White House Points to A 2001 Measure." *NPR*, September 6, 2016, www.npr.org/ sections/parallels/2016/09/06/492857888/when-the-u-s-military-strikes-white-house-points-to-a-2001-measure.

Kelly, William. 2017. "The Diplomatic Reception Room's Historic Wallpaper." *The White House Historical Association*, June 13, 2017. www .whitehousehistory.org/the-diplomatic-reception-rooms-historic-wallpaper.

Kelsen, Hans. 1967. *Pure Theory of Law*. Berkeley, CA: University of California Press.

Kennedy, Liam. 2012. "Seeing and Believing: On Photography and the War on Terror." *Public Culture* 24 (2): 261–81. DOI: https://doi.org/10.1215/ 08992363-1535498.

Kessler, Glenn. 2020. "Introduction: 16,000 Falsehoods." In *Donald Trump and His Assault on Truth: The President's Falsehoods, Misleading Claims, and Flat-Out Lies* by Glenn Kessler, Salvador Rizzo, and Meg Kelly. New York: Scribner.

Kessler, Glenn, Salvador Rizzo, and Meg Kelly. 2020. *Donald Trump and His Assault on Truth: The President's Falsehoods, Misleading Claims and Flat-Out Lies*. New York: Scribner.

Khalili, Laleh. 2013. *Time in the Shadows: Confinement in Counterinsurgencies*. Stanford, CA: Stanford University Press.

Kingsolver, Barbara. 2001. "A Pure, High Note of Anguish." *Los Angeles Times*, September 23, 2001. www.latimes.com/archives/la-xpm-2001-sep-23-op-48850-story.html.

Klein, Stephen A. 2005. "Public Character and the Simulacrum: The Construction of the Soldier Patriot and Citizen Agency in *Black Hawk*

Down." *Critical Studies in Media Communication* 22 (5): 427–49. DOI: https://doi.org/10.1080/07393180500342993.

Klimas, Jacqueline. 2017. "U.S. drops 'mother of all bombs' against ISIS in Afghanistan." *Politico*, April 13, 2017. www.politico.com/story/2017/04/moab-isis-in-afghanistan-237201.

Ko, Hanae. 2012. "The Sweet and Bitter Road: Michael Rakowitz." *Art Asia Pacific* 78. http://www.artasiapacific.com/Magazine/78/TheSweetAnd BitterRoadMichaelRakowitz.

Koppes, Clayton R., and Gregory D. Black. 1990. *Hollywood Goes to War: How Politics, Profits and Propaganda Shaped World War II Movies.* Berkeley, CA: University of California Press.

Kron, Josh, and Mohamed Ibrahim. 2010. "Islamists Claim Attack in Uganda." *New York Times*, July 12, 2010. www.nytimes.com/2010/07/13/world/africa/13uganda.html.

Krygier, Martin. 2016. "The Rule of Law: Pasts, Presents, and Two Possible Futures." *Annual Review of Law and Social Science* 12 (1): 199–229. Annual Reviews. DOI: https://doi.org/10.1146/annurev-lawsocsci-102612-134103.

Kumar, Ruchi. 2017. "Afghans Want More 'Mother of All Bombs'." *Foreign Policy*, April 19, 2017. https://foreignpolicy.com/2017/04/19/afghans-want-more-mothers-of-all-bombs/.

Kwate, Naa Oyo A., and Shatema Threadcraft. 2017. "Dying Fast and Dying Slow in Black Space: Stop and Frisk's Public Health Threat and Comprehensive Necropolitics." *Du Bois Review* 14 (2): 535–56. DOI: https://doi.org/10.1017/S1742058X17000169.

LaCapria, Kim. 2016. "Edward Snowden Said Osama bin Laden is Alive." *Snopes*, May 10, 2016. www.snopes.com/fact-check/snowden-bin-laden-alive/.

Lane, Kimberly, Yaschica Williams, Andrea N. Hunt, and Amber Paulk. 2020. "The Framing of Race: Trayvon Martin and the Black Lives Matter Movement." *Journal of Black Studies* 51 (8):790–812. Los Angeles, CA: SAGE Publications.

Lange, Katie. 2018. "How & Why the DOD Works with Hollywood." *Inside DOD*, February 28, 2018. www.defense.gov/News/Inside-DOD/Blog/art icle/2062735/how-why-the- dod-works-with-hollywood/.

Latifi, Ali M. 2017. "Mother of All Bombs." *New York Times*, April 20, 2017. www.nytimes.com/2017/04/20/opinion/mother-of-all-bombs.html.

Lawrence, J. P. 2021. "Troop levels are down, but US says over 18,000 contractors remain in Afghanistan." *Stars and Stripes*, January 19, 2021. www.stripes.com/theaters/middle_east/troop-levels-are-down-but-us-says-over-18-000-contractors-remain-in-afghanistan-1.659040.

Lawrence, Bruce B, and Aisha Karim (eds.). 2007. *On Violence: A Reader.* Durham, NC: Duke University Press.

Lens, Sidney. 1987. *Permanent War: The Militarization of America*. New York: Schoken.

Levey, Bob. 1983. "When You Can't Decide, You Just Pick Them All." *Washington Post*, November 8, 1983. www.washingtonpost.com/archive/local/1983/11/08/when-you-cant-decide-you-just-pick-them-all/fbd4bf9c-b383-4e55-9bd7-508cb9f69f1b/.

Levin, Sam T. 2020. "What Does 'Defund the Police' Mean? The Rallying Cry Sweeping the US – Explained." *The Guardian*, June 6, 2020. www.theguardian.com/us-news/2020/jun/05/defunding-the-police-us-what-does-it-mean.

Levine, Adam. 2016. "Unprecedented Access to the White House to Relive the Bin Laden Raid." *CNN*, May 2, 2016. https://edition.cnn.com/2016/04/30/politics/obama-osama-bin-laden-raid-situation-room/index.html.

Li, Darryl. 2020. *The Universal Enemy: Jihad, Empire, and the Challenge of Solidarity*. Stanford, CA: Stanford University Press.

Lipset, Seymour Martin. 1963. *The First New Nation: The United States in Historical and Comparative Perspective*. New York: Basic Books.

Lipset, Seymour Martin. 1996. *American Exceptionalism: A Double-Edged Sword*. New York: W. W. Norton

Locher, James R., III. 2017. "Transformative Leadership on Capitol Hill: The Goldwater-Nichols Defense Reorganization Act." In *Reagan and the World: Leadership and National Security, 1981-1989*, edited by Bradley Lynn Coleman and Kyle Longley, 81–108. Lexington, KY: The University Press of Kentucky.

Lockie, Alex. 2017. "How Much the US's 'Mother of all Bombs' Really Costs." *Business Insider*, April 14, 2017. www.businessinsider.com/real-cost-of-moab-mother-of-all-bombs-170-000-2017-4?r=US&IR=T.

Lokaneeta, Jinee. 2011. *Transnational Torture: Law, Violence, and State Power in the United States and India*. New York: New York University Press.

Lokaneeta, Jinee. 2017. "Sovereignty, Violence and Resistance in North East India: Mapping Political Theory Today." *Theory and Event* 20 (1): 76–86.

López, Ian Haney. 2014. *Dog Whistle Politics: How Coded Racial Appeals Have Reinvented Racism and Wrecked the Middle Class*. New York: Oxford University Press.

Loughlin, Martin. 2000. *Sword and Scales: An Examination of the Relationship Between Law and Politics*. Oxford: Hart.

Lowe, Lisa. 2010. "Reckoning Nation and Empire: Asian American Critique." In *A Concise Companion to American Studies*, edited by John Carlos Rowe, 229–44. Malden, MA: Wiley-Blackwell.

Lubin, Alex. 2021. *Never-Ending War on Terror*. Oakland, CA: University of California Press.

Lutz, Catherine. 2009. "Anthropology in an Era of Permanent War." *Anthropologica* 51 (2): 367–79.

Lyman, Rick. 2001. "A Nation Challenged: The Entertainment Industry; Hollywood Discussed Role in War Effort." *New York Times*, November 12, 2001. www.nytimes.com/2001/11/12/us/nation-challenged-entertainment-industry-hollywood-discusses-role-war-effort.html.

Lyrics.com. n.d. "Search Results for 'Shock and Awe'." Accessed October 13, 2021. www.lyrics.com/lyrics/shock%20and%20awe.

Macaulay, Stewart. 1989. "Popular Legal Culture: An Introduction." *The Yale Law Journal* 98 (8): 1545–58.

Mackenzie, Richard. 1998. "The United States and the Taliban." In *Fundamentalism Reborn? Afghanistan and the Taliban*, edited by William Maley, 90–103. New York: New York University Press.

Madison, James. n.d. "June 1, 1812: Special Message to Congress on the Foreign Policy Crisis – War Message" (speech). *Miller Center*. https://millercenter.org/the-presidency/presidential-speeches/june-1-1812-special-message-congress-foreign-policy-crisis-war.

Madsen, Deborah L. 1998. *American Exceptionalism*. Jackson, MS: University Press of Mississippi.

Mamdani, Mahmood. 2004. *Good Muslim, Bad Muslim. America, the Cold War, and the Roots of Terror*. New York. Pantheon Books.

Manderson, Desmond. 2018. *Law and the Visual: Representations, Technologies, Critique*. Toronto: University of Toronto Press.

Manly, Lorne. 2016. "'Eye in the Sky' and 'National Bird' Train Sights on Warfare by Remote Control." *New York Times*, March 10, 2016. www.nytimes.com/2016/03/13/movies/helen-mirren-eye-in-the-sky-and-national-bird-train-sights-on-warfare-by-remote-control.html?_r=0.

Marcoń, Barbara. 2011. "Hiroshima and Nagasaki in the Eye of the Camera." *Third Text* 25 (6): 787–97. DOI: https://doi.org/10.1080/09528822.2011.624352.

Margulies, Joseph. 2006. *Guantanamo and the Abuse of Presidential Power*. New York: Simon & Schuster.

Margulies, Joseph. 2013. *What Changed When Everything Changed: 9/11 and the Making of National Identity*. New Haven, CT: Yale University Press.

Marks, James. 2017. "U.S. Drops "The Mother of All Bombs"; Passenger Dragged Off United Airlines Flight Likely to Sue; Search for the Missing Chibok Girls; "The Fate of the Furious" Roars into Theaters." *CNN Newsroom*. CNN, April 14, 2017, 01:00 ET. http://edition.cnn.com/TRANSCRIPTS/1704/14/cnr.18.html.

Marks, Julie. 2018. "How SEAL Team Six Took Out Osama Bin Laden." *History*, May 24, 2018. www.history.com/news/osama-bin-laden-death-seal-team-six.

Marsh, Allison. 2017. "Meet the CIA's Insectothopter." *IEEE Spectrum*. https://spectrum.ieee.org/meet-the-cias-insectothopter.

Marvin, Carolyn, and David W. Ingle. 1996. "Blood Sacrifice and the Nation: Revisiting Civil Religion." *Journal of the American Academy of Religion* 64 (4): 767–80. DOI: https://doi.org/10.1093/jaarel/LXIV.4.767.

Marvin, Carolyn, and David W. Ingle. 1999. *Blood Sacrifice and the Nation: Totem Rituals and the American Flag*. Cambridge: Cambridge University Press.

Masco, Joseph. 2014. *The Theater of Operations: National Security Affect from the Cold War to the War on Terror*. Durham, NC: Duke University Press.

Mashal, Mujib, and Fahim Abed. 2017. "U.S. Isn't Saying How Much Damage 'Mother of All Bombs' Did in Afghanistan.'" *New York Times*, April 18, 2017. www.nytimes.com/2017/04/18/world/middleeast/us-isnt-saying-how-much-damage-the-mother-of-all-bombs-did.html.

Massoud, Mark F. 2021. *Shari'a, Inshallah: Finding God in Somali Legal Politics*. Cambridge: Cambridge University Press.

Mather, Lynn. 2011. "Law and Society." In *Oxford Handbook of Political Science*, edited by Robert E. Goodin. DOI: https://doi.org/10.1093/oxfordhb/9780199604456.013.0015.

Mawani, Renisa. 2012. "Law's Archive." *Annual Review of Law and Social Science* 8 (1): 337–65. Annual Reviews. DOI: https://doi.org/10.1146/annurev-lawsocsci-102811-173900.

Mayer, Jane. 2009. "The Predator War." *The New Yorker*, October 19, 2009. www.newyorker.com/magazine/2009/10/26/the-predator-war.

Mazzetti, Mark, Julian E. Barnes, and Adam Goldman. 2021a. "Intelligence Warned of Afghan Military Collapse, Despite Biden's Assurances." *New York Times*, August 17, 2021. www.nytimes.com/2021/08/17/us/politics/afghanistan-biden-administration.html.

Mazzetti, Mark, Julian E. Barnes, and Adam Goldman. 2021b. "Amid Afghan Chaos, a C.I.A. Mission That Will Persist for Years." *New York Times*, August 27, 2021. www.nytimes.com/2021/08/27/us/politics/cia-afghanistan.html.

Mbembe, Achille J. 2000. "At the Edge of the World: Boundaries, Territoriality, and Sovereignty in Africa." Translated by Steven Rendall. *Public Culture* 12 (1): 259–84. https://muse.jhu.edu/article/26186/.

Mbembe, Achille. 2003. "Necropolitics." *Public Culture* 15 (1): 19. Durham, NC: Duke University Press. DOI: https://doi.org/10.1215/08992363-15-1-11.

Mbembe, Achille. 2019. *Necropolitics*. Translated by Steve Corcoran. Durham, NC: Duke University Press.

McAlister, Melani. 2002. "A Cultural History of the War without End." *Journal of American History* 89 (2): 439–56.

McAlister, Melani. 2005. *Epic Encounters*. Berkeley, CA: University of California Press.

McArdle, Mairead. 2019. "House Votes to Repeal 2001 Authorization for Use of Military Force." *National Review*, June 19, 2019. www.nationalreview .com/news/house-votes-repeal-2001-authorization-military-force/.

McBride, Keally. 2006. "Riding Herd on the New World Order: Spectacular Adventuring and U.S. Imperialism." In *Tarzan was an Eco-Tourist and Other Tales in the Anthropology of Adventure*, edited by Luis A. Vivanco and Robert J. Gordon, 257–69. New York: Berghahn Books.

McCarthy, Erin. 2002. "Justice." In *Collateral Language: A User's Guide to America's New War*, edited by John Collins and Ross Glover. New York: New York University Press.

McFarland, Kevin. 2016. "*Eye in the Sky* Is the Quintessential Modern War Film." *Wired*, April 1, 2016. www.wired.com/2016/04/eye-in-the-sky-modern-war-film/.

McGregor, Katherine E. 2009. "The Indonesian Killings of 1965-1966." *Mass Violence & Resistance*.

McVeigh, Karen. 2012. "US military facing fresh questions over targeting of children in Afghanistan." *The Guardian*, December 7, 2012. www .theguardian.com/world/2012/dec/07/us-military-targeting-strategy-afghanistan.

Mears, Bill. 2012. "Federal Judge Blocks Release of Bin Laden Death Photos." *CNN*, April 27, 2012. https://edition.cnn.com/2012/04/26/justice/bin-laden-photos/index.html.

Mendelson, Andrew L. 2018. "Lessons from the Paparazzi: Rethinking Photojournalistic Coverage of Trump." In *Trump and the Media*, edited by Pablo J. Boczkowski and Zizi Papacharissi, 59–68. Cambridge, MA: The MIT Press.

Méndez, Xhercis. 2016. "Which Black Lives Matter? Gender, State-Sanctioned Violence, and 'My Brother's Keeper.'" *Radical History Review* 2016 (126): 96–105. DOI: https://doi.org/10.1215/01636545-3594445.

Merry, Sally Engle. 1990. *Getting Justice and Getting Even: Legal Consciousness Among Working-Class Americans*. Chicago, IL: University of Chicago Press.

Merry, Sally E. 1995. "Resistance and the Cultural Power of Law." *Law and Society Review* 29 (1): 13. Beverly Hills, CA: Law and Society Association. DOI: https://doi.org/10.2307/3054052.

Mertz, Elizabeth. 2002. "The Perfidy of Gaze and the Pain of Uncertainty: Anthropological Theory and the Search for Closure". In *Ethnography in Unstable Places: Everyday Lives in Contexts of Dramatic Political Change*, edited by Carol J. Greenhouse, Elizabeth Mertz, Kay B Warren, 355–78. Durham, NC: Duke University Press.

Michael McIntee. 2011. "Obama: Osama bin Laden Dead – Full Video." *YouTube video*, 9:45. http://www.youtube.com/watch?v=m-N3dJvhgPg.

Milbank, Dana. 2003. "Curtains Ordered for Media Coverage of Returning Coffins." *Washington Post*, October 21, 2003. www.washingtonpost.com/archive/politics/2003/10/21/curtains-ordered-for-media-coverage-of-returning-coffins/13375c81–187e-4f91-a565–2ce8f3bf3549/.

Milbert, Jacques G. [1828] 1968. "Picturesque Itinerary of the Hudson River and the Peripheral Parts of North America." Translated by Constance D. Sherman. Upper Saddle River, NJ: Gregg Press.

Miles, Corey J. 2020. "How a Democracy Killed Tamir Rice: White Racial Frame, Racial Ideology, and Racial Structural Ignorance in the United States." In *Gender, Sexuality and Race in the Digital Age*, edited by D. Nicole Farris, D'Lane R. Compton, and Andrea P. Herrera, 99–111. Cham, Switzerland: Springer.

Military.com. 2016. "'Eye in the Sky' Director Gavin Hood Talks Drone Warfare." April 1, 2016. www.military.com/undertheradar/2016/04/eye-in-the-sky-director-gavin-hood-talks-drone-warfare.

Miller, David Lee. 2017. "What is the MOAB?" *Fox News*. April 14, 2017. https://www.foxnews.com/politics/what-is-the-moab

Miller, William Ian. 1998. "Clint Eastwood and Equity: Popular Culture's Theory of Revenge." In *Law in the Domains of Culture*, edited by Austin Sarat, and Thomas R. Kearns, 161–202. Ann Arbor, MI: University of Michigan Press.

Miller, Zeke. 2019. "White House Says Bin Laden Son Killed in U.S. Operation." *PBS*, September 14, 2019. www.pbs.org/newshour/nation/white-house-says-bin-laden-son-killed-in-us-operation.

Minerva Research Initiative. n.d. "Home." Accessed January 09, 2021. https://minerva.defense.gov/.

Mirzoeff, Nicholas. 2005. *Watching Babylon: The War in Iraq and Global Visual Culture*. New York and London: Routledge.

Mirzoeff, Nicholas. 2006. "The Subject of Visual Culture." In *The Visual Culture Reader*, edited by Nicholas Mirzoeff. Abingdon: Routledge,

Mitchell, W. J. T. 2005. "There Are No Visual Media." *Journal of Visual Culture* 4 (2): 257–66. DOI: https://doi.org/10.1177/1470412905054673.

Moore, Sally Falk. 1978. *Law as Process: An Anthropological Approach*. London, England: Routledge & K. Paul.

Moore, Adam. 2019. *Empire's Labor: The Global Army that Supports U.S. Wars*. Ithaca, NY: Cornell University Press.

Morris, Edward W., and Brea L. Perry. 2017. "Girls Behaving Badly? Race, Gender, and Subjective Evaluation in the Discipline of African American Girls." *Sociology of Education* 90 (2): 127–48. DOI: https://doi.org/10.1177%2F0038040717694876.

Mullen, Bill V., and Christopher Vials. 2020. *The US Antifascism Reader*. London: Verso.

Mulrine, Anna. 2008. "Warheads on Foreheads." *Air Force Magazine* 91 (10): 44–47.

Museum of Contemporary Art Chicago. 2017. "Michael Rakowitz: Backstroke of the West." https://mcachicago.org/Exhibitions/2017/Michael-Rakowitz.

Musolff, Andreas. 2016. *Political Metaphor Analysis: Discourse and Scenarios.* London: Bloomsbury Academic.

Nash, Phil Tajitsu. 2003. "Shock and Disgust: Achieving Rapid Restruction." *AsianWeek* 11.

National Archives. 2018. "Vietnam War U.S. Military Fatal Casualty Statistics." www.archives.gov/research/military/vietnam-war/casualty-statistics.

Neiwert, David. 2018. "Patriot Prayer again brings violence to Portland with 'flash march' downtown, rounding out a weekend of far-right violence." *Southern Poverty Law Center*, October 15, 2018. www.splcenter.org/hate watch/2018/10/15/patriot-prayer-again-brings-violence-portland-flash-march-downtown-rounding-out-weekend-far.

Nelson, Deborah. 2008. *The War Behind Me: Vietnam Veterans Confront the Truth About U.S. War Crimes.* New York: Basic Books.

Ngai, Mae M. 2014. *Impossible Subjects: Illegal Aliens and the Making of Modern America.* Princeton, NJ: Princeton University Press.

Nixon, Rob. 2011. *Slow Violence and the Environmentalism of the Poor.* Cambridge, MA: Harvard University Press.

Nolan, Cynthia M. 1999. "Seymour Hersh's Impact on the CIA." *International Journal of Intelligence and Counterintelligence* 12 (1): 18–34. DOI: https://doi.org/10.1080/088506099305205.

NPR Staff. 2011. "Among the Costs of War: Billions a Year in A.C.?" *NPR,* June 25, 2011. www.npr.org/2011/06/25/137414737/among-the-costs-of-war-20b-in-air-conditioning.

Nuamah, Sally A. 2019. *How Girls Achieve.* Cambridge, MA: Harvard University Press.

Obama, Barack. 2009. "Remarks by the President at Cairo University, 6-04-09" (speech). *The White House.* https://obamawhitehouse.archives.gov/the-press-office/remarks-president-cairo-university-6-04-09.

Obama, Barack. 2011. "Remarks by the President on Osama Bin Laden" (speech). *The White House.* http://www.whitehouse.gov/the-press-office/2011/05/02/remarks-president-osama-bin-laden.

Obama, Barack. 2013. "Remarks by the President at the National Defense University." May 23, 2013, https://obamawhitehouse.archives.gov/the-press-office/2013/05/23/remarks-president-national-defense-university.

Obama, Barack. 2016. "Remarks of President Barack Obama – State of the Union Address as Delivered" (speech). *The White House.* https://obamawhitehouse.archives.gov/the-press-office/2016/01/12/remarks-president-barack-obama---prepared-delivery-state-union-address.

Obama White House Archived. 2011. "P050111PS-0210." Flickr, May 1, 2011. www.flickr.com/photos/whitehouse/5680724572/in/album-721576265076 26189/.

Ochsenwald, William L., Jill Ann Crystal, Dawlat Ahmet Sadek, and John Duke Anthony. 1999. "Kuwait: Resources and Power." *Encyclopedia Britannica*, last updated August 26, 2021. www.britannica.com/place/Kuwait/Resources-and-power.

Office of Legacy Management. n.d. "Trinity Site - World's First Nuclear Explosion." Accessed October 13, 2021. www.energy.gov/lm/doe-history/manhattan-project-background-information-and-preservation-work/manhattan-project-1.

O'Kane, Caitlin. 2020. "'Say Their Names': The List of People Injured or Killed in Officer-Involved Incidents is Still Growing." *CBS News*, June 8, 2020. www.cbsnews.com/news/say-their-names-list-people-injured-killed-police-officer-involved-incidents/.

Oliver, Kendrick. 2003. "Atrocity, Authenticity and American Exceptionalism: (Ir)rationalizing the Massacre at My Lai." *Journal of American Studies* 37 (2): 247–68.

Omarkhali, Khanna. 2016. "Transformations in the Yezidi Tradition after the ISIS Attacks: An Interview with Ilhan Kizilhan." *Kurdish Studies* 4 (2): 148–54.

Orford, Anne. 2011. *International Authority and the Responsibility to Protect.* Cambridge: Cambridge University Press.

Orford, Anne. 2012. "Rethinking the Significance of the Responsibility to Protect Concept." Proceedings of the ASIL Annual Meeting 106. Cambridge University Press: 27–31. DOI: https://doi.org/10.5305/procannmeetasil.106.0027.

Orford, Anne. 2013. "Moral Internationalism and the Responsibility to Protect." *European Journal of International Law* 24 (1): 83–108. DOI: https://doi.org/10.1093/ejil/chs092.

Osman, Wazhmah. 2017. "The Military Present (Episode 3)." Interview by Vasiliki Touhouliotis and Emily Sogn. *American Anthropologist Podcast*, May 18, 2017. www.americananthropologist.org/podcast/military-present-episode-3-wazhmah-osman.

Ottaway, David B., and Dan Morgan. 1998. "Gas Pipeline Bounces between Agendas." *Washington Post*, October 5, 1998. www.washingtonpost.com/wp-srv/inatl/europe/caspian100598.htm.

Owen, Wilfred. 1917. "Dulce et Decorum Est." *Poetry Foundation.* www.poetryfoundation.org/poems/46560/dulce-et-decorum-est.

Panetta, Leon E. 2009. "Director's Remarks at the Pacific Council on International Policy" (speech). *Central Intelligence Agency.* www.aclu.org/sites/default/files/field_document/34-4._Exhibit_4_8.28.15.pdf.

Parker, James E. K. 2015. *Acoustic Jurisprudence: Listening to the Trial of Simon Bikindi*. Oxford: Oxford University Press.

Paul, Deirdre Glenn, and Jacqueline Araneo. 2019. "'Orange is the New Black' Comes to New Jersey's Public Schools: Black Girls and Disproportionate Rates of Out-of-School Suspensions and Expulsions." *The Urban Review*, 51 (2): 326–43. DOI: https://doi.org/10.1007/s11256-018-0483-8.

Pawlyk, Oriana. 2017. "After US Drops 'Frankenbomb' on Afghanistan, Questions Linger." *Military.com*, April 22, 2017. www.military.com/daily-news/2017/04/22/after-us-drops-frankenbomb-on-afghanistan-questions-linger.html.

PBS. n.d. "John Chapman and the Kamikaze Attack." Accessed October 13, 2021. www.pbs.org/wgbh/americanexperience/features/pacific-john-chapman/.

Pease, Donald. 2002. "The Patriot Acts." *boundary 2* 29 (2): 29–43. DOI: https://doi.org/10.1215/01903659-29-2-29.

Pease, Donald. 2007. "Exceptionalism." In *Keywords for American Cultural Studies*, edited by Bruce Burgett and Glenn Hendler, 48–112. New York: New York University Press, 2007.

Peltier, Heidi. 2020. "The Growth of the 'Camo Economy' and the Commercialization of the Post-9/11 Wars." Watson Institute for International and Public Affairs Costs of War Project. https://watson.brown.edu/costsofwar/papers/2020/growth-camo-economy-and-commercialization-post-911-wars-0.

Pengelly, Martin. 2019. "'So brilliant, So Smart': Trump Meets His Match in Hero Dog Wounded in Isis Raid." *The Guardian*, November 25, 2019. www.theguardian.com/us-news/2019/nov/25/trump-conan-white-house-dog-baghdadi-isis-raid.

Peters, Gerhard. 2021. "Presidential News Conferences." *The American Presidency Project*, December 20, 2021. Edited by John T. Woolley and Gerhard Peters. Santa Barbara, CA: University of California. www.presidency.ucsb.edu/statistics/data/presidential-news-conferences.

Peters, Jeremy W. 2019. "The Tea Party Didn't Get What It Wanted, but It Did Unleash the Politics of Anger." *New York Times*, August 28, 2019. www.nytimes.com/2019/08/28/us/politics/tea-party-trump.html.

Philipps, Dave. 2016. "Ex-Marine Describes Violent Hazing and the Lies That Covered It Up." *New York Times*, September 29, 2016. www.nytimes.com/2016/09/30/us/ex-marine-describes-violent-hazing-and-the-lies-that-covered-it-up.html.

Philipps, Dave, and Eric Schmitt. 2021. "How the U.S. Hid an Airstrike That Killed Dozens of Civilians in Syria." *New York Times*, November 15, 2021. www.nytimes.com/2021/11/13/us/us-airstrikes-civilian-deaths.html.

Phillips, Macon. 2011. "Osama Bin Laden Dead." *Obama White House Archives*, May 2, 2011. https://obamawhitehouse.archives.gov/blog/2011/05/02/osama-bin-laden-dead.

Pieslak, Jonathan. 2009. *Sound Targets: American Soldiers and Music in the Iraw War*. Bloomington, IN: Indiana University Press.

Pilger, John. 2021. "John Pilger: Afghanistan, the Great Game of Smashing Countries." *Monthly Review Online*, August 26, 2021. https://mronline .org/2021/08/26/john-pilger-afghanistan-the-great-game-of-smashing-countries/.

Pincus, Walter, and Dan Eggen. 2001. "New Powers Sought for Surveillance." *Washington Post*, September 17, 2001. https://jime.ieej.or.jp/htm/extra/ 2001/09/13/20010917/wp-01.html.

Pinfari, Marco. 2019. *Terrorists as Monsters: The Unmanageable Other from the French Revolution to the Islamic State*. New York: Oxford University Press.

Pitcavage, Mark. 2020. "Twenty-five Years Later, Oklahoma City Bombing Inspires a New Generation of Terrorists." *Anti-Defamation League* Twenty-five Years Later, Oklahoma City Bombing Inspires a New Generation of Extremists | ADL https://www.adl.org/resources/blog/twenty-five-years-later-oklahoma-city-bombing-inspires-new-generation-extremists.

Popal, Seelai, Ali A. Olomi, and Laila Rashidie. 2017. "After MOAB, More Afghans Unite to Resist US War and Occupation." *Truthout*, April 20, 2017. https://truthout.org/articles/after-moab-more-afghans-unite-to-resist-us-war-and-occupation/.

Popalzai, Ehsan, and Laura Smith-Spark. 2017. "'Mother of All Bombs' Killed 94 ISIS Fighters, Afghan Official Says." *CNN*, April 15, 2017. https:// edition.cnn.com/2017/04/15/asia/afghanistan-isis-moab-strike/index .html.

Poros, Maritsa V. 2009. "Backlash 9/11." *Journal of Balkan and Near Eastern Studies* 11 (3): 333–37.

Post, Robert. 1991. *Law and the Order of Culture*. Berkeley, CA: University of California Press.

Powell, Colin L., and Joseph E. Persico. 1995. *My American Journey*. New York: Random House.

Powers, Thomas. 2004. "Secret Intelligence and the 'War on Terror'." *New York Review of Books* 51 (20): 50.

ProPublica. 2015. "The FBI Checked the Wrong Box and a Woman Ended Up on the Terrorism Watch List For Years." December 15, 2015. www.propublica .org/article/fbi-checked-wrong-box-rahinah-ibrahim-terrorism-watch-list.

Pugliese, Joseph. 2007. "Abu Ghraib and its Shadow Archives." *Law and Literature* 19 (2): 247–76. Routledge. DOI: https://doi.org/10.1525/lal .2007.19.2.247.

Pulliam-Moore, Charles, and Margaret Myers. 2014. "Timeline of Events in Ferguson." *PBS*, August 20, 2014. www.pbs.org/newshour/nation/time line-events-ferguson.

Pyke, Alan. 2016. "'Eye In The Sky': An Ambivalent, Thrilling Movie about Drones That America Needs to Talk about." *ThinkProgress*, March 9,

2016. https://archive.thinkprogress.org/eye-in-the-sky-an-ambivalent-thrilling-movie-about-drones-that-america-needs-to-talk-about-26456a17cae4/.

Rajah, Jothie. 2012. *Authoritarian Rule of Law: Legislation, Discourse, and Legitimacy in Singapore.* New York: Cambridge University Press.

Rajah, Jothie. 2016. "Law as Record: The Death of Osama bin Laden." 13 *No Foundations: An Interdisciplinary Journal of Law and Justice*, 45–69.

Rakowitz, Michael. 2009. "Strike the Empire Back: Episode IV: The Lord, the Homeland, the Leader." Lowitz + Sons. https://media.mcachicago.org/pdf/J7C8OL5W/strike-the-empire-back-comic-book.pdf.

Ralph, Laurence. 2019. "The Logic of the Slave Patrol: The Fantasy of Black Predatory Violence and the Use of Force by the Policy." *Palgrave Communications* 5. DOI: https://doi.org/10.1057/s41599-019-0333-7.

Ralph, Laurence. 2020. *The Torture Letters: Reckoning with Police Violence.* Chicago, IL: University of Chicago Press.

Ransby, Barbara. 2018. *Making All Black Lives Matter: Reimagining Freedom in the Twenty- First Century.* Oakland, CA: University of California Press.

Rashid, Ahmed. 1998. "Pakistan and the Taliban." In *Fundamentalism Reborn? Afghanistan and the Taliban*, edited by William Maley. New York: New York University Press.

Rasmussen, Sune E. 2017a. "Devastation and a War That Rages on: Visiting the Valley Hit by the Moab Attack." *The Guardian*, April 17, 2017. www.theguardian.com/world/2017/apr/17/moab-bomb-site-afghanistan.

Rasmussen, Sune E. 2017b. "'It Felt Like the Heavens were Falling': Afghans Reel from Moab Impact." *The Guardian*, April 17, 2017. www.theguardian.com/world/2017/apr/14/it-felt-like-the-heavens-were-falling-afghans-reel-from-moabs-impact.

Razack, Sherene H. 2012. "We Didn't Kill 'Em, We Didn't Cut Their Head Off." In *Racial Formation in the Twenty-First Century*, edited by Daniel HoSang, Oneka LaBennett, and Laura Pulido. Berkeley, CA: University of California Press.

Reading the Pictures. 2019. "The Trump Vs. Obama Situation Room Photos", October 27, 2019, www.readingthepictures.org/2019/10/trump-obama-situation-room-photos/.

Reitman, Janet. 2017. "How the Death of a Muslim Recruit Revealed a Culture of Brutality in the Marines." *New York Times*, July 6, 2017. www.nytimes.com/2017/07/06/magazine/how-the-death-of-a-muslim-recruit-revealed-a-culture-of-brutality-in-the-marines.html.

Renshon, Stanley A. 2005. "Presidential Address: George W. Bush's Cowboy Politics: An Inquiry." *Political Psychology* 26 (4): 585–614.

Restad, Hilde. 2015. *American Exceptionalism: An Idea That Made a Nation and Remade the World.* Abingdon, Oxon: Routledge.

Richland, Justin B. 2013. "Jurisdiction: Grounding Law in Language." *Annual Review of Anthropology* 42: 209–26.

Richter, Paul. 1998. "White House Justifies Option of Lethal Force," *Los Angeles Times* October 29, 1998, www.latimes.com/archives/la-xpm-1998-oct-29-mn-37327-story.html.

Robb, David L. 2004. *Operation Hollywood: How the Pentagon Shapes and Censors the Movies.* Amherst, NY: Prometheus Books.

Robinson, Julian. 2016. "British White Widow Terror Fugitive Samantha Lewthwaite 'Mentored All-Female Team of Jihadists' Who Attacked Kenyan Police Station." *Daily Mail*, September 15, 2016. www.dailymail.co.uk/news/article-3791189/British-white-widow-terror-fugitive-Samantha-Lewthwaite-mentored-female-team-jihadists-attacked-Kenyan-police-station.html.

Robinson, Sue. 2018. "Trump, Journalists, and Social Networks of Trust." In *Trump and the Media*, edited by Pablo J. Boczkowski and Zizi Papacharissi, 187–94. Cambridge, MA: The MIT Press.

Rochelle, Safiyah. 2020. "Capturing the Void(ed): Muslim Detainees, Practices of Violence, and the Politics of Seeing in Guantanamo Bay." Doctoral dissertation. Carleton University, Ottawa, Canada.

Rodriguez, Dylan. 2010. *Suspended Apocalypse: White Supremacy, Genocide, and the Filipino Condition.* Minneapolis, MN: University of Minnesota Press.

Roele, Isobel. 2013. "Disciplinary Power and the UN Security Council Counter Terrorism Committee." *Journal of Conflict & Security Law* 19 (1): 49–84. DOI: https://doi.org/10.1093/jcsl/krt018.

Rogin, Michael. 1988. *Ronald Reagan the Movie: and Other Episodes in Political Demonology.* Berkeley, CA: University of California Press.

Rogin, Michael. 1990. "'Make My Day!': Spectacle as Amnesia in Imperial Politics." *Representations* 29 (1): 99–123.

Rohde, David. 2012. "The Drone Wars." *Reuters*, January 26, 2012. www.reuters.com/article/us-david-rohde-drone-wars-idUSTRE80P11I20120126.

Rohlinger, Deana A., and Leslie Bunnage. 2017. "Did the Tea Party Movement Fuel the Trump-Train? The Role of Social Media in Activist Persistence and Political Change in the 21st Century." *Social Media + Society* 3 (2): 1–11.

Roosa, John. 2006. *Pretext for Mass Murder: The September 30th Movement and Suharto's Coup d'Etat in Indonesia.* Madison, WI: University of Wisconsin Press.

Rosand, Eric. 2003. "Security Council Resolution 1373, the Counter-Terrorism Committee, and the Fight Against Terrorism." *American Journal of International Law* 97 (2): 333–41. DOI: https://doi.org/10.2307/3100110.

Rosen, Lawrence. 2006. *Law as Culture: An Invitation.* Princeton, NJ: Princeton University Press.

Rosenberg, Carol. 2019. "Trial for Men Accused of Plotting 9/11 Attacks Is Set for 2021." *New York Times*, August 30, 2019. www.nytimes.com/2019/08/30/us/politics/sept-11-trial-guantanamo-bay.html.

Rosenberg, Carol. 2021. "Trial Guide: The Sept. 11 Case at Guantánamo Bay." *New York Times*, August 23, 2021. www.nytimes.com/article/september-11-trial-guantanamo-bay.html.

Rosenberg, Emily S. 2014. "World War I, Wilsonianism, and Challenges to U.S. Empire." *Diplomatic History* 38 (4), 852–63.

Royster, Jacqueline J., ed. 1997. *Southern Horrors and Other Writings: The Anti-Lynching Campaign of Ida B. Wells, 1892-1900*. Boston, MA: Bedford Books.

Rubenstein, Richard E. 1987. *Alchemists of Revolution: Terrorism in the Modern World*. New York: Basic Books.

Rubio, Marco. 2015. "Rubio: 'But there are over 700,000 Americans on some watch list or another...And that's the problem." *CNN's State of the Union*, December 6, 2015. https://cnnpressroom.blogs.cnn.com/2015/12/06/rubio-but-there-are-over-700000-americans-on-some-watch-list-or-anotherand-thats-the-problem/.

Rudalevige, Andrew. 2005. *The New Imperial Presidency: Renewing Presidential Power after Watergate*. Ann Arbor, MI: University of Michigan Press.

Rumsfeld, Donald. 2003. "Pentagon Briefing." *CNN Live Event/Special*. CNN, March 20, 2003, 11:05 ET. https://transcripts.cnn.com/show/se/date/2003-03-20/segment/08.

Russell, Adrienne. 2019. "Making Journalism Great Again: Trump and the New Rise of News Activism." In *Trump and the Media*, edited by Pablo Boczkowski and Zizi Papacharissi, 203–12. Cambridge, MA: MIT Press.

Said, Edward W. 1978. *Orientalism*. New York: Pantheon Books.

Said, Edward W. [1978] 2004. *Orientalism*. New York: Vintage Books.

Said, Edward W. 1987. "The Imperial Spectacle." *Grand Street* 6 (2): 82–104. DOI: https://doi.org/10.2307/25006961.

Said, Edward W. 1993. *Culture and Imperialism*. London: Chatto & Windus.

Saito, Natsu Taylor. 2010. *Meeting the Enemy: American Exceptionalism and International Law*. New York: New York University Press.

Saito, Natsu Taylor. 2021. "Indefinite Detention, Colonialism, and Settler Prerogative in the United States." *Social & Legal Studies* 30 (1): 32–65. DOI: https://doi.org/10.1177%2F0964663918769362.

Samuels, Richard J. 2005. "Assassination, US Executive Order against." In *Encyclopedia of United States National Security*. Thousand Oaks, CA: SAGE Publications. DOI: https://doi.org/10.4135/9781412952446.

Sanburn, Josh. 2015. "From Trayvon Martin to Walter Scott: Cases in the Spotlight." *Time*, April 10, 2015. https://time.com/3815606/police-violence-timeline/.

Sandhoff, Michelle. 2017. *Service in a Time of Suspicion: Experiences of Muslims Serving in the U.S. Military Post-9/11*. Iowa City, IA: University of Iowa Press.

Santhanam, Laura and Larisa Epatko. 2019. "9/11 to Today: Ways We Have Changed." *PBS*, September 10, 2019. www.pbs.org/newshour/nation/9-11-to-today-ways-we-have-changed.

Sarat, Austin, and Jonathan Simon. 2001. "Cultural Studies & the Law: Beyond Legal Realism?" *Yale Journal of Law & the Humanities* 13 (1): 3.

Sarat, Austin and Thomas Kearns. 1998. *Law in the Domains of Culture*. Ann Arbor, MI: University of Michigan Press.

Savage, Charlie. 2007. *Takeover: The Return of the Imperial Presidency and the Subversion of American Democracy*. New York: Little, Brown and Company.

Savage, Charlie. 2015. "How 4 Federal Lawyers Paved the Way to Kill Osama bin Laden." *New York Times*, October 28, 2015. www.nytimes.com/2015/10/29/us/politics/obama-legal-authorization-osama-bin-laden-raid.html.

Scahill, Jeremy. 2007. *Blackwater: The Rise of the World's Most Powerful Mercenary Army*. New York: Nation Books.

Scahill, Jeremy. 2013. *Dirty Wars: The World is a Battlefield*. New York: Nation Books.

Scahill, Jeremy. 2017. *The Assassination Complex: Inside the Government's Secret Drone Warfare Program*. New York: Simon & Schuster.

Schabner, Dean. 2006. "Debate Heats up over 'Sunsetting' Parts of Patriot Act." *ABC News*, January 7, 2006. https://abcnews.go.com/US/story?id=853909.

Scheppele, Kim Lane. 1989. "Foreword: Telling Stories." *Michigan Law Review* 87 (8): 2073–89.

Scheppele, Kim Lane. 2004. "Other People's Patriot Acts: Europe's Response to September 11." *Loyola Law Review* 50 (1): 89–148.

Scheppele, Kim Lane. 2010. "The International Standardization of National Security Law." *Journal of National Security Law and Policy* 4 (2): 437–53.

Scheppele, Kim Lane. 2013. "The Empire of Security and the Security of Empire." *Temple Journal of Comparative and International Law* 27 (2): 241–78.

Schill, Dan. 2009. *Stagecraft and Statecraft: Advance and Media Events in Political Communication*. Lanham, MD: Lexington Books.

Schmitt, Carl. [1922] 2005. *Political Theology: Four Chapters on the Concept of Sovereignty*. Translated by George Schwab. Chicago, IL: University of Chicago Press.

Schmitt, Carl. [1932] 2007. *The Concept of the Political*. Translated by George Schwab. Chicago, IL: University of Chicago Press.

Schmitt, Carl. 1985. *Political Theology: Four Chapters on the Concept of Sovereignty*. Cambridge, MA: MIT Press.

Schmitt, Eric. 2002. "U.S. Would Use Drones to Attack Iraqi Targets." *New York Times*, November 6, 2002. www.nytimes.com/2002/11/06/

world/threats-responses-battlefield-us-would-use-drones-attack-iraqi-targets.html.

Schmitt, Eric, and Helene Cooper. 2021. "Pentagon Acknowledges Aug. 29 Drone Strike in Afghanistan was a 'Tragic Mistake'." *New York Times*, September 17, 2021. www.nytimes.com/2021/09/17/us/politics/penta gon-drone-strike-afghanistan.html.

Schmitt, Gary, Joseph M. Bessette, and Andrew E. Busch, eds. 2017. *The Imperial Presidency and the Constitution*. Lanham, MD: Rowman & Littlefield.

Schudson, Michael, and Susan E Tifft. 2005. "Orientations: The Press and Democracy in Time and Space." In *The Press*, edited by Geneva Overholser and Kathleen Hall Jamieson, 1–3. Oxford: Oxford University Press.

Scott, James C. 1998. "Seeing Like a State: How Certain Schemes to Improve the Human Condition Have Failed." New Haven, CT: Yale University Press.

Scott, Shirley V. 2009. "The Nature of US Engagement with International Law; Making Sense of Apparent Inconsistencies." In *Routledge Handbook of International Law*, edited by David Armstrong, 210–21. London: Routledge.

Security Council Resolution 1373. S/RES/1373 (2001). www.unodc.org/pdf/ crime/terrorism/res_1373_english.pdf.

Seigel, Micol. 2018. *Violence Work: State Power and the Limits of Police*. Durham, NC: Duke University Press.

Seir, Ahmad, Rahim Faiez, Tameem Akhgar, and Jon Gambrell. 2021. "Taliban sweep into Afghan capital after government collapses." *AP News*, August 16, 2021. https://apnews.com/article/afghanistan-taliban-kabul-bagram-e1ed33fe0c665ee67ba132c51b8e32a5.

Shaw, Michael. 2019. "The Trump vs. Obama Situation Room Photos." *Reading the Pictures*, October 27, 2019. www.readingthepictures.org/ 2019/10/trump-obama-situation-room-photos/.

Shear, Michael D. 2021. "'We Will Not Forgive,' Biden Says, Vowing Retaliation for Kabul Attack." *New York Times*, August 26, 2021. www .nytimes.com/live/2021/08/26/world/afghanistan-taliban-biden-news.

Sherwin, Martin J. 1995. "Hiroshima as Politics and History." *Journal of American History* 82 (3): 1085–93. DOI: https://doi.org/10.2307/ 2945113.

Sherwin, Richard K. 2000. *When Law Goes Pop: The Vanishing Line Between Law and Popular Culture*. Chicago, IL: University of Chicago Press.

Shklar, Judith. 1987. *Montesquieu*. Oxford, Oxfordshire: Oxford University Press.

Sidhu, Sandi, Nick Paton Walsh, Tim Lister, Oren Libermann, Laura Smith-Spark, and Saskya Vandoorne. 2021. "Ten Family Members, Including

Children, Dead after US Strike in Kabul." *CNN*, August 31, 2021. https://edition.cnn.com/2021/08/29/asia/afghanistan-kabul-evacuation-intl/index.html.

Silberstein, Sandra. 2002. *War of Words: Language, Politics, and 9/11*. London: Routledge.

Silverstein, Jason, and Nancy Dillon. 2017. "United States Drops Its Largest Non-Nuclear Bomb for the First Time Ever, on Afghanistan Compound." *New York Daily News*, April 13, 2017. www.nydailynews.com/news/world/u-s-drops-largest-non-nuclear-bomb-time-combat-article-1.3051981.

Singh, Nikhil Pal. 2004. *Black is a Country: Race and the Unfinished Struggle for Democracy*. Cambridge MA: Harvard University Press.

Singh, Nikhil Pal. 2017. *Race and America's Long War*. 1st ed. Berkeley, CA: University of California Press.

Skolnick, Jerome H., and James J. Fyfe. 1993. *Above the Law: Police and the Excessive Use of Force*. New York: Free Press.

Slahi, Mohamedou Ould. 2015. *Guantánamo Diary*. New York, NY: Little, Brown and Co.

Slotkin, Richard. 1973. *Regeneration through Violence: The Mythology of the American Frontier, 1600-1860*. Middletown, CT: Wesleyan University Press.

Slotkin, Richard. 1992. *Gunfighter Nation: The Myth of the Frontier in Twentieth-Century America*. New York: Maxwell Macmillan.

Slotkin, Richard. 2001. "Unit Pride: Ethnic Platoons and the Myths of American Nationality." *American Literary History* 13 (3): 469–98.

Slotkin, Richard. 2017. "Thinking Mythologically: Black Hawk Down, the 'Platoon Movie,' and the War of Choice in Iraq." *European Journal of American Studies* 12 (2): 1–19. DOI: https://doi.org/10.4000/ejas.12000.

Small, Zachary. 2019. "The International Spy Museum Seen through the Eyes of a Human Rights Expert" in Hyperallergic September 4 2019, https://hyperallergic.com/514255/the-international-spy-museum-seen-through-the-eyes-of-a-human-rights-expert/.

Smith, Clive Stafford. 2008. "Welcome to 'the Disco'." *The Guardian*, June 19, 2008. www.theguardian.com/world/2008/jun/19/usa.guantanamo.

Sontag, Susan. 2003. *Regarding the Pain of Others*. New York: Farrar, Straus and Giroux.

Southern Poverty Law Center. n.d. "Patriot Front." Accessed August 27, 2021. www.splcenter.org/fighting-hate/extremist-files/group/patriot-front.

Southern Poverty Law Center. n.d. "The 'Patriot' Movement Timeline." Accessed August 27, 2021. www.splcenter.org/fighting-hate/intelligence-report/2015/patriot-movement-timeline.

Southern Poverty Law Center. n.d. "United Constitutional Patriots." Accessed August 27, 2021. www.splcenter.org/fighting-hate/extremist-files/group/united-constitutional-patriots.

Speckhard, Anne, and Molly D. Ellenberg. 2020. "ISIS in Their Own Words: Recruitment History, Motivations for Joining, Travel, Experiences in ISIS, and Disillusionment over Time — Analysis of 220 In-depth Interviews of ISIS Returnees, Defectors and Prisoners." *Journal of Strategic Security* 13 (1): 82–127. DOI: https://doi.org/10.5038/1944-0472.13.1.1791.

Spector, R. H. 2021. "Vietnam War." *Encyclopedia Britannica*, July 6, 2021. www.britannica.com/event/Vietnam-War.

Spicer, Dale. Forthcoming. *"Consecrating Steel: The Remains of the World Trade Centers and American Civil Religion."*

Spivak, Gayatri Chakravorty. 1988. "Can the Subaltern Speak?" In *Marxism and the Interpretation of Culture*, edited by Cary Nelson and Lawrence Grossberg. Urbana, IL: University of Illinois Press.

Stahl, Roger. 2010. *Militainment, Inc: War, Media and Popular Culture.* New York, NY: Routledge.

Stahl, Roger. 2018. *Through the Crosshairs: War, Visual Culture, and the Weaponized Gaze.* New Brunswick, NJ: Rutgers University Press.

Stam, Robert. 1992. "Mobilizing Fictions: The Gulf War, the Media and the Recruitment of the Spectator." *Public Culture* 4 (2): 101–26. DOI: https://doi.org/10.1215/08992363-4-2-101.

Starr, Barbara. 2003. "U.S. Tests Massive Bomb." *CNN*, March 12, 2003. http://edition.cnn.com/2003/US/03/11/sprj.irq.moab/.

Starr, Barbara, and Ryan Browne. 2017. "First on CNN: US Drops Largest Non-Nuclear Bomb in Afghanistan." *CNN*, April 14, 2017. https://edition.cnn.com/2017/04/13/politics/afghanistan-isis-moab-bomb/index.html.

Stein, Lisa. 2011. "Sculptor Michael Rakowitz: Strange Connections, Fascinating Exhibitions." *Weinberg Magazine.* https://weinberg.northwestern.edu/after-graduation/weinberg-magazine/crosscurrents-archive/2011-spring-summer/sculptor-michael-rakowitz.html.

Steinhauer, Jennifer. 2020. "Veterans Fortify the Ranks of Militias Aligned with Trump's Views." *New York Times*, September 11, 2020. www.nytimes.com/2020/09/11/us/politics/veterans-trump-protests-militias.html.

Stone, Rebecca, and Kelly M. Socia. 2019. "Boy with Toy or Black Male With Gun: An Analysis of Online News Articles Covering the Shooting of Tamir Rice." *Race and Justice* 9 (3): 330–58. DOI: https://doi.org/10.1177%2F2153368716689594.

Struyk, Ryan. 2017. "Here are the 28 Active National Emergencies. Trump Won't Be Adding the Opioid Crisis to the List." *CNN*, August 15, 2017. www.cnn.com/2017/08/12/politics/national-emergencies-trump-opioid/index.html.

Stuff They Don't Want You To Know – HowStuffWorks. 2015. "Did Osama bin Laden Really Die in 2011?" YouTube video, 8:17. www.youtube.com/watch?v=bHhalz3iy7g.

Stumpf, Juliet P. 2006. "The Crimmigration Crisis: Immigrants, Crime, and Sovereign Power." *American University Law Review* 56 (2): 367–419.

Sugars, Stephanie. 2019. "From Fake News to Enemy of the People: An Anatomy of Trump's Tweets." *CPJ*, January 30, 2019. https://cpj.org/2019/01/trump-twitter-press-fake-news-enemy-people/.

Suid, Lawrence H. [1978] 2002. *Guts and Glory: The Making of the American Military Image in Film.* Lexington, KY: University Press of Kentucky.

Sullivan, Gavin. 2020. *The Law of the List: UN Counterterrorism Sanctions and the Politics of Global Security Law.* Cambridge: Cambridge University Press.

Sultan, Ahmed. 2017. "Few Clues on Casualties at Site of Huge U.S. Bomb in Afghanistan." *Reuters*, April 23, 2017. www.reuters.com/article/us-afghanistan-usa-bomb/few-clues-on-casualties-at-site-of-huge-u-s-bomb-in-afghanistan-idUSKBN17P0HX.

Sylvester, Judith. 2020. "President Trump and the Mother of All Bombs — Quickly Forgotten." *Athens Journal of Mass Media and Communications* 6 (1): 23–42. DOI https://doi.org/10.30958/ajmmc.6-1-2.

Syrian Observatory for Human Rights. 2019. "Barisha's Mysterious Night: Aerial Bombardment and Clashes on the Ground and a Landing by the U.S. Forces Led to 9 Casualties Including a Child, 2 Women, and First-Rank ISIS Leaders", October 27, 2019, www.syriahr.com/en/145453/.

Szoldra, Paul. 2016. "This is Everything Edward Snowden Revealed in One Year of Unprecedented Top Secret Leaks." *Business Insider*, April 14, 2017 https://www.businessinsider.com/snowden-leaks-timeline-2016-9.

Szoldra, Paul. 2017. "Fox News Host Says Dropping 'Mother of all Bombs' on ISIS is 'What Freedom Looks Like'." *Business Insider*, September 16, 2016. www.businessinsider.com/fox-host-freedom-looks-like-2017-4?r=US&IR=T.

Tamanaha, Brian Z. 2004. *On the Rule of Law: History, Politics, Theory.* Cambridge: Cambridge University Press.

Taussig-Rubbo, Mateo. 2009. "Outsourcing Sacrifice: The Labor of Private Military Contractors." *Yale Journal of Law & the Humanities* 21 (1): 101. New Haven, CT: Yale University, School of Law.

Taylor, Keeanga-Yamahtta. 2016. *From #Black Liberation to Black Lives Matter to Black Liberation.* Chicago: Haymarket Books.

The Associated Press. 2021. "A Timeline of More than 40 Years of War in Afghanistan." *The Associated Press*, July 2, 2021. https://apnews.com/article/joe-biden-islamic-state-group-afghanistan-europe-middle-east-70451c485d46908ef5c6a83a1de9f0f6.

The Bureau of Investigative Journalism. n.d. "Drone Warfare." Accessed October 25, 2021. www.thebureauinvestigates.com/projects/drone-war.

The Center for Media and Democracy. 2003. "Zalmay Khalilzad: Private Career." Last updated February 5, 2021. www.sourcewatch.org/index.php/Zalmay_Khalilzad#Private_Career.

The Congregationalist. 1895. "The Week in Review: Patriot's Day." *The Congregationalist* 80 (17): 635.

The Editors of Encyclopaedia Britannica. 1998. "kamikaze." *Encyclopedia Britannica*, last updated March 7, 2021. www.britannica.com/topic/kamikaze.

Thomas, Clayton. 2020. "The Washington Post's 'Afghanistan Papers' and U.S. Policy: Main Points and Possible Questions for Congress." *Congressional Research Service*, January 28, 2020. https://crsreports .congress.gov/product/details?prodcode=R46197.

The Editors of Encyclopaedia Britannica. 2001. "Dick Cheney." *Encyclopedia Britannica*, last updated September 20, 2021. www.britannica.com/biog raphy/Dick-Cheney.

The Guardian. 2019. "'Probably the World's Most Famous Dog': Trump Honours Conan at the White House – video." November 25, 2019. www.theguardian.com/us-news/video/2019/nov/25/probably-the-worlds-most-famous-dog-trump-honours-conan-at-the-white-house-video.

Thompson, Mark. 2016. *Enough Said: What's Gone Wrong with the Language of Politics?* New York: St. Martin's Press.

Thomsen, Scott. 2001. "Arizona Man Accused of Killing Sikh: 'I'm an American!'" *The San Diego Union-Tribune*, September 29, 2001. www .sandiegouniontribune.com/sdut-arizona-man-accused-of-killing-sikh-im-an-american-2001sep29-story.html.

Thorndike, Edward L. 1920. "A Constant Error in Psychological Ratings." *Journal of Applied Psychology* 4 (1): 25–29. DOI: https://doi.org/10.1037/h0071663.

Thrush, Glenn. 2016. "Clinton Revamps Stump Speech to Tout Her Role in Bin Laden Raid." *Politico*, January 12, 2016. www.politico.com/story/2016/01/hillary-clinton-2016-bin-laden-raid-217637.

Tierney, Dominic. 2011. "'The Mother of All Battles': 20 Years Later." *The Atlantic*, February 28, 2011. www.theatlantic.com/national/archive/2011/02/the-mother-of-all-battles-20-years-later/71804/.

Tierney, Dominic. 2016. "The Twenty Years' War." *The Atlantic*, August 23, 2016. www.theatlantic.com/international/archive/2016/08/twenty-years-war/496736/.

Tisdall, Simon. 2002. "Reaching the parts other empires could not reach." *The Guardian*, January 16, 2002. www.theguardian.com/world/2002/jan/16/afghanistan.oil.

Trumbull, Jonathan, and Joseph Gurley Woodward. 1896. *Vindications of Patriots of the American revolution.* Connecticut: Connecticut Society of the Sons of the American Revolution.

Trump, Donald J. 2017. "Notice Regarding the Continuation of the National Emergency with Respect to Iran." *The White House.* https://trumpwhitehouse.archives.gov/presidential-actions/notice-regarding-con tinuation-national-emergency-respect-iran/.

Trump, Donald J. 2019. "Remarks by President Trump on the death of ISIS Leader Abu Bakr al-Baghdadi" (speech). *The White House.* https://trumpwhitehouse.archives.gov/briefings-statements/remarks-president-trump-death-isis-leader-abu-bakr-al-baghdadi/.

Trump, Donald J. 2020. "Remarks by President Trump on the Killing of Qasem Soleimani" (speech). *The White House.* https://trumpwhitehouse.archives.gov/briefings-statements/remarks-president-trump-killing-qasem-soleimani/.

Turse, Nick. 2013. "America's Lethal Profiling of Afghan Men." *The Nation,* October 7, 2013. www.thenation.com/article/archive/americas-lethal-profiling-afghan-men/.

TV Tropes. n.d. "Shock and Awe / Video Games." Last updated September 23, 2021. https://tvtropes.org/pmwiki/pmwiki.php/ShockAndAwe/VideoGames.

Ullman, Harlan. 2002. *Unfinished Business. Afghanistan, the Middle East, and Beyond – Defusing the Dangers That Threaten America's Security.* New York: Citadel Press.

Ullman, Harlan. n.d. "Harlan Ullman." Accessed October 13, 2021. https://about.me/ullmanharlan.

Ullman, Harlan K., and James P. Wade. 1996. *Shock and Awe: Achieving Rapid Dominance.* Washington, DC: The Center for Advanced Concepts and Technology.

United Nations Security Council. 2019. "Technical Guide to the Implementation of Security Council Resolution 1373 (2001) and Other Relevant Resolutions." December 27, 2019. www.undocs.org/en/S/2019/998.

UPI. n.d. "Afghanistan Condition Reports Released in Washington." Accessed October 13, 2021. www.upi.com/News_Photos/view/upi/5fa391b286aea47f5c74f00dfc24eb3f/Afghanistan-condition-reports-released-in-Washington/.

U.S. Department of Justice. 2004. "Report from the Field: The USA PATRIOT Act at Work." July 2004. www.justice.gov/archive/olp/pdf/patriot_report_from_the_field0704.pdf.

U.S. Department of State. n.d. "Zalmay Khalilzad." Accessed October 13, 2021. https://web.archive.org/web/20181122112728/www.state.gov/r/pa/ei/biog/287479.htm.

Valverde, Mariana. 2015. *Chronotypes of Law: Jurisdiction, Scale, and Governance.* Abingdon: Routledge.

Vavrus, Mary Douglas. 2013. "Lifetime's Army Wives, or I married the Media-Military Industrial Complex." *Women's Studies in Communication* 36 (1): 92–112. Laramie, WY: Taylor & Francis Group. DOI: https://doi.org/10.1080/07491409.2012.756441.

Verdery, Katherine. 1999. *The Political Lives of Dead Bodies.* New York: Columbia University Press.

Virilio, Paul. 1989. *War and Cinema: The Logistics of Perception*. London: Verso.

Vismann, Cornelia. 2008. "Image and Law - A Troubled Relationship." *Parallax* 14 (4): 1–9. Leeds, England: Taylor & Francis.

Volcic, Zala, and Mark Andrejevic, eds. 2016. *Commercial Nationalism: Selling the Nation and Nationalizing the Sell*. New York: Palgrave Macmillan.

Volpp, Leti. 2002. "The Citizen and the Terrorist." *UCLA Law Review* 49 (5): 1575–600. Los Angeles, CA: University of California at Los Angeles, School of Law.

Von Drehle, David. 2003. "For 'Shock and Awe' Author, Concern." *Washington Post*, March 22, 2003. www.washingtonpost.com/archive/politics/2003/03/22/for-shock-and-awe-author-concern/8bb31575-72d1-4fb7-b1df-1f11ba872e2e/.

Waldrep, Christopher. 2002. *The Many Faces of Judge Lynch: Extralegal Violence and Punishment in America*. New York: Palgrave Macmillan.

Waldron, Jeremy. 2016. "The Rule of Law." *The Stanford Encyclopedia of Philosophy*. https://plato.stanford.edu/archives/fall2016/entries/rule-of-law/.

The Washington Post. 2011. "Breaking Down the Situation Room." Accessed January 7, 2022. www.washingtonpost.com/wp-srv/lifestyle/style/situation-room.html.

The Washington Post. 2017. "James Wade Jr." Accessed October 15, 2021. www.legacy.com/us/obituaries/washingtonpost/name/james-wade-obituary?pid=184652600.

Watson Institute for International and Public Affairs. 2015. "Costs of War: Summary of Findings." https://watson.brown.edu/costsofwar/papers/summary.

Watson Institute for International and Public Affairs. n.d. "Costs of War." Accessed October 13, 2021. https://watson.brown.edu/costsofwar/.

Welsh, Richard O., and Shafiqua Little. 2018. "The School Discipline Dilemma: A Comprehensive Review of Disparities and Alternative Approaches." *Review of Educational Research* 88 (5): 752–94. DOI: https://doi.org/10.3102/0034654318791582.

The White House Office of the Press Secretary. 2001. "President Names Special Envoy for Afghanistan" [press release]. https://georgewbushwhitehouse.archives.gov/news/releases/2001/12/20011231-1.html.

White, James Boyd. 1973. *The Legal Imagination*. Chicago, IL: University of Chicago Press.

White, James Boyd. 1984. *When Words Lose Their Meaning: Constitutions and Reconstitutions of Language*. Chicago, IL: University of Chicago Press.

White, James Boyd. 1990. *Justice as Translation*. Chicago, IL: University of Chicago Press.

Whitlock, Craig. 2019. "At War with the Truth." *Washington Post*, December 9, 2019. www.washingtonpost.com/graphics/2019/investigations/afghanistan-papers/afghanistan-war-confidential-documents/.

Wilke, Christiane. 2017. "Seeing and Unmaking Civilians in Afghanistan: Visual Technologies and Contested Professional Visions." *Science, Technology, and Human Values* 42 (6): 1031–1060.

Williams, Patricia. 1991. *The Alchemy of Race and Rights*. Cambridge, MA: Harvard University Press.

Williams, Raymond. [1958] 1989. "Culture is Ordinary." In *Resources of Hope: Culture, Democracy, Socialism*, 3–18. London, New York: Verso.

Williams, Raymond. 1959. "Culture is Ordinary." In *Conviction*, edited by Norman Mackenzie, 74–92. New York: Monthly Review Press.

Williams, Raymond. [1976] 1983. *Keywords: A Vocabulary of Culture and Society*. London: Fontana Paperbacks.

Wilson, Woodrow. 1917. "War Message to Congress" (April 2, 1917), https://wps.prenhall.com/wps/media/objects/107/110495/ch22_a2_d1.pdf.

Woodrow Wilson. 2009. "Wilson's War Message to Congress" (speech). Delivered in Washington DC, April 2, 1917. *The World War I Document Archive*. https://wwi.lib.byu.edu/index.php/Wilson%27s_War_Message_to_Congress.

Wilson, Scott, Craig Whitlock, and William Branigin. 2011. "Osama Bin Laden Killed in U.S. Raid, Buried at Sea." *The Washington Post*, May 2, 2011. www.washingtonpost.com/national/osama-bin-laden-killed-in-us-raid-buried-at-sea/2011/05/02/AFx0yAZF_story.html.

Wodak, Ruth. 1996. *Disorders of Discourse*. London: Longman.

Wodak, Ruth. 2009. *The Discourse of Politics in Action: Politics as Usual*. Basingstoke, England: Palgrave Macmillan.

World News Daily Report. n.d. "Bin Laden is 'Alive and Well in the Bahamas,' Says Edward Snowden." Accessed September 20, 2021. https://worldnewsdailyreport.com/bin-laden-is-alive-and-well-in-the-bahamas-says-edward-snowden/.

Wright, Robin. 2017. "Trump Drops the Mother of All Bombs on Afghanistan." *The New Yorker*, April 14, 2017. www.newyorker.com/news/news-desk/trump-drops-the-mother-of-all-bombs-on-afghanistan

Wright, Robin. 2021. "U.S. Retaliation for the Kabul Bombing Won't Stop ISIS or End Terrorism." *The New Yorker*, August 27, 2021. www.newyorker.com/news/daily-comment/us-retaliation-for-the-kabul-bombing-wont-stop-isis-or-end-terrorism.

Yang, Anand. 2003. "Indian Convict Workers in Southeast Asia in the Late Eighteenth and Early Nineteenth Centuries." *Journal of World History* 14 (2): 179–208.

Young, Alvin L, and Paul F. Cecil, Sr. 2011. "Agent Orange Exposure and Attributed Health Effects in Vietnam Veterans." *Military Medicine* 176 (7): 29–34. DOI: https://doi.org/10.7205/milmed-d-11-00082.

Young, Marilyn B. 2003. "Ground Zero: Enduring War." In *September 11 in History: A Watershed Moment?* edited by Mary L. Dudziak, 10–34. Durham, NC: Duke University Press.

Zachary, Stacia. 2008. "'Mother of All Bombs' celebrates 5 years." *Eglin Air Force Base*, March 11, 2008. www.eglin.af.mil/News/Article-Display/Article/393148/mother-of-all-bombs-celebrates-5-years/.

Zambernardi, Lorenzo. 2017. "Collateral Damage." *The SAGE Encyclopedia of War: Social Science Perspectives*, 330–33. Los Angeles, CA: SAGE Reference.

Zelizer, Barbie. 2018. "Why Journalism in the Age of Trump Shouldn't Surprise Us." In *Trump and the Media*, edited by Pablo J. Boczkowski and Zizi Papacharissi, 9–16. Cambridge, MA: The MIT Press.

Zevnik, Andreja. 2011. "Becoming-Animal, Becoming-Detainee: Encountering Human Rights Discourse in Guantanamo." *Law and Critique*, 22 (2), 155–69.

Zernike, Kate. 2010. *Boiling Mad: Inside Tea Party America*. New York: Henry Holt and Company.

Zine, Jasmin. 2006. "Between Orientalism and Fundamentalism: The Politics of Muslim Women's Feminist Engagement." *Muslim World Journal of Human Rights*, 3, 1–24.

INDEX

CAMBRIDGE STUDIES IN LAW AND SOCIETY

Printed by Printforce, United Kingdom